TRUTHS THE HAND
CAN TOUCH

Xerox

— into

— 108-9

TRUTHS THE HAND CAN TOUCH

The Theatre of Athol Fugard

by
Russell Vandenbroucke

Theatre Communications Group
New York
1985

To A.C.V. and A.B.V.
For St. Vincent's, Ravinia, The Art Institute,
Proco, and the Cubs

Copyright © 1985 by Russell Vandenbroucke

Truths the Hand Can Touch: The Theatre of Athol Fugard is published by Theatre Communications Group, Inc., the national organization for the nonprofit professional theatre, 355 Lexington Ave., New York, NY 10017.

Acknowledgment

The Drummer © 1985 by Athol Fugard, printed by permission of the author. CAUTION: This play is fully protected, in whole, in part, or in any form, under the Copyright Laws of the United States of America, the British Empire including the Dominion of Canada, and all other countries of the Copyright Union, and is subject to royalty. All rights, including professional, amateur, motion picture, recitation, radio, television, and public reading, are strictly reserved. All inquiries concerning performance rights should be addressed to the author's agent, Esther Sherman, William Morris Agency, 1350 Ave. of the Americas, New York, NY 10019.

Cover photograph by T. Charles Erickson

Designed by Soho Studio

The text of this book is set in Goudy. Display type is Benguiat.

Manufactured in the United States of America

First Edition

Library of Congress Cataloging in Publication Data

Vandenbroucke, Russell.
Truths the hand can touch.

Bibliography: p.
Includes index.
1. Fugard, Athol—Criticism and interpretation.
I. Title.
PR9369.3.F8Z92 1985   822   85-2760
ISBN 0-930452-42-9
ISBN 0-930452-45-3 (pbk.)

Contents

CONTENTS

Preface

I first remember hearing the name Athol Fugard while living in England: A Rhodesian friend urged me to see a group of plays that had recently opened at The Royal Court. Although I can still recall my friend's excitement about this man named Fugard, I ignored his advice until the following August. Viewing *Sizwe Bansi* for the first time proved to be an intellectual, emotional, and sensual experience of the first order—one of those infrequent moments in a lifetime when one's senses are as receptive as possible and one's mind fully stimulated. Standing in St. Martin's Lane after the performance, never before having sought out a stage door, I told John Kani the play *had* to be performed in America. He hoped that it would be.

The following month, September of 1974, I enrolled at the Yale School of Drama. In October, *Sizwe Bansi* received its American premiere at Long Wharf Theatre, located within a mile or so of Yale. By that time I had also met Jonathan Marks, an admirer of Fugard who had edited an issue of *yale/theatre* that had provided the fullest coverage of him up to that point. Through Jon I soon met Mary Benson, a friend of Fugard's who had been the first person to publish an article on his work in the international press.

During a New York visit that autumn, I met Michael Kirby, editor of *The*

Drama Review, who asked if I knew anything about South African theatre. Only a little, I admitted. Nevertheless, he asked me to write a piece for a forthcoming issue on politics in the theatre. Did I know the South African director, Barney Simon? Only by reputation, I replied; I'd been told about the lasting impression Simon had made when he had spoken at Yale some years previously. Kirby suggested that I wait in his office since Simon was on his way down to Washington Square even as we spoke. Following a long conversation, Barney decided to return with me to New Haven for the American premiere of *The Island*. We attended the performance together and afterward he introduced me to his friend, Athol.

I next saw Fugard when he spoke informally at Yale. Jaded professors and cocky students alike were impressed by the man who sat before them. Fugard is short, thin, and wiry; his pointed beard, now salted with gray, does not quite hide rather hollow cheeks; his eyes are without the blinders that isolate many people from the world around them. He played no games that day and assumed no roles—no all-knowing playwright, no renowned authority deigning to offer words of wisdom on pet subjects, no sanctimonious liberal glibly lecturing us about South Africa's problems. He spoke quietly, with great passion, choosing his words meticulously. When the students asked their questions, he seemed as interested in what they had to say as in his replies. Six years later he recalled this occasion rather differently: "I thought I'd let everybody down enormously that day. A mortifying experience. I just felt terrible. I remember it as one of those situations when I just sort of bullshitted instead of giving anybody anything." By this time I realized that such self-criticism is characteristic of Fugard.

Soon after this visit to Yale, John Kani and Winston Ntshona were also invited for an informal talk.

Within three months of seeing my first Fugard play, I had met the author, two of his actors and collaborators, two of his closest friends, and an editor who knew as much about him as anyone in the country. By January I had finished the *TDR* article. Kirby's rejection of it noted, "The impression is that there is no political theatre in South Africa."

However, Simon Trussler of *Theatre Quarterly* liked the article and wondered what else I could suggest on the subject. He subsequently decided to do a "Theatre Checklist" on Fugard and to devote most of an issue of *TQ* to both South African theatre and Fugard. I became his editor, which gave me enough superficial credibility and false confidence to interview some of Fugard's actors: Yvonne Bryceland, Ruby Dee, Bill Flynn, John Kani, Ben Kingsley, Alton Kumalo, Winston Ntshona, Paul Scofield, and Janet Suzman. I also contacted André Brink, Ian Ferguson, and Robert Mohr, who have remained helpful ever since.

Having done all this work on Fugard, it seemed a good idea to write a book about him. After a summer in London doing research, I committed myself to the project. Almost as an afterthought, I wondered if Yale would accept it as my dissertation. They did. Since completing that ur-draft in 1978, this book has expanded and contracted whenever I could find time outside of my responsibilities at the Mark Taper Forum, a large resident theatre in Los Angeles.

I am not a South African, despite my last name, nor have I ever visited that country. This may seem a disadvantage, but one of the theses of this book is that the importance of Fugard's nationality has been wrongly exaggerated. He is usually referred to as "Athol Fugard, South African playwright," with the emphasis on the nationality; Beckett and Pinter are simply playwrights. For far too long, critics and audiences have mistakenly equated the South African setting of Fugard's plays with their ultimate meaning and have thereby emphasized the specifics with which he starts rather than the universals with which he ends.

The structure of this book is loosely chronological. Because it is the first study of Fugard yet to be published, I have tried to satisfy a number of responsibilities: both to introduce Fugard and to examine his plays closely and comprehensively, always remaining conscious that they were created to be seen and heard rather than read; to reveal Fugard's craft as a writer but also as a wright; to record the general shape of his life, especially as it relates to his work; to write a condensed theatre history of the companies with which he has been associated; and, especially, to place his work within an intellectual and historical context, thereby suggesting why the plays have such reverberations and why, simply, Fugard is as important a playwright as any working today. I hope my audience includes those who make theatre as well as those who teach it, study it, and attend it.

Northrop Frye notes that what an author says, as opposed to what he writes, does not have a peculiar authority; but it does have a peculiar interest. I have included many direct quotes from Fugard because of this interest, and also because none of our conversations has been published in itself. Our talks have been factual or about the theatre in general. On only one occasion have we directly discussed the intentions or possible interpretations of his work: In 1981 Dan Petrie and I flew to New York to meet with Fugard in preparation for a Taper production of A Lesson from Aloes that Dan would direct and that I would serve as dramaturg.

Fugard and I have talked by phone, both transcontinentally and intercontinentally. We have met in New York restaurants, hotel rooms, and borrowed apartments. Late at night, in a modest Westside bar, we have played his game of "five questions" and shared our secret selves. Most frequently of all, we have met in New Haven, sometimes in classrooms or his rented house, but usually at his favorite table in Kavanaugh's, a bar and grill near the Yale Rep where Fugard makes his "office" during a production. Every waitress and bartender knows him by name. It is the place he continues his work as a director by talking simply, eagerly, and with an open mind to his actors and designers. Fugard is such a gracious host to those who surround him, including reverential students, that he often tries to pay the tab for everyone. When privacy or quiet are needed— Fugard is hard-of-hearing in one ear and a noisy room makes it difficult for him to hear every word of a conversation—he moves to a table at the rear.

Many people have spent time answering my questions and correcting misapprehensions. Robert Thompson deepened my understanding of South Africa and its history. James Earl Jones and Zakes Mokae took the time to discuss their long associations with Fugard. Lindsay Anderson answered a long letter with an even longer one, as did André Brink, Tone Brulin, Ross Devenish, Jack Grütter, and Stephen Gray. Brian Astbury, Mary Benson, Sheila Fugard, Mannie Manim, Gessler Moses Nkondo, and Barney Simon have all shared with me their special perspectives on Fugard and on South African theatre.

I am indebted to the friendship, humor, and horse sense of Rocco Landesman; to Howard Stein, whose warmth was especially welcome in the chilly New Haven environs; and to Richard Gilman, who was a careful and provocative reader of an early draft of this manuscript. If it contains a good sentence or two, he deserves much of the credit. Had Robert Brustein not created an invigorating crucible in New Haven, I might never have benefited from the contributions of these men.

Help in securing research materials has come from Leonie Prozesky and Jill Ainslie of the National English Literary Museum in Grahamstown; John Crosse, Curator of the African Collection of the Yale University Library; and Helen Mochedlover of the Los Angeles Public Library. Rob Rambout, Dr. Herman Goslins, and Robert S. Kirsner translated the Dutch reviews and theatre programs that Karel von Muyden secured for me from the Nederlands Theatre Institute.

Murray Biggs and Aden Ross gave many hours to their thoughtful reading of an earlier draft. The experience and advice of Helen Merrill has always been calming. Suzanne Shepard loaned me her copy of Fugard's cut version of The Blood Knot. Eileen Blumenthal showed me her notes on Fugard's talk at Yale. Gresdna Doty shared with me her interview with John Kani. A two-month leave from the Mark Taper Forum arranged by Gordon Davidson and William Wingate helped me draft a portion of the manuscript. Finally, I am grateful to my publisher, Terry Nemeth, and to Laura Ross, who edited the book with considerable care.

The support and forbearance of Mary Allison Dilg and Aynsley and Justin Vandenbroucke have been invaluable. No one is happier than they to see this book completed. Were it not for the beautiful and provocative words, characters, and ideas of Athol Fugard, the hours it took to do so would not have been so easily sustained.

R.V.

Introduction:

The
South African
Context

The difference in color is merely the physical manifestation of the contrast between two irreconcilable ways of life, between barbarism and civilization, between heathenism and Christianity, and finally between overwhelming numerical odds on the one hand and insignificant numbers on the other. —D.F. Malan, former Prime Minister

When Alan Paton's *Cry, the Beloved Country* was published in 1948, a review in *The Atlantic Monthly* noted, "There is no large area of the civilized world which we have read less about than South Africa." Twenty years later, Joseph Lelyveld called it "one of the least known countries in the world."[1] Since then, much has been written about South African apartheid, race riots, sports boycotts, bannings from public life of outspoken individuals, censorship, political prisoners, and investments by multinational corporations. Despite worldwide interest in these issues, the complex *chiaroscuro* of South Africa is often reduced to its simple, misleading, black and white outlines.

This superficial familiarity with South Africa has contributed to the widespread confusion about the plays of Athol Fugard and a tendency by critics and audiences to equate their context with their subject. Like other playwrights, Fugard writes about what he knows, and most of his plays are set in South Africa. Consequently, it is easy to conclude they are "about" South Africa. Conditions there are so inflammatory, so ostensibly "dramatic" in their own right, that the background is confused with the foreground, the context taken as the thing itself.

Fugard's reputation is as a South African playwright, with the emphasis on the nationality. Perhaps this is inevitable for the only native dramatist ever to be performed regularly outside the country, but such a reputation also suggests a parochialism that limits the scope of his work. This is especially inappropriate in the cosmopolitan contemporary theatre in which Irishmen and Spaniards write in French, Czechs and Nigerians in English, and an American play may premiere in a London theatre subsidized by the British government. Perhaps Fugard will someday be called a South African playwright in the same spirit that Faulkner is considered a Southern novelist, for both are "regional" writers who use the details of a specific time and place, and their experience in that place, to explore general conflicts and quandaries. The region is a starting point and locus, finally a metaphor, rather than the subject itself.

As universal as they are, however, most of Fugard's works were written for a South African audience, and presume an understanding of that society. A brief summary of the South African context of the plays, and the particular laws, attitudes, and ways of life that inform them, will make it easier in succeeding chapters to examine Fugard's plays as works of art rather than sociological essays or political tracts. South Africa is a country that fascinates as it repulses, a carcinogenic sow that poisons its young even as it suckles them.

South Africa is the richest country on the world's poorest continent, but alongside its booming economy exists a parallel system of sub-subsistence agriculture run by the families of men working in the city, as well as by those blacks unable to work in the city or unwilling to leave their families in order to do so. Workers may share only minimally in the economy's riches, but the government smugly compares local wages with those paid elsewhere in Africa. The split between urban industrialized centers and vast rural agricultural areas is deep, and it has had a profound effect on all sections of the populace. What may appear to be merely a difference in domicile—rural or urban, homeland or township—is actually a complex and far-reaching distinction that extends to religion, politics, education, and culture. In general, rural blacks are more politically conservative and culturally traditional than urban blacks.

Of the many divisions in South Africa, race is the most important, followed in significance by language differences within a racial group. Such distinctions are made in most societies, but what is de facto elsewhere is de jure in South Africa. The 1950 Population Registration Act legislated classification of every individual according to race. Racism exists elsewhere, but nowhere with such steadfast persistence and virulence in so successful an industrial economy. As race is determined at birth, so is a child's future, since there is no mobility among the races except through surreptitious and illegal "passing." Biology is destiny.

The government has determined that there are four racial groups: white, Bantu, Coloured, and Asian. "White" refers to the European immigrants, originally Dutch, French, German, and English for the most part, who now number more than 4.5 million. The "Coloured" people, numbering about 2.8 million, are descendants of the indigenous Khoikhoi (or Hottentots), of slaves imported from Southeast Asia and Madagascar, and of whites—an embarrassing fact in a country where racial purity is an obsession promoted to an ideology. Most of the "Asian" population, which numbers more than 800,000, is descendant from Indians brought to the country as indentured laborers. (Because of an important trade agreement, the Japanese are considered honorary whites.)

The word "Bantu" has a precise anthropological meaning designating a large group of people speaking related languages. However, its everyday use in the apartheid society for everything from Bantu Areas and Bantu Beer to Bantu Radio has pejorative connotations. So does the term "native." With the growth of ethnic pride in the 1960s, a political and consciousness-raising movement similar to "black is beautiful" in the United States, South Africa's oppressed peoples began to assert their racial identity in positive terms. Thus, "non-white" has also been rejected since it implies that whiteness is the norm. At one time South African Negroes preferred to be called "African," but most now favor "black." ("Black" may also now refer inclusively to all oppressed people: black, Coloured, and Asian.)

Although a linguistic relationship exists among all blacks, who number about twenty-three million, there are nine major groups. Apartheid policy is designed to separate races and maintain factions within each race, but one result of industrialization has been the rapid rate of urbanization. As blacks from different groups have been thrown together in townships on the outskirts of the cities, differences and hostilities among them have diminished. Townships are becoming the home of a composite black culture no longer identifiable as simply Xhosa, Zulu, Sotho, or Venda. Indeed, now that millions of second- and third-generation blacks have never lived in rural areas and know little about traditional life and customs, it becomes increasingly ludicrous for apartheid policy to define blacks by language and cultural group rather than race. It is equally absurd to pretend that they truly belong in one of the nine "homelands." More than half of all blacks live outside the homelands, either in the townships or on white-owned farms.

Of South Africa's four provinces, blacks have had a longer period of contact with whites in the Cape than in Natal, the Transvaal, or the Orange Free State. Urban areas have long been centers of black political action, demonstrations, and attempts to end oppression. This has been particularly true around Fugard's Port Elizabeth home in the Eastern Cape. For years this center of the auto and rubber industries was the main stronghold of the African National Congress (ANC).

For blacks born in the homelands, escape from the fetters of sub-subsistence agriculture is the only means to support a family. The choices are three: the mines, the cities, or a white man's farm. By making it easier for blacks to get permission to work in the mines than in the cities, the government guarantees that the manpower needs of the mines are met. Until recently, blacks were barred from skilled jobs and from joining unions. In the all-male mining compounds, blacks are housed according to language group: Since different cultures exist, the argument runs, each must be protected and nurtured. The mere existence of differences becomes a rationale to perpetuate and consolidate those differences.

If the rural-born black man is able to get the necessary permission to work in the city, his wife and children must remain in the homeland, which is still considered his official residence. (His wife might get a job as a live-in domestic in the white suburbs, but even then her husband and children could not live with her.) He will be able to visit them only two weeks of every year. He is permitted to be in the city because of his work, and if he stops working for any reason—health, lay-offs, his firm's bankruptcy, or simply because he quits his job—he loses his right to remain there. Black workers in the cities may have to live, like the miners, in all-male "bachelor" dormitories. Weekend entertainment is found in the community halls, bioscopes (movie houses), government-run beer halls, and shebeens (speak-easies).

By dividing the population into races and the races into language groups, by creating separate departments to administer the affairs of each group, separate schools for the young, hospitals for the ill, courts and jails for supposed transgressors, and by establishing distinct residential areas, the government tells all its citizens, every day of their lives, exactly who they are, where they belong, and what they can and should do. Because so many personal decisions and choices are usurped by the state, psychological certainty and security might seem part of the South African way of life. It is true that most Afrikaners, who are descendants of German, French, and especially Dutch immigrants, have a clear sense of their beliefs, values, and "mission." With the rise in black consciousness and pride, blacks too have an increasingly unified sense of themselves and their goals. However, among Coloureds and, to a lesser extent, English-speaking whites, insecurity and ambivalence prevail. South Africa is the only country in the world where a large group of *native* English-speakers constitute a minority.

Coloureds are not black, nor are they white. Because most of them speak Afrikaans and live in the relatively liberal Cape, they have historically aligned themselves with whites and enjoyed clear advantages over blacks. They have traditionally felt superior to blacks, but have never had the full advantages enjoyed by whites, who accept them as only partial inheritors of the European culture. Furthermore, in recent years black income has been increasing at a faster rate than that of Coloureds, though the latter still earn more than blacks. Since the Nationalist Party gained power in 1948, Coloureds have lost numerous rights and privileges, some of which they had enjoyed for more than a century. As the government continued (until very recently) to rescind those privileges, an increasing number of Coloureds began to identify with blacks and to see their hopes and futures linked in the struggle for liberation. The Soweto Riots of 1976 caused many young Coloureds to unite with blacks.

Among English-speakers there is also considerable ambiguity of identity, as Margaret Bacon has noted: "'Who am I?' a prominent white South African English-speaking writer asks. 'I'm not an Afrikaner, or an African, or an Indian, or a Coloured. I'm nothing.' . . . While the white English-speaking South African would like to think of himself as an African—indeed, what else is he?—his claim to this title is increasingly disputed by all but the liberal Black Africans. Yet unlike the Afrikaner, he does not have the laager of a nationalism into which to retreat for security and reinforcement of his sense of self."[2]

Afrikaners have also had periods of uncertainty. While the crucial division in today's South Africa seems to be between black and white, this has only been so for the last twenty-five years. Before about 1960 the primary struggle was Anglo-Boer. (A "boer" is literally a farmer, but it is a name applied generically to all Afrikaners.) Although blacks may have viewed the 1910 Act of Union—which joined the four provinces, Anglo and Boer—as the means of uniting all whites against them, such unity did not exist until a half-century later. Afrikaners have always outnumbered English-speaking whites, the ration is now about three to two, but English-speakers long held the dominant positions in commerce and industry while Afrikaners were concentrated in rural areas. Many saw themselves as outcasts in their own home until the 1948 ascension of the Nationalists, who represent the opinions of most Afrikaners. It was not until 1961 that the Union of South Africa withdrew from the British Commonwealth and became the Republic of South Africa. The same year the South African monetary system shifted from the pound ($2.80) to the rand, a decimalized currency originally pegged at two rands to the pound. One rand, worth $1.40 in 1961, stayed at approximately that value until 1975. It is currently worth about $.50.

Throughout their history, Afrikaners have been united by the perceived threat of a common enemy—first the English ("liberalism") and now blacks ("Communism"). They have long looked to one another for support and security; such turning inward, a product of both isolation and an obsession with ethnic purity, has had numerous consequences. Through their schools, churches, and political party, the socialization of most Afrikaners is entirely homogeneous. They may be the only people in the industrial world without an ideological or attitudinal gap between generations, although the most ardent and influential opponents of apartheid have often been "detribalized" Afrikaners.

Thus, most Afrikaners persistently distinguish themselves from races that are not white, and also from whites who are not Afrikaner. "In" and "out" groups, "us" versus "them," are part of the Afrikaner's siege mentality. They were first opposed by Great Britain, then by blacks—both in South Africa and elsewhere in Africa—and now by opinion around the world. They see no need to be more defensive today than in the past because they have always felt threatened, both from within and without the country. Instead of growing paranoid as a result of rejection from all quarters, many Afrikaners have grown increasingly self-righteous, convinced of the importance of the divine mission selected for them. Setbacks and defeats, by the British or the blacks, can be perceived as God's will.

Though racism existed in South Africa from the time of its settlement by Europeans, it operated in a sporadic and ill-defined manner until 1948 when the concept of apartheid was elevated to an ideology, a philosophy, and, with the election of the Nationalists, a systematic if inherently inconsistent governmental policy. Although the term "apartheid" (literally "separation") was coined in 1929—and today is often replaced by the euphemistic "parallel development"—it was made popular by a 1948 report. Apartheid has begotten scores of statutes, but the measures particularly relevant to Fugard's plays are the Group Areas Act, the pass laws, the Immorality Act, and the security laws.

While blacks had long been shunted into reserves (later called homelands or Bantustans) and locations (now known as townships), the Group Areas Act of 1950, often amended, was designed to extend physical separation to all four racial groups. Certain areas were declared to be for the use of a particular race and others, "disqualified persons," were forced to move. White areas could have been declared to be for black, Coloured, or Asian use, but in the vast majority of cases the whites remained secure while everyone else was uprooted. Whites comprise approximately fifteen percent of the population, but control more than eighty percent of the land and also retain mineral rights to much of the land they do not control.

Shops and schools were affected by the Group Areas Act, but housing was especially disrupted. For example, Sophiatown was unusual among black locations for permitting freehold ownership. However, a nearby white Johannesburg suburb was growing so rapidly that it was decided that Sophiatown had to be demolished and its residents removed. Mary Benson has described the 1955 scene: "Armed police moved into a few houses and stood over the families as pathetic possessions were removed. Families, soaked through, were huddled with their bundles and bits of furniture on the lorries and driven away to Meadowlands."[3]

The existence of squatter communities on the outskirts of all industrial areas makes the housing shortage especially evident. Sometimes a family can find a place to live within a township, even if only the male worker is officially entitled to live there, but the demand is often so great that illegal squatter communities grow up in prohibited areas.

Unless blacks are born in a township and can prove it, or have lived there long enough to establish residency (ten consecutive years of employment with a single employer), they are only permitted to live in the townships if they are working in the nearby city. Movement and residence are controlled by the various pass laws. Since 1952 a comprehensive system has existed that, with various revisions and amendments, is the cornerstone of government control of blacks and has the greatest effect on their daily lives. Prosecutions of pass offenses exceed a half million per year and constitute nearly a quarter of all cases sent to trial.[4]

All blacks sixteen years of age and over are required to carry a reference book, nicknamed a dom-pass (from "verdomde," meaning "damned"). It indicates an individual's identity number, his employment history, where he is permitted to be, and what taxes he has paid. An employer must sign the book monthly, and no black can leave one job for another without a discharge signature. Because of the limitless discretionary powers given police, any black can be stopped at any time and asked to produce his book. Failure to do so is a criminal offense. (Whites, Coloureds, and Asians have seven days to produce their identity cards.) A rural black may visit the urban areas for only seventy-two hours unless he has a special permit. If he remains longer, he will be "endorsed out" and forced to return to his homeland. Black resistance in South Africa has often been synonymous with resistance to the pass laws. On March 21, 1960, police killed sixty-nine blacks at Sharpeville and wounded 178 others during a demonstration against just such laws.

If the pass laws and Group Areas Acts are the daily instruments of apartheid, the Immorality Act (1927) represents the spirit behind that policy; it has been called the bedrock of apartheid. The narrator of "The Prisoner," a short story by Lewis Nkosi, states, "In South Africa the laws against racial mixing are very strict; one can be forgiven for anything but diluting what the popular imagination conceives as the pure racial strain."[5] In a country that so idealizes racial purity and chooses to classify every citizen at birth according to his race, it is easy to understand the threat that miscegenation poses. Because "race" and "blood" are treated equivalently, miscegenation diminishes the "pure" blood of everyone. To break the Immorality Act is to betray one's racial heritage.

In 1950 the government sought new means to control opposition through the Suppression of Communism Act, which made the Communist Party illegal (its estimated 2,000 members had already disbanded). The act defines Communism as "any doctrine or scheme which aims at bringing about any political, industrial, social or economic change within the Union by the promotion of disturbance or disorder, by unlawful acts or omissions or the threat of such acts or omissions."[6] Only three weeks after the Sharpeville Massacre the government used this act to outlaw the ANC even though it was dedicated to both non-violence and constitutional means to redress grievances.

Other security laws have further crippled the opposition. These include the Riotous Assemblies Act (1956), the Unlawful Organizations Act (1960), the General Law Amendment Act of 1963 (popularly known as the Sabotage Act), the Terrorism Act (1967), and the Internal Security Act (1976). The Minister of Justice now has the power to ban or place under house arrest any person furthering, or likely to further, the aims of "Communism." His accusation needs no proof, it cannot be appealed, and he need not explain it. The government also has the power to control persons it thinks will promote feelings of hostility between the races; to ban organizations, even if they are not "Communist," that jeopardize the safety of the State; to ban individuals for up to five years and to re-impose such bans as soon as they expire; to place the burden of proof of innocence on accused saboteurs; to provide for repeated ninety-day detentions *ad infinitum*, without court order, without trial, and without legal counsel for the detainee.

Although a Minister of Justice and Prisons has claimed there are no political prisoners in South Africa, these laws are clearly directed against political acts.[7] The most serious offenders are sent to Robben Island, but "serious" may mean no more than membership in a banned organization, distributing leaflets, collecting funds, or attending a meeting. These "criminals" often become heroes and martyrs in the minds of their people.

Despite the history of discrimination, degradation, and persecution, violent resistance within South Africa has been surprisingly selective. Most of it has been directed against property, and deaths, except of demonstrating blacks, have been few. Until John Harris's bombing of the Johannesburg railway station in 1964, violence was directed against specific targets for specific reasons.

Effective opposition has been undermined by the large number of informers operating within each racial group. The fear of discovery (like the fear of censorship to the writer) may prevent any action whatsoever. Such fear has resulted in what Fugard calls a "conspiracy of silence," an unwillingness to speak out and act against injustice. The Soweto Riots of 1976 and the reaction to the murder of Steve Biko in 1977 may, however, indicate that smoldering rage is now so intense and widespread that it can no longer be contained.

In a country that systematically separates one group from another, mutual understanding is extremely difficult. For the writer, the problem is obvious. Most of Fugard's works have black or Coloured characters, but since 1964 he has needed a permit to visit the townships and has seldom been granted one. This might be an insurmountable problem for a writer seeking utter verisimilitude. However, race is only one component of the human condition; the suffering and degradation rife throughout Fugard's work is, finally, a poetic image of the plight of all men.

Numerous modern playwrights have abandoned, at least for a time, their native country, among them Büchner, Ibsen, Strindberg, Shaw, O'Casey, Brecht, and Beckett. While Fugard has never left South Africa for a long period, like Genet he is a kind of exile in his own home, estranged from the mainstream of life around him. The separation of man from man that is so ruthlessly imposed by the South African government may not be the root of Fugard's profound sense of man's alienation, but it is confirmation of the anguish resulting from such alienation.

The South African Context

South Africa provides both the setting and raw materials for most of Fugard's writing. His first works in particular—*No-Good Friday*, *Nongogo*, and *Tsotsi*—are based on township life. Later plays touch upon the effect of particular laws: the Group Areas Act in *Boesman and Lena*, the Immorality Act in *Statements after an Arrest under the Immorality Act*, the pass laws in *Sizwe Bansi Is Dead* and *Marigolds in August*, and the Suppression of Communism Act in *The Coat*, *The Island*, and *A Lesson from Aloes*. In nearly every work an insecure character tries to find his identity and assert the dignity inherent in his humanity.

I

Apprenticeship

Early Life, Early Writings

What I knew: a mother, poverty, lovely nights under a sky. —Albert Camus

In Athol Fugard's first major play, *The Blood Knot*, Morrie says of the Karoo: "Dry country, man. White, white thorns and the bushes grey and broken off. They roll about the veld when the wind blows. And, of course, there's the dust as well. Dusty as hell it is, when the wind blows."[1] It was in this semi-desert, sheep-farming area of South Africa's Cape Province that Harold Athol Lannigan Fugard was born on June 11, 1932 in the small village of Middelburg. Fugard recalls that "a primitive shanty with its enforced intimacy and depressing squalor was my original home."*

His mother, Elizabeth Magdalena Potgieter, known as Betty, was a member of a family that had been in Africa for three centuries and had been among the Voortrekkers instrumental in establishing the Transvaal. Potgieters still sit in the South African Parliament and remain among the most honored of the original Dutch *volk*. Betty Potgieter was raised in Knoffelvlei. Fugard says, "You couldn't call it a town. Even 'village' flatters it. I suppose you'd call it a hamlet in the Karoo." His father, Harold David Lannigan Fugard, was the son of im-

*Unless otherwise credited, all quotes of Fugard and his wife were recorded in a series of private interviews, 1974-1984.

migrants from Manchester, England of either Irish-Huguenot, Irish-Polish, or Scandinavian ancestry. Fugard is not sure which, though he often claims "there's a lot of Irish in me."

Fugard, his older brother Royal, known as Roy, and his younger sister Glenda were all named by their paternal grandmother, a British royalist whose last name was Lannigan. "Athol" presumably derives from an Earl of Athlone who had been a British governor of South Africa. After being called Hally throughout his childhood and adolescence, Fugard eventually dropped his first name and also the double last name Lannigan Fugard, which his parents and grandparents used.

Following a visit to England when he was seven or eight, Fugard's father slipped on a staircase during the voyage back to South Africa and severely damaged his hip. By the time he reached port the injury was irreparable and he became crippled for life. His extremely protective mother, Fugard's grandmother, prevented him from leading an active life. The leg was eventually amputated above the knee, and in 1961, when Fugard was twenty-nine, his father died of gangrene that had gone undiagnosed.

When Fugard was three, the family sold its small general store in Middelburg and moved to Port Elizabeth, which, with brief exceptions, has remained his home ever since. He says of this industrial port on the Indian Ocean: "Close on half a million people live here—black, white, Indian, Chinese, and Coloured. It is also very representative of South Africa in the range of its social strata, from total affluence on the white side to the extremest poverty on the non-white. I cannot conceive of myself as separate from it."[2]

Fugard's mother leased the rights to a home that she ran as a boarding house, the Jubilee. In 1941 she sold her rights in it to invest in a cafe at the St. George's Park swimming bath where she sold cigarettes, cakes, and tea. Fugard recalls that the family's relationship with the blacks working there was very good "in the paternalistic South African sense. It was warm and real—but to an inferior; to someone who needed looking after." Fugard was especially fond of a waiter named Sam Semela. Although his father had many prejudices, Fugard says that his mother was color-blind.

Fugard recalls that "circumstances were really dictated by what my mother was doing at that time to keep us going . . . My mother is a remarkable woman. In fact that's got a lot to do with my plays; the woman is always the affirmative element."[3] She was the primary breadwinner, but Fugard's father supplemented her income by playing piano. His first band was the Orchestral Jazzonians. He later appeared with The Melodians, a jazz band that performed at local concerts and dances and in which Fugard's mother played drums. Harold David especially loved Duke Ellington, and Fugard credits his father for his intense interest in music, "which remains one of the most important survival mechanisms in my life."

Although his father played jazz rather than the classics, Fugard is a devotee of both. He has been known to give impromptu lectures on classical music with demonstrations from his favorite records, and has frequently acknowledged Bach's influence upon his writing. Indeed, one of Fugard's first creative compositions was for the piano, when he was ten. He played his tune proudly for his brother, who informed him that exactly the same one had played on the radio the previous week. Fugard never composed music again.

Fugard says of the family's circumstances, "In terms of white South African social categories, my background would be described as lower middle-class—though with pretentions toward something better. Lower middle-class is more or less the bottom social rung because you don't really have a white laboring category in South Africa. Judged by the considerable degree of affluence enjoyed by white South Africa, both in my childhood and still to this day, it was a relatively poor situation."[4]

Fugard sometimes refers to his family as *bywoners*, a term applied generically to all poor whites that literally means "squatters" or "share-croppers." Nevertheless, the Fugards "were very tightly-knit. That in some ways may be the origin of the concern in my work with the nexus of family relationships." In Alan Paton's *Cry, the Beloved Country*, the father of James Jarvis swears to disinherit any child of his who marries an Afrikaner. Fugard claims, however, there was no English-Afrikaner conflict in his home, though he does call himself "a bastardized Afrikaner, a product of cultural miscegenation."[5] The meeting and sharing of cultures and heritages proved enriching.

His father had poor command of Afrikaans and usually conversed with his wife in English, but Fugard remembers, "We spoke both languages with indiscriminate proficiency. Today, after an English education from the age of six onward, I use English with only slightly greater facility than Afrikaans. But I would not attempt to write creatively in Afrikaans." [6] As a young man he wrote some stories and poems in Afrikaans, but none was published. He has since stopped writing in Afrikaans "because I couldn't do it well, and I won't do anything badly."

Fugard speaks with an Eastern Cape accent tinged with Afrikaans and says he is "very conscious of how certain qualities, certain textures, certain moods—in terms of the South African scene—can with total precision be described only by an Afrikaans turn of the word. So before I even put pen to paper I'm involved in a job of translation."[7] In addition to a word or phrase, he must sometimes translate an entire dramatic situation since all of his characters speak English. Because of this, Fugard admits that perhaps some of his plays should actually have been written in Afrikaans. Also, some exchanges between rural and urban blacks might realistically be spoken in Xhosa—if Fugard desired absolute verisimilitude.

Both parents were storytellers: "My father was an avid reader, even late in life—good adventure stories, Jack London, Bret Harte, Bram Stoker—and I used to get those from him. My mother told stories about her own life and all that was happening around her." Fugard credits his father for "a command of the language which I have deliberately chosen to use as a playwright and which is a pleasure, but from my mother as an Afrikaner comes the sense of roots, a sense of the textures of that country which I think the Afrikaner uniquely has."[8]

Fugard was also influenced by her "glorious corruptions" of English: "She does queer things with English, silly things like 'zink' for 'sink,' but actually she also makes the language flower in her mouth. This has been an important factor in my playwriting; in the way I've tried to play with words." Fugard's mother has proudly recalled that, "When he turned eleven, Athol had already been a member of the adult library for some time—he refused to read children's books any longer. He never played any sport and spent nearly all his time reading and writing and studying. Athol was happiest when he had a book in one hand and a pen and pencil in the other."[9]

From the age of about ten to twelve, Fugard and his sister were a ballroom dancing team that held Eastern Province junior titles. During World War II their mother was a member of the Governor General's War Fund, which organized social functions for troops stationed in Port Elizabeth and for sailors who docked there. Fugard recalls, "Glenda and I used to turn up at those occasions as part of the entertainment. They suffered, believe me, and were glad to get back and fight the Jerrys." The favorite dance of the young Fugards was the apache. Glenda recalls that after an argument between them, "Hallie took full advantage of the apache to send me flying across the dance floor, resulting in near catastrophe— what an ovation we received."[10]

Throughout his school years, Fugard lived in an area of Port Elizabeth called Newton Park. He started primary school at Marist Brothers College, a Catholic school, although the family was not Catholic. Fugard recalls, "In early childhood my brother and I were dragooned by my mother into going to the Anglican church. We sang in the choir, but we were able to escape from the church eventually." After several years at Marist Brothers College, Fugard transferred to Albert Jackson School, where he completed Standard Six in 1945. Since his family could not afford to continue his education, he competed for a council scholarship. An essay entitled "Butterfly Hunting in the Amazon River Basin" won him a four year course in motor mechanics at the Technical College of Port Elizabeth: "I was a very keen naturalist even then. Why they awarded me a scholarship on the basis of that essay is curious, but that's the way South Africa works." Although an automobile would figure prominently in important scenes in *Tsotsi* and *The Blood Knot*—and throughout *Mille Miglia*—Fugard's interest in nature has had a much stronger influence upon his writing.

The school had an amateur Dramatic Society, which Fugard calls "a very undernourished and insignificant little number. I did have a crack at directing

4

and acting. I did both even then. If I couldn't direct, I wasn't prepared to act. I've never taken kindly to other directors. One of the plays I did was called *Sundays Costs Five Pesos*. Not surprisingly, no one has ever heard of it. Another was a one-acter set in a Welsh mining village. I played a character who'd had his face blown away in a mine accident."

Fugard was also active in an annual publication called *The Warden*, edited by a student. "One year, miracle of miracles, I was elected head boy and supervised the compilation of that publication. I think I contributed something I'd written, but I'm not sure." Fugard was forced to spend a fifth year in Technical College because he failed mathematics.

Despite the disappointment of having to spend an extra year at school, Fugard made the best of it after he was befriended by the head of the science department, a Mr. James. Sensing Fugard's dissatisfaction with his studies, the teacher invited him to sit in on night classes in advanced zoology, botany, and chemistry. By the end of the year Fugard won both the Principal's Prize for industry and an award for loyalty and service to the school. The science classes and the purchase of his first microscope ended any plans Fugard had of becoming a mechanic. To this day he remembers the excitement he felt when his daughter was old enough to use a microscope: "I couldn't wait for the opportunity to buy her one. I knew it was as much for me as her and that I was going to play with it, which I still do. I can spend hours studying a drop of pond water. It's interesting that there are two optical instruments that give access to other dimensions—the microscope and the telescope. I don't have a telescope. My plays are small plays. Figures, doesn't it?" They do not remain small, however. In his finest work, detailed miniatures assume cosmic proportions.

Fugard enrolled at the University of Cape Town in February 1951, to study philosophy and social anthropology: "My head was full of very big questions, the whys and whats and hows. I did a lot of reading to attempt to answer those questions—Kierkegaard, Sartre, Camus. I studied all the philosophers, but especially the existentialists." Before entering university Fugard had begun to read in this area, but his Port Elizabeth education had been too weak for him to comprehend what he read. The university gave him the necessary skills: "A very remarkable professor of ethics and political history called Martin Versveld enabled me to interpret Sartre and Kierkegaard and Heidegger. I don't mean at a terrifically high level; but just in terms of personal needs, I was equipped finally to get into the heads of those incredible men and understand something of what they were writing about."[11]

At university Fugard met his future wife, a drama student named Sheila Meiring, whom he remembers as "the snootiest and snobbiest woman on campus in her red beret and cape, full of literature and a good English speaking voice. I don't think she was aware of me, though." Born in England of an Irish mother who raised her daughter Catholic, and an Afrikaans father who was a doctor,

Meiring moved to South Africa when she was five. Although they shared no classes, she did remember Fugard. As part of an initiation at his residence, he was forced to wear a cravat and tailcoat as punishment for transgressions. Refusing to conform, he was frequently in trouble and "went through my entire first year in evening dress." Meiring adds, "he was in that outfit long after other students had gone back to ordinary dress. I remember seeing him at a distance and feeling sympathetic, but he was a bit too dangerous to get involved with. It would have been an indignity. I was interested in slightly older men." Fugard wonders if his looks played a part in her wariness: "I was pretty scruffy then. Still am."

For recreation Fugard boxed as a lightweight and almost became a university champion. During vacations, he hitchhiked home: "I was always kind of hard up and didn't want to put the money into a train ticket. I also hitched for jaunts around the country." He won medals for both social science and social anthropology in his end-of-year exams. As a result, he was given financial support for his second year. His second-year exams won him continued support for his third year, but before completing it he decided to leave university. Fugard has often said he was only a couple of months short of his degree, ·vhich he should have completed by November 1953. In fact, he left university shortly after the start of his third year, probably in April.

Fugard recalls that when he left university, "I didn't know then that I wanted to write but I did know that the academic life was not what I wanted." He believes he was headed for a teaching career and now recalls, "I just had a sense that, because of the person I am, the degree and its invitation to an academic life could become a trap. . . . Some instinct must have told me that I was going to try to write. I don't think that that would have happened if I'd ended up with an Honors Degree in philosophy." Aside from his instinct, Fugard had, in fact, already begun to write. Classmate Benjamin Pogrund recalls, "He had been writing for as long as I had known him. But it was the writing of short stories. I cannot remember any details of the ones I read, but I do remember the power of the language and the images."[12]

Fugard does remember his interest in poetry: "One or two short stories had come out as well. But even then, all of those were in a sort of intensely free prose style, which almost made them like long poems. The question of a novel, which cropped up a bit later in my writing career, hadn't crossed my path. . . . There was a fair amount of poetry, none of which, thank God, now exists."[13] Fugard is unsure of the exact chronology of his early writing, but about the time he left university he began a novel about his mother: "She told me marvelous stories about her childhood in the Karoo, about Port Elizabeth, and so on."

Upon leaving university, Fugard and Perseus Adams, a poet who was Fugard's first friend after Sam Semela, set out to hitchhike their way up the continent: "There was a brand of cigarettes then for sale in Cape Town called C to C, Cape to Cairo. That seemed like a pretty good idea, so you can gather our imaginations weren't very fertile." Leaving with ten tins of sardines and about thirty pounds ($84), Fugard hoped first to cover the 6,500 overland miles between Cape Town and Cairo, then to go on to Paris.

On their first day, he and Adams travelled seventy-five miles to Worcester. Fugard recollects, "I hadn't yet reached the heart of South Africa, hadn't even left Cape Town really, but I remember the terrible loneliness of that first night and the sense I had that I was actually going to leave my country for the first time in my life. I was panic-stricken." For the next few days Fugard and Adams rode over 2,000 miles through South Africa and Southern Rhodesia (now Zimbabwe), into Northern Rhodesia (now Zambia) with a copper-belt miner on his way to Kitwe. It then took the pair four weeks to get from Northern Rhodesia to the Sudan, by which time they had eaten their sardines. Their cash remained intact. Having difficulty getting lifts, Fugard talked his way into a ride at one point by saying he was the Pope's emissary. At another point he and Adams lived with pygmies in the Congo.

They entered Egypt illegally and finally reached Cairo, but were arrested by the police and sent back to the Sudan. While Fugard was there, his mother wrote the head of police in Khartoum asking if he could find her son. The policeman promised to try. Fugard adds, "Since we were in the Sudan illegally, the police had every reason to be looking for me and, in fact, already were." While in Khartoum, Fugard and Adams were invited to address a group of students at Gordon University. Fugard tried to speak about philosophy, but the black students were more interested in politics. "They asked me the reasons for the white man's attitude in the Union and I gave in. I told them the situation was more complicated than they presumed. Bottles rained down on me from all sides and the lecture devolved into a riot."

In a letter to his parents from Juba, in Anglo-Egyptian Sudan, dated July 19, 1953, Fugard refers to himself as a prodigal son, mentions some financial difficulties, and alludes to some of his experiences on the trip: the wild animals he had seen, pygmies who had helped drag a tree out of the road that an elephant had pushed over before his eyes, shooting at the tires of a lorry that would not allow him to pass, and his boat trip up Lake Tanganyika. Still, he missed his family and Port Elizabeth: "For myself and my writing I can safely say there will only be one home. I have promised myself that after a week or so in Paris I will return to South Africa. Travelling is all very well for some—but with my whole life dedicated to my art I must return home soon. Don't forget to keep my place at Xmas table. Re my writing I can at least say that the wellsprings of inspiration are still bubbling. When I finish this letter I will turn to a play I have been busy on for some time."[14] Fugard has no memory of this play, and was startled to hear himself quoted about it. He has always assumed he had no interest in theatre until his marriage three years later.

From Juba, Fugard and Adams took a barge down the Nile to Khartoum: "Conditions on the barge were appalling. We were packed in below deck with raw, naked black men. The barge reeked of goat's blood. The Natives slaughtered the goats in our living quarters."[15] The pair had to cope with so much on the trip that they ended up terrible enemies. It took more than a decade for them to speak again. Pogrund recounts Fugard's tale of his arrest with Adams in the Sudan: "It was midsummer and day after day they were locked into a tiny corrugated iron shed, suffocatingly hot. They each sat in a corner, spending the heated hours of each day sitting silent and rigid, just staring at each other. If either had moved a muscle, the other would have been at his throat for the kill. They both knew it and sat and sat until darkness ended the heat."

Upon their release, the two separated in Khartoum, where Adams hid aboard a mailship. Fugard fled from Khartoum to Port Sudan by conning his way onto a BOAC flight. He claimed to be a French journalist doing a background story on the forthcoming Sudanese independence elections. Fugard was broke, but explained that his money was tied up in Port Sudan and that he had arrived in Khartoum too late to arrange a transfer. Because he waited to concoct his story until the middle of an important Moslem feast,[16] Fugard knew there was no way it could be checked with a bank manager. The BOAC officer considered himself a good judge of human nature, believed Fugard's story, and gave him a ticket.

After arriving in Port Sudan Fugard had planned to slip quietly into the native quarter, but the BOAC man had become so concerned about his plight that he had booked a room for Fugard in the Red Sea Hotel, the finest in the city. Fugard did not learn this until he disembarked, but by then he was trapped. He began drinking in the hotel bar, signing for his drinks because by then everyone had heard his story. "After about three days," Fugard continues, "a portly gentleman sat down beside me and asked, 'What's your problem?' I insisted I had none, but he replied, 'Come on, laddie. I've been around quite a bit. What's your trouble?' So I told him my story. He was a Welshman of French Huguenot stock named Hersee, captain of a 6,000-ton tramp steamer, the S.S. *Graigaur*, a Welsh word meaning 'Rock of Gold.' He smuggled me on board and I made my escape."

Fugard's writing of this period has been lost, but it is obvious from this episode that even at this stage of his life he was able to tell a compelling story. His fondness for assumed roles has persisted: "My greatest moment comes on a long flight out of South Africa. There's always someone sitting next to you and they'll ask, 'What do you do?' And I take on totally different identities. I've been a computer mechanic. I've been a buyer for an art museum, I've been a hundred different things. And I have enjoyed those moments so enormously."[17]

In a letter sent to his parents two days before sailing from Port Sudan on the *Graigaur*, probably written about October 12, 1953, Fugard said he was healthy, having a good time, "and writing great poetry." On ship he was paid one shilling per month, which made him subject to the ship's laws and the captain's authority: "I became what is known as the captain's tiger, the person who looks after him, serves his food, runs his bath, and so on. Hersee was a very solitary man who didn't associate with his officers."

After stopping in Colombo, Ceylon, Fugard again wrote his parents, this time from the Malacca Straits a day out of Singapore. The date was October 28, 1953: "I am busy on the completion of the novel started in Cape Town and by the time I come to writing letters I am dog tired with the mere effort of writing. I don't like to repeat myself too much but must say that am deeply satisfied with my writing; there exists no doubt now in my mind that it is the one thing I have always been destined to do, and one does not argue with destiny." Nevertheless, he experienced considerable homesickness, "a weak word to describe the intense longing I relive with every sunset."

The ship's thirty-four man crew was multi-racial: white officers and cabin staff, Malay sailors, and blacks in the engine room. Fugard believes his racial attitudes and assumptions prior to being a seaman had been similar to those of the typical South African, but a brawl in a Singapore pub only two weeks into the voyage began to change this: "I thought I was by myself and then I found two of the Malays from the ship by my side. After that, things were different."[18] Most of his experiences on ship were with the blacks and Malays: "I was the only white on that ship with friendships across the color line."

From Singapore the ship set out for Yokohama, Japan, a three-week journey. Fugard sometimes wrote his mother requesting four or five pounds. In a letter of November 18, 1953 from Niigata, Japan, he informed her that his next stop would be the Fiji Islands and that he was heading, eventually, for Great Britain, but that before being allowed to land, the British government required her assurance that she would pay his passage back to South Africa should it be necessary.

The ship was caught in a typhoon for five days, and by the time Fugard reached Fiji, he had finished the novel about his mother. Upon rereading it, however, he quickly threw it overboard into a lagoon—at no loss to world literature, he is certain. After sailing from Fiji, one of the ship's crew died in the South Pacific. Following an exam in Honolulu, Fugard became an Able Bodied Seaman. He proudly recalls that he eventually ended up at the ship's wheel.

In a long letter to his mother from Honolulu, dated February 6, 1954, Fugard acknowledged her offer of his fare back home:

> I might never be able to repay you, but in the end I hope what I offer will be greater.
>
> My writing is not a thing of the here and now—if I've the strength to fulfil my destiny it will live when I am no more—and through it— you. The silent dedication behind all my work is to you. In you I saw

those virtues which today mean so much to me—courage, an indomitable will and faith. I might fail as a man but my art will be strong because it is inspired by those virtues; it will triumph where you have. . . .

South Africa is my soul. The thought of possibly never getting back again was the most terrible thing I have ever known. I need my land and, maybe, my land needs me. I have learnt a few things on this trip but above all else has been the vision of how stupid I was to ever leave. Never again will I forsake those sacred shores. I've said goodbye to my immaturity and my cowardice. I feel within me a strength equal to the great issues of my land. I am burning with impatience to return. Your reward will come Mom! God grant me the strength. . . .

Give the staff my kindest regards, from someone who is no "master" or "baas," but their friend.

The ship broke down seriously at least twice, and when it reached San Pedro, just south of Los Angeles, Fugard went ashore. After the engine was overhauled, Fugard rejoined the *Graigaur* and sailed through the Panama Canal to the Azores where he joined another ship and worked his passage to Greenock, Scotland. He signed off the ship, made his way to London, and lived off his seaman's earnings while awaiting return fare to Port Elizabeth aboard the *Stirling Castle*.[19]

Upon his return to the family home in Newton Park, Fugard knew more clearly than ever before that he wanted to write. He recalls, "My mother said, 'well, how do we start?' I said, 'Got to have a typewriter, can't be a writer without a typewriter.' She bought me my first one, at a sale. I wish I could connect then and now by saying that I'm still using it, but I write in long hand. The real business of writing gets done in pen and ink."

Fugard's visceral, workmanlike relationship with the tools of his trade is manifest when he describes with relish his Mont Blanc and other fountain pens and the inks of various hues he sometimes mixes from crushed berries gathered in his garden: "It's a very complicated number and I have to be at home, settled for a long spell of writing. When I'm travelling I just blend from different bottles of ink. Store-bought never satisfies me." He uses a new pen for every new work: "I think it's slightly adulterous if you take a pen and write another play with it."[20]

"I was certain I was going to have some relationship with blank paper," Fugard remembers. He looked for work as a journalist and began to freelance: "A sailor has a special relationship with each port. He sees a side of each city that few other people do. I suddenly knew how to move around Port Elizabeth as I never had before. I knew how to find the shebeens, for example. They were much more interesting places to drink than the white bars." After writing an article on this side of Port Elizabeth, Fugard showed it to John Sutherland, editor of the *Evening Post*, who published it. Fugard says that Sutherland "became, in a sense, my guide and mentor. After some other looks at Port Elizabeth, I suggested a piece on night schools for blacks. It was my first commission. I remember asking a man about seventy why he was learning to write. His reply has stuck with me ever since. 'If you can't read the white man's notices you'll land in trouble.' "

Fugard also wrote of his sailing experiences in "Life Aboard a Tramp" and in a vivid and truly dramatic article called "Caught in a Typhoon in the Pacific." In it he writes, "Death strikes a hollow disturbing note at sea. For the issues, the questions you've ignored so long are laid out with the corpse, a cold fact that can no longer be avoided." His concern with death is also evident in an arid and stiffly written account of his visits to local cemeteries in "Turning the Pages of History in Graveyards."[21]

Fugard continued to freelance for about six months. The articles, which carried his byline, filled his mother with pride. She saw an advertisement for a cadet journalist placed by the local office of the South African Broadcasting Corporation (SABC) radio news service. Fugard got the job and began compiling twice-daily regional news bulletins about Port Elizabeth and the Eastern Cape: "It looked like I had a glorious future in journalism. I was promoted and transferred to Cape Town."

After moving, Fugard soon made contact with old friends from his university days, among them Benjamin Pogrund, who remembers Fugard calling his job "a plot on the part of the Government to dominate news coverage so as to undermine newspapers." The group of friends included liberal whites interested in working across color lines, an impecunious advocate, a couple of journalists, and a secretary. Their base, according to Pogrund, "was a flat on the Sea Point beachfront where we would gather to eat, drink and argue. We laughed a lot. Living in the same building was a divorced woman and her daughter Sheila, recently qualified in drama at the University of Cape Town. Round-faced, attractive, an intense reader of books, shy and quiet, but pleasing. The group decided Sheila and Athol were made for each other, so we brought them together." (In fact, Meiring was not living with her mother at the time.)

Although at least two years had passed since Fugard had last seen Meiring, he distinctly remembers first seeing her again about a month after his transfer to Cape Town at the arranged party at Pogrund's house. She was "sitting in a corner, as snooty as ever." After completing her studies, Meiring had taken a job in a local art gallery while looking for acting opportunities. There was then no resident professional theatre in Cape Town, but about that time she was cast in her first professional production. Pogrund's matchmaking proved successful. Following a year's courtship, Fugard and Meiring were married on September 2, 1956, despite her father's fear that Fugard would be nothing more than a hack journalist. Fugard says, "I *was* a hack journalist."

During their courtship, Fugard accompanied Meiring to an audition for *Oedipus Rex*. She did not get the part, but Fugard was cast as the old shepherd: "It was my first experience with truly professional theatre. André Huguenet played

Oedipus. He was very good to me, but could also be very cruel. In rehearsal one day, I came on without my stick. He said to me, 'That stick has more character than you do.' I went on to get the notices my performance deserved." The Fugards also participated in an acting workshop under the direction of Pietro Nolte.

Meiring was cast in a production of Sidney Kingsley's *Detective Story*. When an actor failed to appear one evening, Fugard played a walk-on part of a policeman. Yvonne Bryceland played a lead, but, Fugard says, "I wouldn't describe it as our first meeting. Y was so bloody snooty in her amateur days that she looked down on me as a nondescript hanger-on. She would have nothing to do with me. She was a big-timer in those amateur circles." Bryceland has no memory of either Fugard's performance or his presence backstage with Meiring.

Fugard claims his wife "was totally responsible for my interest in the theatre."[22] There is still no resident professional theatre in Port Elizabeth, and Fugard admits his experience of the theatre prior to meeting Meiring was vestigial: "I had seen perhaps six plays." He contends he was writing only short stories and poems at the time, but she insists, "He was writing bits and pieces of plays when I met him. There was an attempt at a full-length play, which I didn't like very much, and also the beginning of a new play that impressed me. It was very South African: two policemen in a charge office out in the country. It was set on a warm night with the sound of crickets in the background." Fugard has no memory of this early effort.

Shortly after his marriage, Fugard had his first play produced. He calls *Klaas and Devil*, the first of his plays he actually remembers, "an attempt, a bad one, to set Synge's *Riders to the Sea* in a South African fishing village. It was an Afrikaaner play in the sense that, had I wanted to capture all the resonances, to be absolutely accurate with the types of characters I'd created, it would have been written in Afrikaans." Fugard assumed the role of the devil.

Written in prose, *Klaas* was entered by the Bay Dramatic Society in an amateur drama festival at the Scopus Club on October 3, 1956. Sheila directed: "I wanted a realistic setting and because it was a sea story I used fishing nets. But the only ones to be found were real ones that had just been used. They stank. I had to spray them with air freshener." One of the festival judges, Rosalie van der Gucht, found the play interesting "although it did not quite come together, and the acting was not stark enough."[23]

The Fugards and a small group of friends, among them Wilhelm Grütter, Carl Otley, and Ralph Rosen, then began a small theatre company that Sheila named Circle Players. Because the rent was cheap, they booked Sunday evenings at the Labia Theatre, named after an Italian countess who was a local patron of the arts. They tried to make it a platform for indigenous material. Meiring had been trained as an actress, but for Circle Players she functioned as a director and did some of the writing. Fugard acted at first, then contributed two plays. He recalls, "We did sort of way-out, avant-garde theatre. . . . It involved

12

a lot of pretentious prose and impossible settings and so on. But we learnt a lot."[24] Each show was performed twice, production budgets were about $50, and instead of charging for tickets, a collection was taken to defray expenses.

On May 26, 1957, Circle Players' first one-act plays opened: Fugard's The Cell, directed by A. Fouche; an allegorical fantasy called Score for Melody, which Meiring wrote and directed; and Grütter's Afrikaans comedy Met die Eerste Oogopslag (With a First Sight), staged by W.J. Basson. Grütter recalls that his "innocuous" comedy was rehearsed with the other two plays at the Fugards' Bantry Bay apartment, where the sets were also built. Grütter can only remember that for Fugard's play he made some masks, "which the actors wore on a stage dark with significance."[25]

The Cell is a one-act verse drama based on an actual story that happened, Fugard believes, in the Orange Free State: "The police had arrested a black woman and, in classic South African fashion, took her off to jail for the weekend. Because of a language barrier she couldn't make them understand she was on the point of giving birth. The child was born in the cell, died, and by the time the woman was released she had become mentally deranged." The cast consisted of the woman, another black prisoner in an adjoining cell, and a chorus of three, dressed in sheets, that commented upon the action of the play. Fugard and Grütter were in the chorus. Meiring recalls, "Athol got bad reviews. They said nobody could hear because of the white masks, which I had baked in our oven. I remember sitting in the back of the theatre when a black man who looked after the building made the brilliant suggestion that I make the holes in the masks bigger. That's how sophisticated we were."

She recalls of this period, "There wasn't any great jubilation. Nobody said, 'This is an incredible playwright.' Athol and I were young. We had no perception where this involvement would lead. I certainly had no idea what I had initiated or where it would lead. If I had, I don't know what I would have done."

Sixteen years after The Cell Fugard would write another play about blacks in prison. He has said of his first effort, "I'm sorry it doesn't exist any more because it might have contained one or two good things."[26] It actually does exist. "To my considerable displeasure," Fugard says, "Sheila has a copy of both The Cell and Klaas and the Devil. I've allowed her to keep them because she wants them, but I've forbidden that they be shown to anyone. They're very pretentious. They really are bad, believe me. Even The Blood Knot makes me squirm."

The Labia plays have been forgotten, but Grütter remembers the young Fugard as being "incredibly enthusiastic, naïve, and consumed with a pretty forlorn passion. I didn't think he had the slightest chance of becoming a serious playwright." In the years after the group disintegrated, Grütter became a critic for the Cape Times. When The Blood Knot toured to Cape Town (and played the Labia), Grütter went to see the show, but not to review it. He recalls, "It was something akin to a blinding explosion to realize that he had mastered stage technique so well—quite apart from the tremendous significance and intrinsic meaning of the play—and I came away somewhat dazed at the thought that perserverance could bring one so far."²⁷

Throughout his stay in Cape Town, Fugard continued to work as a journalist. Sitting with him in a restaurant in December 1957, Pogrund recalls, "I enthused to him about Johannesburg: It was vital, exciting, I told him, compared with staid Cape Town. There was activity which stimulated the mind and the senses. And there was Sophiatown, approaching the sentence of death imposed by Nationalist apartheid, but still raucously alive and like nothing else in South Africa. 'Come to Johannesburg,' I urged him. 'Your writing needs it.' "

Feeling restrained by the demands placed on a journalist to be objective, and increasingly eager to commit totally to his own writing, Fugard decided to give up his job and move to Johannesburg. He and Sheila travelled there circuitously, via Port Elizabeth to see his parents, then up to the Transkei and Pondoland, through Natal, Zululand, and Swaziland. On the way they conceived a series of radio plays about African wildlife with fictionalized stories: "We developed a couple of themes and ideas and even wrote out a couple of synopses, but no one in Johannesburg was interested. This is the only time we considered writing collaboratively." One of the radio plays, *The White Buffalo of Goyani Ridge*, was actually written, but, as with much of his early work, Fugard professes to be glad it no longer exists.

After settling in Johannesburg, Fugard tried to get a job writing advertising copy at Lindsay Smithers, but lost out to another candidate. He finally turned to civil service and became a clerk in Fordsburg for a Native Commissioner's Court, which exist primarily to administer pass book offenses. Fugard organized proceedings and drew up and endorsed warrants; the job was to have a lifelong effect on him. He found horror unadorned and began to understand how South Africa functioned. Prior to working for the court, he says, "I knew that the system was evil, but until then I had no idea of just how systematically evil it was. That was my revelation. As I think back, nothing that has ever happened to me has eclipsed the horror of those few months."²⁸

Fugard stayed in the job six months. During that time Pogrund, who had been transferred to Johannesburg ahead of Fugard, introduced him to Sophiatown, one of the few black townships that could then be entered without a permit. Pogrund's connections and interests were in the political life of the township, but through a series of coincidences Fugard made contact with a group of black artists. He says, "I was very fortunate in the black friends, the black actors I worked with. I suppose when one looks back on South African literature, there will have to be a chapter on what I would describe as the Sophiatown group. Lionel Rogosin was secretly filming *Come Back Africa* there, with some of them at the same time. The group included writers like Bloke Modisane, Lewis Nkosi,

Can Themba, Nat Nakasa, and one splendid actor in the person of Zakes Mokae."[29] Others in the group included Ken Gampu and Don Poho.

These are not household names in Europe and America, but Nkosi, Themba, and Modisane are among the most frequently anthologized black South African writers; all three have been banned. Nkosi and Modisane are in exile, Mokae lives in the United States, Themba and Nakasa, both journalists, committed suicide.[30] As far as South African culture is concerned, the gathering of these individuals at one time and place might be compared to the Beats in San Francisco, or the Lost Generation in Paris.

The blacks Fugard met were especially interested in film and fiction, but Nkosi and Nakasa had considered forming a theatre workshop to train actors and to allow budding playwrights a chance to hear their work. In the office of *Drum*, a weekly magazine important as an outlet and forum for black writers and intellectuals, Nkosi and Fugard discussed the possibility of starting a theatre group. The two often argued while Sheila watched and listened. "It seems to me quite possible now," says Nkosi, "that Sheila had nothing to say to us because we were so obviously silly and enthusiastically silly at that. On the other hand Sheila, now a poet, was a fine actress: From time to time when she offered to read something with the actors, she created out of flimsy gestures and bare words a whole world of living people."[31]

Mokae was a saxophonist and clarinetist who had been a founding member of the Huddleston Jazz Band. He had acted for a small television company that broadcast in England and recalls that he and a group of friends often congregated at Dorkay House to talk and drink wine. Dorkay House, a warehouse-like former clothing factory, had a small office and plenty of open space. Mokae remembers, "We were messing around with theatre, just playing really. We were more theoretical than practical and would discuss what Beckett, for instance, was trying to say. You might lose an argument because you hadn't even read the play in question, so then you'd run out, read the play, and come back to present your case again."[32] During a visit to Dorkay House, Nkosi introduced Fugard as another person interested in theatre. Mokae recalls, "Athol spoke English, but he was clearly an Afrikaner. We called him 'knappie,' which is equivalent, I suppose, to an Okie or hillbilly. He was fun to be with. The fact that he was white didn't make us suspicious. He was clearly interested in art and besides, he came out with Lewis. Since we weren't doing anything illegal we had no fear of being arrested, and even if we were arrested, Athol would have been involved too. It didn't really matter that he was working for the Native Commissioner's Court."

Fugard calls his relationship with the group "the classic one of the whole South African story—generous, warm, accepting. There were no problems. My job with the court didn't poison my relationships. In fact, I became an important contact at the court for those trying to organize resistance and prevent the removals then taking place with nightly raids on Sophiatown. Related cases were tried in my court and I would slow up the process a bit so the lawyers could arrive in time to present a defense. My superiors never caught on." Fugard would use his familiarity with these removals in *Tsotsi*.

Township Life—The Sophiatown "Trilogy": *No-Good Friday*, *Nongogo*, and *Tsotsi*

The unexamined life is not worth living. —Socrates

As invigorating as their impassioned conversations were, the Dorkay House group soon realized that it had to stop talking about theatre and start making it. Sophiatown possessed no theatre; the few skits and sketches that were performed locally were presented in halls. Mokae recalls the difficulties the group encountered: "We'd say, 'We want to do a play.' 'What's that? You want to come and play in my place? Big guys like you playing?' Even the people at Dorkay House thought we were crazy. Since Athol was going to direct the thing, it made sense that he also write it, though he had to do so as we went along. If he had said, 'Listen fellows, I'll go off and write a play and see you again in four weeks,' our momentum would have stopped, the group would have dissolved, and he might never have seen any of us again."

When plans were first made for *No-Good Friday*, Sheila Fugard was to direct. She recalls, "I'd been to drama school, but it wasn't easy dealing with inexperienced actors who had no idea of movement and for some of whom English was not a first language. Athol thought he should take over, which he did, and I then showed him quite a lot of things—like how to build a box set—not that I knew very much, but at least I had some knowledge. We built that set at an Anglican school, thanks to the support of Fr. Martin Jerret-Kerr. I worked as stage manager, did publicity, and sold tickets."

The group rehearsed at Dorkay House and St. Peter's, a nearby school, usually on Sunday, their day off. Everyone in the cast helped with the various aspects of the production. Mokae says, "There was a lot of exchange between Athol and the actors, but basically he was our pen man. If something didn't work, we'd throw it out and come up with something else. You had the stuff written, you had an idea, and if it didn't work you changed it around. We didn't do much improvisation *per se*."

The plot of *No-Good Friday*, Fugard's first full-length play, runs as follows: Willie Seopelo, whose enrollment in a college correspondence course is evidence of his once fervent dream of a better life, commands the respect of his Sophiatown friends and neighbors. These include his mate Rebecca, his close friend Guy, and Father Higgins, a white priest who asks Willie to help Tobias, a new arrival from the country. When Shark, a local *tsotsi* (township gangster), arrives to collect his weekly "protection money," Tobias claims he needs no protection and is stabbed to death. Unable to forget the incident, Willie breaks the customary conspiracy of silence and reports Shark to the police. Willie vows to buy protection no longer. After Shark promises to return for the money, Willie awaits him fearlessly, having finally found peace with himself.

No-Good Friday is a simple play taking one aspect of township life as its starting point. Strongly rooted in that milieu, the play is filled with realistic touches: A condescending potential employer tells Guy, "You boys is just born musicians;" (122*) both a toadyish local politician and do-good white liberal reveal their impotence; Tobias has moved to the city because there is no work in the reserves; Guy tries to teach him the fawning grin and subservient role the white *baas* (master) expects of the black worker; another worker must compromise himself by apologizing for something he did not do; thugs like Shark operate freely throughout the townships without fear of reprisal because the police have been bribed. Such slice-of-life references were hardly revealing to black audiences, but may have been to whites.

Because of the play's verisimilitude and the palpability of the social moment, there seems to be a cause and effect relationship between the facts of Sophiatown life and Willie's internal struggle. This apparent effect of society upon the individual is more explicit than in Fugard's mature plays, but even here it proves illusory. In a crucial exchange near the end of the play, Willie says, "The world I live in is the way it is not in spite of me but because of me. You think we're just poor suffering came-to-Jesus-at-the-end-of-it-all black men and that the world's all wrong and against us so what the hell. Well I'm not so sure of that any more. I'm not so sure because I think we helped to make it, the way it is." (160-161) Willie neither likes the status quo nor denies there is oppression, "but there's a lot of it we make ourselves and a lot we accept." Thus, despite the emphasis throughout No-Good Friday on crime and social underdogs, it is not simply a Naturalistic work in which downtrodden characters are depicted as the innocent victims of social circumstances. Willie denies he is a product of forces outside himself.

The plot baldly described above appears to make a martyr-hero of Willie, but is is actually no such thing. What might have been the play's emotional climax—either Willie's murder or his triumph over Shark—is conspicuously omitted. Despite the importance of Tobias's murder, No-Good Friday does not so much emphasize the effect of external events upon Willie as it does his internal transformation. The play focuses on his psyche rather than his fate at the hands of Shark.

*Quotations from No-Good Friday and Nongogo are from Dimetos: And Two Early Plays (Oxford: Oxford University Press, 1977).

Willie assumes responsibility for himself, but he refuses to be accountable for others. He will not become their leader and acts only on the basis of personal convictions. Even his use of the plural "we" is undercut when he adds, "This doesn't concern any of you and the sooner you leave me alone to solve it my way the better." (161) Because his friends admire Willie, they cannot easily surrender their presumption that he is either telling them how to act or providing a model for their behavior. However, Willie follows only his own dictates and refuses to be what others, including Rebecca, expect him to be. She tells Guy the correspondence course has made Willie independent: "He just doesn't need anyone. Not you . . . not even me." (123)

The course has not caused the breach between Willie and Rebecca. Rather, it has prompted him to reexamine his life. He declares, "It's just possible that a man can get to thinking about other things than extra pay and a better position. . . . Such as himself. What's he doing? Where does he fit in?" (135) After two years of enrollment, he is still in the first year of his B.A. course. Correspondence school had held out the hope of one kind of independence, but Willie finally seeks another—from illusory dreams, including the dream of upward mobility through personal industry. He tells Guy there is something wrong with a man's attempt to make a decent life for himself "if he uses it as a fire exit every time it gets a little hot." (155) Dreams provide respite from the here and now, but when finally recognized as illusory, they must be discarded.

Willie's dreams are counter-poised by the hopes and future plans Tobias airs in a letter to his wife. Willie wants to tell him the truth that will stop such dreaming: "I woke up a long time ago," he says. (137) He subsequently agrees to write Tobias's widow about the murder only if Tobias's own letter remains unmailed, "because it's full of dreams." (145) Yet even this precondition does not make it easy for the usually articulate Willie to compose the letter: "How do you speak kindly of a man's death when the only truth about it is its stupidity? How do you tell a woman that her man died for bugger-all and that his death means bugger-all." (154) Unlike Good Friday, there will be no resurrection following this no-good Friday. Tobias's false dreams have reminded Willie of the futility of his own. Rejecting both delusive dreams of an ideal future as well as Guy's and Rebecca's misconceptions of the past—"a better Willie that used to be" (137)—Willie decides to live in the present, which he forthrightly faces despite its dreariness.

This theme of dreams and illusions—and the distinctions between past, present, and future that are often linked to it—runs throughout Fugard's work. The dominance of internal rather than external action and character transformation is also the norm.

Another leitmotif first introduced in *No-Good Friday* is self-consciousness of language, not simply on the part of the playwright, but also in his characters. Rebecca learns the difference between admiration and pride from Willie's dictionary. She later complains of the difficulty of arguing with Willie "when you don't even know half the words for the things you want to say." (149) After asking Willie the reason behind his report to the police, Guy adds, "Forget the big words, Willie. . . . I want you to tell me in short ones that I can understand why you went." (154) Watson, the township politician, is worried about a speech he must make and auditions for Guy two "stirring" rhetorical platitudes.

Language facility is most pronounced in Willie. He helps Guy and Tobias spell and is selected to write the letter to the widow. Most important of all, his speech is usually precise and, as Guy says, he has "got the words." (125) But not always. As Willie sees in Tobias his own past dreams, so they share the difficulty of writing a letter. Tobias complains floridly to his wife, "I need words and a word is only a wind. . . . The words, Maxulu, the words. You must know when you read that I have not got the words." (136-37) When Willie must later write the same woman, his words dry up.

No-Good Friday is no longer than a typical Fugard play, but it is plotted, sometimes awkwardly, more heavily than most. Willie's secret attendance of Tobias's funeral is revealed without grace. Tobias is killed without hesitation despite his unfamiliarity with the protection racket, yet Shark suddenly decides to wait patiently before collecting Willie's payment. *No-Good Friday* also contains twice as many characters as any succeeding play. Rebecca is unusual among Fugard's women in that she is weaker than her companion. Like many of the succeeding protagonists, Willie must face alone the imperatives of an uncompromising world. *No-Good Friday* does not end with the hopefulness of a Prometheus ready to solve or transcend the problems of the world, but neither does it end in despair. Willie has finally become conscious of himself.

No-Good Friday's simplicity lies in its directness, not in its presumed examination of an innately good man pitted against a heinous system, nor in some imagined polemic for political action. Nkosi realizes that the play "had very little concern with the politics behind the chronic violence and gangsterism in the ghetto," but this represents, for Nkosi, a limitation. The play, "posed the wrong questions and provided the wrong answers. The problem that Fugard has set his hero—an educated African who must provide some leadership in the community—[is] whether to defy the thugs and refuse to pay up his share, or live forever in fear of the gangs."

In fact, Fugard carefully underscores Willie's refusal to be a leader of his community. A more serious misconception lies in Nkosi's reading of the choice Willie faces. His alternative to paying Shark is not fear of facing the gangs. Rather, Willie would have to confront his personal weakness thus revealed. The pressures impinging on his consciousness are created more by Willie himself than by Sophiatown or South Africa.

No-Good Friday was first performed on August 30, 1958 at the Bantu Men's Social Centre, a site for billiards, ping-pong, and chess located next to Dorkay House.

Mokae remembers that the opening performance "was a disaster because of the music. We taped it. Also, Connie Mabaso [as Guy] never really learned his part and every time we looked up at him we were likely to crack up." Mokae was originally slated to play the role of Shark, but a week before the opening he had to leave Sophiatown to attend a funeral. Bloke Modisane moved into the role. When Mokae returned he played one of the thugs. Stephen Moloi played Willie (not Lewis Nkosi as the published text indicates), with Gladys Sibisi as Rebecca, Preddie Ramphele as Watson, Daniel Poho as Pinkie and Ken Kampu as Tobias. Using the name Hal Lannigan, Fugard himself appeared as Father Higgins: "Since I was the only white around, there was no question but that I would play the part. I used a stage name because I thought it a bit pretentious to be writer, director, *and* actor." Tone Brulin, who would figure prominently in the next phase of Fugard's career, was not impressed with Fugard's acting, "Athol was merely standing in. At least, he gave that impression."[33] For one performance in Pretoria, Fugard could not perform with the black cast without breaking the law. Nkosi assumed the part and, according to Fugard, "acquitted himself very well."

In addition to performances at the Bantu Men's Social Centre and in Pretoria, *No-Good Friday* also played church halls in the townships, almost exclusively to small black audiences, and in the white suburbs. A special reading was organized in Port Elizabeth so that Fugard's father could hear the play. For one performance in the Johannesburg township of Orlando the audience numbered five. According to Mokae, "Sometimes there were as many people on stage as in the audience. We played more to friends than anyone else." This was the rule rather than the exception, according to Fugard. The ease with which he had access to Sophiatown and Orlando contrasts sharply with conditions today. Whites must now have a permit to visit a township, and since 1964 Fugard has often been refused such permission, even to see productions he directed, performed by actors he helped train. *No-Good Friday* was presented over a period of three months, although sometimes a week or two passed between performances.

Thanks to the fund-raising of Benedicta Bonnacorsi, who ran a local acting school, *No-Good Friday* also had a single Sunday night performance at a major Johannesburg theatre, the Brian Brooke. Fugard calls Bonnacorsi "the equivalent of a Johannesburg mother for us. She was a patron in our early years and became a very good friend of Sheila's and mine. I've never mentioned her often enough, if at all. She was a very important person in our lives." The reviews following the performance at the Brian Brooke were not enthusiastic: "Clear-cut simplicity more than compensated at first for a certain fulsomeness of dialogue. . . . People and plot got bogged in a rather celebrated emotionalism which could be more justly labelled 'after Tennessee Williams' than something out of Africa."[34]

During the run of *No-Good Friday*, Fugard also established important friendships with two men who saw the production: Barney Simon, who had been hired as a copywriter for Lindsay Smithers in the very position that Fugard himself had sought, and Tone Brulin, a Belgian director brought to South Africa by the National Theatre Organisation (NTO) to begin a Chamber Theatre (Kamertoneel) in Pretoria, where he directed a series of productions in Afrikaans and English. Founded in 1948, the NTO was the first national theatre in the (then) British Commonwealth. Though unimpressed with Fugard's acting, Brulin had been excited by the production of *No-Good Friday* and suggested that Fugard acquire more professional experience.

As early as April 1958 he had sought a position with the NTO in public relations, acting, or stage management. Following Brulin's recommendation, the NTO hired Fugard on October 25, 1958 to serve as stage manager and "The Voice" for James Ambrose Brown's *Seven against the Sun*. Fugard was paid 12 pounds per week. Following the scheduled run, he was appointed publicity officer for a tour of the play. He was paid fifty pounds per month, one pound allowance for every day on the road, and a five percent ticket commission. The tour, according to Fugard, "kept the wolf away from the door for quite a long time because it went on tour. In those days a tour in South Africa meant a six-month stint of one night stands." Tours of Kamertoneel productions were unusual, Fugard says, because "it was a venue for presenting work that was regarded by the standards of that time as avant-garde and couldn't be done in a large theatre, couldn't be done on tour to rural areas. I worked with Brulin most on Flemish and Dutch plays and German plays in translation. It was European avant-garde as opposed to English or American." Brulin eventually moved in with the Fugards.

The job was more than a means to escape the Native Commissioner's Court. Because the NTO was a large organization, indeed the first fully professional theatre with which he had been associated except for the Huguenet *Oedipus Rex*, Fugard received invaluable experience and "an enormous opportunity to learn about the practical side of theatre." The NTO served as his drama school: "It was educational learning how directors get work out of actors, so was the sheer exercise of watching a show every night from the wings. Some of the plays were well written, so there was also an important lesson in craftsmanship." For the Labia productions and *No-Good Friday*, "you simply had to teach yourself everything, how to build a set, how to light a show—though in some of the places this was very simple. One switch. Off or on." He stage managed *The Chairs* by Ionesco, Saroyan's *Cave Dwellers*, Paul Osborn's *Mornings at Seven*, and *Bruide in die More (Bride in the Morning)* by Belgian Hugo Claus. In addition, Fugard recalls, "I was suddenly in the company of professionals—actors like André Huguenot, actors like Bill Brewer, Michael Turner, Arthur Hall, Frank Wise, Peter Gildenhuys."[35]

While working for the NTO, Fugard wrote and directed his next play, *Nongogo*. It opens as Johnny, a door-to-door salesman, visits Queeny in her township shebeen. She is so impressed by his hopes and dreams of starting a decorating business that she begins to share them and even lends him some money. He responds to her trust by confiding both the horrors he experienced as a young man in the all-male mining compounds, and his desire for "a clean woman." Sam, part of Queeny's life in "the old days," resents Johnny's intrusion into her life and plots to reveal her past. To convince Johnny she is willing to change her life for him, Queeny closes the shebeen to celebrate their new venture, but their dreams evaporate when he discovers her past. She had been a nongogo: She slept with any man for twenty-five cents. (In early performances, both Sam and Johnny died at the hands of Blackie, Queeny's helper, but this was subsequently changed.)

Nongogo is a play about the actuality of the past and forlorn hopes for the future. The two are linked by Johnny's decorating business of the present, which he and Queeny hope will fulfill their dreams of independence, freedom, and an escape from the past, especially the sexual degradation both experienced at the mines. Queeny's willingness to give up her successful shebeen for Johnny indicates it has not been as satisfying as she had hoped.

Even before hearing Johnny's grand plan, she admits to Sam that she does not have everything. Other women have a man. She confides that she might not mind being told where to go and what to do. Her anger towards a patron named Patrick can be perceived as an indirect reflection of her aspirations towards a normal life: She identifies with the pregnant wife he has left alone. Queeny quickly determines that Johnny is not married.

Queeny is intoxicated by Johnny's dreams and captivated by the way he treats her. Blackie wonders if Johnny "is going to make you like other women?" (85) Johnny is confident she can learn to sew: "Other women can, you can. You're the same as them." (88) He holds out the promise of the respectable life Queeny never had. Trying to become the clean woman he seeks, Queeny has found some purpose in life.

She anxiously hopes to conceal her past, and Sam reassures her that while people are curious to know her real name and from where she comes, "they're not getting any wiser." (68) Unable to forget her past, Queeny is incensed to think Sam can forget his. Johnny, of course, cannot forget his either, but at least he discusses it openly with her. She is initially incapable of such candor and says the shebeen is "the only thing you or anybody else can point at in my life." (109) She also deceives Johnny about the length of time she has operated it.

Time—whether it is the past to be escaped, the present to be seized, or the future that promises so much more than the present—is referred to throughout the play, indeed, throughout Fugard's work. Blackie steals a chiming clock for Queeny. She gives Johnny a wristwatch. Twenty-four hours after he and Queeny meet, their dreams of a new life end when he learns about her previous life. They resign themselves to the impossibility of escaping their pasts. Johnny's optimism about change and the future is suddenly transmuted: "The future. It's a waste of time talking about that. The only future we've got is tomorrow if we're unlucky enough to wake up." (107)

Johnny finally precipitates her confession with the simple statement, "There is a name for everything." (113) As with Fugard's only novel, *Tsotsi*, *Nongogo* is about a name and what it means to live with one, or without one. Fugard has called the ability to name something, "a small act of possession." This concern with names appears frequently in his writing. While getting drunk, Patrick tries to name his child. As soon as Johnny mentions the possibility of owning a shop, Queeny urges that they name it. She is eager about future names, but not those of the past or present: "There's been times I never knew what day it was in here . . . Monday or Tuesday, maybe Friday? It didn't make any difference. Giving it a name didn't make it any different from the rest." (91)

As Queeny nears her confession, the tension grows along with the constant knocking on the door by potential customers. However, her description of life as a nongogo is not quite the climax for an audience it might at first seem. The play's title minimizes the surprise of her revelation, at least for a South African audience, and the unsavoriness of her past is alluded to long before Sam's machinations begin. Only Johnny lacks full awareness of it.

Furthermore, it is not simply Queeny's past that destroys the dream of a new life. Before she fully explains her past, Johnny says, "Let's blame the stinking bloody world out there that makes us what we are. Let's blame what sent us into this world because nobody with any sense would choose to come. . . . Sometimes I get the crazy idea that a man can change the world he lives in. Hell. You can't even change yourself." (109) Thus, the obliteration of their dreams is largely foreordained. *Nongogo* is the only truly Naturalistic play in the Fugard canon. As if written to conform to Zola's dictates in "Naturalism on the Stage," Johnny and Queeny have been mechanically predetermined by their milieu. As Johnny wants to blame a stinking world, so Queeny later says, "I did it because I was hungry." (113) As in other Naturalist works, sex is central and moralistic judgments are avoided. *Nongogo* does not so much tell a story or present a new relationship as expose a thin slice of township life.

In *No-Good Friday*, Willie actively and consciously surrenders his dreams by recognizing them as mere illusions. Johnny and Queeny have theirs passively stripped away, as if against their wills. Environmental contingencies can never be circumvented, but this is not the reason Willie stops dreaming. Whereas he states that the world "is the way it is not in spite of me but because of me," (160) Johnny declares, "I didn't make myself." (112) He implies he is not responsible for what had happened in the past, nor capable of controlling what will happen to him in the future. Queeny echoes him in her confession: "no one's given me a chance." (113) She too disclaims responsibility for the way she is: "I don't suppose it's my fault, or even Sam's. (*Pause.*) Then who . . . who the hell do you swear at and hate?" (64) Thus, while Sam appears Machiavellian and the apparent agent for wrecking hopes and dreams, he is merely the proximate cause of what is, ultimately, inevitable.

Nongogo and *No-Good Friday* both concentrate on "exotic" aspects of township life. The theme of individual enterprise and upward mobility is central to both. So is the distinction between dreams and reality. Yet, assumptions about the relationship between man and his society are very different. Many of the characters Fugard creates in the years ahead are also concerned with their pasts. Several attempt to escape it. Unlike Johnny and Queeny, however, the lives of future characters are never again so contingent upon social and environmental imperatives, as opposed to metaphysical and cosmic ones.

As with many of the plays to come, *Nongogo* focuses on two characters and is neoclassical in spanning little more than a day and being confined to a single room. Sam's plot is the first of many games to be played by Fugard's characters. Although this charade is a serious one, intended to wreck illusions by revealing the past, it can be compared to subsequent happier games in which the past is recovered through the imagination.

Nongogo is a conventional story of a woman with a past she tries to hide but cannot—as in *Lady Windermere's Fan* and *The Second Mrs. Tanqueray*—and of the prostitute with a heart of gold. Such women are usually remorseful about their pasts, have changed their names, and are the focus of a contrast between experience and innocence. The fallen women of this tradition often try to make good, but usually fail. There is also something of Shaw's Mrs. Warren in her. Although the shebeen has made her financially secure, she decides to transform herself back into the "old" Queeny: "There are a lot of streets I haven't walked, lampposts I haven't stood under, faces I haven't smiled at." (114) As with Mrs. Warren, hunger had forced Queeny into the business, and like her she remains in it after her stomach has been filled.

Nongogo rehearsed at Jan Hofmeyr, a school for social workers next to the Bantu Men's Social Centre, where it opened on June 8, 1959. It later had a short run in Darragh Hall of Johannesburg's Anglican cathedral. Mokae recollects, "Tone Brulin did the set for us, we had some lights, got reviews, and the audience liked it. Things began to get tight. It was fun to be in one place. Being in town, whites came to see us. That's when the Dorkay people started to say, 'these people aren't so crazy, they might be up to something.' It was nice playing regularly and to larger audiences, maybe a hundred on the weekends. Tickets were sold at a small fee, and though I don't think we were ever paid, we were happy just to work."

David Langa composed "Johnny Boy," which used a traditional Shangaan instrument, the mbela. It was tape recorded by Thandi Kumalo and used before the play, during intermission, and to indicate the passage of time. The cast included Sol Rachilo as Johnny, Thandi Kumalo as Queeny, David Phetoe as Sam, Connie Mabaso as Patrick, and Mokae as Blackie. Fugard says that, "while working with Zakes on *No-Good Friday* we discovered a close bond. In writing *Nongogo* I specifically saw him in the role of Blackie."

Fugard now calls *No-Good Friday* and *Nongogo* "inflated verse dramas by a liberally-informed white." (Both are written in prose.) In an undated letter to Richard Rive, he mentions, "I've reread them and find them immature, gauche, derivative and in a hundred other ways unsuitable for publication. Quite honestly, I'd like to forget I ever wrote them."[36] Fugard considers the characters to be two-dimensional stereotypes and the central dilemmas to be obvious and clichéd: "Both plays were written fairly quickly, without any radical reexamination. There was none of the diligence and minute attempts to rewrite and reexamine a speech or page of dialogue. This started when I rewrote *The Blood Knot* and has been an absolute fact of my existence as a writer ever since. For these early plays there weren't the innumerable drafts that I now find myself writing." He also considers both plays derivative of his excitement at first encountering O'Neill, Williams, and other American playwrights.

It is unlikely that either play would now be staged except out of curiosity. (In addition to the original South African productions, they were presented in Sheffield, England, in 1974; *Nongogo* was revived in the Transvaal in 1970, in New York in 1978, and in Cape Town in 1978-79.) These are obviously minor plays, rather simplistic, but of interest in comparison to Fugard's succeeding plays. As conventional as they now appear, in 1965 Bob Leshoai referred to them as "experimental theatre."[37] Leshoai's comment is less a reflection of his misunderstanding of the plays, or of what might truly be called "experimental," than it is of the standards then prevailing in South Africa.

After the run of *Nongogo*, Brulin and the NTO asked Fugard to become resident stage manager of the Cape Town branch, which was just opening at the Bellville Civic Centre, where they presented some of the shows already done at the Kamertoneel. Fugard's experience at the NTO and with the two early plays was valuable, but it also contributed to his and Sheila's decision to leave South Africa, perhaps for good: "I had a sense of the widening horizon of the theatre, but the experience I could get at home was limited. There was also a sense of adventure inside the two of us."

In November 1959, they boarded the *Orangefontein* in Port Elizabeth, which stopped in Cape Town before sailing to Southampton via Madeira. Sheila would be outside South Africa for the first time since her arrival as a girl. Fugard recalls the emotion of leaving Cape Town: "For me there wasn't quite the strong sense of loneliness there had been in Worcester at the start of my hitchhiking trip. It was very disconcerting to be back on a ship, but not as a crewman. I tried hard to make friends among the sailors, but they wouldn't have anything to do with me."

After settling in an attic room off London's Finchley Road, Fugard began to look for work in the theatre: "I didn't presume to think the Royal Court would take me on as a stage manager. I'd gladly have been a stagehand, but they'd have none of me." Kenneth Rae of the International Theatre Institute in England arranged for Fugard to observe the work of an experimental theatre club in Leatherhead. Fugard remembers it as "British theatre at its stodgiest." John Hale of the Bristol Old Vic also invited Fugard to visit.

The nearest he got to a theatre job was working backstage for Joan Littlewood, to whom he had sent a play he had written in South Africa called *A Place with the Pigs*: "It was the first of my attempts at an Immorality Act story. It centered on the reaction of a little Afrikaans community to a man who had a love relationship with a Coloured woman. I eventually tore it up." The job with Littlewood fell through.

With their finances dwindling, Sheila began work as a typist. Fugard signed on with an agency for out of work actors that sent him out to houseclean and scrub floors. Because sailors live in a confined space, they become very tidy and careful. Fugard recalls, "I did cleaning so well all the elderly ladies asked me to come back." Whenever possible, the Fugards went to the theatre. They had seen early works by Pinter and Osborne in South Africa, but found most of the plays that they saw in England less adventurous formally than the European plays in translation they were accustomed to at the Kamertoneel.

Also in London at that time were David Herbert, an actor Fugard had met while stage managing in Cape Town, and his wife Jonne Finnemore. After Brulin came to London, having recently moved back to Belgium, the group decided to set up a little South African company called the New Africa Group. They would create a theatre piece and take it to the Continent where Brulin had contacts. "The question then became," Fugard remembers, "what piece of work? David was as interested in writing as I was." Both decided to write plays very quickly. They would perform the better one. Fugard's was a modern allegorical treatment, set in South Africa, of the Magi looking for the virgin and child. One wiseman was Indian, another black, and the third Coloured. "The play has vanished from the face of the earth," says Fugard, "and good riddance. David's was much better. In fact, I think it was a bloody good play. I'm amazed it has disappeared. I'd have thought it still had life in it."

Written in a series of short scenes, Herbert's *A Kakamas Greek* centers on the relationship between Gabriel and a man he befriends who claims to be Akadis, a Greek from Kakamas, a remote town in the arid Karoo. It is gradually revealed that Gabriel is really an albino black, and Akadis is actually Okkie, a Coloured man trying to pass as white. Both are possessed by fear of the dark side of their heritage. They are joined by a black man named Skelm, who remains silent throughout the play, but who evolves from being the projection of their inner-consciousness to the acknowledged reality in their thoughts. With Skelm and Gabriel as catalysts, Okkie eventually accepts his Coloured destiny.

26

Following rehearsals in Brulin's Brussels apartment, where the group lived, they began the tour Brulin had arranged. A *Kakamas Greek* opened in Brussels at the Palais des Beaux Arts on May 24, 1960 as part of the Festival of Avant-Garde Theatre, which included troupes from Germany, France, Belgium, Poland, and Holland. The following week it received single performances, always in English, in Amsterdam, Antwerp, Ghent, Mechelin, Rotterdam, The Hague, and again in Amsterdam. This tour, according to Fugard, taught him much of what he knows about theatre craft.

Under Brulin's direction, Herbert appeared as Gabriel with Clive Farrel, a black actor from Sierra Leone, as Skelm and Fugard as Okkie. Sheila Fugard served as stage manager. One critic wrote that Herbert and Fugard "played their roles with intensity of expression and with great verbal and physical range." Another added that the production received an ovation rather than, simply, applause.[38]

Brulin's memories of A *Kakamas Greek* remain vivid: "There were whispers of giving us a first prize for best play and best production, but because of fear of the South African Embassy, they didn't do it. Athol's acting in *No-Good Friday* hadn't impressed me, but for A *Kakamas Greek* the intensity and strength of his everyday personality carried over and grew on stage. The group broke up because, in spite of apartheid, there was nostalgia for home."[39]

Fugard returned to London, but soon went back to the Continent without Sheila. The Amsterdam host of A *Kakamas Greek*, Toneelgroep Puck, decided to produce Brulin's play *De Honden* (The Dogs) in its weekend series beginning November 13, 1960. (It had already been published in the magazine *Podium*.) Because of other commitments, Brulin asked Fugard to direct. According to Fugard, "Dutch is close enough to Afrikaans that I had no trouble with the language. It was the first time I'd directed another writer's play, but I did a pretty good job. It was well received and ran about four weeks."

The play reflected Brulin's encounter with South Africa, especially the way blacks guilty of minor passbook infractions are treated on forced-labor farms. It was generally not as favorably received as Fugard remembers. Despite its good intentions, *De Honden* was criticized for being over-written and needlessly complicated. Its episodic structure and frequent scene changes prevented fluid progression. One critic complained that after forty-five minutes he hadn't the faintest idea what was going on. Fugard himself was praised by another critic for doing everything to give the play an edge.[40]

The Sharpeville Massacre on March 21, 1960 had prompted the Fugards to begin to think it was not the time to be away from South Africa. That autumn, Sheila learned she was pregnant and they decided to return home. "There was a sense," Fugard remembers, "that the only place I could really have an identity and live my life was on South African soil. Had I pulled out my roots, I would have stopped writing. This may be a limitation, but when I realized that I belong in South Africa, I felt better."[41] They sailed from Southampton aboard the *Stirl-*

27

ing Castle: "The moment was charged with an ominous presentiment of a dark future—and we were sailing to the Cape and sunshine." They arrived in Cape Town on December 15, 1960.

The only play Fugard had written during his sojourn, the three wisemen allegory, had gone unproduced, but while in London Fugard began one of the most important writing exercises of his life, his notebooks: "It became a daily ritual to record anything that happened to me which seemed of significance—sensual fragments, incidents, quotations, speculations. Writing now, I find in them the content of all I can possibly say about my work."[42] They also contain some of his most joyous utterances—a celebratory note Fugard sometimes finds lacking in his other writing.

The notebooks were started in London, but most of the entries, like the plays, have been written in Port Elizabeth "at the table at which I usually work. Even though the notebooks are a haphazard and discontinuous exercise, I can only pursue them at home, with a few exceptions in Johannesburg and London. When I took the fellowship at Yale [spring term 1980], I thought that for once I'd try and keep an absolutely accurate log of a production. I started and the notes came out very nicely, for instance my assessments of the actors. But then I had to make a cast change and ended up throwing out all those pages." Although Fugard "never consciously used the notebooks as a playwright," he admits that "everything is reflected there—my plays come from life and from encounters with actual people. But I found that as soon as I got deeply involved with writing a play, I either forgot the notebooks completely or had no need of them."[43]

The notebooks reveal both Fugard's love of the physical beauty of his homeland and an eye and ear sensitive to events around him. The celebratory note mentioned above is especially evident in this entry: "Mom doctoring Maria with Bob Martin's (for dogs) conditioning pills. Maria has been complaining about pains in her legs. When Mannie Swart heard about Maria's trouble he fished a little bottle of the Bob Martin's pills out of his waistcoat pocket. Says he was put on them by relatives in the Transvaal. Mom: 'They work. She could hardly walk . . . now she runs.' Also: 'But you must remember to order for the "medium dog." You get them for small dogs, medium dogs, and big dogs . . . you know, Grey Danes and those things. Well the medium dog is the one for human beings.' "(10-63*) The appreciative tone of this humorous entry suggests the anecdotal storytelling ability of Fugard's mother, which had once prompted him to try and write a novel about her.

---

*The date for each quotation from the notebooks will be indicated parenthetically. The printed sources for these include: introductions to Fugard's plays; "Athol Fugard Notebooks," *The Classic*, 3, No. 4 (1977), 66-82; "Fugard on Fugard," *yale/theatre*, 4, i (1973), 41-54; "Writer's Notebook," *Sunday Tribune*, December 11, 1966; theatre programs for various programs; and unpublished entries. Entries dated only by the month are from the edited version published by Knopf (New York, 1984).

While shaping the notebooks for publication, Fugard edited out some personal sections and omitted or changed the identity of people mentioned in any entry of a political nature. He also became aware that "something was creeping into them that hadn't been there before, and it was making what had been a very important exercise in disciplining my life into a sterile one. I was becoming self-conscious."[44] Sensing that he had begun to write for posterity, Fugard admitted in 1980 that he had stopped keeping a notebook. By 1982 he had begun them again "on a very different basis."

The first entry in his notebook proved to be the genesis of *The Blood Knot*. Aboard ship on his way back to Port Elizabeth, Fugard also made notes that led to his novel, *Tsotsi*. These included: "*The idea for a story*—criminal: completely shrouded in darkness. At a moment—a stab of light and pain. This followed, developed, in the span of a short time leads to the full Christian experience;" (12-9-60) "Madondo was his name—a long time ago. A name dimly remembered. Finally, the value—life=love is found and clung to, guarded, cherished;" (12-12-60) "Tsotsi—progression is an admission of an ever deeper dimension to his living. Tsotsi—a freedom (1) to choose his victim. (2) Not to have a victim." (1-10-61) For the only time in his career, Fugard began to write two works simultaneously, *Tsotsi* and *The Blood Knot*: "I've tried it a couple of times since, but the results have been a waste of time. If I can't hand myself over to one project, I screw it up."

Fugard says that he cannot remember any moment actually spent writing *Tsotsi*, and that after finishing the manuscript he did not try to get it published. He assumed he had thrown it away until Sheila found a draft when the National English Literary Museum and Documentation Centre (NELM) at Rhodes University asked if there were any papers Fugard would give it for safekeeping.

The story of the *Tsotsi* manuscript and its eventual publication is as complicated as it is fascinating. The text was handwritten, some of it on the backs of stock inventories for Cyril Lord Carpets (where Sheila had worked briefly in London), some on the backs of record inventories (Sheila had also worked in a record store), and still other sections were written on the backs of swimming programs from the pool where Fugard's mother had her cafe. After discovering the manuscript at Rhodes, Stephen Gray edited it for publication in 1980. Every word remained Fugard's, but the text was cut fifteen to twenty percent.

After Gray delivered the manuscript to the printer, Fugard produced a second draft that was sharper and more mature. Gray writes, "That meant two things: First, a more considerable time and amount of energy had gone into the drafting of *Tsotsi* than anyone including Fugard had remembered; it had been done with extensive care and conscientious planning—any doubters who felt that it must have been composed in a slapdash fashion could rest at ease. Secondly, it meant a possible last-minute cancellation of all existing arrangements, followed by the establishing of another, yet more definitive text."[45]

Fugard appointed Sheila and Ross Devenish, a friend and film director, to make editorial decisions on his behalf and to oversee Gray's work. Fugard claims never to have reread the novel, but he did read two chapters in Grahamstown in the spring of 1978 at a public celebration of a visit by Ezekiel Mphahlele. When, shortly after *Tsotsi's* publication, Sheila claimed she had never written a play (though she actually had in the days of Circle Players), Fugard countered "I've never written a novel." Reminded of *Tsotsi* he teased, "that was by somebody else."

The story opens as a group of *tsotsis*—Boston, Die Aap, Butcher, and Tsotsi, their leader—plot their strategy for the night. After they kill a miner for his pay packet, Boston begins to probe Tsotsi's past with questions Tsotsi cannot answer.[46] He viciously beats Boston, then finds his way to a grove of trees where a woman thrusts an infant upon him and disappears. The child evokes a long-suppressed memory of a dog. Unusual as a memory is for Tsotsi, even stranger thoughts strike him as he becomes curious about his past. After stalking a cripple named Morris Tshabalala, Tsotsi surprises himself by asking Morris questions instead of robbing or murdering him. Returning home to the baby, Tsotsi kidnaps a woman to nurse it. He again thinks of the dog and remembers the time when he, a ten-year-old boy named David, fearfully ran away from home. As Tsotsi's reveries about his past continue, he seeks out Boston to help him explain the recent turn in his life. The next morning, after visiting a church, Tsotsi dies trying to rescue the baby from the rubble created by a slum-clearance squad.

From the age of ten onward, Tsotsi had been most concerned with keeping his body alive, but in the span of the novel his attention shifts to the life of his soul. Tsotsi's journey towards rebirth through consciousness and light, away from insensitivity and darkness, is initiated by questions and propelled by memories. Following the miner's murder, the gang visits a shebeen where Tsotsi tries to assure himself nothing has changed. He realizes, however, "It had no longer *felt* the same. Boston had something to do with it . . . and Tsotsi knew why. It was because of his questions." (16*) Boston's questions and "the light of his eyes" lead Tsotsi to "a world in which no one, not even Tsotsi himself, had ventured." (23)

Boston, like Johnny in *Nongogo*, is a common figure in the Fugard canon: the outsider who acts as a catalyst. Soon after joining the gang he had asked simply, "What's your name Tsotsi . . . your real name?" (16) Tsotsi hates such questions because he does not know their answers. Three rules have ordered his life. The first is to check his knife upon awakening. The second is "never to disturb his inward darkness with the light of a thought about himself or the attempt at a memory." His third rule, that he tolerates no questions from another, is the rule Boston breaks: "Those questions sounded the vast depths of his darkness,

*Tsotsi, (Johannesburg and London: Ad. Donker, 1980).

30

making it a tangible reality. To know nothing about yourself is to be constantly in danger of nothingness, those voids of non-being over which a man walks the tightrope of his life." (32) Yet, following Boston's questions, Tsotsi sets out to recover his real name and, by implication, his real identity. He will discard the generic ones he adopted at the age of ten.

Once it begins, Tsotsi cannot retreat from the journey into his past nor prevent the gradual metamorphosis of his character. Unexpected sensory associations between present realities and past memories become increasingly frequent: As the baby reminds him of a dog in his past, so does Morris Tshabalala's oath, "Whelp of a yellow bitch" when Tsotsi steps on the cripple's hand. The association is compounded when Tsotsi recognizes the similarity between the dog's paralyzed hindquarters and the labored crawling of the beggar.

The admission of the baby into Tsotsi's life is one turning point. His interaction with Morris is another. Boston had warned Tsotsi that one day he would feel something—and not know what to do. "One day" turns out to be the next day. Tsotsi begins to feel for Morris, his victim. He insists to himself that he doesn't care a damn for Morris, but the narrator adds, "It had never been necessary to say this to himself before. He had to now, and it was because of the feeling." (79)

After relentlessly pursuing Morris, unnerved by this new sensation of feeling for another man, Tsotsi experiences sympathy, a novel emotion he compares with light and its ability to reveal. When the two finally confront each other, Tsotsi breaks the silence by, of all things, asking a question: "What do you feel?" (86) Morris replies, "Sunshine in stones. The warm stones of the streets. I felt it tonight at the end of the day. I must feel it tomorrow. If my hands don't feel I'll make a hole in my trousers and sit with my soft bum to feel, or lay my face on the ground. . . . Do you understand now. I want to live." So does the baby. So did the homeless boy named David.

Morris then poses the same question Boston had: "How old are you?" Instead of responding angrily or with his fists, Tsotsi admits he does not know, "but I will find out." Tsotsi's three rules had given his life at least the semblance of order. His contact with Morris begins to erode this order: Tsotsi starts to ask some questions and to answer others.

When Butcher and Die Aap try to learn about their next job, Tsotsi becomes conscious of them in a new way and discovers that decisions involve choice; alternatives are possible. His life had been dominated by resignation to the inevitable, but he begins to learn that some things are avoidable. When Morris asks why he must be killed, Tsotsi is again confronted with a choice: "The alternatives were even greater than he had imagined. It was not just the sort of job, a choice of the ways and victims—killing itself was a choice. A question shot with the impact of a bullet into his mind. When had he made that choice?" (91) Despite the pathetic circumstances of Tsotsi's childhood, the novel is not, like *Nongogo*, deterministic. Rather, like Willie in *No-Good Friday*, Tsotsi realizes that he is responsible for his life and capable of altering at least some aspects of it.

The softening of Tsotsi's character and dawning of his consciousness develop through contact with his past. As in several of Fugard's subsequent works, confrontation with the past becomes a way to fathom the present. As Tsotsi holds the baby, as unlikely a father as Silas Marner, the narrator states, "Its function that moment went beyond giving him a hold on an actual moment of the living, urgent present. He had become the repository of Tsotsi's past. The baby and David, himself that is, at first confused, had now merged into one and the same person." (131) The baby's link between past and present is solemnized moments later when the parentless Tsotsi gives the orphan baby his own name, David. Tsotsi, too, is thus reborn.

As Tsotsi's first words to Morris had been put as a question, so he seeks out Boston to ask other questions. Upon finding his bruised cohort, Tsotsi carries him in his arms, as he had the baby, back to his room where he removes Boston's soiled pants, also as he had with the baby. When Boston regains consciousness, Tsotsi starts hesitantly as he tries to ferret out the meanings of the baby, Morris, and the dog. Boston's answers begin slowly: "You are different. . . . You are changing. . . . You mustn't be frightened. It happens, man. . . . You are asking me about God." (152) As Tsotsi has recovered his past, so Boston leaves in search of "the green fields of my youth." (153)

This sudden turn to religious piety continues in the novel's last chapter, but Tsotsi's regeneration, which had been largely internal and solitary, has been essentially completed before he arrives at the church and learns about sin and Jesus. By then Tsotsi has already disbanded the gang, for example. Moreover, while peering in a store window at his reflection during the pursuit of Morris, Tsotsi had begun to identify with his fellow man. When the baby needs to be nursed a second time, Tsotsi goes to Miriam and stares at her so that she understands he is asking her. The shift from an abduction to a request suggests the extent to which Tsotsi has changed.

His transformation had begun at night in a grove of trees. It ends in the light of morning. The miner had died with a disfigured face because of an obscenity Tsotsi has whispered in his ear; Tsotsi was then known for the purity of his evil. He dies wearing a radiant smile.

Tsotsi is sometimes naïve and simplistic, like its protagonist in the last chapter. The use of light and dark images, often as a metaphor for Tsotsi's state of consciousness, is apt, but the images occur so frequently that their freshness and vigor dissipate. The book is sometimes unwieldy in its transitions, especially when the focus shifts away from Tsotsi and when it changes from the present to incidents from his past. The story of Boston's education and expulsion from school, though interesting in itself and for what it reveals about his character, is poorly integrated. As the novel nears its conclusion, it begins to resemble a gyroscope on the brink of spinning out of control.

Nevertheless, *Tsotsi* is an affecting if modest work, a good first novel. The prose is clean and evocative, as in this description of the Bantu Eating House that Morris visits: "It was a cheerless room, and reflected the poverty of a people who measured their essentials and excesses in the smallest unit of the white man's money. Everything sold in the shop was a multiple of the humble penny." (71) As already mentioned, Fugard is a keen naturalist and two of the novel's best similes reflect this. Tsotsi recalls his first glimpse of the baby, its "hands adrift in the small boxed world like anemones in a dead sea." (46) When Tsotsi later touches the baby's hands, "the fingers closed on his like the tendrils of a lazy anemone." (95) (Fugard's use of the same image twice does diminish its effectiveness.)

Fugard is especially good at creating dramatic tension, as in the moments leading up to the miner's murder, when Tsotsi seems about to rob a general store, and when he pursues Morris down sidestreets and alleys—an episode as suspenseful as any thriller. The arrest of ten-year-old David's mother and his growing sense of fear is one of the finest scenes in the novel. Butcher and Die Aap are small, sometimes two-dimensional characters, but the writing is never condescending toward these black underlings. Fugard has become intimate enough with his characters to write them from the inside out. Miriam is another of Fugard's strong women, though as a character she is only a sketch of goodness embodied.

Fugard faced numerous problems in creating a central character who is often inarticulate. He better handles this challenge later in his career with characters such as Zachariah Pieterson and Boesman, but Tsotsi is vivid and his inner life is gradually revealed despite his taciturnity. The narrator, of course, enters Tsotsi's mind and acts as an intermediary between him and the reader, but his omniscience is never intrusive. As David Hogg notes, "Fugard's prose-narrative is dramatic, in that it offers, or strains toward offering, the tale without the teller."[47]

Fugard's future work is also anticipated by *Tsotsi*'s simple structure, essentially a series of one-on-one interactions between Tsotsi and Boston, the baby, the Indian shopkeeper, Morris, Miriam, his mother, and the church sexton. In the plays to come, Fugard repeatedly focuses on two characters. Also, as many of the plays are neoclassical in their adherence to unity of time, *Tsotsi* opens late on a Friday afternoon and closes the following Tuesday morning.

Tsotsi is unique among Fugard's writings because of its form and the naïve piety (reminiscent of *Cry, the Beloved Country*) with which it ends. Yet, it could hardly be mistaken for the work of anyone else. In addition to a common Sophiatown setting, it embodies themes found in *No-Good Friday* and *Nongogo* while introducing others that figure prominently in subsequent works, though a decade will pass before Fugard again sets a full-length play in a black township.

These themes include the acceptance of responsibility for one's life, the recovery of past memories that lead to affirmation of the present, and the heightening of individual consciousness.

Tsotsi's memories lead to the recovery of his family life. The loss of his own mother does not prevent him from mothering the infant. He has begun to create his own family and dies trying to protect it. Families are especially prominent in Fugard's next three plays.

II

Brothers and Other Lovers: "The Family"

Life can only be understood backward; but it must be lived forward. —Søren Kierkegaard

The Johannesburg group of actors involved with *No-Good Friday* and *Nongogo* continued to perform in Fugard's absence. Mokae recalls, "Athol was a lousy correspondent after he ran out on us, but by then we were so involved with theatre there was no stopping us. We began working on other projects, including a folk thing we did at Witwatersrand University. Athol came to see us, and you could see things were tough. He really did have to scrub floors in London, but we said, 'Good for you.' We gave him hell: 'Trying to sneak out on us, leaving us back here, you didn't even tell us.' Still, we had a good laugh."

While in England, Fugard had written P.P. Breytenbach, Director of the NTO, "I must say I am very impressed with the standards of acting, and the faultless quality of the direction. It is not, however, very exciting. By local standards, one season of the 'Kamertoneel' is decidedly avant garde experimental theatre. . . . I still definitely feel that the Kamertoneel is my spiritual home in theatre."[1] While on the Continent he had acquired the rights to some Flemish play that required only a small cast and one set. He hoped to direct them back in South Africa.

On the eve of his departure from England, Fugard wrote Breytenbach that he wished to resume his association with the NTO. After arriving in Cape Town on December 15, 1960 Fugard received his response: The three speaking parts in Bridget Boland's *The Prisoner* had already been cast, but he was offered a job as stage manager at seventeen pounds per week. He declined because he did not want to be on tour while Sheila was pregnant and also because, as he wrote the NTO Production Manager Michael Grobbelaar, "I have always thought that you and Mr. Breytenbach realized that the period during which I stage managed for you was, as it were, my theatre apprenticeship. . . . My debt of gratitude to NTO is that you gave me that chance. Frankly Michael, I consider my apprenticeship finished. I studied extensively on the continent and also worked in professional theatre . . . the latter reaching its climax for me with my direction of Tone's play for one of the foremost Amsterdam companies. My work was measured against the finest European standards . . . and as you see, my notices were excellent."[2]

After he had left home, Fugard's parents rented their big house in Newton Park and took a modest two-room flat on Bird Street. Fugard and his pregnant wife moved in. Although he had no money, he hoped to avoid a regular job. Since there was no directing position with the NTO, he turned instead to a new play he had begun thinking about while in Europe. His mother supported him and Sheila during the seven months he spent writing it. He gave the play a name, *The Blood Knot*, after Lisa's birth on May 27, 1961: "The writing of the play lasted as long as gestation."[3] Six months later, his father was dead.

Fugard's notebook contains an extraordinary account of Lisa's birth and of sharing that experience with his wife. (Details about nursing mothers in *Tsotsi* suggest that it too was completed after Lisa's birth.) A year later Fugard noted, "Her birth has settled some of the problems, finally. I have a family—for the rest of my life a home. These two realities will, between them, determine the pattern of ninety percent of my living." (6-62) Fugard has remained devoted to his daughter, though few of his characters have children.

The Blood Knot was not conceived as the first part of a trilogy, but Fugard later recognized the interrelationship of it to *Hello and Goodbye* and *Boesman and Lena* as a cycle of plays about "the nexus of family relationships." In addition to this connection among the three plays, they share many themes and stylistic traits.

Brothers Past, Present, and Forever:
The Blood Knot

There is no man who differs more from another than he does from himself at another time.   —Blaise Pascal

Fugard's first thoughts about *The Blood Knot*, indeed the first entry he made in his notebook, include the following: "No streets, names or numbers. A world where anything goes. . . . In one of these shacks the two brothers—Morrie and

Zach. Morrie is a light-skinned Coloured who has found out that to ignore the temptations to use his lightness is the easiest way to live. . . . In contrast, his brother Zach—dark-skinned Coloured, virtually African in appearance. . . . Zach can never be anything other than what he is—a black man. There are no choices for him." (1960 [London]) Fugard recalls that writing *The Blood Knot* "was a compulsive and direct experience and this note is the only reference I can find to it."[4]

His note reflects the setting and nucleus of the play. Its story runs as follows: Having returned home to Zach after some years apart, Morrie fosters the dream of their purchasing a farm together. Zach has adapted to Morrie's manipulations and the changes he has effected, but he still remembers a past that was not limited to the womanless world of a Korsten shanty. Morrie suggests he get a pen-pal, Ethel. She turns out to be white. When she writes that she is planning to visit, Zach proposes that Morrie pass himself off as a white man and pretend that *he* is her pen-pal. Their farm savings pay for the fancy clothes Morrie will need, and Zach convinces his finely-dressed brother to learn "whiteness" by playing the role of the condescending *baas*. Even after Ethel cancels her visit, the role-playing continues until Morrie and Zach abandon their dreams of an illusory future and embrace their brotherhood.

The initial image for the play, according to Fugard, was "a man on the road and all the possibilities. He was a Coloured man. He was possibly even myself, confused, going somewhere." Fugard has also admitted that *The Blood Knot* "is really a personal statement. It is basically myself and my brother . . . when I developed an enormous guilt thing about him because he was going through a hard time. . . . There was just the sense of responsibility for another man, for another existence." He has added, "Zach did not need Morrie and my brother did not need me."[5] Royal Fugard had been a slow learner who failed his major exams.

The Blood Knot explores new themes even as it reflects Fugard's previous interest in hopes, dreams, and the presence of the past. The brothers are temporarily uncertain about their shared distant past, their childhood. Morrie is additionally troubled by those years from the recent past that he spent away from Zach; he hopes to expiate the guilt he feels for ever having left him. Connected to this uncertainty about his past is Morrie's insecure identity as either Coloured or white. Morrie imposes on Zach his own desires for the future, especially the two-man farm, as a means to escape an unaccommodating past and present. Through the use of imaginary games and role-playing, Morrie and Zach reconcile themselves to their personal histories and true identities, discard illusory dreams of an ideal future, and learn to live in the present.

Morrie precipitates most of the play's action: His return to the Korsten shack has caused its disruption, the guilt is his, and the farm and pen-pal are his ideas. When Zach mentions his old drinking friend Minnie, Morrie tries to change the subject; he is so jealous of anyone or anything that might threaten the marvelous future he has planned that he tries to destroy Zach's memories of his old friend with lies and speculations. Early in the play it is Morrie who persistently deflates Zach's reveries of a golden past; later, Zach will help destroy Morrie's dream of an ideal future.

Zach's past life of sensual pleasures had been wholly different from the monasticism Morrie has imposed. Zach's recollection of Minnie quickly leads to memories of women. Again Morrie tries to change the subject. The intrusion of any outsider might usurp his position or diminish his function. Zach is the breadwinner, but Morrie is the head of the household. Zach ignores Morrie's attempts to make him forget his palpable past experiences with women. It is these memories, these perceptions of an absence in Zach's life, that lead Morrie to suggest a pen-pal.

He manipulates Zach to insure the future he has planned. Morrie's behavior can also be explained by his personal history before his return to the Korsten shack. The facts of his immediate past are gradually revealed throughout the play, especially towards its end. At first Morrie's musings are opaque and obscure. Although Zach is asleep, Morrie cannot forthrightly admit what he has done because his guilt is too oppressive. What he cannot openly admit to himself cannot yet be revealed to the audience, although the vagueness of his words arouses curiosity about his apparent piety, sense of guilt, and feelings of responsibility. This obscurity is Morrie's, not Fugard's. The way Morrie gradually accepts what he has done and explains and admits it directly is the same deliberate process by which Zach and the audience are led to understand his past.

At first Morrie mutters and stammers. He wants to escape or at least forget his past, but he later admits. "There is no whitewashing away a man's . . . facts." (58*) After counseling Zach to remember *his* facts, however difficult they are to accept, Morrie finally admits openly that he had used his light complexion to "pass" as a white man until he was caught—not by the law, but by his burdensome guilt and the sense of responsibility it had engendered. By caring for Zach he seeks atonement for what he perceives to be the betrayal of a Cain, the desecration of a blood relationship. The guilt living on in him is only one indication of the presence of the past. Sublimation, however often attempted, is impossible.

Whereas Zach wants to escape the consuming ennui of his life through immediate satisfaction of his senses, Morrie believes in delayed gratification—saving money for the future. His dream is so compelling that he has been able to foist it onto Zach, thus altering Zach's inclination to live for the day. Morrie has apparently traded the illusion of passing as white for the illusion of the farm, but he fails to recognize that he has only switched dreams and not transformed the dreamer. Morrie is initially unable to objectify his experience and learn from

*All quotes throughout this chapter are from *Three Port Elizabeth Plays* (New York: Viking Press, 1974)

it; his self-consciousness is limited. He thinks he has forsworn his past games, but he will soon play them again.

Imaginary games and role-playing are the primary means by which Morrie and Zach finally affirm the present and their true identities. Morrie had made his debut in the role of the white man many years before, but within the play Fugard also indicates the ability of Morrie and Zach to perform, as in, for example, their reenactment of a childhood game, a scene that also advances the theme of time.

Their imaginary car ride triggers the memory of other childhood games, but Morrie and Zach have done more than rediscover their youth and distant past.[6] They have also verified the present, their fraternal bond: Although they had different fathers, which explains their different pigmentation, they had the same washerwoman mother. Without this blood relationship Morrie might not suffer from the guilt of his presumed betrayal, but without a brother he would also lose a purpose for existence. After acknowledging their bond, calmness reigns; the struggle for dominance and to impose one will on another ceases, at least temporarily. Morrie and Zach have not yet fully accepted themselves, but they are adjusting to each other.

The car ride is a pivotal scene because it affirms the present. It is also stylistically important. Morrie and Zach self-consciously play themselves. They relive their childhood imaginatively and begin to indicate an objectivity towards themselves, an ability to be self-critical, that was not previously evident. Self-deception gives way to reflection and insight. As in art itself, imagination makes truth accessible.

Morrie and Zach do not write their own play, the way Hamlet does, nor are they as theatrically self-conscious as many of Pirandello's and Beckett's characters. *The Blood Knot* is not anti-illusionistic, but Morrie and Zach do collaborate, in a sense, with Fugard in their own dramatization. From the car ride on, Morrie and Zach "play" with increasing frequency; they repeatedly use their imaginations, ephemeral internal means to escape concrete external circumstances. Merely corresponding with Ethel is a kind of game, as is Morrie's planned imitation of a white man. Sometimes they simply mimic: Zach coyly keeps one of Ethel's letters from Morrie, who responds with his own childish tricks and feigned indifference; while explaining the way a man courts a woman, Morrie mimes a tea service; and upon returning with the new clothes, Zach acts out the roles of customer and salesman. However, these are mere sophomoric turns, audition pieces, compared to the role-playing that lies ahead. Twice they reenact the South African ritual of the arrogant white *baas* abusing the black "boy."

The first of these is undertaken to teach Morrie "whiteness," but before this Morrie himself takes on the role of teacher in helping Zach understand his identity. Morrie has wanted to help Zach and be needed by him for so long that he cannot quite believe Zach's plea for help. For perhaps the first time since Morrie's return, Zach truly needs his brother. What follows is an incisive Socratic inquiry in which Morrie's hard questions and exhortations lead Zach to understand his "facts." The scene is between tutor and pupil. Zach is coached and coaxed until his dream of meeting a white woman is exorcised and he realizes he can never have her. Zach understands and accepts, "I'm black all right." (62) He finally recognizes that, "after a whole life I only seen me properly tonight." (64) It remains for Morrie to discover and accept his true identity.

The identity that Zach has found with Morrie's help may be a limiting one defined primarily by his race, but Zach at least has the security of that identity: "Black days, black ways, black things. They're me. I'm happy. Ha Ha Ha! Do you hear my black happiness?" (62) Morrie envies that certainty and happiness.

Morrie dominates the early scenes, but Zach can also get his way. Despite Morrie's objection, Zach replies to Ethel's letter. This letter is truly Zach's in a way the introductory one was not. (In playing Zach's Cyrano, Morrie had initially all but appropriated the pen-pal for himself.) Zach gets his way again after suggesting they use the money saved for the farm to buy "white" clothing. Despite his initial opposition, Morrie begins to warm to the idea. By the end of the scene he has switched from resistance, through passivity, to an active desire to meet Ethel and once again try passing.

With his appropriation of the "future tin" in which they keep their savings, Zach takes charge. In the first scene Morrie had interrupted Zach's memories of Minnie. Now, in an exact reversal, Zach interrupts Morrie's musing on his own past. Morrie's acquiesence in spending the farm money is the first sign of his willingness to live in the present. He is ready to don the costume of a white man and play the role of the white man on the dirt floor stage of a Korsten shack.

After purchasing the new outfit, Zach plays tutor: Morrie had taught Zach "blackness," now Zach will teach Morrie "whiteness." In the past Morrie had not discovered the "inner whiteness" that supposedly pervades the white man's demeanor. Every actor knows that a costume helps create a character, and *The Blood Knot* audience has also been alerted to the link between the clothes and the man: As Zach sleeps, Morrie puts on his brother's coat and says, "You get right inside the man when you can wrap up in the smell of him." (21)

Until Morrie unleashes an abusive taunt, he and Zach rehearse a brief episode of a white man purchasing nuts from a black man. The derision Morrie directs at Zach is a kind of self-hate. The role-playing ends, but Morrie finally explains to Zach in the clearest terms yet exactly why he had left home. The scene is wonderfully ironic and complex. Morrie and Zach are playing—and they are not. Illusion and reality meld to the point where it is impossible to ascertain where one stops and the other begins. Their games are always deeply rooted in an external reality; their wakeful, everyday life is dominated by dreams of escape. They have thoroughly learned the black and white roles by observing and playing them in the outer world—Morrie by passing, Zach by kowtowing to his boss.

Morrie has sworn at his brother and been forced to recognize the persistence of his desire to pass. This old dream remains, as does the new one of pastoral retreat, but the farm money has been spent. Morrie decides to leave Korsten again. He has been unable to expiate the old remorse and thinks he has again betrayed his brother by abusing him. To meet Ethel would be to invite additional feelings of guilt.

Zach perceives only part of the cause of Morrie's dejection, the threat of Ethel's visit. When they learn she is not coming, the worry about discovery is removed and Morrie is ecstatic. His readiness to resume the old illusions seems to indicate he has learned nothing. Zach even suggests he dress again in the white man's costume and that they repeat their game: "We're only playing now." (87) However, it is not really the same game since before they had been preparing for Ethel; now it appears to be play for its own sake, just for fun. It is actually no such thing. When initiating this game Zach says—"*slyly*" according to the stage direction—"You looked so damn smart in that suit Morrie. It made me feel good." (87) Zach is disingenuous for the first time. Instead of interacting spontaneously, he is now consciously plotting.

This game starts where the last one ended, with Morrie abusing Zach, but now the game is different. As teacher in the fifth scene, Zach had delivered a lesson about whiteness. He now has another lesson and shows Morrie an additional side of the stereotyped black man Zach had played. In response, Morrie pretends to walk and walk, fervently believing that he has left Zach, Korsten, and his past behind. But Zach follows. He is as inescapable as Morrie's past and the true identity Morrie will soon discover and accept.

Throughout much of the play Morrie has had an answer for everything. Now Zach answers each of Morrie's questions and rebuffs his attempts at escape. As Morrie becomes cold, lonely, and afraid, he prays for forgiveness and Zach prepares to attack him. The foreboding and tension of the confrontation are finally broken by the alarm clock; as in their previous game, Morrie and Zach are shocked back to reality.

Through Zach's instruction, Morrie recognizes and understand's the inner meaning and implication of his hopes, not simply their external form. He abandons the fantasy of the farm, the illusion of living in the future, and says, "It's a good thing we got the game. It will pass the time. Because we got a lot left, you know! (*Little laugh.**) . . . I mean, other men get by without a future. In fact, I think there's quite a lot of people getting by without futures these days." (96) Morrie will live in present time.

The most obvious symbol of *The Blood Knot*'s time theme is Morrie's alarm clock, which breaks the silence of the play's opening and catapults Morrie into one of his housewife routines. The clock dictates life in the shack. It fails to command immediate attention only after the brothers become disoriented by the

---

*Italicized parenthetical words such as these indicate stage directions.

first dress-up game. The calendar is another way Morrie regiments life. He serves fish every Thursday and polony (baloney) on Friday. A break in the routine indicates something important has transpired. The disheveled appearance of the room at the beginning of the last scene, an objectification of Morrie's befuddlement, suggests the turmoil to come. This signal of a change in Morrie, both past and impending, is strengthened when he holds up the clock: "It's stopped. Like me. What time shall we make it?" (86) Morrie is in control of the clock instead of it being in control of him. Time becomes subjective rather than objective.

The time theme is also implied elsewhere, as in the moths Morrie describes. In addition to flying into the whiteness of light where they are burned, both Morrie and the moths undergo transformation through time. The latter end up ugly moths, but there is always the possibility that a plain caterpillar will evolve into a beautiful butterfly. Morrie ponders the human equivalent: "worms lying warm in their silk to come out one day with wings and things! Why not a man?" (79)[7]

By the play's conclusion Morrie and Zach begin to live in the present, brother and brother. Should they continue to play their little game, they will do so without taking it seriously, without deluding themselves through the illusion of true or final escape. The game will simply be part of the routine, along with footsalts and the alarm clock. The game is recognized as a game, an end in itself rather than a means.

Morrie and Zach will live in the present with the one certainty that has existed throughout their lives, but that was sometimes unrecognized. Morrie speaks the last lines of the play: "You see, we're tied together, Zach. It's what they call the blood knot . . . the bond between brothers." (97) When all else fails, the symbiotic bond of blood and love remains. Meager as this may be, it is more than many of Fugard's subsequent characters will have.

"Brother" is not the only word emphasized in The Blood Knot. Morrie teaches Zach the meaning of terms such as "insult," "injury," "inhumanity," "prejudice," and "injustice." Fugard has a penchant for such loaded words: In Tsotsi, Boston stresses "decency;" Boesman is fond of "freedom."

Zach also likes to listen to the lines Morrie has memorized, and he responds to Zach's requests with short recitations of sentimental verse Fugard has made up. (He says, "It's easier to write something yourself than to scour about and find the right quotation from someone else.") In contrast to Morrie's verse, Zach's words, even in the song "My Skin is Black," (48) tend to be assembled into simple, declarative statements of fact.

Quoting lines and learning new words are games the brothers play to pass the time. Morrie truly believes talking helps and that words are an adequate—indeed ideal—substitute for action, the thing itself. He has faith in the word as purgative and suggests that Zach satisfy his need for female companionship through a pen-pal, more words. When he first hears Ethel's self-description, Zach complains, "I can't get hot about a name on a piece of paper. It's not real to me," (23) but Morrie quickly recaptures Zach's interest by quoting Ethel's words, "I am eighteen years old and well-developed." Morrie relies on words for their impressionistic and euphonious sense, but also by attempting to argue with Zach logically. After discovering Ethel is white, Morrie wants to throw away her letter, but Zach successfully counters with, "What sort of chap is it that throws away a few kind words? Hey, Morrie? Aren't they, as you say, precious things these days?" (43) These letters are as important as those Willie must write in *No-Good Friday*.

The language of Morrie and Zach is often metaphorical, but there are problems with it—not its pitch or lyricism, but its sheer quantity. Some scenes are too long. Moments of delightful humor—selecting a pen-pal, writing Ethel, and the car ride, for example—provide respite from emotional self-indulgence. Morrie's reveries and speeches are often repetitious. Unsure of the evocative power of his language, or, perhaps, because he had fallen in love with it, Fugard often repeats himself, as if afraid the audience would otherwise mistake his intentions. *The Blood Knot* is not his last play to have this problem, but over the years Fugard gradually diminishes it. From *The Blood Knot* through *Statements after an Arrest under the Immorality Act*, an eleven-year period, each of Fugard's major plays is more condensed than its predecessor.

This process of refinement has been conscious. In 1980 Fugard admitted that in *No-Good Friday* and *Nongogo* he was concerned not so much with language but with the craft of dramatic structure, his models being O'Neill, Williams, and Odets: "Somehow the question of dramatic structures was, after I'd written those two plays, not exactly solved, but I was able to find it instinctively. I didn't have to work away at it like an apprentice making a chair. But a different apprenticeship started with *The Blood Knot* and continues even now with *A Lesson from Aloes*. . . . I see this apprenticeship in terms of working on the *word*, making that line as spare as it needs to be."[8]

Fugard is aware of the excesses of *The Blood Knot* and says, "Anybody who was to do that play as written now would be an absolute lunatic. It's overwritten, monstrously overwritten."[9] For the first American production, director John Berry cut some of the text, and Fugard realized that he was absolutely right, but that he hadn't been bold enough and that a lot more had to go. In 1966, as he was preparing a second London production, Fugard cut the text by twenty-five percent, rearranged its seven scenes into three acts (the second scene, for example, was inserted into the first), and severely trimmed Morrie's long rhetorical turns. His part is now more nearly equal to Zach's. (None of the lines or actions Fugard cut has been cited.) The revised text has only recently been published by Samuel French, in an acting edition. It is an unusual writer who would throw his first novel into a lagoon in Fiji, forget entirely about his first plays, and presume his second novel had been discarded. It is not unusual, however, for a playwright to be more concerned with the performed text than the published one.

Fugard was apparently aware of other inadequacies, since the play contains unsuccessful attempts to solve them. Most of these relate to plot developments. With one exception, Fugard's plots are never of the mystery-story, what-will-happen-next variety. He does not cleverly complicate stories or situations, then unravel them in the last scene in order to impress with his deftness. Ethel, the threat of her visit, the clothes purchased to meet her, and the relief that settles when she does not come, are not so much plot elements as character ones. (They are catalysts that elicit from the brothers their differing reactions.) However, *The Blood Knot* does tell a story as it develops, and its "revelations" are sometimes awkward, especially regarding Ethel's race and Morrie's light complexion.

Despite these problems, *The Blood Knot* is an astonishing work from a twenty-nine-year-old playwright active in theatre for only five years. Its promise and craftsmanship are especially impressive because the theatre has often been a medium for the mature writer: It was not until Ibsen and Shaw were in their late thirties, and Pirandello and Beckett in their late forties, that they indicated the full range of their dramatic skill.

Fugard attributes the improvement of *The Blood Knot* over his earlier plays to his encounter with European theatre. In addition: "Those one-acts and *Nongogo* and *No-Good Friday* were written ready-made for a group. *The Blood Knot* was the first time that, as a playwright, I sat down and faced a very private situation, without there being any prospect of a production. It was what I call 'the inquisition of blank paper.' I just wrote. For myself."[10]

The Blood Knot dramatizes a psychological and ontological condition. In one of his introductions to the play Fugard writes, "If there is a human predicament, this is it. There is another existence and it feels, and I feel it feels, yet I am impotent. . . . I don't feel innocent. So then how guilty am I? . . . Maybe guilt isn't all *doing*. Maybe just *being* is some sort of sin. I'm sure Morris says that somewhere. If he hasn't, he should."[11] Morrie has suffered because he tried to pass, because he does not accept himself, because he has indulged in illusory dreams, but most of all he suffers because he exists. To suffer is, in part, the meaning of his life, as it is for many of Fugard's characters.

Morrie and Zach will not live happily ever after, but their illusions have ended. They are resigned, but not defeated. Naïve optimism, unfounded faith, and self-delusion give way to perspicuity and consciousness. It is this self-reflection that indicates their kinship to tragic rather than comic characters. Throughout the play, action and cognition are opposed—distinguished by the very personalities of Zach and Morrie—but thought and deed are finally joined through their role-playing. Action leads to cognition. They recognize and accept their true identities.

Morrie and Zach finally possess the lucidity of Sisyphus on the way back down the hill. Camus has influenced Fugard so profoundly that it is impossible to record every cross-current, but two years after completing *The Blood Knot*, Fugard himself noted one connection: "Far from 'leaping,' Morrie and Zach wake up to find themselves heavy, hopeless, almost prostrate on the earth. . . . What is more obvious than that I should be drawn, be overwhelmed by Camus? Morrie and Zach at the end of *The Blood Knot* are two men who are going to try to live without hope, without appeal. If there is anything on that stage before the curtain drops it is lucid knowledge and consciousness. In effect, Morrie says: 'Now we know.' "(12-19-63)

Racial and individual identities are so rigidly linked in South Africa that Morrie has surely absorbed from that society the notion that he is not a full person; Zach's apparently poor education can also be attributed to the society. However, *The Blood Knot* is not a parable. It contains many truths, but the most important ones are not racial. In writing the play, Fugard was more concerned with a personal statement than a political one: "My major concern was a question of a self faced with the problem of another existence. And in a way I think that South Africa just invented the perfect device for showing how different two men are. If I'd been writing an absurdist piece of play, I might have done as Ionesco did, given one man two noses or a green face. But my context was a certain amount of realism and South Africa gave me the biggest chance of making one man different from another man. Give the one a black skin—the other a white skin."[12]

Nkosi interprets the play much differently. He considers *The Blood Knot* "a supreme South African achievement" and "primarily a work of art," but he also views it as a paradigm of South African racial relationships. He objects that Zach's physical and sensual qualities are emphasized over his intellectual ones, that "not once in this play is the very morality of color or *white* as a standard of what is beautiful or desirable, questioned." He is troubled that Zach agrees with Morrie's final rejection of the future and that he has "no intention of rebeling against his status."[13]

Nkosi fails to realize that Zach's personality is more successfully integrated than Morrie's. Zach knows better than Morrie how to live in the present without phony hopes or idle delusions. Throughout the play, Morrie becomes more and more like Zach, and thus ends up more stable, better adjusted, even happier. *The Blood Knot* is not a simple battle between two temperaments, but to the extent that it is, Zach's is victorious. He is more a model for Morrie than vice versa. Zach's rape of a girlfriend is abhorrent, but except for this action from his past, his emotional and interpersonal life is more normal than his brother's asceticism.

Nkosi is also wrong to suggest that the play holds up whiteness as any kind of standard. Concerning racial roles and classifications, *The Blood Knot* emphasizes one simple truth: Accept yourself, don't try to be someone else. Zach's affirmation of his race could be proudly uttered by any "black is beautiful" advocate. Associated with Morrie's passing are the moths that fly into the whiteness of light where they burn to death. When Morrie seeks whiteness he feels guilty. Far from promoting passing, *The Blood Knot* suggests that whiteness is not worth attaining.

To those optimistic about changing the South African *status quo*, Morrie's resignation—"I think there's quite a lot of people getting by without futures these days"—seems pessimistic and despairing. Moreover, Fugard does write in his notebook that there are no choices for Zach. However, the ones Morrie has, passing and dreams of the future, are revealed to be illusory. The futility each experiences is a reflection of the condition of all men, not simply of all oppressed people.

There is no reason to define Morrie and Zach as racial archetypes in the apartheid state. The consistency of Fugard's image of man will become clearer in the plays ahead. Whether white, black, or Coloured, male or female, middle class or poor, all his characters are isolated, alienated, and powerless in the face of their fate—existence itself. Zach's statement about his predicament with Ethel could be uttered by many of Fugard's characters about their plights: "What have I done, hey? I done nothing." (58) He is "guilty" because he is alive.

Fugard directed *The Blood Knot* and played Morrie to Zakes Mokae's Zach. The similarity between their names is no coincidence since, as Fugard says, "there was only one actor, as far as I was concerned, who could handle that role. People laughed at me and said, 'Zakes is no actor.' " Mokae first heard about the play upon Fugard's return from London. They began rehearsing at Braes O'Berea, the name of the apartment block in the Hillbrow section of Johannesburg, where the Fugards lived. Because of their worries about neighbors and fear of the police, Mokae sometimes had to sneak in and out of the apartment. It was illegal for him to stay overnight, but he did so anyway.

Fugard and Mokae continued their rehearsals at Dorkay House. At first there was no intention of performing there, but on September 3, 1961 the play did open on the top floor of Dorkay House in a space Fugard christened The Rehearsal Room. Barney Simon served as Fugard's "third eye" or assistant director. Simon had seen *No-Good Friday* and *Nongogo* and recalls that when he finally met Fugard: "There was instant rapport. I responded to those plays because of their directness and their access to humanity. I'd wanted to leave South Africa, but they gave me a sense of place and direction." Simon spoke about Fugard so frequently that his friends became irritated: "Lots of people saw the Fugards as rather shoddy. They were not well dressed."

The facilities at Dorkay House were rudimentary. The first performance was lit by Simon's bed lamps. He recalls another problem: "We were told that egg cartons covering the windows would deaden the traffic noise from Eloff Street, one of Johannesburg's busiest. That was bad advice. We finally put up some heavy costumes. The west side of the room was also lined with windows so we had to contend with the glare of the sun. What's more, outside these windows was a recreational area for workers in the mine compound nearby."[14] Fugard vividly recalls the contrast between twentieth-century traffic noise on one side and traditional drumming and singing on the other.

Initially, the play ran four hours. According to Simon, Fugard and Mokae had to improvise at times because they did not know their lines. Mokae recalls, "We must have been crazy. The people had to sit on hard chairs. There was no ventilation and no intermission, but nobody walked out. It was so quiet, there were no coughs. When there was finally applause you didn't know where you were at. We drank ourselves to oblivion after the first night."

In his review in the *Star*, Oliver Walker called *The Blood Knot* "a very remarkable new play" and added, "Mr. Fugard's own playing of this tormented role was a tour de force. It is true he mistakes length for significance, and that if he cut some scenes by half he would double their meaning. But for all its unwieldy length the play never flags. Even its literary patches are permissible and some of them have the luminosity of real poetry."[15] This review brought much attention to the production, which played to invited audiences. The tiny theatre seated only about sixty, but the integrated audience was sometimes double that even though there was no advertising budget. No admission was charged, but a collection was taken.

Under the aegis of Toby Kushlick and Leon Gluckman, the production moved from Dorkay House to the Y.M.C.A. Intimate Theatre on November 8, 1961. One critic called it "one of the most entrancing pieces of theatre to have been staged in Johannesburg for a long, long time. . . . *The Blood Knot* is a significant addition to South African theatre—authentic, original and completely stimulating." James Ambrose Brown wrote that the play "has given the South African play international status."[16]

The production then toured the country, opening in Cape Town at Fugard's old home, the Labia, on February 12, 1962. Mokae recollects: "Since Athol and I were still living together, we'd interject things that really affected us. Those long speeches of Morrie are typical. On the trains during the tour, Athol would be in the first class and I'd be in second. At the stops he'd buy alcohol, run back to my compartment and give me some. I tried to make him feel rotten, but I'd take it."

Late in March, *The Blood Knot* opened in Port Elizabeth, the last stop on the tour. After 140 performances, an unusually long run for a serious drama in so small a country, the production closed and Fugard remained at home. In addition to the merit of the play, the production itself was a milestone, since it had been traditional in South Africa for whites in blackface to play the roles of blacks and Coloureds. Mokae's performance challenged this custom. Four years later such mixed casts were prohibited, but the original production of *The Blood Knot* challenged at least one prevailing mode of apartheid.

Recalling the production, Nadine Gordimer writes of "the white audience, streaming in week after week to sit as if fascinated by a snake before Athol Fugard's *The Blood Knot.*" The play was to the stunted South African theatre what O'Neill's *Beyond the Horizon* was to the American theatre in 1920—the most important work of theatre in the history of the country to this point. Fugard took his first step into the company of the finest contemporary playwrights. According to him, *The Blood Knot* "marks my discovery of myself as a writer."[17] Not even an unsuccessful London production in 1963 could destroy this epiphany.

During the South African tour, publisher André Deutsch saw the play and wanted to publish it, but since he did not usually publish plays, he suggested that Fugard write a novel. He began one about a cousin whose personal problems "gave me most probably my first information about a certain loneliness. We once sat on a bench in Port Elizabeth and he told me about his pain." After completing a draft, Fugard noted, "The novel was aborted. Read what I had written to Sheila last night. Her silence and my own feelings as I progressed from one muddled paragraph to another were enough. I don't consider the work wasted. The characters are with me now. They'll come out one day. In any case this business of writing 'prose' because a publisher wants 'prose,' is wrong. I'm a playwright." (5-14-62)

The Past Revisited—Children and Parents: *Hello and Goodbye*

*Children, this day your father is gone from you. All that was mine
is gone. You shall no longer bear the burden of taking care of me—
I know it was hard, my children. And yet one word makes all
those difficulties disappear: That word is love.*   —Sophocles

Following the *Blood Knot* tour, Fugard began to write *People Are Living There.* He completed a draft in March 1963 and began actively seeking a production by June, but the play remained unproduced until 1968. (It will be discussed in the next chapter.) For his next project he contemplated several ideas: one about the Mille Miglia road race, another about a Port Elizabeth character named Johnnie, and a third about a group of hoboes. He noted, "These periods between the finish of one play and the real start of the next one—these false starts, playing around with and examining ideas—are finally very important in their quiet and unobtrusive way. What they amount to, I suppose, is the equivalent of the

training sessions and exercises of an athlete—keeping him fit for the next effort."
(7-63)

By September 1963 Fugard had begun *Hello and Goodbye*. In his notebook
he describes a man named Johnnie who nurses his crippled father following the
old man's injury while working for the South African Railways: "One night—
after ten or fifteen years' absence—[Johnnie's] sister arrives unexpectedly at the
run-down little house. . . . She believes the old man was paid 'hundreds of pounds
compensation' by the S.A.R.—'compensation'—for his accident. It is in a box under
his bed. . . . She wants the money—wants to steal it and eventually is prepared
to kill the old man to get it. Neither of these things happens. She leaves Johnnie
and the old man together." (9-16-63) Although the play was not completed for
another two years, this remains a concise summary of the plot, such as it is,
with one exception. The father has died prior to the start of the play, but Johnnie deludes his sister Hester into thinking he is alive, lying in the next room,
and still in need of Johnnie's nursing.

Like *The Blood Knot*, *Hello and Goodbye* is set in a single room and is a two-
character play in which a sibling who is an outsider returns home to a brother
after a long absence. Family life is recovered through childhood memories, and
once again a guilt-wracked brother lives in self-imposed isolation, keeps house,
and is nurtured by illusions while he denies his true identity. Fugard was aware
of the resemblance: "At one level this worries me a little because it means the
inevitable comparisons with *The Blood Knot*." (9-26-63) He was also concerned
about a stock pattern in his plays, "*growing desperation* leading to *emotional crisis*
leading to the *leap*." (12-63) The similarities between the two plays are not due
to his use of a pat formula, but to the wholeness of Fugard's artistic preoccupations and vision. In his notebook he asks, "How many themes does a writer really have? How *few* can he have?" (9-25-63) Like many of Fugard's characters, Johnnie and Hester are lonely searchers, uncertain about their past, present, and future.
Seeking their identities, they relive the past, their personal histories, in a long
night's journey into their interior selves.

Although Johnnie and Hester are white and Afrikaner and thus have greater
social stature, freedom, and mobility than Morrie and Zach, they are no better
off either economically or metaphysically. Despite visits to the city square and
beach, Johnnie is as lonely as Morrie and Zach. He assiduously avoids interaction with others and doesn't even open his mail. He is as asexual as Morrie.
Johnnie and Hester, both friendless, are "the second-hand Smits of Valley Road."
(139) Their dark, cockroach-infested, three-room cottage without plumbing is
as barren as the one-room Korsten shack. Their poverty, as much cultural as
economic, is equally devastating. Yet *Hello and Goodbye* is not so much the story
of their sibling relationship, of their blood knot, as it is of their separate personalities and different relationships to their past, especially to their father who
was the most influential element of it.

Despite the individual differences between Morrie and Zach, they finally discover their interdependence and the strength of the bond that links them; at the end of *The Blood Knot* they renew their relationship. Hester and Johnnie are complete opposites; at the end of *Hello and Goodbye* they separate, perhaps forever. They are brought together only long enough to say "hello," Hester's first line, and "goodbye," her last. She returns for only a few hours, but this is long enough to relive her lifetime.

Hester seeks answers as persistently as Johnnie avoids them. She yearns to discover and remember while he strives to escape and forget. He is as lost to reality as she is engaged with its coarseness. His piety and habit of quoting the Bible are countered by her atheism. They cannot agree on either their childhood or their parents' marriage. Hester's *apparent* hatred of her father and the raging bitterness she embodies are the opposite of Johnnie's manifest devotion, selflessness, and meekness. She is as strong and fierce as he is weak and unassuming. Johnnie attempts to avoid suffering but Hester accepts it, even embraces it, as an inevitable part of life.

Hunched over the kitchen table as the play opens, Johnnie maniacally attempts to escape life's exigencies by distracting himself with numbers and time, little games and strategies that occupy his mind. (Playing with words also passes the time.) When these fail to engage him fully, he focuses his attention on inanimate objects and becomes especially emotional while describing a steam engine. Later he tries advertising jingles. He hopes concrete reality will shield him from thoughts about himself and his father. However, these escape mechanisms contain his mind only temporarily. On the verge of losing control, Johnnie wonders if he is going mad, but determines through a contorted syllogism that he is not: People who are truly mad don't know they are; he knows that he is; therefore, he isn't.

Throughout his opening monologue Johnnie debates with himself. He would like to be protected from certain thoughts and memories, but his consciousness is inevitably drawn to that event he is striving to avoid: the death of his father. The father's dependence had given Johnnie's life meaning; his death is the cause of Johnnie's disorientation and attempted escape fantasies. Without a job, shunted away in the cottage where he has spent his entire life, Johnnie foresees nothing but an empty future. He has spent his life passively watching and listening to his father, but Johnnie had also actively lent him support. Now he can only observe and audit. Isolated from life outside and the act of living, Johnnie has become a complete spectator, whether looking at his father's body or watching a bus conductor kiss a girl.

After Hester introduces the phrase "nothing to do," (112) it becomes a refrain for both of them. Time's emptiness is clearly established in Johnnie's opening monologue as he counts off seconds. His games and free associations have their own logic, and his blather returns to the word or idea with which it started.

Moments of insight and self-analysis sometimes intrude into his make-believe world; he reveals himself as his thoughts inevitably, if obliquely, return to his deepest preoccupation, the person who had given his life purpose.

Johnnie's deception of Hester begins when he ignores her questions about their father. An honest answer would be an admission Johnnie cannot yet accept. He says, "I'm all ears," (119) but answers her selectively and only hears what he wants to hear, retreating when necessary into the isolation that protects him from reality and from Hester's intimate probing. He persists in believing the old ways still prevail and assures her, "He needs me." (115) Johnnie feels so keenly the loss of his father that he deceives not just Hester, but also himself. He must hide from both of them the fact that his life has become idle and vapid.

Fugard's notebooks suggest that it was Johnnie who first intruded upon his imagination. Asked what "set off" the play, Fugard replied, "My father was a cripple; the father in the play is a cripple. . . . Of the three children I think I had the closest relationship. He was very dependent on me and very solitary. When the time came to leave Port Elizabeth and go to the university, I had a vision of a sort of loneliness that my leaving would create for him."[18] The published text contains no dedication, but in his notebook Fugard wrote, "To my father, who lived and died in the next room." (1-11-65) Johnnie was also based on a Port Elizabeth derelict who had a habit of standing on street corners and at the Queen Victoria statue in Market Square. He was killed when a carload of men from Johannesburg poured a pint of brandy down his throat.

As work on the play progressed, however, Hester became at least as important as Johnnie. Fugard's notebook reveals his search for the play's focus: "Yes, that is it. What I am searching for in the new play is the moment when Hester 'wakes up' and finds herself prostrate on the earth. Three experiences: loss of hope; knowledge of death; the only certainty=the flesh." (12-19-63) Fugard later added, "Hester gives me a chance for the ruthless honesty I so admire in Faulkner's *Wild Palms*—statements of Camus's 'courageous pessimism.' " (9-4-64)

After twelve years in Johannesburg as a prostitute,[19] Hester says that she has returned for her share of the compensation she once heard her parents discuss. Yet this is only a rationalization for her homecoming, since the compensation she seeks is not money so much as something to make up for an unhappy past, a boring present, and an unpromising future. Hester is consumed by her needs, but these are only partially financial and sexual. Above all else they are emotional, psychological, and finally metaphysical.

Were Hester returning only for the money, she might have planned on a brief stay. In fact, she has considered a permanent return, has given up her Johannesburg room, and has brought all her belongings to Port Elizabeth. The image of a woman holding a suitcase was one of the first Fugard had for the play: "When Hester opens that suitcase, I had a moment and I defined Hester. If you look at that little moment, what she put into that suitcase, what she packs, what she says, the way she says it, her character is defined."[20] For some productions subsequent to the original, Fugard has directed Hester to unpack on stage rather than in a separate room as the text indicates. The audience then sees how little she has.

Hester seeks her heritage more than her inheritance. Fugard's notebook reads, "What does Hester want? To begin with, the compensation. *To begin with*, because she walks into that room unconscious of her life." (1-11-65) Late in the play Johnnie asks what she will do if she doesn't find "it" (meaning the compensation), and Hester admits, "I don't even know what it is yet. Just one thing that's got a good memory. I think and think. I try to remember. There must have been something that made me happy. All those years. Just once. Happy." (146-47) She has completely forgotten about the money, the mere pretext for her return.

Initially, Hester is unconscious of her life, but like Tsotsi, she does not end this way. She is "searching for something she *doesn't* know, *can't* identify—a meaning to her life?," (1-11-65) but this is so not because she avoids self-understanding, but because her needs are so many, consuming, and desperate that no single thing or person can ever satisfy them. Hester is need personified.

Her bitter outbursts often lead to at least the articulation of these needs. "None of you know me," (125) she says, then she admits she doesn't even know herself: "What does Hester Smit mean?" In a solitary room with her customers she can only "Lie there, let it happen, and wait. For a memory. . . . Suddenly there's going to be a memory of you, somewhere, some other time. And then you can work it all out again. In the meantime, just wait, listen to the questions and have no answers . . . no danger or pain or anything like that, just something missing, the meaning of your name." (128) Tsotsi had also lost his name and its meaning.

Hester hopes to find that "somewhere" in her old Port Elizabeth home, that "some other time," when she was a child. Perhaps there she can discover happiness and the meaning of her name. Hers was not the childhood of Morrie and Zach, remembered with joy and abandon. Painful as some of her memories are, however, she cannot escape them nor does she desire to. Rather, she will challenge Johnnie's memories of the family with her own.

The childhood Hester rejects and Johnnie clings to was one of strict Calvinism, which helps explain his frequent allusions to God and her vehement rejection of Him. Hester is both a prodigal daughter and a prodigal Afrikaner. After she had left home, her father had said, as Johnnie recalls, " 'We won't speak about her any more.' You weren't a real Afrikaner by nature, he said. Must be some English blood somewhere, on Mommie's side." (125)

Hester reviles her past but returns to it to understand her present better. She cannot escape her roots despite her rejection of her family's sexual and religious mores. In contrast to his taciturnity, she forthrightly lectures him: "The fairy stories is finished. They died in a hundred Jo'burg rooms. There's man. And

I'm a woman. It's as simple as that. You want a sin well there's one. I Hoer [whore]."
(132)

The boxes Johnnie brings out for her inspection yield no money, but they are filled with relics that stir Hester's memory to the point of rage. She scorns the family habit of saving clothes for the future, then castigates wives, families, marriage, and child-bearing. Like Morrie and Zach, Hester and Johnnie relive their childhood, but for them there is as little joy in the memory as there was in youth itself.

Hester claims to care about nothing, but the ferocity of her cynicism suggests that she does care. Her hatred is allied to love rather than being its opposite. Hester experiences life too deeply ever to be indifferent; raging hatred is perhaps her most salient characteristic. Johnnie finally acknowledges that she is his sister by recognizing, of all qualities, her hatred.

Hester is remembered for her hatred, but she too remembers the hatred directed against her by her father and by a childhood playmate. Whether or not Hester actually was hated matters less than the fact that she believes she was. She attempts to get Johnnie to admit his hatred, but he says, "I don't love, I don't hate, I play it safe. I come when called, I go when chased, I laugh when laughed at." (154) Johnnie anesthetizes himself from reality and emotional risks. He cannot admit hating his father because to do so would be to admit the absurdity of his long years of service.

After examining a photo album, that most common object used to preserve the present with an eye toward its later resurrection, Hester discovers a dress that she recognizes by smell as her mother's. She had been the one person who had provided succor in Hester's childhood and respite from harshness and ugliness. Her only pleasant memories are of her mother and the refuge she had provided. Hester claims the dress as a memento, a tender act that marks only the first break in her facade of bitterness. Later, she carefully protects the dress shoes and ribbons she wore as a child. Hester has forgotten neither her mother's smell nor the pain Hester had caused her. Like most familial loves, Hester's is saturated with guilt and remorse over what she should have said or done or felt, but did not.

As Johnnie recalls his father's death, so Hester relives her mother's funeral. Fugard's stage direction is another indication that Hester is not quite as formidable as she would like to appear: "*She is talking with the calculated indifference of someone not sure of their self-control.*" (149) Guilt mingles with the past in the memories of Johnnie and Hester. Their parents are phantoms palpable enough to haunt the present.

Hester avers nothing. Upon rediscovering her childhood without happy memories she asks, "why the hell did we go on living?" (140) After she claims that birth and death are mistakes, Johnnie dares her to commit suicide, the seemingly reasonable choice for one who finds meaning in nothing. Hester ignores him; it is a question, no doubt, she has already resolved for herself.

Throughout the play Johnnie admits to caring only about his father, but as Johnnie helps reveal Hester's secrets, she causes him to admit his continuing interest in the railroad. In this respect, too, Johnnie is his father's son. For the only time in the entire play Johnnie becomes passionate about something outside the family and indicates the life he might have had. (For Afrikaners, the building of the railroad was a kind of latter day reenactment of the Great Trek, complete with mythic and religious implications.[21])

Johnnie's decision to remain a doting son nursing his father instead of enrolling in railway school might be seen as one of filial love and selflessness, but his devotion has become an abnormal obsession. When Johnnie finally admits the father is dead, he explains, "I'm ashamed. Of me. Of being alone. Just me in my whole life. It was so different with him. He was in there, something else, somewhere else. Even tonight, just pretending it helped." (160-61) Johnnie's sense of responsibility has not ended with his father's death.

Although Johnnie is now on his own, he is too weak to live without some hope, illusion, narcotic, or pipe dream. Consequently, he trades one self-delusion, that his father is still alive, for another, that the father's ghost will come back. Throughout the play Johnnie has been haunted by that ghost. Instead of exorcising it, he completes the identification process by actually pretending to be his father.

Hester has claimed her mother's dress as a memento; Johnnie claims his father's crutches. Finally pulling himself up onto them he says, "Why not? It solves problems. Let's face it—a man on his own two legs is a shaky proposition." (162) Man's "shakiness" is implied throughout Fugard's work, but Johnnie's solution to this is continued self-delusion. Unlike Morrie and Zach who finally step out of their fantasy worlds, Johnnie retreats further into his. By pretending to have been crippled in an accident he will be "a man with a story," (162) but that story, that history, is a false one. Johnnie's appropriation of it is irresponsible. Instead of the Oedipal pattern in which the son kills his father, in *Hello and Goodbye* the dead father continues to maim his son.

"Resurrection," (163) the final word Johnnie speaks, is one of Fugard's cruelest ironies. Its religious overtones subtly echo back to the beginning of the play when Johnnie computes the number of seconds that have passed since Christ's birth. As alone at the end of the play as he had been at the beginning, Johnnie's presumed moment of triumph is actually one of abject personal failure. He has surrendered his life to remain in limbo. His apparent resolution marks, instead, continued irresolution. Early in the play he had claimed with no apparent irony, "Always onwards. That's me in a nutshell." (121) This ability to deceive himself persists throughout the play. By its end he has yet to emancipate himself from idleness and fantasy. He has hope, but there is none for him.

The boxes are revealed to be as empty as Johnnie and Hester's lives, or their father's bedroom. Since Johnnie and Hester are differentiated in almost every regard, it is no surprise that they reach different solutions in approaching the brink while standing in the piles of rubbish that are the detritus of their past. Whereas Johnnie cloaks himself in additional fantasies, Hester faces and accepts herself, naked and independent. Isolated from her family, without friends or a blind faith in a god, Hester knows that she is wholly responsible for her life. She is her own maker. Johnnie lives in the fog of the past and the miasma of some future divine salvation. He plans his tomorrows by concocting a story of his yesterdays. His is the third-person life of a detached and distinterested narrator; Hester's is the first-person life of a vital participant. She embraces her life despite its pain and disappointment.

Fugard has said that Hester's triumph is to confront her fate and not squeal.[22] She realizes she can neither alter nor avoid the imperatives of her life, but learns better to live with them. Hester does not despair, but she is resigned. She is one of several Fugard females whose strength is Herculean.

It is her strength to face life without illusory hope that most clearly distinguishes her from Johnnie. She is no big-hearted whore purified through the experience of true love; she does not even give up her profession. Nor is she the self-possessed prostitute of the Mrs. Warren variety. At first glance Johnnie is a nicer and more likeable character, but Hester commands respect. Her forthright honesty and directness is clearly preferable to Johnnie's continuing, even increasing escape and self-delusion. He remains an existential coward unable to face truth. Like Peer Gynt, a patron saint of fantasy and self-delusion, Johnnie is guilty of halfness. Since he and Hester are left utterly alone without support or companionship, *Hello and Goodbye* may seem more pessimistic than *The Blood Knot*, but Hester's fortitude, persistence, and courage are examples of human potential in the face of overwhelming odds.

It is one of *Hello and Goodbye*'s ironies that it is Hester, the prostitute who has learned the faked response, who experiences life so wholeheartedly and feels, mostly pain, so intensely. In one of her final lamentations she cries out, "All the hardships, the hating. I couldn't stop hating and it hurts, it hurts." (156) Pain and hatred are linked, as are pain and love, the flip side of Hester's capacity for hatred. The extent to which she feels pain is one with her ability to hate so fiercely and, though it is less obvious, love so desperately. Johnnie's one-dimensional paternal devotion pales in comparison.

He has determined to *be* his father, but it is the prodigal daughter who has the most in common with the old man. They are united by their pain. Fugard considers the seeds of the play to be notes about his crippled father made two years before he actually began writing *Hello and Goodbye*: "He knows it, the anatomy of pain, the way other old people know their pets. The secret places where it plays—the chest, toe-nails, stump, cramp in the good leg. This and the habit of dependence, the habit of humiliation, of loneliness. A man withdrawn, marooned finally on the last unassailable island of the individual consciousness . . . pain." (5-11-61) Except for the dependence, this could apply to Hester. Her pain has no physical cause, but may be more absorbing and intense because of that; there is no narcotic or fantasy that can mask its effect upon her.

Hester cannot simply ignore her father. Although she had presumed his rejection of her, she has hardly accepted it. Her return home can be viewed as an attempt at *rapprochement*. In beating Johnnie upon learning their father has died, she is not simply revenging herself for Johnnie's deceit, but acting out the grief and remorse of a great loss. Hester's heart truly is, as Johnnie says, "the heart that hurts." (158)

Hello and Goodbye was first performed in the dining room of a condemned Johannesburg mansion that was home to a group of students. It subsequently opened October 26, 1965, at Johannesburg's Library Theatre, then went on tour. Fugard played Johnnie with Molly Seftel as Hester under the direction of Fugard's friend, Barney Simon. Simon named the group Phoenix Players and recalls, "Athol referred to us as a green leaf on a burnt tree." The name has been used subsequently by groups unconnected to either Simon or Fugard.

The play more than confirmed Fugard's theatrical promise. He was hailed as South Africa's finest playwright. Lional Abrahams wrote, "Fugard stands in virtual isolation as a native master of the medium." Robert Hodgins claimed, "Athol Fugard is, flatly, the best playwright South Africa has."[23] Such praise is hardly surprising given the stature of South African theatre, but *Hello and Goodbye* does mark a clear advancement in Fugard's technical skill. It is far more tightly written than *The Blood Knot*. Without becoming wordy, its few long speeches effectively open the play to past events and places outside the claustrophobic cottage.

Between the 1961 production of *The Blood Knot* and the 1965 opening of *Hello and Goodbye*, the South African law regulating theatres and public performances changed. In 1961 mixed casts and audiences were legal, though unusual. To inform foreign writers of this custom, Fugard wrote "An Open Letter to Playwrights" in September 1962, at the time of the opening of Johannesburg's Civic Theatre. He stated, in part, "Your plays are being made to fit neatly into this scheme of things. . . . I have written this letter in the very first instance because we want to see your plays. The Whites-Only ruling, with an occasional special performance as a sop to the more liberal consciences, does not make this possible." By the following June, with the support of The Anti-Apartheid Movement, 276 playwrights from around the world had refused performing rights "in any theatre where discrimination is made among audiences on grounds of color."[24] However,

Proclamation R26 of February 12, 1965, extended the Group Areas Act to pro-hibit both mixed casts and mixed audiences in public theatres. (Integrated aud-iences were still permitted in the small private theatres that fell outside the law's scope.) Thus, the performance conditions sought by the boycott were made il-legal (until 1978).

Most foreign playwrights have continued the boycott despite the new law, though it has been openly debated from time to time. For South African playwrights, however, the statute presented a quandary. "It was a question," Fugard explained in 1973, "of either accepting this compromise or doing nothing at all. I decided on the former. Since *Hello and Goodbye* all my plays have gone before segregated audiences, on the condition that whenever staged, both white and non-white communities be given a chance to see them."[25]

As heinous as censorship is, poets, novelists, and essayists can still work at their typewriters and, perhaps, find publishers abroad. However, no play can truly live without actors and an audience. Fugard's choice between segregated performances and none at all was a difficult one, often reconsidered, but for a man so nurtured by his native land and dependent on it for his creative energy, the choice was really whether or not to remain a playwright.

Fugard has frequently questioned his decision to allow segregated perfor-mances. He was attacked as an "ally of apartheid" and for having contributed to the "erosion of human decency." (12-19-65) Nevertheless, he noted, "I can't escape talking to South Africa—even under the compromising conditions of segregated performances. What am I trying to say? That a man can't ever escape the need to talk to his brother? (Himself?) And this involves love—not politics, or morals, or slogans." (12-66)

In a letter to Benson about his decision, Fugard wrote, "*I am not sure. I do not know.* I don't think I ever will. But to sit in moral paralysis while the days of my one life, my one chance to discover the brotherhood of other men, pass, is obviously so futile and pointless, it is not worth talking about. So . . . relying only on an instinct (blind as it is) . . . I have chosen to act." Fugard admits that he has often felt rotten with compromise, but he persists in thinking, "I would rather go on talking, even in compromised circumstances than be silent. . . . Silence is, I think, a sort of treason in my country."[26]

Nevertheless, Fugard has prohibited production of his plays under certain circumstances. He refused to allow the Performing Arts Council of the Transvaal to stage *People Are Living There* at a time when it had never been performed. In recent years Fugard has allowed productions in state-subsidized theatres. In general, he admits, "No consistent principle informs my dealing with segregated versus integrated audiences. The occasions when I've said 'no' and when I've said 'yes' relate, I suppose, to my sense of survival in those particular circumstances. Also, when I finally did get around to letting a state theatre do one of my plays,

I made them agree to take productions into the black ghetto areas, which they had never done before. Both The Space in Cape Town and Johannesburg's Market Theatre, where six of Fugard's plays have premiered, have always been integrated.

On June 13, 1967, Fugard's passport was withdrawn. He was never given an explanation, but thinks that "the act was meant to intimidate and so force me into leaving the country permanently on a one-way ticket, the so-called 'Exit Permit.' " Petitions calling on the government to return Fugard's passport were drawn up by Frank Bradlow, chairman of PEN in Cape Town, and Bobbie Melunsky of Port Elizabeth. Tables were placed outside theatres and 4,000 signatures were collected. Such public pressure, coupled with press attention and the appointment of a more tolerant Minister of the Interior, finally prompted the return of Fugard's passport on May 29, 1971 so that he could direct the Royal Court production of his new play, *Boesman and Lena*. In retrospect, Fugard considers the loss of his passport a fortunate accident. "I was cut off from the degree of lionization that I might have enjoyed if I could have got out of the country. . . . Heaven knows, there was certainly a gratifying recognition of my work, but nothing like the pressures that Osborne and Pinter had to deal with in terms of being the heralds of a new birth of a new English drama."[27]

Lifemates: *Boesman and Lena*

She was, she became, she became nothing.   —Peter Handke

Boesman and Lena begins as two Coloured itinerants arrive on the bank of the Swartkops River. They have walked many hours since their eviction that morning from their shanty. Such treks have marked the times and places of their relationship, yet Lena is uncertain about her identity and her past, which concerns her more than her future. She repeatedly presses Boesman with questions, but he replies with hostility and derision rather than answers. As they prepare for the night, an old black man wanders into the campsite and is adopted by Lena, who communes with him intimately through the night until his death. As Boesman prepares to flee, afraid he will be suspected of murder, Lena declares her independence from him, then chooses to join him on yet another trek.

As in *The Blood Knot* and *Hello and Goodbye*, indeed many modern plays, nothing much "happens" in *Boesman and Lena*. Plot is less important than character. Instead of new events and relationships being created, past ones and states of mind are gradually revealed. An additional character, Outa (old man), has been added to the two character format of *The Blood Knot* and *Hello and Goodbye*, but the foreign language he speaks is incomprehensible. The claustrophobic setting of a shabby room in the earlier plays has been replaced by a riverbank, but Swartkops is just another bivouac, albeit a thoroughly isolated one. The play could be set in any of Boesman and Lena's other "homes": Coega, Veeplaas, Missionvale, Redhouse, Kleinskool, Bethelsdorp, or the Korsten hovel where they had spent the previous night.

Like *Hello and Goodbye*, *Boesman and Lena* presents a long night of reckoning, a journey of self-discovery toward dawn. The second act of each play takes place an hour after the first, but both could be presented as long one-acts; any neoclassicist would approve of the unity of place and the way the ticking of a clock can be imagined throughout each play. Like *The Blood Knot*, *Boesman and Lena* ends with the recognition of human interdependence. The characters are again poverty stricken, but Boesman and Lena are more abject than the Pietersens or Smits, lacking even the distinction of a surname. Yet neither their wretched state nor the ignobility of their environment prevents them from piercing eloquence, lyricism, and final heroism.

Fugard began writing the play in October 1967, but his notebooks date several images and incidents as early as 1963, when, for instance, he mentions itinerants selling empty bottles. Fugard also recalled a story his mother had told him concerning a Coloured couple travelling in a donkey cart who were about to have a child. Mrs. Fugard helped the woman deliver, but when she returned the next morning with food and rags, the donkey cart had gone. "It's a very simple story," Fugard says, "but the image stayed—Lena saying, 'I didn't even have rags.' "[28]

Fugard's perception of the way poor people invest mundane things with great meaning was also influential. Driving home from the trial of one of his actors, he offered a ride to a black woman with a heavy bundle. It contained "an old zinc bath, there was half a bottle of tomato sauce, some cleaning fluid, *bits and pieces*. My God—burdened as she was, you know, she couldn't abandon any of it. . . . She packed up her life on her head and walked off."[29] Fugard also noted about the woman, "No defeat. Great suffering and pain, but no defeat." (8-11-65)

The play

In his notebook Fugard remarks, "Ontological insecurity: Lena in her demand that her life be witnessed. Not just a sense of injustice and abuse." (8-21-68) It is the consuming nature of this insecurity, so much more than merely social or political, that animates Lena's search and makes it so desperate and insistent. Lena strives to locate herself as an autonomous being. Having done so, however tentatively, she can go off with Boesman, taking a middle course between that of Hester-Johnnie and Morrie-Zach: neither choosing an entirely separate life nor depending utterly on the warmth, support, and succor of a kinsman.

Lena yearns to end her disorientation in time and space. She is certain of today and Swartkops; she also makes specific sensory associations with places from her past: collecting pears at Redhouse, chopping wood at Veeplaas, the mountains near Kleinskool, and the mud of Swartkops. (Zach, too, remembers through physical and sensory associations.) However, these are not enough for Lena. To understand her present better, she must rediscover the order of her past. She presumes this order will give her life a pattern, certainty, significance, and sense of integration. Frank O'Connor writes of man in mnemonic, pre-literate cultures, "The greatest possible nightmare is the loss of his identity, which may occur at any time as a result of a loss of memory."[30]

Lena searches for both a history and a heredity that are ultimately generic rather than merely genetic. Her condition is that of all men: the product of a past and external forces she could not alter, for which she is not personally responsible, from which she cannot possibly escape. Hers is the problem that lies behind all tragedy—existence itself. Disoriented in a world she cannot fully comprehend, she is alone, a foreigner in what she would like to believe is her true home. The more that certainty and affirmation are lacking, the more fervently they are sought. Her life and the meaning of it must be confirmed, somehow. Lena desires community, a way of sharing her plight, and a means to become part of something greater than herself. A mangy dog and a dying old man are preferable to both the anesthetizing effect of wine and the sharing of a solitary pallet with the life's companion she takes for granted—almost as easily as she is taken for granted by him.

Lena's quest begins with a question—"Here?"—the first of more than a hundred she directs to Boesman, Outa, and herself. In her search for truth, she is an unwitting practitioner of the Socratic method. Many of her questions are rhetorical: She knows Boesman will not reply, Outa doesn't understand her, and she cannot verify what she does not comprehend. Interspersed with such arbitrary questions, however, are the probing interrogative pronouns that dominate her consciousness. Boesman recalls their first trek: "I was tired. I wanted to sleep. But you talked. 'Where we going?' 'Let's go back.' Who? What? How? *Yessus*! On and on." (173-74) Lena is words, Boesman is silence.

She has yet to satisfy the needs these questions reflect. Finally, she forthrightly asks Boesman to help her. His sarcastic responses—"What? Find yourself?" (180) and "One day you'll ask me who you are" (181)—pinpoint Lena's most pressing need. She shrugs off his replies because she prefers to pose factual questions about where she has been to the more intimate and revealing, "who am I?" She knows, "I'm Lena," (182) but an external identity is insufficient. She has yet to achieve the resignation and torpor of Boesman; for him a mere name is enough.

Lena initially assumes that Boesman has some of the answers when, in fact, he seems unconcerned with the questions. He and Lena are equally lost and their fates are objectively the same, but Boesman generally refuses to admit confusion, uncertainty, or doubt. Wholly resigned to his impotence and passivity, he is past the point of caring about abstract ontological quandaries; the here and now are all that matter to him. Lena, of course, does not recognize that her search is ontological, but it is precisely this nonetheless.

She yearns for the human contact, consolation, and interdependence that Boesman can no longer give her. In a world where nothing else may be certain, at least there are other human beings. Man need not be entirely alone, which is why Lena prefers the community of Veeplaas to the solitude of Swartkops. She calls out into the night seeking vitality and finds, instead, a dying old man. When Boesman threatens to kick him out, Lena bribes Boesman with her share of the wine, trading the inanimate for the (temporarily) animate. As she has apparently done with other strays, she brings Outa into her life for her own sake: "I'm not thinking of him." (184) He presents Lena with an opportunity for satisfying human intercourse.

Outa is Lena's sounding board and his foreign words are a kind of Rorschach test: She projects onto them as she pleases and hears what she wants.[31] Lena reveals those parts of herself and her past that she longs to disclose to a fellow human's sympathetic if uncomprehending ears, but sometimes she deludes both herself and Outa. Their duologue is actually a stream of consciousness monologue during which Lena utters some of Fugard's most eloquent prose. In her most emotional moment she mentions her child that had lived for six months, then continues, "The others were born dead. (*Pause.*) That all? *Ja.* Only a few words I know, but a long story if you lived it. . . . One night [pain] was longer than a small piece of candle and then as big as darkness. Somewhere else a donkey looked at it. I crawled under the cart and they looked. Boesman was too far away to call. Just the sound of his axe as he chopped wood. I didn't even have rags! You asked me and now I've told you. Pain is a candle *entjie* [stump] and a donkey's face." (193)

Lena reaches out to the old man for reassurance that she is human, alive, and not completely alone. Echoing her name by rote, he provides enough certainty and calmness to assuage her distress temporarily. Besides being her audience, he can play the role of witness to Lena's judge-prosecutor-defendant in her trial of her life. He is the projected moderator of her inner debate. His apparent attention and interest allow Lena to infer some sense of self-worth. His frailty gives her a chance to mother him, thus temporarily satisfying one of her unappeased needs. They face the night protected by a threadbare blanket and the radiating warmth of human contact.

With Boesman staring at them silently from inside the *pondok* (lean-to shelter), Lena and the old man huddle about the campfire, share a mug of tea, and break bread. This tableau marks the end of the first act, but its dim religious overtones were accidental, or subconscious. Fugard noted, "kept hearing [Lena] say, 'This mug . . ' 'This bread . . ' 'My life . . .'. Suddenly, and apparently irrelevantly, remembered Lisa the other day reading a little book on the Catholic Mass. There it was. Lena's Mass—the moment and its ingredients became sacramental, the whole celebration of her life." (8-23-68) The tea-and-bread service provides a moment of rest and tranquility for Lena, but Boesman's brooding presence is superimposed upon it. The sacrament, far from being one of transubstantiation, is reminiscent of Johnnie Smit's false and ironic resurrection at the end of *Hello and Goodbye*. The celebration Fugard refers to is preordained to be short-lived.

Lena clings to Outa for many reasons and in so doing discovers an effective way to strike back at Boesman. Initially, he had merely laughed at the old man, another object for his *"cruel amusement."* (185) Gradually, however, Boesman's derision, contempt, and sense of superiority turn to jealousy. This is surprising at first, for upon arriving at Swartkops he had cheerfully invited Lena to leave him. However, his indifference then had been feigned; Lena's worth increases in his eyes as soon as the old man becomes her ally.

Boesman wants her back, though he cannot admit this so bluntly. His jealousy becomes increasingly manifest as he drinks. Rather than causing the jealousy, wine is the agent that releases it. Boesman feels threatened by Lena's independence and fears he has lost control over her. That Outa is old, feeble, and "black people" rather than "brown people" make his usurpation of Boesman's position additionally galling. The mere presence of the old man threatens Boesman. A stage direction indicates, *"For the first time he is unsure of himself."* (197) This will not be the last time.

Throughout the first act, Boesman is a personification of brutality and insensitivity; he seems to care about nothing. Another side of him is revealed during the second act. Nourished by two bottles of wine, the silent and sullen Boesman becomes a voluble but articulate railer. He too begins to ask questions and gradually reveals a percipience and sensitivity not seen before. The alcohol has not created new feelings, but revealed those a sober Boesman could supress.

Lena considers the demolition of the Korsten shantytown that morning a "sad story." Boesman had found it funny: "It was bioscope [movies] man! And I watched it. Beginning to end, the way it happened. *I* saw it. Me." (202)[32] At the place his *pondok* had been, he had found "room for me to stand straight. You know what that is? Listen now. I'm going to use a word. Freedom! Ja, I've heard them talk it. Freedom! That's what the whiteman gave us. I've got my feelings too, sister. It was a big one I had when I stood there." (203)

Boesman is partially able to accommodate the experience of his life by adopting a superior and seemingly objective posture; as much as possible, he denies that such experience is *of* him as well as *around* him. The pose is a means to exert control over himself when surrounding events are beyond his command. Boesman's pleasures are tied to the humiliation and degradation of others. While Lena can laugh *with* the old man, it is Boesman's habit to laugh *at* Lena, which Fugard specifies in several stage directions.

When Boesman is the object of laughter rather than its agent, he becomes unnerved. Lena relates the incident of the broken bottles: "I would have been dead if [the workmen] hadn't laughed. When other people laugh he gets ashamed." (188) Thus, she chooses her words carefully when she makes a brief claim for independence: "When you walk I'm going to laugh! At you!" (219) She would make an object of him as he has made one of her. This is her last act of revenge before taking up the yoke they bear together.

Humor provides a break, the instant liberation of a laugh, for both the characters and the audience. Sometimes a laugh saves Boesman and Lena from the brink of madness. As the mundane physical is joined to the cosmic spiritual throughout the play, so laughter is united with anguish. Huddling around the fire with Outa, Lena tells him, "Sit close. Ja! Hotnot and a Kaffer got no time for apartheid on a night like this." (207) Fugard's only use of the word "apartheid" in his entire canon is ironic and off-hand, as is Lena's use of the offensive terms "hotnot" (for Coloured) and "kaffer."

Throughout much of the play, Lena manifests her sense of loss while Boesman refuses to admit uncertainty or confusion, but finally he can no longer hide these and other feelings. Upon recognizing his dejection and momentary vulnerability after he mentions freedom, Lena interjects an acutely sarcastic riposte: "You lost it? (Boesman doesn't answer.) Your big word? That made you so happy? . . . So that's what we were looking for, that dwaal [directionless confused state] there in the back streets. Should have seen us, Outa! Down one, up the other, back to where we started from . . . looking for Boesman's Freedom." (203-04)

After arriving at Swartkops, Lena had accused Boesman of not knowing where he had been going. She thinks he had ignored her questions about their destination, "Because you didn't know the answers," (171) but Boesman had insisted he knew precisely where he was going, to Swartkops: "I'm not mix-up like you. I know what I'm doing." The exchange occurs so early in the play that one is inclined to believe him, if only because of the forcefulness of his manner.

However, Boesman actually had been lost, at least uncertain about where to go. The options freedom had implied had provided some respite. Wandering about Korsten, trying to decide where to go, Boesman had played out in his mind the luxury of choice, a notion apparently as new to him as it had been to Tsotsi. The possibilities seemed many, but Boesman had gradually realized none would make a difference. Reconciled to this, he had trekked off on the familiar route to Swartkops.

Thus, at least while meandering through Korsten, Boesman and Lena had been equally lost. She can honestly admit confusion upon arriving at Swartkops; he cannot. In a drama of inaction such as Boesman and Lena, it is such internal moments of consciousness, or its absence, that distinguish characters. Yet it is only a temporary distinction between Boesman and Lena, for he later admits his uncertainty: "Show it to me! Where is it? This thing that happens to me. Where?" (210) His pleas echo those Lena voices throughout the play.

Other similarities between them become clear when Boesman tells Lena, "I'm thinking deep tonight. We're whiteman's rubbish. . . . He throws it away, we pick it up. Wear it. Sleep in it. Eat it. We're made of it now. His rubbish is people." (205) The idea is readily accepted by Lena, who has previously said "Time to throw it away. How do you do that when it's yourself." (172) She later decides to keep an old bucket: "Might be whiteman's rubbish, but I can still use it." (220) Fugard has added, "That's possibly one definition of man that the anthropologists have never thought of: an animal that produces rubbish. And very definitely now, human rubbish."[33] For the original production, he gathered his props from a dump.

During the birth that Lena describes to Outa, Boesman had been "too far away to be called," which, coupled with what has been revealed of his character up to this point, implies that he was not even concerned. However, in another flurry Boesman tells Lena their life is dumb: "Like your *moer* [womb]. All that came out of it was silence. There should have been noise. You pushed out silence. And Boesman buried. . . . One day your turn. One day mine. Two more holes somewhere. The earth will get *naar* [sick] when they push us in. And then it's finished. The end of Boesman and Lena." (212)

Previously laconic, though never quite as taciturn as Tsotsi, and seemingly insensitive, Boesman suddenly unleashes a caustic diatribe against life's absurdity. Lena is not the only one capable of articulating deep emotions. She has wanted to be a mother, perhaps even a madonna—a donkey had attended one of her births, and she says, "I want to be Mary;" (181) now it is clear that Boesman had yearned to be a *paterfamilias*. Through fundamental needs such as these they come to represent *ur*-Earth Mother and Father. *Boesman and Lena*, in the words of Stanley Kauffmann, "converts almost protozoan characters into vicars for us all."[34]

Although convinced that he and Lena are worthless, Boesman had nevertheless hoped for an heir and the consequent postponement of his family's putrefaction and eradication. Without a permanent home or offspring, he knows they will eventually disappear without a trace. He and Lena are not sterile, but the death of their children represents a kind of castration. Moreover, if Boesman's alcoholism has made him sexually impotent, this merely complements the weakness and helplessness that prevent him from acting decisively or effectively in other spheres of his life. As if in reaction to society's expectation that he act like a good "boy," Boesman strives to attain fulfillment as a man through acts of *machismo*: beating Lena or Outa, getting drunk, fathering a child. All end in failure.

Boesman is capable of momentary outbursts, but he also recognizes the futility of opposing the inevitable. His passivity is a reasonable response to the terms of his life, which are always and in every way beyond his control. Fugard has called passivity "Boesman's survival kit."[35] In the first act he tries to convince

Lena that only the here and now matter, but she finds this inadequate: "I know I'm here now. Why?" (174) Gradually, she too accedes to the inevitable: "You're right, Boesman. It's here and now. This is the time and place. To hell with the others. They're finished, and mixed up, anyway. I don't know why I'm here, how I got here. And you won't tell me. Doesn't matter. They've ended *now*. The walks led *here*. Tonight." (206)

Such acquiescence becomes clearer throughout the rest of the play. Lena remains impassive when Boesman offers her his tea and also when he threatens to strike her. Her resignation is a prelude to her final choice and indicates the inner journey she has made throughout the night.

She is able to remember neither the distant past nor the frantic events surrounding the demolition of the *pondok* that very morning. When Boesman cannot diminish the pleasure she enjoys with Outa by any other means, he reveals that he had beaten her for her supposed carelessness with the empty bottles, even though he was actually the one who had broken them. The cruelty has been well calculated, and Lena later admits, "You were clever to tell me. It hurts more than your fists. You know where you feel that one? Inside. Where your fists can't reach." (217-18)

Lena revenges herself by convincing Boesman he will be suspected of murdering Outa. Boesman's innocence makes Lena's revenge especially apposite since she too has suffered without reason. Boesman can find no relief, not even from beating the dead body.[36] His disclaimer of responsibility in Outa's death echoes Zach's response to Ethel's proposed visit: "What have I done, hey? I done nothing." (58) Both are "guilty" by circumstances. Morris Tshabalala had asked Tsotsi, "What have I done to you?" (84) The implied answer is "nothing."

Although Boesman seems stronger than Lena, her fortitude can never be doubted. By merely opening her life to the old man, then keeping him despite Boesman's objections, she indicates her independence and self-sufficiency. She also recognizes Boesman's dependence on her, which means, as she sings in her impromptu song, that "Lena's got a Boesman" (208) rather than the other way around.

Lena's decision to trek off with her lifemate is not the triumphant "yes" of Molly Bloom, but nor does it indicate weakness or fear of being alone. Her persistent desire to know when and where she has been is not a question of geography nor of simply reliving her past and recovering lost time. Rather, she believes her past will help explain her present. When Boesman finally explains the proper order of their past journeys, Lena realizes as Boesman had long before, "It doesn't explain anything." This could be the motto of Boesman and Lena—and of the entire play. Lena's triumph is to recognize then accept the fact that existence is incomprehensible, inexplicable, and implacable.

Fugard writes in his notebook, "Boesman—self-hatred and shame, focused on Lena, who is, after all, his life . . . tangible and immediate enough to be beaten, derided, and worst of all, needed." (10-21-67) Interviewed in 1973, he explained, "What really fascinated me was just how a relationship based on incredible reciprocity—the fact that Boesman loves Lena, needs her, totally depends on her—how a relationship like that can turn into hate."[37] He has also called Boesman and Lena "victims of a common, a shared predicament, and of each other. Which of course makes it some sort of love story. They are each other's fate." (7-19-68)

Given the brutality and vituperation so rife through *Boesman and Lena*, it seems paradoxical to call the play a love story. As in *Hello and Goodbye*, however, harsh words and bitterness cannot mask sensitivity, acute consciousness, and the capacity of characters to experience life and each other deeply. Such qualities distinguish most of Fugard's characters. Boesman's hatred of Lena, like Hester's of her father, is only apparent. His jealousy towards Outa suggests the depths of Boesman's love. The bond between him and Lena, though not one of blood, and perhaps not even sanctioned by church or state, is indivisible.[38]

There are no high expectations for Boesman and Lena's next journey, no new worlds to conquer. Their next stop—another bend of the river, the next shantytown, a new *pondok*—will be physically but not metaphysically different from Swartkops. Lena learns "it doesn't explain anything," but *Boesman and Lena* has no resolution; there has been no significant external change from one state of affairs to another. On the next day, too, the peripatetic Boesman will stop on a bare patch of ground followed many steps behind by a heavily burdened Lena, his loquacious punching bag.

The structure and language

Each of the plays of "The Family" trilogy begins with an arrival: Zach after a day at work, Hester after twelve years away from home, Boesman and Lena after their trek. Both *Hello and Goodbye* and *Boesman and Lena* end with a departure. The frequency of such arrivals and departures is reminiscent of Chekhov, and also as in Chekhov, the pre-existing situation remains unchanged. For both playwrights, the use of circular plots suggests the impossibility of escape. White men had destroyed the Korsten *pondok* in the morning; Boesman demolishes the Swartkops one in the evening. At the end of *Godot*, Didi and Gogo "do not move." Boesman and Lena do, and keep moving constantly, but as if on a treadmill—movement for its own sake.

Between the beginning and end of a classical tragedy, change, usually for the worse, has transpired. Catastrophic endings characterize many such plays, but in *Boesman and Lena* and many other modern plays of inaction, nothing so dynamic transpires. Stasis is the ruling principle. *Boesman and Lena* begins with a situation in which the characters exist, in which they have long existed, and in which they will continue to exist. They play unravels through time, but Lena's condition does not; it is all of a piece. Circumstances do not change; what do change are a character's consciousness of the circumstances and the audience's consciousness of both the circumstances and the character. The distinction is between physical actions and momentous events on the one hand, and internal psychological ones on the other.

Boesman and Lena does not so much create and dramatize a new situation as explicate a pre-existing one while exploring its implications for the characters trapped within it; like the situation, the characters may end badly, but they begin badly as well. Instead of a triumphant moment of recognition in which everything is explained, only limited recognition and understanding are possible. Lena's "it doesn't explain anything" is less a climax than an anticlimax.

Furthermore, the endings of *Boesman and Lena* and plays like it do not, in a sense, really matter. They do not depend on suspense. An audience is curious and engaged, but not breathless to discover *the* answer to Lena's questions, as if one existed. There are no surprises in store, no penultimate climax followed by denouement. "It doesn't explain anything" is merely the open admission of what has long been evident. It is reminiscent of the non-arrival of Godot and the failure of Chekhov's three sisters to get to Moscow. Such plays end in ir-resolution instead of the neat clarification that satisfies conventional expectations. There are no ready answers to the struggles and voyages of these ontological astronauts.

Because *Boesman and Lena* does not conform to dramatic "laws" presumed to be immutable, lacking as it does the development and, especially, resolution of a conflict, it may not be thought to be a "good" play. Such laws and conventional terms are irrelevant to *Boesman and Lena* because other principles determine its structure, not because it has none. "A new form," writes Robbe-Grillet, "will always seem more or less an absence of any form at all, since it is unconsciously judged by the consecrated forms."[39]

The plots of Fugard's plays are seldom either complicated or of great importance. They establish a situation and provide an excuse for characters to gather together at a particular time and place when and where the effect of their being together is explored. The clearest clue to the structure of *Boesman and Lena* and plays like it is the shift in the kind and importance of plot: Aristotle promoted the *propter hoc* plot, one event on account of another, but *Boesman and Lena* has a *post hoc* structure, one event merely *after* another. The cause and effect order created by the *propter hoc* plot is clearly alien to both Fugard's world view and his dramatic purposes.

Boesman and Lena has an apparently orthodox structure, and Fugard himself has said: "It's made up of what Marshall McLuhan called mechanical linkage; B follows A, C follows B, etc. It's turning the pages in the book and following the story."[40] Nevertheless, *Boesman and Lena* is a *post hoc* play. Outa must arrive before he dies, and he must die before Lena finds a way to revenge herself on Boesman, but these are exceptions, among others, in a play in which contingency does not for the most part function. The situation of Boesman and Lena is homogeneous from beginning to end. There are no pronounced hierarchies of experience.

Boesman and Lena are pawns in a world where physical acts import nothing and can change nothing. Because nothing seems to happen and because momentous incidents are missing, the play may appear talky. This impression forms because Boesman and Lena do less than is common in many plays, not because they say more. Since, however, they express themselves with great economy, clarity, and potency, their words make an especially strong impression. They achieve significance through words rather than deeds, and the rhythm of the play is not determined by action, rising and falling, but by the level of the language.[41] Internal modes again prevail over external ones.

It is in their moments of greatest anguish and loss that Boesman and Lena grow especially eloquent and lyrical. Lena reflects on being at Swartkops again, "After a long life that's a thin slice. No jam on that one." (175) Considering her many treks, she confides to Outa, "Those little paths on the veld . . . Boesman and Lena helped write them. I meet the memory of myself on the old roads. Sometimes young. Sometimes old. Is she coming or going? From where to where? All mixed-up. The right time on the wrong road, the right road leading to the wrong place." (192-93)

Boesman's and Lena's speech is especially intense, piercing the darkness around them and the invisible wall separating actors and audience, when their memories turn to their dead children: Lena's "One night it was longer than a small piece of candle and then as big as darkness;" Boesman's, "You pushed out silence. And Boesman buried it." Even in his caustic vehemence, Boesman's language can be magnificent. His and Lena's words are as memorable as the deaths of their children.

Their recourse to such heightened language when they are under extreme duress suggests that it is their primary means for accommodating their plight. Boesman and Lena rely on nothing so confidently as they do on their words. It is through their words that they establish relationships and express passion; it is their words that help them assimilate and understand their experience; and it is their words that momentarily allow them to transcend that experience. Outa is he who, within the context of the play, has no words; he cannot communicate.

By placing a character with heightened consciousness of language in each play, Fugard creates a conduit for his own voice. In *Tsotsi* it had been Boston, in *The Blood Knot* Morrie (and finally Zach), in *Hello and Goodbye* Johnnie. Now it is Boesman who is especially sensitive to the sound and meaning of words, though Lena has some of this facility too. Boesman resists Lena's endless interrogations because they demand his attention, energy, and patience, but also because she prattles.

Had Fugard not established this sensitivity to language, Boesman's ruminations on so grand a concept as freedom would be unexpected and too simplistic a contrast to his lack of freedom. However, as with Morrie's attraction to the sound of "brother," Boesman's "freedom" is not simply an abstract idea. For at least a moment after the workmen had razed the shanty, freedom seemed a concrete reality, possibly even a new mode of existence. The word itself had provided a moment of respite for Boesman, until the illusory nature of the concept itself became inescapably manifest to him.

Boesman has his words and his fists. The two are related since, as Lena says, "When Boesman doesn't understand something, he hits it." (218) He comprehends through verbal assimilation, through his ability to name a thing: "I'm Boesman. . . . That's who. That's what. When . . . where . . . why!" (182) By naming a thing, Boesman exerts a kind of shamanistic control over it. When the thing cannot be named, like Outa's death, he responds with his fists. Lena's response to the death reveals the importance of speech to her: "Outa, why the hell you do it so soon? There's things I didn't tell you, man." (220) If it is language that provides some respite for Boesman, it is also language—or, rather, Lena's inability to either answer or ignore certain words, tiny interrogative pronouns— that compels her inexorable search.

In his notebook Fugard writes about a Coloured woman who had been employed by his family, quit, then returned some months later seeking work. Learning there was none to be had, she had trekked back to the bush. Fugard thought of Lena: "A walk into the final ignominy of silence, burdened at that moment as never before by those unanswerable little words . . . Why? How? Who? What?" (7-13-68) These interrogative pronouns accrue additional meanings each time she utters them. Like the silence of Lena's womb, or the silence of the dead old man, the silence of this void is resounding. Such quiet emptiness has been especially emphasized in Fugard's own productions: "My whole sense of the play is that it must have a core of silence."[42]

The primary language problem Fugard faced with *Boesman and Lena* was that of writing it in English when "Afrikaans would have been possibly a richer medium. With *Hello and Goodbye*, no—those Smits down in Valley Road . . . that's sort of half-English, half-Afrikaans, and I used a very corrupt English there. . . . But with *Boesman and Lena* specifically I can remember having a sense on my side that . . . it should almost be in Afrikaans. . . . The play was in fact translated before it was written."[43]

The world view

Fugard's plays center upon characters who live rather than those who die, such as Tobias in *No-Good Friday*, the father in *Hello and Goodbye*, Outa in *Boesman and Lena*, or Lydia in *Dimetos*. Yet the "ignominy of silence" that Boesman and Lena enter is a kind of death. Throughout the play, Lena is concerned with her present and past, but she must also face her future. Outa's death makes her ultimate fate especially palpable. (The play has Fugard's oldest group of characters.) Lena will carry the memory of his death, as she has the deaths of her children, for the rest of her life. Her ultimate death becomes an intrinsic part of her here and now. Boesman's fear of death is characteristic—he cannot name it, and therefore cannot understand it—and so are Lena's abstract musings. While Boesman cannot believe Outa did not even cry, Lena offers a calm, "Maybe it wasn't worth it." (213)

Lena's willingness to face her final destiny marks the zenith of her consciousness. Having "come through a day that God can take back, even if it was my last one," (209) there is nothing left to startle or threaten her. Ready to trudge onward, this twentieth-century Mother Courage says to Boesman, "Next time you want to kill me, do it. Really do it." (221) Lena is not asking to die, but she is resigned to it.

It is often assumed that death must be the ultimate fate in tragedy, even if Oedipus does not die until he is an old man at Colonus and Aristotle specifically prefers the misfortune-changed-to-good-fortune ending. The horror of death is related to the importance attached to life. Death may simply be a means of escape—the road to heaven or an end to suffering. In the decaying and chaotic cosmos of *Boesman and Lena*, life is so painful and that pain so unavoidable, that escape through death may be preferable; it happens only once in a lifetime whereas life must be endured daily. The real tragedy of the Hedda Gablers of the world, Shaw once remarked, is not that they die, but that they go on living. Boesman and Lena submit to life, to the inescapable present, but both the death of most classical tragedies and the continuing life of *Boesman and Lena* are irreparable: In the one, death is the last fact, finally achieved at the end of a life; in the other, death is the first fact, and life is played out through resignation to that fact.

Fugard's vision of man and the universe is part of a broad and essentially modern intellectual tradition. *Boesman and Lena* presents a world in which God may or may not be dead, but in which he is certainly irrelevant, as irrelevant to the resolution of Lena's struggle as social welfare legislation or an end to apartheid. Discord, confusion, and alienation are metaphysically permanent.

Fugard writes, "I don't know if there is or isn't a god. What I do know is the question is the most idle and meaningless I could ever find." (5-63) In *Boesman and Lena* a prime mover is absent, but also missing is any explicit cause of Boesman and Lena's plight. It is, simply, in the nature of things, a consequence of the fact that they are alive. It obeys only its own imperatives. The certainty and order of a Newtonian world are implicitly discarded as wishful thinking everywhere unsupported by experience. Cartesian rationality provides no answers and hence no succor. Particular actions may indeed have effects, but the way the one causes the other to happen cannot be determined with any certainty. The absence of a causal plot reinforces this lack of contingency.

"A world that can be explained even with bad reasons is a familiar world," writes Camus, "But, on the other hand, in a universe suddenly divested of illusions and lights, man feels an alien, a stranger."[44] Camus's perceptions again saturate Fugard's imaginative world. *Boesman and Lena* presents not the proposition of absurdity but the fact of it, deeply and instinctively felt at every moment.

Fugard depicts the conscious struggle of man to understand his state of being, not to overcome it, which in any case is impossible. Since the play projects a world without order, none can be confirmed, nor can suffering be resolved. This is often precisely the point: "It doesn't explain anything." Lena's understatement is characteristic of the play. If melodrama can be defined as emotional effects without sufficient cause, *Boesman and Lena* is distinguished by the absence of emotional effects when cause exists for ranting, moaning, and hair-tearing. Instead, torpor and impassivity are characteristic responses. Ineffectual and impotent, Boesman and Lena can do nothing else.

Since they have not authored their fate and cannot change it, they appear to be innocent. However, distinctions between innocent victim and culpable perpetrator are obviously arbitrary when life itself is sufficient reason for suffering: Lena is beaten although Boesman broke the bottles; he is fearful although he did not murder Outa. There is no causal chain of events beginning in specific personal or social defects that leads to a catastrophe, no discrete flaw causing disharmony in the universe, the state, or the individual himself. Hence, there can be no simple expiation by which, to the strains of harmonious celestial music, certainty and order are restored.

This is not a world of Calvinist predestination, nor of the social determinism of the Naturalists, and yet great actions and transcendence are impossible. Boesman and Lena have the physical ability to act freely, but they know, either innately or from past experience, that their actions can change nothing. When changes do occur, they are not the result of particular, intentional human acts. Effective action being non-existent, passivity, impotence, and stasis pervade. Instead of growing powerful through his life, man in the world of *Boesman and Lena* is enervated. The protagonist of classical tragedy does not always achieve what he intends, but he at least resolutely intends something. Boesman and Lena are involved in a contest they know they will lose. Another king of Thebes or wiser ruler of Britain might have escaped the fate of an Oedipus or Lear. No king, queen, priest, or shaman could escape Lena's.

It is sometimes assumed that outcasts like Boesman and Lena lack the intellect to understand themselves and their world. John Gassner writes, "We cannot have truly tragic enlightenment when the character's mental and spiritual endowment is so low that he cannot give us a proper cue for vision, or cannot set us an example of how high humanity can vault."[45] Regardless of Boesman's and Lena's mental and spiritual endowments, their consciousness is enlightening. It is not they who are lacking, but the world itself. Humanity can no longer run, let alone vault. It can, however, be conscious of its predicament.

Lena is no intellectual, but she is finally able to perceive the limits of her life. She has located herself, if in a void, and has partially satisfied her need for answers, if only by realizing there are none. Implying both surrender and acceptance, her resignation to the fact that respite is unattainable provides in its own way a kind of respite. Consciousness of the absence of abiding answers is also an abiding answer. Consolation is impossible, but acceptance of this is a kind of consolation.

Lena does not discover her identity as clearly as does Oedipus, but this is more a distinction between the cosmological assumptions lying behind the two plays than it is of the characters themselves. Although doomed to final failure from the start, Lena's search has been every bit as insistent as that of Oedipus. A sometime dreamer and maker of illusions, Lena finally perceives the immutable and inconsolable nature of existence. She abandons her search for reason and cause, finally realizing that "it doesn't explain anything." Rationality is merely a notion that man projects onto himself and his environment as a pretense of understanding. Life lacks a clear and definite purpose, or if it has one, it can never be known. Such is the world-view implied by Fugard so potently throughout the play.

Boesman and Lena have certainly been influenced by the social and political environment that has nourished and starved them. The pleasure Boesman derives from degrading Lena is not simply sadistic. At least towards her, he need not be obsequious.[46] She is the sole element of his life that he can control, at least until Outa's arrival. Boesman has learned to take the brutality directed towards him, augment it, and send it on to her. Their relationship reflects the power of men in all patriarchal societies. Moreover, he acts towards her as the white "masters" presumably act towards him. Boesman and Lena also assume that because they are "whiter" than the old man, they are better. Their feelings of superiority parallel those of the white man towards them.

Nevertheless, it is sophomorically reductive to think that the play is essentially a passive mirror of South African society. Boesman and Lena's plight is not primarily social. As itinerants they live, by definition, isolated from any society except that of their own making. From Lena's condition, like that of every man, there is no escape. Because it is not merely temporary, man-made, or social, there is no religious, political, or social "ism" that will resolve it.

"If I were to write a play protesting what has been done to the Coloured people in South Africa," Fugard has wondered, "why did I have to choose such a loathsome individual? Why didn't I choose somebody intact? Why didn't I find a Coloured man who'd been evicted from a nice home by the Group Areas Act, who had a decent job, who was clean living and decent? Why did I have to look for, and use to make my point, somebody as unpleasant as Boesman?"[47] The obvious answer is that, ultimately, Boesman and Lena does not focus upon the plight of Coloureds, the effect of the Group Areas Act, or the evils of apartheid. Such issues have little importance in the play. Anti-apartheid sentiment alone cannot explain the ability of Boesman and Lena to startle the intellect as well as the emotions.

Throughout their performances Fugard and Bryceland used less and less make-up to make them look Coloured. Boesman and Lena could be white, middle-class, or productively employed. Some of the details of the play would have to be changed, but its essence would not. The junk they have accumulated is not so different from that lying on the kitchen floor in Hello and Goodbye. Hester and Johnnie are "the second-hand Smits of Valley Road;" (139) Boesman and Lena are "whiteman's rubbish." In a sense, they are flotsam drifting down the Swartkops past the Smits' Valley Road bungalow and the Korsten shack of Morrie and Zach. In the sea they become one with the other souls drifting in the abyss. Up against an existential wall, Fugard's characters fight for a time, then resign themselves to the inevitable. Boesman and Lena have wandered about on the darkest night in one of the universe's blackest holes. They keep on trekking, but it is a night, and a hole, from which there is no escape.

Boesman and Lena neither affirms nor resolves man's lot in a chaotic universe, but simply confirms through its dramatic experience that it is of a particular kind. This is not pessimistic, which implies a kind of moralistic judgement. Nor is it despairing. Fugard is not gloomy; things are as they are and have always been. The impossibility of change is neither good nor bad. It is, however, alien to the the hopeful instincts of cosmic engineers constantly constructing new vistas to escape the old, instead of reconciling themselves to the immutable and implacable. Boesman's and Lena's resignation leads to freedom from the disappointment and frustration inherent in the struggle to escape the inevitable.

Nietzsche writes that in tragedy, "The truth once seen, man is aware everywhere of the ghastly absurdity of existence. . . . Then, in this supreme jeopardy of the will, art, that sorceress expert in healing, approaches him; only she can turn his fits of nausea into imaginations with which it is possible to live." He goes on to state that Dionysiac art, tragedy, "forces us to gaze into the horror of individual existence, yet without being turned to stone by the vision: A metaphysical solace momentarily lifts us above the whirl of shifting phenomena. For a brief moment we become, ourselves, the primal Being, and we experience its insatiable hunger for existence."[48]

As much as art changes—and has to change—it remains the same. This is so, according to Richard Gilman, "because content seen too long from the same perspective, or possessing the same form, loses its meaning. Innovation in the arts gives us new perspective on what has always been true."[49] Despite the differences between Boesman and Lena and those post hoc plays generally accepted to be tragedies, both their representations—the ontological struggle, man's condition, Nietzsche's "horror of individual existence"—and the effect of those representations—Nietzsche's "metaphysical solace"—are akin. If there is such a thing as modern tragedy, *Boesman and Lena* is a prime example. It is the finest play written since *Waiting for Godot*.

Boesman and Lena premiered July 10, 1969, at the Rhodes University Little Theatre in Grahamstown during a conference on South African writing in English. Fugard directed the production and played Boesman with Yvonne Bryceland as Lena and Glyn Day as Outa. On opening night the cast took eight curtain calls.[50] The play was first produced in America at New York's Circle in the Square beginning June 22, 1970. After Fugard and Bryceland paid their own fares to England, it opened at the Royal Court on July 19, 1971. A film version of the play, directed by Ross Devenish, was released in 1974.

The Nexus of Family Relationships: "The Family"

They endured.   —William Faulkner

The Blood Knot, Hello and Goodbye, and *Boesman and Lena* were not conceived as a trilogy, although Fugard once noted that they should be called "The Family." (9-11-68) They were not even written consecutively: *People Are Living There* was completed, though not produced, between *The Blood Knot* and *Hello and Goodbye.* During this period Fugard also became involved with Serpent Players and began directing plays for them. By 1967, two years prior to the completion of *Boesman and Lena,* he had presented his first collaborative work with them. Hence, the interrelationships among "The Family" are not due to a master plan but to the wholeness of Fugard's world view and to the persistence in his imagination of certain artistic, psychological, and philosophical questions.

Fugard knew that *Boesman and Lena* had to survive on its own merits, but he also recognized its link to the two previous works. All emphasize the nexus of family relationships, first "between the children themselves . . . i.e. brother and brother as in *Blood Knot.* Secondly there is the relationship between child and parent . . . as in *Hello and Goodbye.* Finally there is the relationship between two people not knotted to each other by blood (the parents). . . . It just may be that I am saying something about this in Boesman and Lena. Do you understand me? They could be the parents of . . . ?"[51]

It is not evident in any of the published editions of *Boesman and Lena,* but Fugard has called it "the only play of mine [up to this point] that has a dedication. It's dedicated to my wife, Sheila." A decade after completing the play he added: "I've found, from my personal life and from watching other relationships, how selfish and how gross the male dominance in a man-woman relationship can be. How, to speak about myself and my wife, bullying I've been in a sense. . . . I've written about the original male chauvinist and that, obviously, is what I am."[52]

In writing about the family, Fugard "mined the one real stock of capital life had given me."[53] The influence of his mother upon his work has already been mentioned. In addition, his relationship with his brother informs *The Blood Knot*, that with his father influences *Hello and Goodbye*, and that with his wife bears upon *Boesman and Lena*. His notebooks contain another revealing comment about families. In the period between *The Blood Knot* and *Hello and Goodbye* he wrote about the idea of parents trying to live the child's life: "Doesn't this really only point to an earlier cannibalism? The child having swallowed up the parent's life? I do not know a single relationship in my life in which I wasn't eating or being eaten. . . . Lisa comes at my life hungrily—a blind, ravenous hunger to eat into and possess my life. I have to defend myself. If I don't and she does eat me up then I will be in her bowels, parasitic upon her, for as long as she lives. There are certain things to be said about the parent-child relationship." (10-28-63)

Man is always beset by the physical suffering of his inevitably decaying body or by the ravaging destruction of an indifferent physical world. Joining with others in the creation of families and societies, he can share his agony if not mitigate it, but through such bonding he also risks betrayal, cruelty, and disappointment. Freud writes that the unhappiness that stems from human relationships is "perhaps more painful than any other; we tend to regard it more or less as a gratuitous addition, although it cannot be any less an inevitable fate than the suffering that proceeds from other sources."[54] There is no permanent relief from the terminal affair that is life, only the brief vacation of a laugh, a song, a dance, or a play. The men and women of "The Family" are pilgrims searching for the means to satisfy basic human needs: continuity, dignity, meaning, and a true identity. Through persistent self-analysis they find at least some answers to "who" and are better able to endure the indeterminate "why" and "how."

In each of Fugard's plays, intimate relationships among family, friends, or lovers inevitably lead to the exposure of a character's innermost needs, pain, and weakness. His tramps and outcasts live detached from society or at its periphery. Alone in a cosmic void, they cling to one another. Instead of being mawkish, these bonding relationships are an instance of the most fundamental of all human needs and aspirations. They are the emotional complement to the basic physical needs—shelter, food, drink, and clothing—that also play a prominent role in each play. Well aware of this primordial level of her existence, Lena tells Boesman, "Just your clothes, and each other. Never lose that" (175); and later, "You've had the wine, you've got the shelter. What else is there?" (206) Shelter is obviously of special importance in Fugard's only play set entirely outside.

For Boesman and Lena, the disparity between the visceral level of their lives and the cosmic nature of their metaphysical struggle is only apparent. On the one hand are the Swartkops mud, Lena's bruises, insipid tea, cheap wine, a tiny fire, ragged clothes, and a makeshift shelter; on the other are love, death, and the search for intelligibility. Yet the need for these defines what it means to be human no less than the need for food, clothing, and shelter. It is the dramatization of this essence that is Fugard's primary concern throughout his work, though it is never again so clear, forceful, and condensed as in *Boesman and Lena*.

The three plays of "The Family" also have numerous technical similarities. Fugard never employs more than a limited number of characters inhabiting a simple set. His concern with elementary human existence is reinforced by his minimal use of theatrical accoutrements. Because they are so sparingly used, properties—such as Morrie's alarm clock, the crutches of Johnnie Smit's father, or Lena's tea and bread—become extremely important. Stripped of everything inessential, Fugard's plays depict minimal man in a stark environment forced to face the fundamental nature of existence; there is little else to demand the attention of either his audience or his characters. They are fashioned from clay as primordial as the Swartkops mud.

In his notebook Fugard writes, "To master the idiom—thought and speech—of a character. The problem is never 'what' Hester and Johnnie think but 'how' they think. A constant challenge in all the plays." (2-28-65) Speech is used to distinguish one character from another. It is also language—often lyrical, sometimes rhetorical, seldom simply colloquial—that makes Fugard's work more than simply realistic. While struggling with *Hello and Goodbye* he noted, "Have always squirmed within the realistic convention." (1-64)

With its concentration of siblings, children, parents, and mates, and enough apparent verisimilitude to permit some easy recognition and immediate identification, "The Family" seems to be a textbook example of the domestic realism genre. It should be remembered, however, that *Oedipus Rex*, *King Lear*, and *Othello*, indeed most great plays, also have domestic contexts. Plays of domestic realism have usually concentrated on middle-class characters; Fugard's are selected from the bottom of society, but they are no more atypical than the kings and warriors of classical tragedy. Instead of implicitly possessing nobility and herosim because of great social stature, Lena earns these attributes.

In his study of Proust, Beckett writes, "Allusion has been made to his contempt for the literature that 'describes,' for the realists and naturalists worshipping the offal of experience, prostrate before the epidermis and the swift epilepsy, and content to transcribe the surface, the façade, behind which the Idea is prisoner."[55] Pure realism can suggest that meaning is self-evident and that, therefore, the artist need merely present or describe people and events instead of interpreting them. Fugard's realism, however, is only the pretext, the outer style through which he fathoms the inner Idea.

With the exception of *Nongogo*, his plays are not Naturalistic. They are not enslaved by what Delacroix calls "the fetish for accuracy that most people mistake for truth."[56] Characters cannot be explained through sociobiology; they are not mechanistic products of their social environments.

Totally absent in Fugard is the subtle condescension implicit in many works in which middle-class intellectuals write about peasants and proletarians. Even when such works emphasize milieu, they often suggest that the degradation or disease inheres in a particular class. Fugard has wondered if he were making capital from the misery of others. He realizes, "I'm going to be measured by my work as a writer. If I have told any lies, if I have in any way been dishonest, if I haven't handled that misery with reverence and respect then I'm obviously guilty. I've got a feeling that I haven't. I know that I've felt myself reverent and respectful in the presence of some of the pains I've tried to write about."[57] While the misery Fugard writes about parallels certain instances of suffering in South Africa, that suffering is ultimately a catalyst for his imaginative constructs.

Fugard uses the family not as a locus for normal everyday activity, but as a cauldron of intense human experience as insistently overwhelming as the ontological struggle in which his characters engage. The concentration of bourgeois tragedians on the family was an alternative to the emphasis of classical tragedians on the state. Fugard's characters live at the periphery of society itself, in constant proximity to a cosmic abyss, in some cases already within it. All his characters exist outside social hierarchies and class distinctions as dispossessed, unaccommodated, and naked men.

Boesman and Lena marks the end of a phase in Fugard's career inasmuch as he will no longer be concerned with the nexus of family relationships. However, each of his subsequent plays, like his previous ones, depicts men and women isolated in an alien world as they seek to establish bonds with one another and strive to satisfy fundamental human needs.

III

Time's Toll

Time—a condition of resurrection because an instrument of death.   —Samuel Beckett

In a note preceding a work-in-progress extract of *Boesman and Lena*, Fugard writes, "Also 'time.' Past revealed in Present, Present defining (?) Future. The three experienced simultaneously."[1] His note might have prefaced *The Blood Knot* and *Hello and Goodbye* as well. Fugard's characters are not historically determined, but throughout his work the past both yields up truths about the here and now and provides temporary respite from a consuming present. In resurrecting their pasts, his characters are sometimes freed from them, at least in part. Fugard's obsession with time has been alluded to frequently. It continues to figure prominently in *People Are Living There*, *The Occupation*, and *Mille Miglia*. *People* and *The Occupation* were composed in the period between *The Blood Knot* and *Hello and Goodbye*, *Mille Miglia* was written between *Hello and Goodbye* and *Boesman and Lena*. (The works examined in this chapter have been grouped outside the chronological order of Fugard's career so that "The Family" could be considered as a unit.)

78

People Are Still Living There:
People Are Living There

*Then she thought that there was a beginning, and a middle. She
shrank from the last term. She began once more—a beginning. After
that, there was the early middle, then middle-middle, late middle-
middle, quite late middle-middle. In fact the middle is all I know.
The rest is just a rumor.*   —Saul Bellow

The day that Fugard aborted the novel about his cousin, he wrote in his notebook,
"How many false starts before one finds a beginning that leads through to an end!
But I am hopeful. One image has resurrected an old complex of ideas: Milly's panic
when she realizes late at night that she's spent the whole day in her dressing gown.
Her *cri-de-coeur*: 'Is this all we get?' Hurt or outrage? Obviously both. Certainly not
despair." (5-14-62)

This resurrected image dates back to 1958 when Fugard was employed by the
Native Commissioner's Court, first getting to know Sophiatown, and living with
his wife in a Johannesburg rooming house at the bottom of Hospital Hill in the
Braamfontein section. The characters in *People* and most of its incidents are literal
transcriptions of his experiences there. In 1978 he wrote that the play "has neither
a Port Elizabeth setting nor, seemingly, a socio-political context of any significance.
It deviates from my other work in still a third respect: It was written more directly
from life than any of the other plays. . . . However, the play is in no sense an 'aber-
rant' work. For six years my attempts to understand the possibility of affirmation
in an essentially morbid society were dominated by and finally invested in three
women: Mildred Constance Jenkins was the first, Hester Smit the second, and Lena
the culmination."[2] In addition to living in Milly's rooming house, Fugard had been
raised in another, The Jubilee, run by his mother.

People's seedy boarding house is home to five fumbling souls: Don, an aloof cynic
with a penchant for sophomoric psychology, who is capable of some insight into
his housemates; Shorty, an inept but optimistic postman seemingly content with
his unconsummated marriage to Sissy, a castrating bitch who humiliates him in
public; and Ahlers, a small businessman never actually seen on stage who has just
ended a ten-year love affair with Milly, the slatternly and pathetic owner of the
rooming house. Milly seeks happiness, an escape from boredom and meaninglessness,
and a way to revenge herself upon the man who consumed ten years of her life
before discarding her. After calling Don and Shorty into her lonely life as allies,
she plans to celebrate her fiftieth birthday and thus prove to Ahlers that she can
enjoy herself and plod on without him. Shorty is belittled at the party, and Don
and Milly berate each other, yet they retain some ability to laugh and sneer at
themselves and a disappointing world around them. In the end, their lives remain
as unchanged as their state of (un)consciousness.

When Fugard first conceived the play it was titled *The Silkworms*, and the characters were called Mitzi, John, Shorty, and Ethel. Although these names were changed, silkworms remain the central metaphor: of metamorphosis, of the inexorable passage of time and process of aging, and of people as victims.

After the hostilities of the party subside, Shorty is about to feed his pets before realizing they are in silk. Milly wonders what he will do with them now that they have served their purpose. The silkies will eventually be discarded, as Shorty has been by Sissy and Milly by Ahlers. Apparently useful only during the time they spin silk, they become unwanted, like Milly herself, and turn into ugly common moths, then die. They evolve into what they are and must be. Nor can Milly be other than she is, though she sometimes tries to be.

People's time theme is also emphasized, as in previous plays, by Fugard's use of the device of reliving the past. Here it is embodied by Milly, who looks back with nostalgia, in contrast to Don's apprehension of the future. Her past evaporated quickly; in looking ahead Don seems to wonder, "Will the present ever pass?" For him there is so little difference between one hour and another, one day and the next, that he cannot fathom her anxiety about time.

Milly cannot remember *the* deciding moment of her past, but she does recall a day when she was eleven, a day whose happiness she had tried to retain. However, she cannot will happiness into her life forevermore nor guarantee that the party will be joyous.

Milly's reveries of a happy moment from her youth, a fleeting recovery of that youth, are reminiscent of Morrie and Zach's imaginary car ride, but she immediately juxtaposes her sweet memory of what had been lost with the inescapable nature of her present. Unable to forget the ten lost and seemingly wasted years with Ahlers, Milly finally reveals the reason he discarded her. Like the silkworms, Milly has undergone a transformation: first through puberty from little girl to adult, and then, apparently quite recently, through menopause from fertility to barrenness.[3] Ahlers's response had been immediate; since he wanted a family he had thought it best to break off with Milly, though he stressed that they could remain friends. (None of Fugard's heroines is a mother. Hester has had an abortion, Lena's children have died either in the womb or soon after birth, Melton's wife in *Marigolds in August* has borne two children, one of whom is buried during the film. No other woman conceives.)

Milly's self-revelation near the end of the play is a moment of high emotion that helps explain the vehemence of her earlier denial—"No! There was no baby. And I don't care, because I don't want babies. Understood? Finished. Settled." (29*) Her disclosure also explains, in retrospect, her reply to a toast in which she insists she is not an old woman. Her spirit is willing even if her flesh is weak: "Somebody once said you start to die the moment you are born. The fact re-

People Are Living There (London, New York, Cape Town: Oxford University Press, 1971)

mains however that the best years are the middle years, somebody else said. I side with him. . . . There are plenty of kicks left in the old girl!" (48-49) She has unintentionally confirmed Don's earlier "The sound of doom, Milly. Seconds becoming minutes, minutes becoming hours, days, months, years. . . ." (36) By the end of the play she wants Ahlers back not forever, but only for tomorrow.

Milly's fixation on the ten lost years is frequently evident. She boasts that she sometimes forgets Ahlers for hours on end—as if this were a significant accomplishment. She calls him a thief; he has stolen her time. Don makes the emptiness of the ten years especially palpable when he computes the days Milly and Ahlers have spent together as well as the amount of beer and sausage they have consumed. As if this were not blunt enough, he informs her that a dress she was planning to wear is old-fashioned and that "you've started to get old woman odors . . . . It's nearly twelve o'clock and then you're a year older. And there's not many more left where that one came from. You're in the home stretch, Milly!" (58) The birthday party itself, of course, also suggests time and the process of aging.

Finally, the passage of time is implied by the numerous references to death. Ahlers sells his plastic flowers to undertakers. Milly thinks Don's room is like a morgue. She asserts that "Waking up is a cold business in an empty house. Put out the light and you're as good as in your grave." (5) Sleep is the simplest way to escape her fears, boredom, loneliness, and rejection. She briefly toys with the idea of suicide, the final sleep. Milly's undertones are especially grave when she refers specifically to the failed party: "I've been cheated. The whole thing was just a trick to get me to go on. Otherwise who would? Who wants to get up tomorrow if this is it? If this is all?" (59)

Don is also obsessed with mortality. He thinks time is subtracted from the point of death rather than added to the point of birth. Given his saturnine temperament, it is no surprise when he suggests the image of a coffin: "All you need is four walls, and a lid." (70) This is especially apposite following a birthday celebration that is "more a wake than a party."[4] Don's final suggestion to Milly, albeit a facetious one, is suicide.

Asked in an interview about this obsession with time, Fugard replied that he considered man's central dilemma to be the fact that life dies: "To the extent that one can come to terms with time, one comes to terms with the prospect of ultimate oblivion. . . . One of [the] basic games in life is an attempt to escape time, to stop the clock, or to forget or try and drown the noise of the clock ticking away."[5] There is also an autobiographical influence. Early in his notebook Fugard records his father's "twenty-four hours a day of nothing" as he fills his life with solitaire: "Anything to pass the time, darling. Anything at all." (1960)

By conjuring imaginary moments from Milly's past, Don provokes many of her self-revelations. Though he is not quite her conscience, his frequent challenges and ripostes are effective goads to her subconsciousness. He is her inquisitor general, she his check and balance. They take an almost sadistic pleasure in their mutual sarcasms, a game they have obviously played before—and will play again. Don keeps score, but both know the rules well: no holds barred.[6]

Fugard has described Don as "a pimply-faced pseudo-cynical student with a superficial command of Penguin-book psychoanalysis." He is an admixture of Fugard himself and Perseus Adams, his hitchhiking companion.[7] Don drops the names of Sartre and Darwin as well as catch phrases such as "dilemma of our age" and "Age of Crisis." (4) Don does not possess the verbal facility and language consciousness found in many of Fugard's characters, but he so revels in his cleverness that he writes down his most "astute" observations. A pipe-smoking pseudo-intellectual, Don is often pretentious and asinine, but he does possess some knowledge. For example, he is correct in stating that silk comes from the insect's head rather than its bowels, as Shorty contends.

Don is capable of incisive perceptions, but his foolishness often masks his occasional lucidity. He is "a Cassandra doomed to have accurate insights that are dismissed because of his silly manner."[8] He has difficulty understanding himself, but this does not prevent him from dissecting others. Don's attempts at Freudian analysis are ludicrous, whether he is trying to interpret Shorty's dream or deducing that Milly's secret must have something to do with rape or incest. It is not until he abandons his pseudo-psychology that he forces Milly to make revealing disclosures about herself.

Don persistently searches for the particular cause of Milly's unhappiness. Although on this night, especially, she has a specific reason to be sad and lonely, he does not realize that her anguish is all-embracing. The would-be scientist and deep thinker is incapable of induction.

Don and Milly have much in common. They enjoy their mutual antagonisms and are equally pathetic. Don claims there are fates worse than death, and Milly would certainly agree that being forgotten before one's time is such a fate. Both attempt to circumvent boredom through sleep, a manifestation of their depression.

Nevertheless, the differences between Don and Milly are significant. She refuses to accept the immutability of circumstances he perceives to be outside his control. Fugard has distinguished Milly from Don (and Shorty) by her "disgust and impatience at their resignation to their respective fates."[9] A stage direction describes Don's "*Body and movements without virility.*" (2) At one point he claims his sexual urge is intact. Perhaps, but his sexuality is detached. Milly alludes to his masturbation (57), and many of his "profound" observations refer to sex and women. Shorty and Sissy apparently have no sex life, but Milly has obviously enjoyed an active relationship with Ahlers, which makes his rejection of her for sexual-biological reasons especially devastating.

Don's inactivity, his virtual impotence, is far-reaching. Murray Biggs notes, "He speaks and 'acts' in negatives: 'nothing,' 'never,' 'nowhere.' "[10] After adopting a superior and condescending position throughout the play, Don finally admits the pervasiveness of his emotional paralysis: "When things happen, I watch. Even when it's to myself. . . . I used to think the right word for me was Numb." (70) Don's haughty pose of superiority successfully distances him from the activity around him and prevents it from making emotional inroads upon him. Milly, conversely, experiences everything deeply and personally. In contrast to her gregarious desperation, he is detached and afraid of human intercourse, even in his recurring dream of being at a party.

The title of *People*, like the later *Sizwe Bansi Is Dead*, is a declarative sentence, an apparent statement of fact. However, Milly is not altogether certain whether she is a person or a meaningless object. Near the end of the play she declares: "I'll make it loud, make them stop in the street, make them say: People are living there! I'll remind them. Tomorrow." (71) The lines can be read several ways, but coming from Milly, the emphasis seems to be on "people." She is finally sure. It is an assertion of self, even a small triumph. Since earlier in the play, after describing her loneliness in the empty house, she had concurred with Don's perception: "You saw yourself—an object called Milly in an object called chair—but knowing the names didn't help because everything went on being useless, including yourself." (31)

Such deep purposelessness is one of *People*'s themes. Don is acutely aware of the lack of purpose and meaning in life, but he accepts this and attempts to convince Milly it is inevitable: "It happens long before you are dead. . . . You lose your place in the mind of man. . . . Who remembers us? At this moment? Ahlers? . . . Or Sissy? . . . When they walk in and find us again, it will be the way you find something old and forgotten and almost useless." (33-34) His outlook is too extreme for Milly and she rejects it: "Nobody gets forgotten like that. One thing I can assure you, it's not happening to me." (34) However, it is happening to her, as she realizes at some primal level. Now that Ahlers has discarded her she cannot quite ignore it. Suspecting that he has already forgotten her, she schemes so that Sissy and Ahlers will return to find that "*they're* forgotten because *we* are having a good time." (42)

Don realizes the absurdity of Milly's scheme, warns her it won't work, and suggests she drop the idea. Besides, they have no reason for a party. Milly claims her birthday is reason enough, but this party is as preordained to failure as the lives of its participants. After a lame start, Milly suggests they start the party again. She, Don, and Shorty must rehearse what comes naturally to others for this is a make-believe celebration with only imaginary fun. A crucial interlude transpires in silence as Milly begins to recognize the disparity between the party she had imagined and the one that is actually taking place. Fugard's use of this silence to project the party's dullness is especially effective on stage.

The melancholy pervading the party is also reflected in the songs sung during it: "Pack up your troubles in your old kit-bag and Smile, Smile Smile;" "Roll out the barrel, we'll have a barrel of fun;" "When Irish eyes are smiling;" and

"Why was she born so beautiful, Why was she born at all?" Shorty does sing "For she's a jolly good fellow," but the one song conspicuous in its absence is "Happy Birthday." As the party disintegrates, Milly dredges up parts of her sometimes-happy past before the merry-makers attack each other. This celebration is as disastrous as that of Johnny and Queeny in *Nongogo*; Don finally declares it a fiasco.

At first, Milly no more accepts this perception than she had Don's earlier ones about life's lack of purpose and the ease with which people are forgotten. While watching Don and Shorty devour the cake and wine, she begins to perceive that something has gone awry, but Milly refuses to relinquish her hopes for the evening. She challenges Don and Shorty: "Nobody goes to bed until I've laughed!" (51) For her, life's ultimate pleasure is to be happy, its ultimate crime is to be forgotten. Preferable to being ignored is notice of any kind, even ridicule.

In Milly's mind, laughter and happiness are one. She is convinced that the best way to get back at Ahlers is by appearing to enjoy herself, but the harder she tries to have a good time the more elusive her goal becomes. Ironically, one of the few times Milly does laugh freely, after boxing with Shorty, she considers it a trick to make her forget Ahlers. She wants Ahlers to think she has forgotten him, but she has no intention of actually doing so.

Milly declares by fiat that she, Don, and Shorty will have a good time. It is characteristic of her to give orders, and on this evening her frequent use of military language is a further indication of her siege mentality and of the soberness of her plan. Ahlers is the enemy as is Shorty, temporarily, for fraternizing with him. Milly refers to the "zero hour" (16) and orders, "Stand by for action," (20) "Action stations," (44) and "all hands on deck." (67) She accuses Don of being a deserter; he wants an armistice.

The contrived nature of this rooming-house party is reminiscent of Pinter's *The Birthday Party*, although *People* lacks its aura of potential physical danger. Instead, there is the danger of imminent psychological attacks and unmaskings, such as those in a number of American plays with pretend parties: Albee's *Who's Afraid of Virginia Woolf?*, Mart Crowley's *The Boys in the Band*, and Jason Miller's *That Championship Season*. All are plays of psychological realism in which characters' innermost secrets are revealed during the course of long, presumably festive evenings.

However, there is an important distinction between these plays and *People* in the means by which frazzled nerves are revealed and psyches bared. The American tradition is insistently *in vino veritas*. The convention of the soliloquy has been replaced by one that encourages characters to bare their souls when they are drunk. Milly, however, has only half a bottle of Muscadel. It may be hard, as Lena claims, "to make a party without a *dop* [tot]," (207) but this is precisely what Milly, Don, and Shorty attempt. They have imbibed no magic truth serum that allows them to expose themselves in the evening, yet claim the following morning, "I was so drunk I didn't know what I was doing."

Fugard's characters can never escape responsibility for what they do. Instead of resorting to the mechanical trick of an elixir, he creates situations that demand heightened consciousness and personal candor. As a result, the pain, frustrations, and inadequacies of his characters seem all the more pervasive and inescapable.

To race-obsessed critics, as many of Fugard's have been, *People* appears quite different from *No-Good Friday*, *Nongogo*, and *The Blood Knot*. It actually has much in common with them both thematically and technically, as it does with the subsequent *Hello and Goodbye* and *Boesman and Lena*. As in *Nongogo*, *Hello and Goodbye*, and *The Blood Knot*, the interior set is quite bare. Again there is a small cast and a slim plot. Although some time elapses between the two acts, action is almost continuous. As in *The Blood Knot*, the dialogue is still over-written and the language sometimes verges on the florid. As in *Hello and Goodbye* and *Boesman and Lena*, a woman is the central character; again there is no possible escape for her or her companions. As with other Fugard characters who never appear on stage, such as Ethel Lange in *The Blood Knot* and the Smit patriarch in *Hello and Goodbye*, Ahlers is a catalyst for much of the play. In addition to the device of returning to the past, Fugard again uses games, notably Milly's pretend party. Characters also arrive at and leave a "home," which is again both the locus of a play and a place characters strive to make a haven of security. Although Milly, Don, and Shorty are not blood relatives, they live together intimately and are thus familiar, as in "The Family," with one another's deepest secrets and fears. Fugard remains concerned with besieged loved and unloved characters who search for happiness, reassurance, and meaning.

People is permeated by the world view of *The Blood Knot*, a perspective that becomes more insistent in *Hello and Goodbye* and *Boseman and Lena*. For this reason its darker side and similarities to these plays have been emphasized. Yet, as in Fugard's other plays, there is also much humor amidst the pain. Indeed, despite its themes of loss, loneliness, fear, and frustration, *People* is the most comic play Fugard has written (until *Master Harold*). In 1974 he stated that comedy, on the whole, "has been a very serious omission in my statement so far."[11]

Henri Bergson writes, "A comic character is generally comic in proportion to his ignorance of himself. The comic person is unconscious."[12] There is less shift in the consciousness of *People*'s characters than in any other Fugard play. Despite the disclosure of their secrets, fears, and frustrations, they end as they began: Milly continues trying both to revenge herself upon Ahlers and to make him feel guilty; Shorty goes off meekly with Sissy, resigned to her continued condescension, belittlement, and refusal to have sex with him. With the chiming of midnight, Milly embarks upon her fifty-first year. Some tranquility returns, but the status quo has been preserved. Milly, Don, Shorty, and Sissy remain unchanged, living in "Jo'burg," at least alive, if not happily and productively so.

In "The Family," characters end in the external physical situation in which they begin, but their self-consciousness changes, except for Johnnie Smit's. Instead of avoiding their lives, they confront them. Milly attempts such forthrightness only temporarily before retreating into her vain search for *rapprochement* with Ahlers and for good times, which Don realizes are an illusion.

Milly's questions, "Why? Why me? Why this?" (59) are similar to Lena's, as is her perception that "I suppose it's more of a mystery really. Life." (71) Also, a stage direction at the end of the play indicates that Milly is *"suddenly conscious of herself and her predicament,"* (71) but this consciousness does not approach Lena's final lucidity. Milly's quest is more limited than Lena's and less consuming. Milly's problems are not as fundamental as Lena's, and they can be easily remedied. Were Ahlers to take Milly back, all would be well. She has not pursued an insistent search so much as embarked upon a casual, self-pitying perambulation. Even in the midst of apparently serious observations, her mind is evidently elsewhere; by asking Don, "What's the score for tonight," (71) she suggests that she has been playing all along.

Horace Walpole has written that "the world is a comedy to those that think, a tragedy to those that feel." Both comedy and tragedy are present in plays like *People*, sometimes called tragicomedy or, J.L. Styan's term, "dark comedy."[13] Both the writers of such plays and their characters may be oppressed by their situation, but they continue to contemplate it as they experience it emotionally.

The tradition of grave comedy extends back through Molière and Jonson to Euripides. In much modern drama, thought is fused to the tears and laughter: In Chekhov, Brecht, and Beckett, the mingling of tears and laughter is the rule rather than the exception. When serious subjects are treated with some levity, the effect is to make the serious even more so.

While working on the manuscript of *People*, Fugard noted on the title page a quotation from Charlie Chaplin: "If the flesh does not laugh in mockery and delight at the world around it, and finally even at itself, it dies." One of the surest signs of mental health is an ability to laugh at oneself. "There is no fate," Camus reminds us, "that cannot be surmounted by scorn."[14] In *Endgame*, Nell says, "Nothing is funnier than unhappiness, I grant you that." By the end of *People*, Milly can laugh at herself freely and wholeheartedly. She remarks, "you could do something with the lot of us if you had a sense of humor." She then *"breaks into laughter . . . her laughter grows enormous."* (72)

Shortly after he began *People* in 1962, Fugard wrote Benson, "I fully expect a rather bewildered public reaction over here if and when it reaches the stage. Bewildered because it might seem to be about nothing—and I know everyone is waiting for more controversy. I couldn't care less." His anxiety about getting the play produced anticipated the difficulties he eventually faced. On June 9, 1963 he wrote in his notebook, "I have sufficient distance now to believe quietly, and unshakably, in *People Are Living There*. It is very real and meaningful despite Ian Bernhardt's stupid remark: 'It is a good play but I don't know why you wrote it.' " (Bernhardt had been one of the organizers of Dorkay House.) In 1968 the Johannesburg Repertory Players found the play to be "lacking social content and not suitable for Johannesburg audiences."[15]

The Oxford edition of *People* indicates that it premiered at Cape Town's Hofmeyr Theatre on June 14, 1969, but Robin Midgley had directed it at Glasgow's Close Theatre, where it opened on March 13, 1968. One critic wrote, "The inner loneliness of four people in a boarding house is savagely and expertly laid bare. But Fugard has maintained a strong vein of humor throughout. His wit prevents too sombre an atmosphere." The production was also seen in London on April 28, at the Mermaid Theatre for a single charity performance to raise money for a South African actor, Mulligan Mbiquaney. When it finally was produced in Cape Town, with Fugard directing and playing Don, one critic called the production, "what might be described as the start of a new era in South African theatre."[16]

Fugard had some difficulty casting Milly—three well-known Johannesburg actresses turned down the part—but he thought that the primary obstacle to getting the play done at first was the eagerness of producers and the public for another *Blood Knot*. *People* is the first of Fugard's plays about whites, the only previous white character being Father Higgins in *No-Good Friday*. Fugard may have hoped that *People* (and *Hello and Goodbye*) would ease his escape from the pigeon-hole of "black theatre." Following the American premiere of *People*, one critic wrote that *People*, "deals only with the whites of Johannesburg, and it suffers seriously from that fact."[17]

Although Fugard had difficulty securing a South African production, *People* was almost done on Broadway in 1965. Irving Schneider was to produce it and Lindsay Anderson to direct. Fugard noted that Schneider "was appalled at the changes I had made and urged me to get back closer to the original." (9-64) There was a great deal of dialogue among Schneider, Anderson, and Fugard. He says, "The text we have today owes quite a lot to that dialogue."

Schneider's first choice for Milly was Maureen Stapleton, who eventually dropped out of the project. A year later Bette Davis became interested, and she invited Anderson to her Connecticut cottage to approve him. He recalls that she was "nervy and nervous, and had evidently made a personal identification with the role of Milly that was not based on a very close study of the text. She explained that she saw the end of the play differently from the author. Milly was to be left alone on the stage 'screaming.' I pointed out, with temerity, that in the play she was *not* alone on the stage, and she was laughing. Miss Davis said she saw the play as a tragedy. I said I thought it should definitely be approached as a comedy—even if we were using the word in a Chekhovian sense." After considering the project for a week, Davis announced her acceptance. Anderson recollects, "My heart sank, but we embraced with words of optimism. I returned to London, apprehensive. A week or so later I was greatly relieved to receive a telegram from Irving Schneider announcing that Bette Davis had withdrawn from the project, because of her 'disagreements with the director.' I am sure the whole thing would have been catastrophic had we gone ahead."[18]

There was also talk of turning *People* into a film. In 1972 or 1973 Roy Sargeant, a professor of drama at Rhodes, approached Fugard about doing an adaptation. He declined, but André Brink did complete a screenplay. It has yet to be produced. Following his 1964 American premiere production of *The Blood Knot*, director John Berry attempted to get backing for a film version of that play with Richard Burton and James Earl Jones. Although Berry thought he had raised the money, it was not forthcoming. Neither of these films was ever made, but for his next project Fugard did turn to writing for the camera's eye.

Two Teleplays: *The Occupation* and *Mille Miglia*

Time rushes forward from the past, which no longer exists, into the present, which has no duration, and into the future, which does not exist; in eternity there is no time. —St. Augustine

While awaiting word about a possible stage production of *People*, Fugard wrote Benson in 1963, "To keep the home fires burning, the wolf from the door and bread in the bin, I am writing a TV play. . . . It's a good idea—four derelicts—hoboes—in an abandoned house where they doss down for the night. What is it really about? Walls, I suppose. Why we build them, imprison ourselves and live our lives away behind them, why we hate, need, even destroy them. This is of course a completely new field and one in which I might prove quite talentless."[19] Stimulated by *Last Year at Marienbad*, a film by Alain Resnais and Alain Robbe-Grillet, Fugard began what he calls "an exercise in researching the possibility of the writer dominating the film medium."

By July he was writing every morning, and the following month he castigated himself for trying to describe the work to Pieter du Preez: "'I must guard against this and make silence an inflexible rule when working on an idea. Talk *always* dissipates." (8-63) While working on a second draft, Fugard noted, "no aversion to this medium—the screen—now that I am working for it. Whether I have any real ability or not is of course another matter. The medium is in no sense novel—I

feel the experience gained in the small lifetime wasted away watching bad films."
(8-63)

After finishing *The Occupation: A Script for the Camera* in September, Fugard sent it to Benson and Michael White, *The Blood Knot's* London producer. Although they were encouraging, it has never been filmed or adapted for the stage, though it has been published twice.* The story runs as follows: Under Cappie's (Captain's) leadership, Koosie, Barend, and Serge (Sergeant) smash their way into an old house as if they were on a combat maneuver. They find only rubbish, a dove, and a bed, the existence of which Barend tries to hide from the others. Their security is threatened when a "native" carrying a club appears outside, but the enemy passes without becoming aware of their presence. As Cappie begins to drink, he reveals how deeply World War II combat has affected him. His mind and emotions have been so wrecked that he becomes enraged by Barend and jealous of his ability to hope and dream. When Barend's bed is discovered, he forces the others out of the room claiming it as his own.

As in other Fugard works, there are few characters in *The Occupation*. They are also poor, live in an environment strewn with debris, and exist outside society's mainstream. As in *Boesman and Lena*, they trek back and forth along the open road from city to city. Again there is a person (the black man), who does not physically appear, but his importance is much less than the emotional presence of Ethel Lange, Ahlers, and Johnnie Smit's father. Again there is a pronounced concern with time as well as evidence of the way significant past events influence the present.

As with other Fugard characters living together closely, the hoboes are intimately familiar with one another. Strong bonds are present (Cappie has sex with Serge), but there is an important distinction between the relationship Fugard emphasizes in this work and those stressed in his others. Instead of his usual exploration of interdependent relationships, such as those between Cappie and Serge or Cappie and Koosie, Fugard focuses instead on the differences between Cappie and Barend, especially Barend's independence and the antagonism it causes. Besides refusing to indulge Cappie's military fantasies, Barend mouths none of the martial phrases sprinkled throughout the script, and he rejects Cappie's hegemony. His explicit defiance of Cappie's authority portends ill, but still more threatening to Cappie are the challenges thrown up by Barend's emotional and psychological independence. Tired of his rootless existence as a hobo, he is as eager to secure a home as Morrie and Hester are.

*It originally appeared in *Contrast*, 2, No. 4 (1964), 57-93, but quoted below is the more widely available edition in Cosmo Pieterse (ed.), *Ten One Act Plays* (London: Heinemann, and New York: Humanities Press, 1968), pp. 255-93.

Cappie's military swagger and domineering ways contrast with his complexity and intelligence. He says far more than any other character, although the camera does not give equivalent attention to his person. Most of the dialogue consists of bits and pieces, short questions and replies, and brief observations. Cappie's revealing harangues are the script's only long speeches. In the first of these he maniacally conjures up the past residents of the house in images that meld with his obsession with time: "The air in here was so thick with living it choked them! (*Pause.*) But the clocks were ticking. They were warned. Waking at night, in the neither today, nor yesterday, nor yet tomorrow. A moment in a sleeping house . . . except . . . what is that? You listen hard. Yes. The old clock ticking away on the landing. Ticking. That's all. Ticking away. . . . Nothing is heavier than time, my boys." (265-66)

As with Morrie's speech about passing for white, or Johnnie's about his father's death, Cappie's speech is obviously disjointed and frantic. Despite its confusion, however, it reflects his state of mind and prepares for subsequent revelations and a final confrontation with Barend. Dreams that never materialized, hopes that were never fulfilled, the pressures of time, the longings for a future that proved to be a delusion, these are the obsessions that rule Cappie's mind.

His deepest self-revelations grow from an imaginary letter to Koosie's father: "That is war, Mr. Rossouw—time and helplessness. And ruins. At the end of it all—ruins. Man is a builder of ruins. I remember Rome. Went up there when it was over. Rome! The Glory that was Greece and the Grandeur that was Rome. . . . We're also ruins. The guns have left our hearts in ruins!" (286-87) Ancient Greece and Rome lay in ruins, the occupied house is in ruins, Cappie's, Serge's, and Koosie's lives are in ruins, and Monte Cassino, where both Cappie and Serge apparently saw action, also lays in ruins.[20]

Fugard deviates from the pattern of his earlier work by clearly specifying the war as the cause of Cappie's behavior. Social factors that help explain behavior always exist, as influences if not absolute determinants of character. Previously, however, these had only been implied; there had been a merely tacit indication of the relationship between society and the individual, of the way the one influences the other. Like *Nongogo*, *The Occupation* is different: not because sociopolitical factors are shown to have been influential, but because an explicit causal relationship exists between them and a character's behavior and state of mind. Individual responsibility is diminished as blame is placed on an external event.

Although Barend speaks only a few hundred words throughout *The Occupation*, the camera often dwells on him. It is also intended to reveal his inner life, but no camera could do all the work Fugard expected of it. (He was influenced by the extreme detail of Robbe-Grillet's shooting script.) For instance, while Barend stares at the sunset, "*We begin to feel it desolates him.*" (271) During Barend's recollection of his discovery of the bed, "*something intensely personal is happening*

90

to him. *We sense the contours of a blind and desperate hope. The function of the camera is to find this and relate it to the physical reality of the man—the old shoes; the coarse, calloused, empty hands; the unlovable face."* (272)

The Occupation ends with Barend sitting on his bed. He says, simply, "It's late! Tomorrow. . . ?" (293) Tomorrow is an uncertainty, as open a proposition as Barend's entire future. Tomorrow the occupation will be Barend's past, a memory of a decaying house and four derelicts, himself among them. Cappie, who had previously claimed, "I'm in tune with the past," (262) may already have suggested the nature of that future memory. He says about the house, "This, Serge, is another man's memory, and what's the bet he hates it." (263) The same fate may await Barend. His future is likely to be as empty as his hands, as empty as the lives of his companions.

The Occupation is an anomaly in the Fugard canon. It is the only unproduced script he has allowed to escape from his study. As in many of his plays, there is considerable talk about time. However, the resurrection of the past usually affords Fugard's characters the opportunity finally to free themselves from it. Cappie's past dominates him. Furthermore, while Fugard usually reveals a character's hopes and dreams to be illusions preventing him from achieving self-consciousness, Barend's continuing hopes both distinguish him from the others and elevate him above them. In this work, Fugard invites respect for Barend *because* he is a dreamer.

The Blood Knot's first London production in 1963 was not well received, but a second one in 1966 with Fugard directing and playing Morrie was. As a result, the BBC telecast the play on June 12, 1967. Robin Midgley directed. The BBC then commissioned Fugard to write a teleplay, *Mille Miglia,* based on Sterling Moss's strategic victory in the Italian roadrace of the same name on May 1, 1955. Midgley again directed.

Unlike closed-circuit races, the Mille Miglia was held on public roads, which gave the native Italian drivers a clear advantage. Moss decided that no matter how much he practiced, he would never be able to memorize the course well enough to take every curve, hill, and corner as fast as possible. Therefore, he devised with Denis Jenkinson, a racing journalist and experienced passenger in sidecar championships, a series of signs by which Jenkinson, as passenger, would alert Moss to the conditions of the road ahead. During five practice runs, Jenkinson used a revolving drum to note various landmarks and the road conditions he could expect until the next landmark.

Fugard read about Moss's victory when he was in London in 1960. He became fascinated by the story and conceived of it from the start as a teleplay. His experience with motor mechanics at Port Elizabeth Technical College gave him some background, "but the car Moss drove was a very, very special number. I had to do a lot of research into that."[21] However, it was not the car that fascinated Fugard but the men inside it, their relationship, their strategy, and the appeal of the sport itself.

He first made notes on the subject as early as 1963, but did not actually begin to work on the script until soon after *The Blood Knot* aired. On September 13, 1967 he wrote in his notebook, "*Mille Miglia*: Jenkinson finally realizes that what has happened is that the game becomes life. The rest is waiting." Fugard finished a draft later that month.

The withdrawal of Fugard's passport on June 23, 1967 prevented him from travelling to London for pre-production consultations. Consequently, Midgley wrote Fugard detailed progress reports that included suggested script changes. He first wrote Fugard on October 4, 1967, shortly after receiving the draft. Midgley was enthusiastic, but he wondered if the script were too short: "I am sure that since the play operates on a largely philosophical level, the exploration of character under tensions, we can take much more of the opposite side of the coin—the humdrum, detailed, meticulous preparations, actions which in themselves are non-dramatic but become all the more so because they are 'waiting' activities."[22] Midgley also yearned to see more of the effect that waiting had on the men and their relationship: "Moss becoming more ascetic, Jenkinson, the ordinary man, more extroverted and frenetic." In another letter, Midgley described the central relationship as "two men artificially locked together, reacting to each other, and in a way, creating each other. Because, though Moss is the soloist, surely even a soloist responds to his accompanist—indeed a good accompanist can liberate the 'genius' in the soloist."

On first glance *Mille Miglia* is a half-breed piece, neither an entirely "original" story nor a documentary. After completing the production, however, Midgley acknowledged that he had decided, "this was clearly a play and not a documentary, and interesting though the individuals were, they were of necessity only background to us and it was the play we were doing."

Since Moss was the first Englishman to win the race, Fugard assumed the audience would know its outcome. Moreover, he was less interested in the drama of the race than the preparations for it and the personal relationship between Moss and Jenkinson, especially the development of trust between them. They are actually shown in the car only when it is in the garage. Instead of presenting the story chronologically, making a climax of the victory, Fugard uses flashbacks, going back as far as preparations made in the February before the race. As in "The Family," he scrutinizes an intense personal relationship, human interdependence, and the imminence of death.

According to Benson, Fugard was especially provoked by two statements Moss had made: "Death is like a piece of furniture in a familiar room. You know it's there but for a long time you've not noticed it;" and, concerning speed and danger: "It's life. The rest is just waiting." Fugard's fascination with these observations led him to try to penetrate racing's appeal to a driver and the absence of fear in him despite impending danger. One review of the telecast was entitled "Philosophy of Moss."[23]

Moss and Jenkinson are neither nervous nor apprehensive while awaiting the race, but a great sense of anticipation fills their hotel room. Moss admits in his last speech that he wants to beat the other drivers, but that he is really up against himself: "It should be possible to live that way—flat out—where the choices and decisions really matter—all the time. Maybe I'd give up racing if I knew how to live like that. But I don't." (80*) Jenkinson asks: "So the game becomes life. . . . And the rest?" Moss replies, "You said it earlier . . . waiting."

Of course, Moss does win, covering the 1,000 miles at an average speed of 97.8 miles per hour. A projected text at the end of the film reads, "This was a new record for the Mille Miglia and will stand for all time. This race was abandoned two years later as being too dangerous." (82)

Mille Miglia was telecast August 5, 1968 with Michael Bryant playing Moss and Ronald Lacey as Jenkinson. The production has not been preserved on either film or tape. Moss and Jenkinson appeared in person later the same evening on a show entitled "Late Night Line-up." A newspaper account reported that Moss "said he was dead embarrassed by it, and that it did not represent what happened. He and Jenkinson agreed that all their humor and fun had been left out and that as represented the two men were very glum characters indeed. In fact, they said, they did not quarrel and their discussions, far from being agonized were strictly practical. . . . Their opinions of the play were far more entertaining than the play itself."[24]

Moss and Jenkinson were disappointed with *Mille Miglia*'s lack of verisimilitude, but Fugard was deeply frustrated by the need to be truthful. He was unable to manipulate the situation as he felt necessary and has stated, "The moment I start getting involved in history I have to pay some attention to facts, and I don't know how to cope with this really. The one writing experience I let myself in for where I had to be careful about set facts was the TV thing I did about Sterling Moss. I found this an inordinately frustrating experience. I could never escape the facts. Couldn't make my own words. . . . It's the plots that I don't want to surrender control over. I don't want to have to follow something.[25]

Within ten years, however, Fugard wrote another filmscript, *The Guest*, also based on an episode in the life of an historical figure. He also used portions of a received story in his collaborative experiment, *Orestes*. However, in these and other works with some basis in history or myth, Fugard controls the "facts" in a way that does not fetter his imagination.

*The manuscript is in the collection of NELM.

Critical response to the teleplay was mixed, but one reviewer noted that Moss and Jenkinson were "real heroes engaged in a real life or death struggle and in consequence this small-scale television piece made all the film epics about racing look the silly melodramas they are." Still working as a journalist two years after the premiere of *Rosencrantz and Guildenstern Are Dead*, Tom Stoppard wrote that *Mille Miglia* and the discussion that followed were "the experience of the week. . . . On the whole, the BBC blurb that Mr. Fugard 'has great insight into people and a special talent for being able to write about them truthfully' seemed well confirmed."[26]

Following the suggestion of Brian Astbury and Yvonne Bryceland, *Mille Miglia* was adapted into a short play called *Drivers* by David Muir, who had been Fugard's cameraman for the film version of *Boesman and Lena*. Muir directed the play in July 1973, at The Space in Cape Town. It was also staged by the Performing Arts Council of the Transvaal at the Arena Theatre in Doornfontein. As recently as 1977, Fugard's disappointment in *Mille Miglia* was evident when he declared that it would never be published.[27]

IV

The Playwright-Director and His Actors

*These lines upon lines of print that call themselves plays are but
inadequate records of the full effect that author and actor conspire
to produce.* —Harley Granville-Barker

Fugard is best known as a playwright, but he is a complete man of the theatre
and his writing has been deeply influenced by his work as an actor and, especially,
as a director. Following Circle Players, his association with the black actors he
met at Dorkay House led to *No-Good Friday* and *Nongogo*. These in turn helped
prepare for *The Blood Knot*, the actors' workshop at The Rehearsal Room that
followed, and its Port Elizabeth counterpart, Serpent Players. Both The Rehearsal Room and Serpent Players are important in themselves, as part of South
African theatre history, and for their direct influence upon Fugard. Following
No-Good Friday and *Nongogo*, his writing moved in the direction of chamber plays
for actors, then total collaboration with them.

Collaboration Begins:
The Rehearsal Room and Serpent Players

*My involvement with the theatre is, I like to think, a total one, as
a director, actor, writer.* —Athol Fugard

Financial and artistic support for Fugard's township plays had been minimal,
but it was at last forthcoming through the Union of South African Artists, which

made its home in the Johannesburg factory building called Dorkay House. Begun to prevent the exploitation of black musicians, Union Artists was first run by Dr. Guy Routh. Following his dismissal from a government post and subsequent emigration to England, Ian Bernhardt assumed the leadership.

Union Artists was responsible for the 1959 production of *King Kong*, an original "African Jazz Opera" based on the life of a popular black boxer. Like *No-Good Friday* and *Nongogo*, which preceded it, *King Kong* explored township life. The income from this production helped Union Artists create the African Music and Drama Association (AMDA). By May of 1961, its student body of messengers, servants, factory workers, and teachers included 200 enrolled in music and thirty-five in drama. One of the students explained, "We are trying to find ourselves to realize our souls. Drama lessons will only teach us the tricks of the game, and we are not interested."[1] Besides *King Kong*, Union Artists mounted large-scale commercial productions of Tagore's *The King of the Dark Chamber*, O'Neill's *The Emperor Jones*, and Alan Paton's *Sponono*, in which Fugard coached the inexperienced AMDA actors while Krishna Shah directed the entire production. Fugard no doubt used the skills he had developed from working with untrained actors on *No-Good Friday* and *Nongogo*.

In addition to its large-scale commercial endeavors, Union Artists also sponsored modest productions at The Rehearsal Room, which Fugard called "our only chance—Zakes and myself and those like us who see in theatre something more than an alternative to Bio [movies] for the jaded palates of the whites." Following The Rehearsal Room's 1961 opening with *The Blood Knot*, productions included Pinter's *The Dumb Waiter*, with Zakes Mokae and Connie Mabaso; Steinbeck's *Of Mice and Men*, directed by Barney Simon with Mabaso, David Phetoe, and Basil Somhlahlo; and a production of *Waiting for Godot* that Fugard mentioned in a letter to Benson: "This production has been as important an event in my life as *The Blood Knot*. I have always loved the play—I was able to get quite fantastic performances from the cast—my old troopers: Connie Mabaso, David Phetoe [as Didi and Gogo], Gilbert Xaba [Pozzo], and two newcomers, Job Musi [Lucky] and Philemon Hou [Boy]. The public was most generous in its response."[2]

Godot opened October 18, 1962. By the following year Fugard considered The Rehearsal Room "the most important thing happening in South Africa today."[3] That same year he directed Sartre's *Men without Shadows*. Performances were always for multi-racial audiences.

Another Rehearsal Room production was to be a double bill of *Anna*, a play Simon had written for Molly Seftel, and Ghelderode's *Escurial*, directed by Fugard. Only days before opening, Fugard cancelled *Escurial* when he realized his actors would not be prepared in time. With Simon directing, Fugard performed *Krapp's Last Tape* in its stead—without his dentures, and without knowing all his lines. Simon stayed backstage to prompt and to make the sounds of bottles opening.

Whenever Fugard deviated from the text, Simon recalls, "I'd gesture to him and he'd exit into the wings, which Krapp does anyway. While I made the popping noises, Athol would study the script, then go back on stage. It was a breathtaking performance."

Fugard's work at The Rehearsal Room meant that he had to spend much of his time in Johannesburg, but he continued to make his home in Port Elizabeth, where Norman Ntshinga visited him to request that they do a play together. Fugard noted, "I say 'request,' actually it is hunger. A desperate hunger for meaningful activity—to do something that would make the hell of their daily existence meaningful. . . . When he sat opposite me, I realized I was making contact again with South Africa for the first time since my return from London. I found his presence 'strange'—his well-known 'blackness' strange—it was like meeting a well-loved and hated friend after a long separation." (5-13-63) After Ntshinga returned with four friends from New Brighton, a black township about twenty miles from Fugard's Port Elizabeth home, Fugard recalls that he "despaired really, I was very tired after the tour [of *The Blood Knot*] and I really didn't feel like getting involved with the actors again so soon—it's very exhausting—but they were persistent, and I felt guilty."[4]

For their initial project the group decided to perform Machiavelli's *Mandragola*. Their talent and enthusiasm so encouraged Fugard that he noted after the first rehearsal, "I look forward with pleasure to the three weeks ahead. I am very glad I committed myself. It is a positive act—creating hope and meaning—it cannot but make life richer and more significant for me. It balances some of the selfishness with which I live." (7-17-63) As the actors gathered for a first reading of the play, five Special Branch (S.B.) policemen burst in, recorded everyone's name and address, read the play themselves, and sorted through Fugard's papers. They would continue to scrutinize the group's activities in the years ahead.

Machiavelli's play was adapted to a township setting and called *The Cure*. The rich cuckold was given a name Fugard had previously used in *Tsotsi*, Tshabalala. Fugard described the production as "hilarious and deliciously vulgar. I am staging it very strictly in the Commedia dell'arte style—bare stage, a few props but lots and lots of fun." *The Cure* played three consecutive days beginning August 15, 1963, in the old Port Elizabeth Museum and Snake Park, which had been taken over by the local branch of Rhodes University.[5] The audience of friends from New Brighton and the university community was one of the first racially mixed ones ever in Port Elizabeth, and the production was a popular and critical success. Fugard considered the acting at least up to Johannesburg standards and vowed to work with the company again: "But possibly the most rewarding aspect of the venture has been the success of my production and my deliberate attempt to reproduce the style—lightness, elegance, tempo—of the period piece. A completely bare stage except for one black applebox, and then the actors—on and off, running about, etc. in a series of short, pithy scenes. For the first time I feel I really sense the potential in truly improvised theatre." (8-17-63)

With the first production also came a name. In an undated letter to Ian Ferguson, Fugard explained the christening: "There's a sweet little story to the origin of the name 'Serpent Players.' The very first performance of the group was given in the abandoned open-air snake-pit of the old Port Elizabeth Museum and Snake Park in Bird Street. We needed a name for the group. The choice was obvious."[6] The pit, designed so that people could stand around the rim and watch men handle snakes in the center, was a natural auditorium. The name stuck even though the troupe never performed there again.

For their next production Serpent Players took on *Woyzeck*. It was presented November 25-29, 1963, in Crispin Hall, controlled by the predominantly Coloured garment-workers union. The rudimentary auditorium was set up with 400-500 chairs, although audiences were only fifty to seventy-five percent of capacity. The proceeds helped support the Port Elizabeth School Feeding Fund.

The production included an original jazz score by Mike Ngxocolo and lyrics by Fugard. "It's the only time I've tried that and I don't think I'll try it again. I can't, thank god, sing you any of the songs." Woyzeck (Welcome Duru) was portrayed as a black laborer and the Drum Major as a Boss Boy. The cast also included Mabael Magada as Marie, Simon Hanabe as the doctor, and Ngxcolo as the Boss. The production received good reviews, but Fugard was not satisfied. "The acting failed completely to catch the subleties, the light and the shade in Marie and Woyzeck. Although for the group this production was a step forward after Machiavelli, the final result wasn't anywhere near as satisfying. A long way to go." (12-63)

Serpent Players initially met at night in a lecture room at Rhodes. They later used a small gymnasium in Korsten. Because it was located in a Coloured area, neither Fugard nor his actors needed a permit to attend. During the period between shows they met only once or twice each week, "always with a couple of jugs of Tassenberg red wine," Fugard says. "My name is synonymous with it in Port Elizabeth." When preparing for specific productions they rehearsed more frequently as they neared their performance dates, finally meeting every day for the last two weeks of the eight- to ten-week rehearsal period. On weekdays, however, they could only work from five to nine in the evening. Attendance was complicated by transportation problems, by police harrassment, and by the regular jobs the actors held as teacher, bus inspector, factory worker, lawyer's clerk, and domestic servant, to name a few. Tickets were only a few pence and paid for the hall, properties, flyers, and carfare for the actors. Production budgets were so small that when money for simple programs was unavailable, the names of characters and actors were announced from the stage. Fugard recalls, "If our whole production budget hit R100 ($140), we were in the big time."

He had initially been apprehensive about working again with amateurs, but the New Brighton actors were different from those at The Rehearsal Room: "There I spent half my time dreaming and bitching. . . . Here we act. Also, these men are so much more responsible. I can see now how the patronage and 'help' of well-meaning whites has sapped away the initiative in Dorkay House." (8-17-63) Inexperienced as they were, the Serpent Players were free of theatrical tricks and clichés and open to new challenges and experiments. The same was true of township audiences, as Fugard stated: "Paradoxically, because they have no preconceptions about theatre we have never felt too far out with them. Not so when we played before White Port Elizabeth, whose theatre consists mainly of an amateur diet of thrillers and drawing-room comedy." Fugard was soon to realize, "I can go further with this group than with any group of white professionals or high-class amateurs," and that "had it not been for the stimulation of Serpent Players I would not be as involved with the practical theatre as I am, and I would suffer as a writer—I am sure of that."[7]

In 1964 Robert Loder invited Fugard to Northern Rhodesia to direct *The Caucasian Chalk Circle* for a drama festival in Lusaka. Loder, who had helped fund The Rehearsal Room and AMDA, hoped to initiate a Rhodesian equivalent to Union Artists, the Zambian Arts Trust. In May, however, Fugard was threatened with deportation from Rhodesia and the production was abandoned. After a rehearsal, while in a bar with Loder and Theodore Bull (who ran a community center that was to host the production), Fugard declared that he had encountered more prejudice from blacks towards whites in Rhodesia than he had in South Africa. His statement was published and the authorities intervened.[8] In retrospect, Fugard admits the poor timing of his outburst since the government was then negotiating independence, which would turn Northern Rhodesia into Zambia five months later.

That September, while commenting on the dominance of African theatre by colonialists, Fugard described another episode of his Rhodesian encounter: "I thought of using the local African dialect in the production. My suggestion was vetoed on the grounds that it was an 'English-speaking' festival. Box-office returns of the past proved that our audience would consist almost entirely of whites, none of whom would understand the vernacular. This was in a country in which the black man out-numbered the white by more than ten to one."[9]

The Rhodesian production was aborted, but Fugard continued to work on *The Caucasian Chalk Circle* with Serpent Players. They presented Brecht's play in late November, again at Rhodes, and in early December at New Brighton's St. Stephen's Hall, which had been home to a single performance of *Woyzeck* and would be one of the venues for subsequent Serpent Players productions. Grusha was portrayed as a domestic servant, the Iron Guard wore police helmets, and the palace clique donned white masks.

On December 10, 1964, the day of the first performance in New Brighton,

Welcome Duru, cast as Azdak, was assaulted by the police in his home and dragged off to jail. Fugard wrote Benson, "I felt suicidal. The whole substance of my life seemed rotten—no, *was* rotten—with self-indulgence. My simplest pleasures turned sour. If I hadn't had to go on as Azdak I don't know what I would have done. As it is this Xmas with its 'tidings to all men' can now provoke nothing but hollow mocking laughter on my side. What a farce!"[10] Nevertheless, Fugard considered the production one of the best he had ever mounted. This was the last regular Serpent Players production he was able to see within a township, where it played perhaps ten times, moving from one hall to another. "If you wanted an audience," according to Fugard, "you had to go to it. Transport is difficult now, but in those days it was almost impossible."

By the time of the next production, Norman Ntshinga and Sipho Mguqulwa had also been arrested for petty offenses such as belonging to a banned organization, attending its meetings, or distributing pamphlets. Three Serpent Players were eventually sentenced to Robben Island—including Ntshinga, despite Fugard's testimony on his behalf. After his trial, an incident occurred that would figure in a later Serpent Players work: An elderly man convicted of charges similar to Ntshinga's took off his old coat, gave it to Ntshinga's wife, and charged her to find his family and tell them to use the coat.

The next Serpent Players production, Sophocles's *Antigone*, was mounted in July 1965. The cast included Nomhle Nkonyeni in the title role, Mabel Magada as Eurydice, George Mnci as Creon, Mike Ngxcolo as the leader of the chorus, and John Kani as Haemon. Kani was promoted from a mute soldier to his first speaking-role when Simon Hanabe was arrested shortly before the opening. Mulligan Mbiquaney acted as assistant director. By this time a new Group Areas Act had been passed that prevented the cast from simply selling tickets at the door in white Port Elizabeth. Instead, Serpent Players played to invited audiences of sponsoring organizations that had a definite membership. Nor was Fugard able to secure permission to see the production in New Brighton. He admits, however, "We do manage to give a few white friends a chance to see our work by way of private performances."[11]

By February of 1966, following the run of *Hello and Goodbye*, Fugard had accepted the invitation of Loder to start a London-based theatre company of Africans from all parts of the continent: Kenya, Nigeria, Ghana, Zambia, Uganda, Sierra Leone, and South Africa. It was to be affiliated with Dennis Duerdin and a London branch of AMDA called African Music and Drama Trust. Fugard sought both trained and amateur actors eager to explore and nurture their skills.

These workshops were conducted at the Round House and eventually led to a production of Wole Soyinka's *The Trials of Brother Jero* with Zakes Mokae as Jeroboam. Fugard had hoped to mount another short Soyinka play to complete the program, but this fell through. Instead, a recital of South African music and poetry accompanied *Brother Jero* when it began a two-week run at the Hampstead Theatre Club on June 28, 1966. Fugard recalls, "While it was exciting to be working in this cosmopolitan African context, it also provided problems of its own. Personal rivalries and misunderstandings, particularly in the last two weeks of rehearsal, almost got out of hand at times. I personally walked out on the whole venture at least twice and on another occasion had the same done to me by a few of my most important actors."[12]

Fugard was also persuaded by Loder and Michael White to mount *The Blood Knot* following *Brother Jero*. Fugard directed and played Morrie with Mokae as Zach. After a short run at the Theatre Royale in Brighton, it opened at the Hampstead Theatre Club on July 11, 1966. This week-long run utilizing the cut and rearranged text was better received than the previous London production. For the first time, Africa's two finest playwrights, Fugard and Soyinka, were performed back-to-back in the same theatre. The company called itself Ijinle, a Yoruba word meaning "depth." After nearly six months in England, Fugard spent a month on Crete before returning home.

Upon his return to South Africa and Serpent Players, Fugard was provoked again by an image that had been nagging at him: the prisoner's coat. He and Ntshinga's wife had promptly told Serpent Players about it and from time to time the group kept the idea alive through improvisations. On September 23, 1966, he noted, "*The Coat*: moving on to foolscap paper. Notes becoming extensive—possible form also emerging."

When a Port Elizabeth theatre appreciation group asked to see the work of Serpent Players, the company agreed to present a reading of *Brother Jero*. However, the actors needed a permit to appear before whites, and the terms turned out to be so insulting that it seemed inappropriate to them to continue. Before cancelling the reading, however, one of the actors suggested that they present *The Coat*, which could pointedly use the humiliating circumstances.

After deciding to proceed with it, Fugard worried about possible repercussions: "And if there are, what were my motives?—vanity, foolhardy recklessness, plus a genuine desire to shatter white complacency and its conspiracy of silence." (11-25-66) Two days later he added that what should have been the last rehearsal "was instead a moving, absurd, sensible and idiotic discussion—given all the pros and cons—of whether, with the possibility of the S.B. being in our audience, we should proceed with *The Coat* as a group venture or as a reading by myself alone."

The Coat: An Acting Exercise from Serpent Players of New Brighton was presented to an audience of 150 at Dunne Hall of Port Elizabeth's Hill Presbyterian Church on November 28, 1966. To protect their identities from the Special Branch, the actors adopted the names of their best roles from previous Serpent Players productions—Marie from *Woyzeck* (Mabel Magada), Jingi from *The Cure*

101

(Humphrey Njikelana), Haemon from *Antigone* (John Kani), Aniko (Nomhle Nkonyemi) and Lavrenti (Mulligan Mbiquaney) from *The Caucasian Chalk Circle*. The day after the reading, Fugard noted, "My faith in the actors, in our subject, the shape and content of the audience's experience of us, completely justified. . . . If I am right and the group was dead, then it is either a resurrection or a moment of posthumous glory." (11-29-66)

During the year that had passed between the original incident with the coat and this public reading, Fugard had begun to work with Serpent Players as a writer as well as a director and teacher. The company continued to perform adaptations of the classics, but it also began working improvisationally to use the stage "for a much more immediate and direct relationship with our audience than had been possible with the 'ready-made' plays we had been doing."[13] During improvisations Fugard acted as "scribe": initiator, catalyst, and critic, as well as recorder of the actors' words and actions. (When *The Coat* was first published, Serpent Players was listed as author.) Questions were posed, challenges raised, discussions pursued, and excesses eliminated. With one actress, Fugard recalls, "I made a little note and handed this to her and said, 'Take it away. Come back same time, same place, next week. Think about it. See if you can fatten it, fill it out a bit.' She did and next week we provoked her and she reenacted the scene for us. Then we provoked her again by questions and a little bit of discussion . . . and that's how it grew." (4*)

The primary challenge of the exercise was the one the prisoner himself had made: His family should use the coat. Instead of specifying one use, several possibilities were presented to the audience during the reading, but presented as a reenactment of the improvisations conducted in rehearsal. Improvisation itself did not continue during the staged reading.

Despite such potentially explosive topics as political prisoners, poverty, and apartheid, *The Coat* tries desperately to be objective. In his introductory remarks the narrator says, "There are certain facts: We will give you them. There are a lot of questions, we tried to find the answers. Listen and judge for yourself." (8) Such quasi-impartiality is also a product of *The Coat*'s anti-illusionism. Properties are introduced as such and the audience is frequently reminded that it is watching actors. After *The Coat*'s only truly emotional speech the narrator attempts to deflate its passion: "That's moving Aniko . . . but how much of that is you, how much the wife? We're not interested in what you would *like* to see happen, but in what *does* happen." (24)

The Coat, of course, has much to do with the real lives of the actors as well as life in New Brighton; any attempts to negate or minimize this make the paradox

---

The Coat: An Acting Exercise from Serpent Players of New Brighton (Cape Town: A.A. Balkema, 1971). Subsequent quotes are also from this edition, although it was published after the one in *The Classic*, 2, No. 3 (1967), 50-68. The editions are the same.

all the more forceful. The quandary is inescapable. The more adamantly neutrality and objectivity are exclaimed from the stage, the more difficult they are to achieve. Emotions are eventually expressed in *The Coat* that, no matter how "true," are not neutral and cannot be. A coat may be a mere object of clothing, but through scrutiny it becomes the symbol of a man, a people, and a way of life. After donning Zach's coat, Morrie says, "You get right inside a man when you can wrap up in the smell of him." (21)

The Coat ends with the narrator saying, "We didn't do too badly. Because it was just a coat we struck a good balance between reason and emotion. Our boredom kept us objective." (25) The actor playing the son asks, "Are you saying that we must be bored with these things before we can understand them, or do anything about them?" Serpent Players and their mentor were evidently aware of the box they had built around themselves, of the difficulty of being neutral about grave matters that affected them personally. Fugard noted that *The Coat*, "lent itself admirably to not wasting time on cultivating illusions, staying instead with an immediate reality."

However, during the impassioned speech of the prisoner's wife when she must finally sell the coat, the actress "lost herself to the extent that I felt it was totally blurred. I felt that there was a way of delivering that moment that would have been objective, that would have communicated the full sense of it to the audience, but would have been much simpler. As actors, we hadn't kept abreast of the ideas we were trying out." (5) There was apparently too much identification between the actress and her character. This attempt at distancing is clearly Brechtian, and Fugard's notebook reveals the influence of the *Messingkauf Dialogues* upon his thinking about *The Coat* (9-27-66), though he generally considers Brecht "a challenge rather than an influence."[14]

The Coat was meant to be didactic in the purest sense of the word: to reveal certain facts about New Brighton life, and to do so objectively. Effective as it is in dramatizing those facts, because it is neither objective nor impartial in so doing, it is a failure on its own terms. Still, it is a fascinating exercise, and at the end of the presentation, according to Fugard, "you could have heard a pin drop." (6)

Following *The Coat*, Fugard and his company continued to make theatre pieces collectively. In May 1968 they decided to do Genet's *Deathwatch*. Mulligan Mbiquaney did much of the directing, with John Kani and Winston Ntshona acting together for the first time as Serpent Players. The third cast member was Nomhle Nkonyemi. Mulligan Mbiquaney did much of the directing. Fugard noted that the performances "make more meaning of that cell and the relationships between the three men than any of my readings of the script have been able to. Possibly the most sustained, convincing, and committed performances that Serpent Players have ever produced." (9-68) The production also marked one of

Fugard's first sustained interactions with Ntshona and Kani who, Fugard remembers, "borrowed a pair of handcuffs from his father, who was a policeman. During the first performance they couldn't get them off."

The group decided that the second half of the evening should be an improvised piece. One of the actors described the New Brighton children he saw each morning buying stale bread at reduced prices. Expanding on this, he suggested a man and his family living below the poverty line: "On Thursday night there is no food in the house. He sacrifices the few cents he'd put aside to buy himself something to eat at work next day. It barely produces enough to stop the children crying from hunger. There is still the problem of Friday—morning and afternoon—what will the family eat until he comes home in the evening with his pay? He does the last thing possible—sacrifices his busfare so that they can buy two loaves of stale bread. He will walk to work." (5-7-68)

Fugard considers the evening this idea was conceived one of the most exciting he ever spent with Serpent Players. After *Friday's Bread on Monday* was performed, Fugard noted that this "improvised essay into hunger and desperation in the townships," which utilized little dialogue, considerable mime, and no sets or props, "had good qualities. It was more than didactic. We moved into the realm of almost valid theatre." The father, played by Winston Ntshona, was named Robert Zwelinzima, a name Ntshona would resurrect for *Sizwe Bansi*. A critic wrote of a 1970 revival of *Friday's Bread* (on a bill with *The Cure* and *The Bacchae*), "The attitudes reflected in the piece were firm and unsentimental; it was neither a wail nor a self-indulgent cry of anger."[15]

Another collective work was *The Last Bus* (1969), which Fugard helped initiate, but which the group completed without him when outside commitments intervened. He described it in his notebook: "Four characters: night-watchman, old woman, two Ciras with a pushcart. (Cira=African trying to pass for the lowest of skollie-type Coloured.) Explored what set the Ciras apart from a poor African." (3-69) Kani and Ntshona again acted together. Neither *The Last Bus* nor *Friday's Bread on Monday* has ever been published.

Fugard acknowledges his debt to these early collaborative works, but admits they were two-dimensional pieces dependent on facts that, however important, were "flat and lacking in the density and ambiguity of truly dramatic images. The reason for this limitation was that I relied exclusively on improvisation in its shallowest sense. I had not yet thought seriously about alternative methods of releasing the creative potential of the actor."[16]

He says that all Serpent Players productions, whether classical adapations or improvised originals, "had an urgent relevance to the lives of the people of the township." Other productions included a studio version of *Coriolanus*, directed by Mulligan Mbiquaney for New Brighton schoolchildren who were studying the play; Schnitzler's *La Ronde*, as a reading only, at Fugard's home; Strindberg's *The Father*, though not adapted as the other plays had been; *The Bacchae*, by

Collaboration Begins

Euripides; and Camus's *The Just*, performed in Port Elizabeth, Grahamstown, and at The Space, in June of 1972. One critic called *The Just*, "perhaps the most tightly controlled and shattering piece of theatre ever to have hit Cape Town, judging by the appalled silence of the largely White audience."[17]

The involvement of white directors and administrators in black theatre groups has been severely criticized by some blacks. A 1973 article reported that the black theatre movement had become "cynical and suspicious of white support. Some even refer to Phoenix [Players] as 'that white group that gives jobs to blacks.' "[18] Such criticism is part of the backlash against white liberalism, but it is also true that in some groups the top positions have been held by whites. Even *King Kong*, which was considered a pioneering work in 1959, was written, directed, designed, and choreographed by whites. Besides the cast, only the composer was black. It must be remembered, however, that Fugard did not initiate his involvement with Serpent Players.

His relationship with the troupe was clearly symbiotic. He may have committed himself out of guilt, but he soon realized that he was learning while teaching others. Little in the other theatre work around him nourished his artistry or stimulated his intellect. He has written that aside from Barney Simon, Serpent Players "is the only significant provocation and stimulus to myself as writer and director that I have encountered in South Africa." He has also claimed, "They've kept me alive," [19] an assertion of more than symbolic importance since he was without a passport from 1967-1971 and thus unable to leave the country.

Initially, Fugard was not enthusiastic about working with yet another amateur troupe, but he now realizes, "It was one of the most important things that ever happened to me in my theatre career because the relationship with Serpent Players began to develop, and *Sizwe Bansi Is Dead* and *The Island* could not have happened had it not been for that knock on the door." Ironically, their enormous success led to the group's demise. During the American tour of the plays in 1974 and 1975, *S'ketsh'*, South Africa's black theatre magazine, noted "the Serpent Players seem to be dormant."[20] After nearly a decade, Fugard's association with the company culminated, then ended—although the group ventured on without him for a short time.

On his passport Fugard had long described himself as either an actor or director. Only at some point after 1974, he is not sure when, did he officially begin to call himself a writer. As a stage actor he has always directed himself except for his early work at the Labia, Huguenet's *Oedipus Rex, A Kakamas Greek*, and Simon's productions of *Krapp's Last Tape* and *Hello and Goodbye*. His roles have included "a laager-minded egotist" in Peter du Preez's *A Place of Safety*,[21] Azdak in *Caucasian Chalk Circle*, Krapp in *Krapp's Last Tape*, and in his own plays Father Higgins, Morrie, Johnnie, Don, Boesman, Errol (in *Statements*), Dimetos, and

Steve (in *A Lesson from Aloes*). On film he has been directed by Peter Brook in *Meetings with Remarkable Men*, by Richard Attenborough in *Gandhi*, by Roland Joffe in *The Killing Fields*, and by Ross Devenish three times: as Boesman, as Eugène Marais in *The Guest*, and as Paulus in *Marigolds in August*. The BBC version of *The Blood Knot*, in which Fugard played Morrie, was directed by Robin Midgley. In addition, Fugard's voice was heard in a BBC radio broadcast of Sheila Fugard's *The Castaways*, adapted by Mary Benson.

With a few exceptions, Fugard has directed only his own plays or productions by the black theatre groups with which he has been connected. The exceptions are Brulin's *De Honden*; du Preez's *A Place of Safety*, presented with *The Cure*; and a double bill of *The Third Degree*, by Fugard's friend Don Maclennan, and *Krapp's Last Tape*. He has had other directing opportunities, such as Soyinka's *The Lion and the Jewel* at the Royal Court, and Lorca's *Blood Wedding* at Britain's National Theatre, but he has thus far declined such invitations. He claims to have "no interest in directing other people's plays. I don't think I do a bad job with them, but I'm in no sense a special director when it comes to work other than my own." In fact, Fugard has vowed from time to time never again to direct even his own plays.

Fugard has directed the premiere productions of all of his plays except *The Cell, Klaas and the Devil, Hello and Goodbye, People,* and *The Drummer.* It is often considered unwise for a playwright to direct his own work, but Fugard is an unusual playwright: "A play is not so many words on paper; a play is an experience in a theatre. I have absolutely no reverence for words on paper, texts. . . . I look at a man and see a body in the first instance. I would take away words from him if a simple gesture, a simple pause—the way he put on a sock, the way he took off his scarf and rolled it and put it into his raincoat pocket—said it all."[22]

Asked how he functions in rehearsals, Fugard once replied, "If you were to ask the actors, they would tell you that they have not been with a playwright; they've been with a director, a director who does not seem to have a lot of reverence for the text. 'That's not working? All right, so what do we do about it? Do you think we can make it better?' There's no reverence for the word at all in the rehearsal room."[23] To answer an actor's question about the text, Fugard sometimes quips, "I'll have to call the author and ask him. I think he's in Paris."

This hesitancy to explicate his own plays is also manifest in Fugard's tendency to get his actors up on their feet the second day of rehearsal. He says, "I think you make your important discoveries out on the floor. Plays aren't about ideas discussed at a table. Get the actors out there in space and silence to try and understand what is happening—or what should happen. I don't waste much time sitting around a table. A hell of a lot of talking gets done—but let that run parallel to the exploration of space and silence."

He also admits he does not possess *the* interpretation of a script: "When I pass from being author to being director, I have to choose. But as author . . .

106

I could point to five or six directions that a specific moment could go with equal validity. As a director I can't play all of them. The one I choose reflects only my face as a director at that time." Fugard claims that some of his best directing occurs after rehearsal while having a drink with his actors. He calls his approach as a director "very individual. Every actor has his own specific vocabulary. I discover the nature of his vocabulary and work with it. . . . They are like drivers in a Formula One car race revving their engines. I see that they are happy and relaxed. 'Go' is when the house lights go up. Then they are on their own and you hope nobody crashes."[24]

Fugard says that he writes plays to become involved with actors and to create a living experience of the theatre: "I am not addicted to the privacy of myself and blank paper. . . . [Acting has] taught me to write for actors. Taught me to think about them. Taught me to listen to rhythms. You know, I couldn't have written the way I have written if I had been concerned with myself only as a literary figure."[25]

Actors are "as precious as a Stradivarius for me," says Fugard. He had worked as an actor and director long before Serpent Players, but his association with them presented an opportunity to perfect his directing skills and expand his understanding of acting and actors. The depth of this understanding, coupled with his devotion to actors, helps explain why he has written so many excellent parts for them. He has often been fortunate to have his plays enacted by consummate craftsmen, but he also deserves some of the credit for the awards and praise they have garnered so frequently.[26]

Despite the breadth of Fugard's experience with actors and his sincere and profound love of them, he concedes that until 1970, "I had not yet thought seriously about alternative methods of releasing the creative potential of the actor. This came with my reading of Grotowski."[27] This reading led to an immediate empathetic response.

Grotowski and *Orestes* /

> *When I hear someone talking about loving the theatre, I turn aside and look for a place to throw up.* —Jerzy Grotowski

Grotowski's theories—if not their realization—are too well known to need repeating, but some of the ideas that must have especially impressed Fugard are worth noting. Grotowski contends that it is the actor-audience relationship "of perceptual, direct, 'live' communion" (19*) that is the essence of theatre. Costumes, scenery, makeup, lighting and sound effects, even a writer and an established text, can be eliminated; the actor cannot. Because mechanical and technical

*All Grotowski quotes are from his *Towards a Poor Theatre* (New York: Simon & Schuster, 1968).

wizardry is unnecessary in the theatre and, in any case, is inferior to that used in film and television, Grotowski proposed "poverty in theatre." (19) He also promoted a chamber theatre of physical intimacy between actor and spectator.

Grotowski aroused such passion and admiration in the European and American theatre throughout the late 1960s that one need not actually have seen any of his productions or read his writings to know about his work and be stimulated and influenced by it. During this period, however, Fugard was confined to South Africa without a passport. Far from the Fringe and Off-Off Broadway paths of theatrical fad and fashion, he was unaware of the stir Grotowski was causing, though he had heard him talked about.[28] In 1970, Benson and Simon sent Fugard a copy of _Towards a Poor Theatre_ and copious notes on Grotowski's New York lectures, along with a copy of Jean-Claude van Itallie's _The Serpent_ from Joseph Chaikin's Open Theatre. Fugard recalls "looking at these two men and their work and realizing how unbelievably bold and imaginative they were in their attempts at storytelling and using the space and silence of the stage, and, by comparison, how dead and orthodox my occupation of it was. Grotowski caused me enormous inner tension and distrust of my worth—a sense at one stage that I hadn't explored as effectively and richly as I should the possibilities of space and silence in telling a story."

Nevertheless, nine years before reading Grotowski, Fugard had explained his own idea of a perfect theatre in a small South African journal that spelled his name "Fougard." Prefaced to an extract from _The Blood Knot_ were the four paragraphs that remain a succint explication of his aesthetic. His vision eerily anticipates Grotowski's:

> In terms of playwriting—the craft involved in what actors say and do to each other and to themselves on a stage, before an audience—_The Blood Knot_ is the nearest I have yet come to my one conscious ideal in Theatre. This is a return to what I prefer to think of and talk about as "the pure theatre experience." I have used the word "return." My reasons for doing so will be obvious in what I have to say. Let me therefore define what I mean by "the pure theatre experience."
>
> This experience belongs to the audience. He is my major concern as a playwright. The ingredients of this experience are already partially revealed in what I have said and are very simple—their very simplicity being the main justification for using the word "pure" in the context of a form as open to adulteration as Theatre: They are the actor and the stage, the actor on the stage. Around him is space, to be filled and defined by movement; around him is also a silence to be filled with meaning, using words and sounds, and at moments when all else fail him, including my words, the silence itself.
>
> I write plays because I believe implicitly in the potential of this "experience" as a means to approaching and transmitting Truth, and in

a way and with a force unique to the drama. I believe equally strongly that this potential is at its greatest when the tricks associated with so much of present day theatre are reduced to a minimum. A lot needs to be said today about *how much the "miracle of electric light," "the ingenious use of off-stage sound" and "clever decor," have hindered and reduced this potential.*

To repeat myself, but using different words: The cathartic possibility in theatre needs nothing more than the actor and the stage. For the miracle to happen it must come from within the actor. A good play will plant the seeds there. Externals will profit the play nothing, if the actor has no soul.[29]

Fugard has frequently expressed his debt to Grotowski, although he has never seen any of Grotowski's productions. He sometimes leaves the impression that Grotowski was a startling revelation, and that subsequent plays such as *Orestes, Sizwe Bansi, The Island,* and *Statements* were entirely due to that influence. This is simply not so. Fugard was not transformed like Saul on the road to Damascus. Grotowski was not a prophet of a new theatrical religion different from the one Fugard was already practicing. Rather, he was an envoy whose message Fugard was predisposed to accept because it was so similar to his own.

Both emphasize the actor and the relationship between actor and spectator; both recognize that the text is not essential—an astonishing admission for a playwright; Fugard seeks a pure theatre, Grotowski a holy one; Grotowski is determined not to teach actors predetermined skills or a "bag of tricks;" Fugard, too, yearned to eliminate gimmicks (one is reminded of the Rehearsal Room actor trying to avoid the "tricks" of traditional drama lessons); Grotowski wanted a chamber theatre, and the small casts and reduced physical scale of Fugard's plays certainly demand intimacy between the audience and the stage; Fugard, like many directors before and after him, was making "poor" theatre long before the term became fashionable, as much out of choice as necessity. Early Serpent Players productions were done on budgets of $50, but Fugard relishes working under limited circumstances: "My aesthetic probably comes out of having a theatre in South Africa with nothing, but even if I had resources, my inclination may be not to use them."

The similarities between Fugard's pure theatre and Grotowski's poor one, coupled with their manifest devotion to the actor, are so startling that one is tempted to fantasize about their direct exchange of ideas. Their affinity is not, however, found in any direct personal contact, but in their independent yet complementary relationship to world drama. Shunted away in a dusky South Africa made even darker by the playwrights' boycott, Fugard, like Grotowski, was confronted with a staid European theatre. Neither approved of what he saw. The renewal that Grotowski sought would come "from people who are dissatisfied with conditions in the normal theatre, and who take it on themselves to create poor theatres with very few actors, 'chamber ensembles' which they might transform into institutes for the education of actors; or else from amateurs working on the boundaries of the professional theatre and who, on their own, achieve a technical standard which is far superior to that demanded by the prevailing theatre: in short, a few madmen who have nothing to lose and are not afraid of hard work." (50) Fugard had pursued such renewal through these methods long before Grotowski delineated them.

The artistic desire to reduce and do without is deep-seated. The search for purity, a term like "nature" that assumes different meanings from one age to the next, is constant. Neoclassicism in any art can be defined as an attempt to shed the extraneous and to rediscover pure and necessary form, often the form of the past; Fugard writes of the "return" to the pure theatre experience. The "less is more" architecture of Mies van der Rohe can be interpreted as such an attempt. Minimalists like Giacometti present as little as possible, or remove as much as possible. Each of Beckett's plays is simpler and more severe than its predecessors; his characters are, if nothing else, minimal man; his theatre is certainly a poor one.

Clearly Fugard, like Grotowski, has a place in this modern aesthetic movement that transcends any single art. The ideal he seeks is "the sentence that needs the gesture: the line by itself incomplete, the gesture by itself incomplete." In an interview he remarked similarly, "It's very noticeable how smaller and smaller the little book has got. . . . The inevitable thing, the thing that must happen to any artist as he progressively comes to terms with the elements of his medium, is a drive for purity, for simplicity."[30]

After the eleven characters of No-Good Friday, no more than five appear in any subsequent play. Two and three characters are most common. Space and, especially, time become increasingly restricted and the use of properties reduced. None of Fugard's plays requires an elaborate set. Costumes are never more than everyday clothes, and they are dispensed with almost entirely for the nudity of Statements. Fugard's plays have also become shorter. Furthermore, this evolutionary process began long before he had read Grotowski.

Grotowski has written that "the strength of great works really consists in their catalystic [sic] effect: They open doors for us, set in motion the machinery of our self-awareness. My encounter with the text resembles my encounter with the actor and his with me." (57) Fugard's encounter with Grotowski had a similar catalytic effect; acting as "scribe" for the collaborative works, he functioned in turn as a catalyst for his actors. While Serpent Players may never have achieved the purity and total dedication of Grotowski's holy actors, Kani and Ntshona certainly approached the intensity and transubstantiation of Grotowski's troupe in Sizwe Bansi and The Island. Fugard believes, "The last holy brothel is the theatre; the last holy prostitute the actor."

Grotowski helped crystalize notions and instincts Fugard had long possessed. According to Fugard, his encounter with Grotowski coincided with a crisis in his relationship to his work and his increasing dissatisfaction with the type of theatre he had been making. Grotowski gave Fugard the confidence "to do something I had wanted to for a long time . . . turn my back on my securities, which is to write a play in total privacy, to go into a rehearsal room with a *completed* text which I would then take on as a director and which actors—under my direction—would go on to 'illustrate,' to use Grotowski's phrase." Grotowski provoked Fugard to be less orthodox in the way he created plays: "My work had been so conventional! It involved the *writing* of a play; it involved *setting* that play in terms of local specifics; it involved the actors assuming false identities . . . etc., etc. I wanted to turn my back on all that. Permanently or not I didn't know. I just knew I wanted to be free again."[31] In his first play after reading Grotowski, Fugard began to seek this freedom.

Orestes is a performance piece rather than a conventional play. Fugard had great difficulty transcribing it onto paper and it has been preserved only in a detailed description Fugard wrote to Bruce Davidson, an American photographer, rather than as a conventional text. It would be easy to overlook the importance of *Orestes* since it lasted only eighty minutes, had a text of only 300-400 words, has only been performed a few times, in 1971, for audiences no larger than seventy, and only in South Africa. However, Fugard has frequently discussed its importance to him and its influence on his subsequent work. *Orestes* is the bridge between the small-scale improvisational works such as *The Coat* and the more ambitious *Sizwe Bansi* and *The Island*.

Fugard and his actors, Yvonne Bryceland, Val Donald, and Wilson Dunster, were supported by Capab, the Cape Town Performing Arts Council, to engage themselves in experimental work of Fugard's choosing. There was no commitment to public performance. He finally had the opportunity to create a theatre experience without a formal text or set rehearsal period. After ten weeks in a rehearsal room, the group gave its first "exposure": "The experience of those ten weeks forced us eventually to jettison a fair amount of the useless baggage we were carting around as 'theatre pros' . . . pseudo-terminology disguising half-truths, self-deception, and vanity being among them. We stayed working on and exposing the project for another six weeks by which time money ran out and we had to disband." (3*) The group was called the Capab Experimental Theatre Lab, no doubt an intentional echo of Grotowski's Polish Theatre Laboratory.

Fugard calls *Orestes* "an attempt to articulate, by way of dramatic metaphor, very primitive if not archetypal experiences." (4) One of these is the destruction of innocence by evil. The basic idea for the play developed from John Harris's 1964 bombing of the Johannesburg train station that killed an old woman. Fugard says, "I superimposed, almost in the sense of a palimpsest, this image on that

* "*Orestes* Reconstructed: A Letter to an American Friend," *Theatre Quarterly*, 8, No. 32 (1979), 3-6.

of Clytemnestra and her two children, Orestes and Electra. There was no text. Not a single piece of paper passed between myself and the actors." *Orestes* utilized "almost somnambulistic action" and became "a series of strange dream images unfolding."[32]

The minimal text included a statement from the testimony of Harris and one quote each from R.D. Laing's *The Divided Self* and *Bird of Paradise*. Because the words were so few and were carefully placed within periods of silence, they became extraordinarily important. Fugard discovered "what weight you gave to a line, to a statement, if you set it in silence." He recollects that "the words are crucial, and some of them remain for me today charged with a pain that really makes me shiver—and I can say this because they weren't my words."[33]

The importance of *Orestes* to Fugard lay in its process as much as the final product. It was an experiment in methodology, an attempt to engage the actor as a fully creative instrument instead of a passive conduit. Like Grotowski, Fugard believed that the actor has been largely reduced to an interpretive instrument rather than a creative one.

Fugard began rehearsals with some very clear ideas about what he wanted to do, but he chose not to have a script. He again called himself a scribe. Each day he challenged the actors with an idea. Iphigenia's murder was handled simply. Fugard said to Bryceland, who was playing Clytemnestra, "Imagine there was somebody in your life you called to, you said their name every day until suddenly, one day, she didn't answer." Bryceland calls this typical of the suggestions Fugard makes when he is directing: "He will find your point of pain and remind you about it. That moment was terrible for me; I can hardly think about it now. We managed to do the play night after night because Athol had been able to touch wells in us that could be repeated in the same pain—without any technical tricks or things like that. Clytemnestra went mad for this child that would never answer her again."[34]

Agamemnon never appears in *Orestes*, but his destruction is symbolically enacted. Fugard recounts the rehearsal when he first gave Bryceland a chair that represented Agamemnon: "This is unique, Y. There is not another one like it in the world. It is useful, a 'good' thing. It will hold and cradle the full weight of you. And because it is useful it is also beautiful. Get to know it. Explore it until you get to know every crack in its wood, every creak from its joints, every scab of peeling paint. Love it. And as you love it look for its flaw, its imperfection, its one fatal weakness." (5) After Bryceland had done so, Fugard asked her to destroy the chair with her bare hands. He also created a metaphor for the station bombing: Dunster, as Harris, threw wadded-up balls of newspaper at the audience.

A *Cape Times* reviewer found the preliminary "rehearsal" he watched obscure. After the production opened at Cape Town's Castlemarine Auditorium on March 24, 1971, another journalist noted, "Communication had its strongest impact through action—the chair, the newspaper-throwing—but I was left with the feeling that although we can communicate on some levels through words and actions, deep down where it is most meaningful (i.e. the essence of ourselves) each man is an island."[35] This image of man alone had been present in each of Fugard's previous plays and would remain prominent in the works to come.

Orestes freed and stimulated Fugard's imagination. It confirmed his ability to work in a different direction and break, though never completely, with his past. He had moved from the wordiness and inaction of *The Coat* to mime and silence; he had used historical material as in *Mille Miglia*, but this time it did not oppress him with the tyranny of facts.

Socio-political innuendoes and overtones had existed in most of Fugard's previous plays. From *The Coat* onward, these would be especially prominent in his collaborative works. Yet, even in *Sizwe Bansi, The Island, Statements*, and *A Lesson from Aloes*, the most ostensibly "political" of his plays, this element does not supplant others. *Orestes* too has a clearly political theme, but, by drawing a parallel between the John Harris bombing and the Orestes myth, Fugard suggests forces that are timeless, perhaps unavoidable. They are not simply due to the socio-political circumstances of a given time and place.

Orestes was a new way for Fugard to create plays. It suggested new "techniques for releasing the creative potential of the actor" and also represented for him a new logic of dramatic structure. Fugard's dissatisfaction with the theatre he had been making was partly due to what he perceived to be the conventional structure of his plays. He credits Grotowski for the right stimulus: "The ABC manner of logical story-telling was not the only way we could communicate experience in theatre—so much more could be done in space and silence."[36]

Fugard had used flashbacks in *Mille Miglia*, but this was a conventional use of the medium. In *Orestes* he escaped the oppression of the neatly linear plot for the first time. Although plots *per se* are of limited importance in Fugard's plays, they do exist, sometimes awkwardly like so many knobby bones poking through the flesh. His previous works had unfolded in a straightfoward sequential manner even if there were no Aristotelian *propter hoc* causation.

As early as 1968, Fugard had written in his notebook, "Pound . . . Image is that which releases an emotional and psychological complex in an instant of time." (7-23-68) The juxtaposition of disparate scenes, characters, and locations in *Orestes* can also be called Imagistic. In his book on Pound, Hugh Kenner writes that "juxtaposed objects render one another intelligible without conceptual interposition,"[37] which clearly happens in the juxtapositioning of the House of Atreus with the John Harris bombing. Two subjects commingle to create a third as the relationship between them is explored.

There was in Fugard, as there had been in Pound before him, a desire to "make it new." Fugard, however, was not as original as he apparently thought in finding a way to communicate other than through the logical ABC story.

Stream-of-consciousness in the novel, montage in film, and collage and cubism in painting were all attempts at both new form and new structural logic. All utilized the juxtaposition of images. Still, it was a new style for Fugard. He never again utilized a structure as free as that of *Orestes*, but he did explore dislocation further in *Statements* and *Sizwe Bansi* before returning to sequential structure. He returned by choice, not because he thought his plays *had* to be so ordered.

V

Collaboration Culminates and Ends

To be in hell is to drift; to be in heaven is to steer.   —George Bernard Shaw

*O*restes had suggested methods for greater use of the actor's creativity, but Fugard emphasizes that during his collaborative period the writer was never jettisoned: "It was never a question of coming together with the actors on a 'let's make a play' basis. The starting-point to our work was always at least an image, sometimes an already structured complex of images about which I, as a writer, was obsessional." (xi*) Looking back on his next three collective projects, *Sizwe Bansi Is Dead*, *The Island*, and *Statements after an Arrest under the Immorality Act*, Fugard says that "instead of first putting words on paper in order to arrive eventually at the stage and a live performance, I was able to write *directly* into its space and silence via the actor." (xi)

While on holiday in November 1971 with Yvonne Bryceland and her husband Brian Astbury, Fugard learned the details of Astbury's plan to open a small theatre in Cape Town, The Space. Astbury recalls "three realizations—which remain the crowning achievements of The Space—came from that day. [Athol]

---

*All quotes throughout this chapter are from *Statements: Three Plays* (London and Cape Town: Oxford, 1974).

115

told us of the librarian and the Coloured schoolteacher; of the photograph of the man with the pipe in one hand and the cigarette in the other; and of how one of the members of his group—Serpent Players—had been arrested for a 'political' crime, sent to The Island where he had entertained his cellmates by acting out the production he had been rehearsing when arrested—*Antigone*." Each of these situations turned into a play that Fugard premiered at The Space. Yet another Fugard play was the inspiration for the entire enterprise. Astbury writes, "It all began with *Orestes*. Without *Orestes* there would have been no Space."[1]

Despite his friendship with Astbury, Fugard initially claimed he would be unavailable either to write a new play or to direct one of his old ones for The Space's premiere. Astbury decided to open with *People*. While searching for a director, Bryceland called Fugard, but he was still unwilling to redo *People*. Instead, he offered a new play, *Statements*. The Space opened as planned on March 25, 1972, but Fugard was never satisfied with this version of *Statements*, and in the months that followed he considered abandoning the play altogether. Before it was produced a second time he completely rewrote it. (Because of the extent of these changes, *Statements* will be discussed after *Sizwe Bansi* and *The Island*.)

Interviewed in South Africa while Serpent Players was still a nascent and relatively unknown group, Fugard stated, "This is an experimental involvement. I do not think the full impact of Serpent Players on my writing has yet realized itself; but it is there, building up, and it will come out soon."[2] He had been functioning with the company as scribe since 1966, but it was not until 1972 and 1973 that the full impact of Serpent Players on Fugard's work "came out" in *Sizwe Bansi* and *The Island*. These plays were not written by Fugard, but "devised" by him, John Kani, and Winston Ntshona.

What's in a Name:
Sizwe Bansi Is Dead

To know oneself is to foresee onself; to foresee oneself amounts to playing a part.   —Paul Valery

Kani and Ntshona had been active with Serpent Players since 1965 and 1967 respectively. (They had met at New Brighton's Newell High School, where they had first acted together in a play called *The Old Custom Never Dies*.) By 1972 they hoped to give up their regular jobs and devote all their time to acting, which they determined would be possible if they could earn R100 ($130) per month. Fugard agreed to help, and he secured a Sunday evening club performance at The Space. He initially sought an existing play written for two actors, or one that could be adapted for two actors, but he also suggested developing a piece in the manner of *The Coat*. When Fugard could not find an appropriate ready-made play, he mentioned an idea for one; the trio decided to work on it together, with Fugard writing and rehearsing simultaneously. The piece would focus on two waiters at the Royal Hotel in Grahamstown awaiting the arrival of the customers: arrogant, vulgar, and self-satisfied white university students.

After a single rehearsal, Fugard feared he would produce something as "shallow, trick and cliché-ridden" as the first production of *Statements* had been for him. Instead, he hoped to turn the initial idea into a mandate and work as he had with *Orestes*. Kani, Ntshona, and Fugard rehearsed at the Moslem Institute, where Serpent Players had also rehearsed *Antigone*. The dramatic subject of two waiters in a lounge was jettisoned eighteen days before the scheduled date at The Space. Instead, Fugard turned as he had so often in the past to a specific image with which he had a long-overdue appointment. He recalled a portrait he had seen in an African photographer's window: "It was a man, sitting at a table with a vase of flowers, wearing a very special hat—a big hat—with a pipe in one hand and a cigarette in the other. It was a very celebratory image, affirmative, full of life—the sort of life that is still intact in New Brighton, despite what it has to cope with." (3)

Fugard, Kani, and Ntshona improvised and engaged in a Socratic dialogue about the possibilities behind this smile. *The Coat* had also evolved through a series of questions, but the attempted neutrality and objectivity of that play gave way in *Sizwe Bansi* to a more openly partisan point of view and to clear answers: They decided the man was happy because his passbook was in order.

Sizwe Bansi was not actually written down until the year following its premiere. Fugard believes it might never have been scripted were it not for the pressure of a successful London production. He had tape-recorded some of the performances and had also written down especially crucial parts of the play. Even so, capturing the play on paper was "very very hard because one of the results of working in this collaborative way is that you can, if the method is successful, generate a very special life and vitality for which there is no way of recalling, no way of notating."[3] This problem exists with most collective efforts. Fugard always speaks of "play-making" rather than "playwriting" when he refers to *Sizwe Bansi* and *The Island*; *The Coat* is subtitled "An Experiment in Play-Making."

Fugard has sometimes been fully credited with creating *Sizwe Bansi* and *The Island*, but he is quick to assert that writing is only part of the process of producing a play. Moreover, he has difficulty distinguishing his contributions from Kani's and Ntshona's: "Because I am the eldest and most professionally experienced I bring possibly an excess contribution to our work at the moment. I know something about what dramatic structure involves, and obviously I did a hell of a lot of the actual writing. . . . I would now find it impossible to say at what point did John Kani's autobiography end and did I then embellish and elevate; and at what point did Winston Ntshona's contribution in terms of facts turn into what he, in fact, turns Sizwe Bansi into."[4] Kani's autobiography, for example, includes a seven-year stint with the Ford Motor Company. He also had a 101-year-old uncle. In addition, Fugard was dependent on his actors because he has not been allowed to enter black townships for many years.

Kani's version of the genesis of *Sizwe Bansi* differs from Fugard's. He says that Winston told a story, a joke, about a smiling man in a photograph who was happy because his book was in order. The subject was so hot politically, according to Kani, that they went to Fugard and asked him to look at what they had done. He said the piece would not survive the censor board and began to oversee the work of the actors. Kani recalls Fugard saying, "Find a simpler statement. Disguise this statement. That is politics. Try and find the artistic value of the piece. There is humor in your situation. Find it." Kani claims that he and Ntshona worked with Fugard only one day a week because, "He was busy writing *Dimetos* then . . . so he would give us Sunday only. Finally, we said we're ready, you can organize an audience. It was only fourteen or fifteen people, neighbors, maids, old ladies, Sheila and Lisa. . . . We then got set-up for one performance at The Space. At first the credit read '*Sizwe Bansi* by Serpent Players, assisted in staging by Athol Fugard.' It was not until the London production as we prepared for a wider and more sophisticated audience that we enlisted Mr. Fugard as director. That is when he took over completely."[5]

Fugard was not writing *Dimetos* when *Sizwe Bansi* first evolved, but some of Kani's story can be partially verified. A review of the production in Johannesburg referred to Kani and Ntshona as Fugard's "playwright/players" and noted that the play was "largely improvised by its two actors, Winston Tshona [sic] and John Kani, under the guidance of Athol Fugard."[6]

Over time, Kani has increasingly minimized Fugard's role in *Sizwe Bansi* and *The Island*. Interviewed in 1976, Kani insisted that he and Ntshona were more responsible for the play than Fugard and that instead of the actors collaborating with Fugard, "it was rather the reversal." In another interview Kani said that Serpent Players was founded "way before the 60s" and that "Mr. Fugard joined in 1961 and became an honorary member."[7] Fugard says, simply, that when Norman Ntshinga knocked on his door in 1963 "Serpent Players didn't exist."

Sizwe Bansi opens in a photography studio run by Styles. In a long monologue he recreates scenes from the car factory where he used to work and tells anecdotes about his current business. He is visited by a man calling himself Robert Zwelinzima who wants to send a photograph to his wife. In a flashback, "Robert," now called Sizwe Bansi, visits a friend of a friend named Buntu. Bansi explains to him the difficulties he has had with the police and his passbook. No longer allowed to live or work in Port Elizabeth, Bansi is supposed to return to his original home in the country. After reveling at a local shebeen, Buntu and Bansi discover a body. The man's passbook identifies him as Robert Zwelinzima. Buntu convinces Bansi to switch passbooks with the dead man, whose papers are in proper order. He is thus able to stay in Port Elizabeth by assuming the identity of a dead man. This ends the flashback, and in a final tableau, Styles snaps "Robert's" photograph.

As in the plays written solely by Fugard, the cast of *Sizwe Bansi* is limited and the set is bare. Unlike Morrie, who merely yearns for the freedom and independence a farm might bring, Styles actually achieves some autonomy through his own business as he manages to join the (black) middle class. Like Zach, Bansi is less articulate and more conscious of his body than his companions. Like Lena, he lives in a nether world without a true home. *Sizwe Bansi* continues Fugard's exploration of human identity and dignity. Games, role-playing, and brief "performances" are even more prominent in *Sizwe Bansi* than in Fugard's previous plays, and they provide a key to understanding the play. The most obvious role is the one Bansi assumes when he adopts the identity of Zwelinzima, but this ultimate game is anticipated by numerous others played by Styles and Buntu.

During his opening monologue, Styles's narration of an incident quickly melds into the reenactment of it. He is especially fond of mimicking the factory General Foreman, Mr. "Baas" Bradley. Bradley assumes he is in control of his workers, but as Styles says of him, "Good man that one, if you knew how to handle him." (4) As Bradley condescends towards the workers, so Styles cunningly patronizes him. In recreating Henry Ford, Jr.'s visit, Styles contrives numerous laughs by duping Bradley.

Nkosi has written that in their portrayal of "simple blacks," many white South African writers fail "to see and underline the fantastic ambiguity, the deliberate self-deception, the ever-present irony beneath the mock humility and moderation of speech." *Sizwe Bansi* clearly shows the façade as façade. Styles realizes he must appear subservient, but he has not internalized feelings of inferiority. By only playing at being obsequious, he remains in full control of his actions, which allows him consciously to create the impression he desires; the other workers do the same. After Bradley orders Styles to tell the workers in their own language that they should look happy, Styles says to them, "You must see to it that you are wearing a mask of smiles. Hide your true feelings, brothers. You must sing. The joyous songs of the days of old before we had fools like this one next to me to worry about." (7) Fugard's glossary describes the song as "an African work-chant," (109) but according to Cosmo Pieterse the song was sung in the resistance movement.[8]

(*Sizwe Bansi* contains other veiled but significant allusions, the most notable of which is the title. There is no such word as "bansi" in Xhosa, and the play was called *Sizwe Banzi* until a misspelled poster from Port Elizabeth prompted the Royal Court unintentionally to re-name the play. In Xhosa, "sizwe" means nation while "banzi" means broad, wide, or large. Thus, the title is ironic since the large nation of blacks is vigorously alive. Also, "Buntu" means humaneness, which is implied by Styles's description of him "always helping people." [18])

Styles and the other autoworkers have learned by rote the roles expected of them, but the white managers also adopt a subservient posture upon the arrival of Ford. Styles tells the audience, "I looked and laughed! 'Yessus, Styles, they're all playing your part today!' " (8)

The ebullient Styles plays other roles while describing his photography studio: the cockroaches that had infested the room, the man who had sold him insect spray to drive them away, and a family of twenty-seven that had come for a group portrait. Styles becomes a hard-driving but likeable salesman when convincing his customers they need an extra photo or two. He also mimics his children begging for money and convinces "Robert" that he should look like a chief messenger to impress his wife and children. (Dressed in the clothes Zach has bought him, Morrie also hopes to impress a woman by appearing more prosperous than he really is.)

Buntu also plays roles, primarily to convince Bansi he must assume the identity of the dead man. Like Styles, Buntu imitates the actions of white officials. When Buntu pretends to be a paymaster, Bansi answers for the first time to the name Robert Zwelinzima. Buntu continues his persuasive charade as a salesman at a clothing store catering to indigent workers that is similar to the one where Zach buys Morrie's "outfit for a gentleman." Buntu also plays a preacher and finally a policeman; Bansi passes inspection because his new passbook is in order. Throughout these episodes, Fugard's stage directions repeatedly emphasize the element of play.

Ultimately, these games are much more than playful. As the imaginary car ride in *The Blood Knot* had been a means for Zach and Morrie to rediscover their brotherly bond, and the imaginary and aborted party in *People* had helped Milly better perceive her life, so games and role-playing are thematically integral to *Sizwe Bansi*: The transience of a superficial human identity is made manifest and emphasized through acts of imagination.

The illusory nature of these roles links them to the illusory dreams present throughout the play. The shebeen Bansi and Buntu visit is called Sky's; Bansi is so overwhelmed by the hospitality there that the evening seems to him almost like a dream. When "Robert" enters his studio, Styles says in an aside to the audience, "A Dream!" (17) and plays upon "Robert's" imagination by suggesting he might one day become a chief messenger or company head. As "Robert" is deluded, so he deceives his wife by pretending to be a "man about town" (21) and happier than he actually is. His contented façade is little different from the countenance the Ford workers are expected to wear in the presence of the white *baas*. Styles also tells the audience that his studio is a strongroom of dreams, and adds, "Something you mustn't do is interfere with a man's dream. . . . Start asking stupid questions and you destroy that dream." (13)

The photographic images emphasized throughout the play include both those Styles creates in his studio and the one on the passbook that allows Bansi to assume the identity of the dead man. It is often assumed that a photograph is an objective and utterly truthful record of a particular reality, and that the lens presents an object in its black and white essence. However, the unexposed film is not simply a *tabula rasa* awaiting the image an opened shutter will reveal. Rather, as Styles embellishes his stories with detail, imposing on them his perspective and interpretation, so he manipulates the camera and its subject to create, ultimately, *his* picture. Photographs nourish dreams, as Styles suggests. They also create an image that leads to a kind of immortality—perhaps the only kind possible when a name is less important to officialdom than a number, and when most citizens are treated as a uniform, faceless mass lacking any individuality or identity. As important as photographs may be during a man's life, after his death they become graphic proof that he once lived.

Death is palpable throughout *Sizwe Bansi*: It is present in the play's title and, as Benson notes, "Sizwe Bansi has to kill his name in order to survive." While playing a preacher, Buntu promotes membership in a burial society; Bansi is afraid of being killed in the mines; Styles relates the deaths of his father and of the elderly patriarch; and Buntu mentions a funeral sermon he had recently heard.[9] Death is so tangible and proximate that the characters embrace life at every opportunity and take risks to augment its meager proportions.

Both Styles and Buntu describe indignations their fathers had had to suffer. These stories emphasize the difference between appearance and essence. Styles has not internalized feelings of inferiority, but he has grown tired of even appearing subservient. After having decided to leave the factory, he had explained to his father, "Daddy, if I could stand on my own two feet and not be somebody else's tool, I'd have some respect for myself, I'd be a man." (10)

Soon after Buntu discovers the body, Bansi turns to the audience and pleads "I'm a man. I've got legs. I can run with a wheelbarrow full of cement! I'm strong! I'm a man." (35) In the BBC telecast of the play the line was delivered, "Does this book say I'm a man? Does this book say I'm a human being?" Bansi's desperate query emphasizes the importance of the passbook and the pathetic degree to which it and his identity have become one in his mind. The white officials are only concerned with the book and its number, not the man holding it.[10] Allowed no identity but that defined by the identification card, the man and card become one. To give up his name is to lose the only thing truly Bansi's own. He perceives the choice between *his* card and identity and those of the dead man as one between personal dignity and survival itself. Despite the pressing needs of his family, he is at first too proud to contemplate a change of name.

In contrast to the play's dreams, illusions, and acts of imagination, *Sizwe Bansi* ends with the rejection of self-delusion. (The "City of the Future" before which the new Robert Zwelinzima stands is obviously phony.) A profound and inalienable sense of identity finally replaces a superficial one. One critic believes that "the text is sometimes ambivalent in its belief that South African Blacks deserve a bolstering of illusions rather than reminders of reality," but the ambiguity is eliminated by the end of the play. Unlike Ibsen's *The Wild Duck* or O'Neill's *The Iceman Cometh*, *Sizwe Bansi* does not imply that man needs his illusions and pipedreams in order to live. Sizwe is not destroyed by abandoning a delusive sense of identity; his dream of supporting his family becomes a reality, at least for a time. He has chosen, in the words of another critic, "between the realism offered by Buntu and the fantasies offered by the photographer."[11]

Such contrasts between characters—Buntu and realism, Styles and fantasy—exist throughout the play and are especially pronounced in Bansi's personal relationships. Rustic and uneducated, he speaks "*with the hestitation and uncertainty of the illiterate. When words fail him he tries to use his hands.*" (23) Both Styles and Buntu are literate and articulate. Lumbering in body and speech, Bansi is a foil to their sophistication and loquacity. His naïveté and shyness are the antithesis of Styles's guile and flamboyance; his innocence is countered by Buntu's savvy and immersion in the realities of day-to-day existence. While Bansi is an idealist, Buntu argues for pragmatism; Bansi is slow, Styles and Buntu quick-witted. Such contrasts echo those in *The Blood Knot*.

Like Johnnie Smit in *Hello and Goodbye*, Bansi finally assumes a dead man's identity; unlike Johnnie, he is fully cognizant of what he has done. He has not truly become someone else; he is merely playing at it by using the government's identity system against itself. It is a pretense born of necessity, a reasonable choice given the parameters of potential action. Through Buntu's direction and the process of making his decision, Bansi alters his consciousness and superficial sense of self. He finally realizes that human identity transcends a mere name, number, or government designation. Moreover, he has no illusions that the ruse will go undiscovered. Since his "skin is trouble," (43) as Bansi himself says, the police will eventually arrest him and discover that his fingerprints do not match those of the real Robert Zwelinzima. As with Shen Te in Brecht's *Good Person of Setzuan*, Sizwe Bansi is forced to abandon illusions. Like her, he assumes a second identity merely to survive. The decision is a practical one. He is transformed, externally, in order to live.

Structurally and technically, *Sizwe Bansi* is fairly simple. Unlike most of Fugard's work, a strong plot line is emphasized and a character, Bansi, undergoes significant external as well as internal change. Like *Orestes*, the play does not unfold chronologically. The time shifts demarcated by Bansi's dictation of the letter to his wife are mildly nonrealistic and meld, as such, with the play's anti-illusionistic device of addressing the audience directly. (In performance, Kani used direct address more often than is indicated in the text.)

Such additions have been common throughout the production history of *Sizwe Bansi*. In particular, the opening monologue has been adapted to current events of the time and place of a performance. Ntshona and, especially, Kani have often added lines, dropped them, and spoken them in an order slightly different from the published text.

The original South African production sometimes lasted as long as four hours. Brian Astbury recounts that for the first performance at The Space, Kani was scheduled to do twenty minutes of newspaper improvisations at the start of the play: "An hour-and-a-half later he was still there, the audience in the palm of his hand. Offstage, Winston was in a fury—Athol walking up and down in the lighting-box, twisting his beard. Finally he sent Winston on in the middle of another of John's hilarious stories and we were into the actual play at last."[12] Fugard recalls, "Those early performances certainly were marathon. John finally stopped the game, but at times when the audience didn't satisfy him, he bloody well punished them by keeping them for about three hours. I wasn't pleased when it got that long because there aren't enough guts, enough meat in the story to occupy that much time." The BBC telecast of the play ran only seventy-five minutes rather than the two hours common in most performances.

Despite this process of refinement, the major inadequacy of the text remains its repetitiveness. Consequently, a fairly short play sometimes feels rather bulky. The drunk scene and Bansi's disorientation last too long. As a newcomer to the city he is unfamiliar with many of the regulations governing him, and these are duly explained. Because a non-South African audience could be presumed to be unfamiliar with the intricacies of Influx Control and the passbook system, the need to include some of this expository information is understandable. Repeated references to these laws also reinforce their daily importance in the lives of blacks. However, so much factual information is imparted that the text becomes overburdened and briefly threatens to become a general survey of black living conditions in South Africa.

The proud assertion of blackness and brotherhood has been sounded frequently in the United States, but such forthrightness was rare in the South African milieu of 1972. At the time of the original *Sizwe Bansi* production, the theatre, like much of South African society, acquiesced in what Fugard has called "a conspiracy of silence." For one of the play's first performances 900 blacks packed a 450-seat hall in New Brighton. Certain that a police raid was imminent, many of them fled as Styles's monologue progressed. Such directness is now quite common in South African black theatre. Mshengu has called *Sizwe Bansi* the main watershed of a new theatre that is "almost exclusively urban in idiom and increasingly political in subject matter."[13]

In coping with Influx Control or the bureaucratic process of opening a photographic studio, Bansi and Styles are treated as mere ciphers. In this context, *Sizwe Bansi* is an indictment of the depravity and inhumanity of apartheid. Styles's experiences in the car factory are further instances of the degradation of the individual. However, such bureaucracies, factories, drudgery, and degradation exist in all mass societies and industrialized economies. Ironically, Styles

123

escapes the routine of the assembly line by opening his own photography studio where he must spend part of his time repetitiously printing numerous copies of a single negative. Family cards are "Good for business. Lot of people and they all want copies." (14) Dehumanization of workers is not limited to South Africa. As always happens in Fugard's work, heightened specificity of time and place leads to a general statement about the plight of all men.

Interrogating himself, Styles asks, "What did I see? A bloody circus monkey! Selling most of his time on this earth to another man." (9) His complaint could be voiced by factory workers around the world. Although his description of the Ford factory seems to imply an indictment of capitalism, he escapes his boring job through free enterprise. Styles may have few alternatives, but he quickly learns the ways of the businessman. Bansi also contemplates free enterprise, selling potatoes, as a means of circumventing his passbook troubles. As in *The Blood Knot*, there is an implied belief, especially with Styles, in delayed gratification through the accumulation of capital.

Behind such recourse to small business enterprises lies confidence in the possibility of individual initiative. Willie in *No-Good Friday* had also hoped to get ahead by enrolling in correspondence courses; in *Statements*, Philander does the same. Their attempts are eventually abandoned, like Johnny's small business in *Nongogo*. In *Sizwe Bansi*, however, the autonomy Styles gains from his studio, as well as Bansi's challenge to the passbook laws, suggest that one man can, if not beat the system, at least sidestep it temporarily. To the extent that individual action can make a difference, *Sizwe Bansi* is far more hopeful and optimistic than the plays written solely by Fugard.

The photograph that provided the original impulse for the play had been joyous, affirmative, and full of life. These qualities are quickly established in Styles's studio. Even the way he dupes Baas Bradley is more mischievous than vicious. Such radiating warmth and celebration of man exist throughout the play. Fugard says, "In addition to being an assault on the conscience of our audience, *Sizwe Bansi* also invites a certain celebration of the basic impulse of life, which is that it refuses to die."[14] It is more celebratory than many of Fugard's plays, but loving humor is used in all his work. However bleak the plays may first appear, and despite the restricted prospects of his characters, laughter and pathos exist side by side. The characters laugh at themselves and their surroundings, embracing the incongruities and absurdities of their existence. It is one of their means of survival.

In *Sizwe Bansi*, tension between the characters and the audience is minimal; when the white man's ways and laws are directly attacked, audiences (predominantly white when the play has been performed outside Africa) have not felt personally threatened or castigated. Despite moments of caustic condemnation and unbridled anger, *Sizwe Bansi* is more loving and ingratiating than strident; it embraces man instead of rejecting him. The affection that grows between Bansi and Buntu ultimately encompasses the entire audience. It is amused rather than insulted when Styles says Buntu is "always helping people. If that man was white they'd call him a liberal." (18)

When *Sizwe Bansi* stresses black dignity, solidarity, and pride, it does so without the bitterness and antagonism that characterize many American black plays of the 1960s. Ironically, such antagonism did exist when *Sizwe Bansi* was performed in Butterworth, in the Transkei, where Kani and Ntshona were detained on October 8, 1976, exactly four years after *Sizwe Bansi*'s first performance—and eighteen days before this homeland became "independent." Kani and Ntshona apparently altered their discussion of Ciskeian Independence (30-31) to Transkeian, and perhaps embellished it as well. They were released after two weeks.

As a statement about a group of people and the quality of life in a restricted time and place, *Sizwe Bansi* might be compared to Camus's *The Plague*. At the end of that novel the reason Dr. Rieux has compiled his chronicle is finally revealed: "So that he should not be one of those who hold their peace but should bear witness in favor of those plague-stricken people; so that some memorial of the injustice and the outrage done them might endure; and to state quite simply what we learn in a time of pestilence: that there are more things to admire in man than to despise"[15]

Following *Sizwe Bansi*'s Sunday evening premiere on October 8, 1972, in the small theatre at The Space (115 seats), half the audience remained behind to discuss the play. Additional late-night performances for special club members were scheduled, it toured Johannesburg, and returned to The Space's big theatre (250 seats) for a two-week run. After the police informed Astbury that *Sizwe Bansi* could not play to open audiences, one performance was cancelled. However, the Argo Film Circle came to Astbury's aid. In only four days, 1,500 new members were enrolled and the run continued as a club event, although the police again tried to stop the show.

After hearing about *Sizwe Bansi* from Nicholas Wright and Donald Howarth, who had seen a performance, Oscar Lewenstein of The Royal Court phoned Fugard in Port Elizabeth and asked to read the play. It still had not been put into the form of a script, but Lewenstein nevertheless offered Fugard a date in the Theatre Downstairs. Fugard held out for the smaller Theatre Upstairs because, "I found it difficult to believe that a story as South African as this could have significance outside my country and I was plain scared. I wanted to stay in a small space with an audience of seventy of people or so."[16] During rehearsals, Lewenstein suggested doing *Sizwe Bansi* downstairs after its run upstairs, and asked to read another play he had heart about, *The Island*. Again there was no script, but Fugard offered a tape recording of a performance. After responding positively to it, Lewenstein then asked about a third play, *Statements*. All three were eventually presented as a South African Season in the Theatre Downstairs. *Sizwe Bansi* premiered in London on September 20, 1973. Thirteen years earlier, ✗ Fugard had been unable to secure a job as a stagehand at the same Royal Court.

Human Dignity Transcendent: *The Island*

No man is an island, entire of itself; every man is a piece of the continent, a part of the main.   —John Donne

While awaiting passports for the London production of *Sizwe Bansi*, never certain they would be given permission to leave South Africa—or rather to return if they did—Fugard, Kani, and Ntshona began work on a new play. As with *Sizwe Bansi*, there were several false starts. Initially, Kani says, "We were intellectualizing. We were not honest. We were not commanded by truth. And thus Athol came up with the idea that there is a place we never talk about, no one can write about, the press cannot talk about, not even white South Africans, free as they are, can talk about. It is the nightmare of every member of Parliament. What will happen to it in the end? That is Robben Island."[17] Kani is referring to the infamous prison in the Atlantic Ocean, seven miles from Cape Town.

Peter Rosenwald has described Fugard's improvisational use of a blanket in rehearsal to create the metaphor of a "sacred ground": "Time and again Fugard would halve the space of the blanket until at last there was just room for the two actors to stand. Then he asked them: 'What do you think it means?' Their answer was that it was a cell, that he had shrunk their liberty to move. They knew instantly where this was leading and they decided to follow: 'To take the island and to say something about it. We joined our hands, closed the garage door and after two weeks, fourteen days, we were on stage in Cape Town,' Kani says."[18]

Kani has subsequently remembered the play's evolution somewhat differently: "Again it was one day with Fugard, six days with us because we can't exceed a certain number of hours visiting a white man. We had an eighty percent contribution. In *Sizwe Bansi*, he was the overseer. *The Island* is where we worked directly with him in the creation of the play."[19] Fugard says they worked together every day.

The creation of a play in so little time is unusual, and Fugard says it might not have been possible if the trio had not worked in a similar way on *Sizwe Bansi*. Moreover, he had already written a prison play in 1957, *The Cell*, and notebook entries dating back to 1963 indicate his continuing interest in the subject. When art lecturer and muralist Harold Strachan was arrested on sabotage charges, Fugard visited his friend in a local jail, then noted, "More than anything else one was conscious of, and embarrassed by, the indignity." (4-4-63) Also, Fugard once considered writing a play for Zakes Mokae about the mutual dependence between a "good" warder and an *agter-ryer*, a prisoner singled out by the warder to help keep other prisoners in line.

Fugard's contact with prisoners also included the trial of Serpent Player Norman Ntshinga, which had led indirectly to *The Coat*. In December 1966, Welcome Duru, who had been arrested shortly before the opening of Serpent Players' *Caucasian Chalk Circle*, was released from prison. He explained to Fugard the cramped transportation of prisoners between Port Elizabeth and Cape Town on their way to Robben Island, and also described the way work teams were organized there. In addition, Ntshinga's wife recounted her annual trip to the prison and her half-hour visits with her husband.

Ten days after Ntshinga's release, he visited Fugard and acted out his "hilarious-terrible" stories of life on The Island. He described the "chain of sympathy" that developed as men tended one another's injuries and tried to raise one another's spirits. Fugard recorded the weather forecast and news bulletin delivered by one prisoner: " 'It will be warm from Mngandi Street to Walmer. Kwazakele will be cold. . . . Bulletin! Black Domination was chased by White Domination, and beaten. Black Domination lost their shoes and will go barefoot to the quarries tomorrow.' " (9-2-67) On subsequent visits, Ntshinga also told Fugard about imaginary phone calls to the outside world and about improvised movies such as "the fastest gun alive" that helped pass the time. During his months at sea, Fugard had learned that sailors, too, love to rehash films they have seen.

On June 17, 1970, Fugard began to outline a new play he planned to call *Sea Island*: "Elements: 1. Norman—his release. The farewell party. The speech from the young boy. 'You will forget.' 2. Bioscope (in the cell) and Concert (for the warders). 3. Solitary (a fly in the cell). 4. Work. (Meaningless activity. Emptying the sea into a hole. Five men trying to push over a tree.) 5. Let's all hang ourselves." (6-17-70) Three years later Fugard approached the subject from a different perspective as he noted first the cramped journey of two prisoners from Rooi Hel (Red Hell, The Port Elizabeth prison) to Robben Island, then added, "Somewhere tonight the same two men confront each other, shocked over the simple fact that one has been reprieved, and can start to count days, while the other . . .". (3-6-73)

The play that finally emerged was called *Hodoshe Span*, "Hodoshe" being the nickname of a notorious Robben Island guard as well as the Xhosa word for a green carrion fly. The new play was kept very quiet, played three weeks at The Space in June and July 1973, and only to limited audiences. Kani's and Ntshona's wives first saw it in the United States. (The production may have been covert because of the legal problems of publicly discussing the South African prison system. For example, the Prisons Act, Section 8 of 1959, obligates newspapers to prove the accuracy of their statements. When the Prisons Department denies access to its reports, or unilaterally refutes the sworn testimony of prisoners or warders, newspapers can be prosecuted for publishing false or unproven material. This happened to the *Rand Daily Mail* in 1965 following a series of articles on the brutal prison experiences of Strachan.)

After selected performances at the universities of Sussex and Leicester, the play moved to the Royal Court. By then, *Hodoshe Span* was renamed *The Island*, most of the Afrikaans and Xhosa dialogue that had been prevalent was translated into English, and instead of calling their characters Bonisile and Zola, Kani and Ntshona lent their own names.

The play opens with a long mime of John and Winston futilely digging sand. After returning to their cell, they discuss their production of *Antigone*, which will be presented at a prison concert. While rehearsing several nights later, Winston declares that playing the title part is an insult to his manhood. His argument is interrupted when John is called to the warden's office and informed that an appeal has led to a reduction of his sentence. Ecstatic at first, Winston later compares his own life sentence with the few days remaining for his friend. In the final scene he and John present their version of the *Antigone* to the other inmates and prison dignitaries.

Instead of simply documenting intense suffering, *The Island* makes it palpable. All of Fugard's plays make minimal production demands—sets, costumes, and properties; in *The Island* this spareness accentuates the facts of prison life. Like *Sizwe Bansi*, *The Island* was quickly devised through extended improvisations and intimate collaboration with Fugard acting as scribe; in addition, both plays focus upon the degradation and dehumanization of man and the ultimate transcendence of human identity, dignity, and pride. As Bansi ultimately discards his superficial understanding of identity, so Winston transcends his rigid sense of masculinity. Again there is a strong and loving bond between two characters, and the role-playing device is once more employed, here in the traditional play-within-a-play form. As in *Sizwe Bansi*, characters have broken the law, though here they have been caught. The Pass Laws restricting Bansi's movement place him in a kind of prison; John and Winston are confined to a real one.

Dressed in shorts, John and Winston are made to look like schoolboys. They do not even wear numbers, which might give them the semblance of individuli-ty. Nor do they have last names. *Sizwe Bansi*'s passbook system of external identi-fication has been eliminated. The inmates have no identity or individuality what-soever in the eyes of the prison officials. The effect of *The Island*'s costumes, which mirror codes on Robben Island for political prisoners, is similar to that sought by Grotowski in *Akropolis*: "Through their similarity the costumes rob men of their personality. . . . There is no hero, no character set apart from the others by his own individuality. There is only community, which is the image of the whole species in an extreme situation." (64, 73) Fugard's repeated use of society's outcasts can always be seen as a means to portray the condition of all men. Moreover, John and Winston recognize both their individual manhood and their place in the community of men.

The inmates must endure hard labor, brutal treatment, and daily humiliation. Short pants are one form of degradation; another is demonstrated when a guard visits the cell and John and Winston drop their shorts and face the wall: standard procedure, one assumes. They have grown accustomed to such treatment.

As in *Sizwe Bansi*, they know they must project a certain posture without necessarily internalizing it. However, routine masking of one's pride is quite different from the ignominy that Winston believes he will have to endure playing Antigone. After donning her wig and breasts, his suspicions are confirmed when John bursts into laughter. Winston insists that even the guards want only to make him a boy, not a woman. John argues unconvincingly that he laughed merely to prepare Winston for stagefright, but he continues in a more serious vein: "Just remember this brother, nobody laughs forever! There'll come a time when they'll stop laughing, and that will be the time when our Antigone hits them with her words." (61)

As Buntu had convinced Sizwe Bansi of the distinction between appearances and reality, so John tries to persuade Winston that his dignity cannot be undermined; appearances do not define his manhood. Unconvinced, Winston claims *Antigone* is a child's play, but John counters, "That's Hodoshe's talk. . . . That's what he says all the time. What he wants us to say all our lives. Our convictions, our ideals . . . that's what he calls them . . . child's play." (62) Winston finally realizes the authorities cannot truly damage what lies deepest within him. He plays Antigone the following day. Human dignity transcends oppression and degradation. As in *Sizwe Bansi*, profound truths are revealed and rights asserted when they are recognized as inalienable.

As a comedy team, the pair is the classic double act: They evoke Laurel and Hardy or Didi and Gogo; John is the comic and Winston the straight man. Humorous episodes are juxtaposed with sober ones. The contrasts highlight each mood separately while emphasizing, simultaneously, the disparity between them. Before going to sleep each evening they take turns entertaining each other—a nightly ritual similar to the Bible-reading in *The Blood Knot*. (Like Morrie, John also nags and worries about housekeeping.) As a result of John's performance while placing an imaginary phone call to their friends in New Brighton, Winston grows uncontrollably excited and projects himself back to a time of joy and a place of freedom. (Their friend, Sky, is no doubt the proprietor of the shebeen Buntu and Bansi had visited. The undertaker named Scott may be the same one who had urged Styles to open his studio.) The make-believe games provide a momentary respite from the here and now. However, as usually happens with

Fugard fantasies, the game turns serious—in this instance when John asks that he and Winston be remembered to their wives. The phone conversation winds down to John's tenuous assertion that his wife be told "this was another day." (58)

Playful fantasy leads, almost against the will of the players, to sobriety. In some cases, however, the games are disingenuous and calculated; insight has preceded rather than followed the act of play. Such was the case with the roles Buntu had played to convince Bansi to become "Robert." The same is true of the performance of *Antigone*. The other inmates may be expecting pure entertainment, but it is clear from the start that John, the author of the adaptation, has a didactic purpose. The lesson of his play is predictable, but this does not make it any less effective. The ineluctability of Antigone's sentence—"Take her from where she stands, straight to the Island!" (77)—is like the certainty of a tragedy's catastrophe. The audience is transfixed because of the inevitability, not in spite of it. In this *Antigone*, the good guys and the bad are as obvious as in the cowboy movies John and Winston had reenacted.

According to Fugard, Robben Island is not simply a depressing place, but rather a symbol of the fight: "For the lifer on Robben Island to finally stand there and say, 'Right. I know what it's about,' for me seems possibly the last heroic stance man is capable of in this godless century. It's a form of courageous pessimism."[20]

"Courageous pessimism," borrowed from Camus, is one of Fugard's favorite phrases. There are echoes of *The Myth of Sisyphus* throughout Fugard's writing, but these are especially clear in *The Island*. The opening mime at the sand pit is a triumph of determination over interminable physical labor. John and Winston are conscious of what they must endure, and this also links them to Camus's Sisyphus: "The lucidity that was to constitute his torture at the same time crowns his victory."[21]

Comparing his own life sentence to John's imminent release, Winston almost breaks, but he recovers and says, "*Nyana we Sizwe* [Brother of the Land]" (72) Unlike Sisyphus, Winston is not completely alone. He has his cellmate and, even after John's release, his bond to his community. No prison can break this union.

The strong interpersonal bond between John and Winston is similar to those found in previous Fugard plays. Their camaraderie does not imply a sexual relationship, but a deeply affectionate one. Their personal bond is a microcosm of the play's much broader racial bond, which represents a new consciousness in Fugard's work. There had been a hint of it in *Sizwe Bansi*. Buntu says to Bansi about the dead man, "If there *are* ghosts, he is smiling tonight. He is here, with us, and he's saying: 'Good luck Sizwe! I hope it works.' He's a brother, man." (43) However, Bansi's commitment and sense of responsibility is directed towards his immediate family. *The Island*'s family includes an entire people.

John and Winston call each other *broer* and brother throughout the play.

When they say *"Nyana we Sizwe"* it is a motto that embraces other members of their race. John reminds Winston, "you put your head on the block for others." (72) John has more than Winston in mind when he declares, "People must remember their responsibilities to others." (56) His implied sense of responsibility contrasts sharply with Creon's as a "servant" to his people.

Fugard's characters are often paired, and John and Winston are literally manacled hand and foot. However, their spirits are free to return to shore and unite with their people. Although more physically isolated than any of Fugard's other characters, John and Winston consider themselves part of a community. It is this solidarity (rather than the dramatization of prison's horrors) that makes *The Island* more political than any other Fugard play. In his previous works characters are alienated from society, but John and Winston are not.

Nor are they as impotent as Morrie and Zach, or Boesman and Lena. Like Bansi, John and Winston have taken an active hand in their fate by contravening the law. They are victims of a political and judicial system like Creon's, in which they do not face an accusing witness. Still, they are not passively powerless. Action is possible, and they hope to effect change. It is their deeds that have caused their imprisonment, and on Robben Island they continue to act through the presentation of their play. Like Antigone herself, they have accepted, even embraced in the manner of civil disobedience, the consequences of their actions. They have contravened only the laws of the state, not transcendent human ones.

The Island ends as it began, with a siren wailing and John and Winston manacled together. The play is not a call for revolutionary upheaval, yet it is more hopeful and optimistic than any of Fugard's others. The "City of the Future" in Styles's studio is obviously an illusory one; Bansi knows his assumed identity will one day be discovered. The future John and Winston seek for their children may someday be achieved. Although their hopes may prove illusory, the play does not insist that they are. Such hope distinguishes them from other Fugard characters and from Camus's Sisyphus for whom hope is a delusive means of escape. As Robben Island itself is a symbol and affirmation of struggle, so is *The Island*.

The innate difference between experiencing a play in the study and in the auditorium is especially great with *Sizwe Bansi* and *The Island*. Both perform better than they read. Fugard is aware of the emotional and, especially in *Sizwe Bansi*, rhetorical indulgence of these exercises in "play-making." Asked in 1974 how they would differ had he written them entirely himself, he replied, "On the credit side, I think they might have had a more economical structure. On the debit side, having written them and having presented them to actors, such as John and Winston, the very special energy that they use in performance might have been inhibited. . . . Their truth eclipses my aesthetics." In 1980 he added,

"Looseness and skimpy structural organization informs both those plays. Because you rely on the actor so much, there's a danger also of losing that marvelous ambiguity of metaphor."[22]

When *Sizwe Bansi* was revived in 1977, Fugard returned to London with some ideas about updating it to keep pace with recent events, especially the Soweto riots. He discovered that the play had a life of its own: "If anything, the experience has been worth it just to discover that. I've always rated *Sizwe* fairly low, a play which walked the tightrope between poetry and propaganda. Maybe I'm wrong. That first amble through the text on a bare Royal Court stage was very moving. Its structure and style remain clever—its essential honesty and humility still radiant—and, miracuously, John and Winston hand themselves over to it, are taken over by it, with the same spontaneity of four years ago. I am as confident of the integrity and honesty of its 'witness' now as I was then and, equivalently, am just as sustained by it." (1-77)

In 1980 he admitted that *Sizwe Bansi* and *The Island* were "an enormously liberating experience: It got me past a very severe block I experienced immediately after *Boesman and Lena*, when somehow the juice in me had dried up and just being alone with the paper was something I found intolerably painful."[23] The London production also encouraged his return to *Statements*, a play he had almost abandoned.

Exposures of Love and Death:
Statements after an Arrest under the Immorality Act

Love and death, a fatal love—in these phrases is summed up, if not the whole of poetry, at least whatever is popular, whatever is universally moving in European literature. —Denis de Rougemont

Statements, like Fugard's other plays, was stimulated by specific images: six police photographs in an Afrikaans newspaper of a naked white librarian and Coloured schoolteacher caught as lovers in 1966 at De Aar, near Fugard's birthplace. He recalls that they were "jumping around like—I just remembered frog legs to which you've put electrodes. You know the way you make a frog's leg twitch; that was pretty horrendous."[24] Because they were first offenders, both were given suspended sentences of six months. The man later committed suicide. ✳

These images lived vividly in Fugard's imagination for five years. Upon learning late in 1971 about Brian Astbury's plans to open a theatre in Cape Town, Fugard described what he then called *Three Statements after an Arrest under the Immorality Act*. He eventually agreed that his new play could open Astbury's theatre. Although much of *Statements* was written in the privacy of his study, he was unable to finish the play by the time rehearsals began. On March 24,

based on fact

1972, the day before the scheduled opening, he and Bryceland appeared in Astbury's office. Fugard confided, "It's not working. I'm not sure we have a play. I'm going to change the whole structure tonight."[25] That evening the set was removed and a long reading from Genesis was prefaced to the play.

Statements opened The Space the following evening and played to good audiences for five weeks, but the production was premature. One critic called it "a mixture of fairly realistic dialogue and portentous rhetoric, illumined by an occasional flash of dramatic expression, but on the whole simply damnably dull." A critic of a rival paper countered that *Statements* was "damnably fascinating." He added, "This stark and disturbing play should be staged again soon, because it deserves far more public attention than this. It is the stuff that real and meaningful theatre is made of."[26]

Like most playwrights, Fugard has always refined his plays during rehearsals for an opening, and again between a first and second production. However, the revisions of *Statements* were more radical than for any of his other work. Fugard's notebook offers a fascinating analysis of the play, his struggle with it, and his despair over ever getting it right. He considered the first production his most incomplete and careless work ever. Fugard isolated two flaws in his production and text: "the placing of equal emphasis on the policemen with their typewriter, and the relationship between man and woman. Reduce the typewriter to the meaningless and stupid detail it is in *their* story. . . . The second flaw—not as easy to define, but again a question of emphasis—of their fear and apology and explanation to the audience being equal, if not even greater, than their relationship to each other." He concluded that the play required the depth and detail of *Boesman and Lena*: "B and L = the hell of being together, of 'No escape.' Frieda and Errol = the hell of not being together, of not being able to have the other." (5-72)

Fugard's perception of the play fluctuated radically. He considered abandoning it as a flawed work he would never get right, then determined to put the play aside for at least a month before deciding its fate. Concentrating on the central images of Philander and Joubert's story, Fugard noted that he wanted to explore the subtext of the six photographs, which emphasized "twenty seconds of Hell which start with them together and end with them irrevocably apart; the twenty seconds that it takes to pass from an experience of life to an intimation of death. . . . I have simply not been able to break the ice and drown in depth—I have not been able to escape cheap and superficial sociology and women's magazine cheap sentiment, and live inside the terror and panic of those six instants—caught and frozen for all time by the camera." (8-8-72)

After resolving this impasse, Fugard began preparing for a second production (at the Royal Court), but he continued revising the script throughout rehearsals. Fugard claims sole authorship, but admits that the Royal Court production and the text that developed from it were totally dependent on the methods he had evolved during *Orestes*. The final form of *Statements* also depended on encounters with his actors in the rehearsal room. He sometimes refers to *Statements* casually as "the play Yvonne [Bryceland] and I wrote." This mixture of independent writing and collaboration has not been repeated, though Fugard believes, "Many things came together there in just the right balance—my attempt to make the actor creative without eliminating myself as the writer."[27]

Statements opens as a man and woman lie naked on the floor. Their friendship had begun when Frieda Joubert, a white librarian, had helped Errol Philander, a Coloured school principal, with books for his B.A. correspondence course. They later became sexually involved. Joubert's religion and Philander's marriage, as well as the Immorality Act prohibiting sexual relations between whites and members of any other race, make them feel guilt, but their need for each other—which is intellectual as much as sexual—is too great for them to separate. A policeman enters as they embrace. In a sudden shift of time forward, he placidly explains to the audience both the charges against the two and the way they had been arrested. The arrest itself, as well as Joubert's and Philander's reactions to it, are then enacted: As an unseen police photographer takes snapshots for evidence, Joubert and Philander are exposed—first physically, then emotionally and psychologically. They immediately confess and compulsively try to explain and justify their relationship, but only succeed in compromising and demeaning themselves while surrendering their dignity.

Despite the basis of *Statements* in fact, Fugard was not concerned with the trial of the couple and its consequences. Rather, he explores the nature of their relationship in the play's first half, and the moment of their arrest and their reactions to it in its second half. The lovers are threatened by legal and social circumstances surrounding them, but these are simply given. As in his other works, Fugard is more concerned with the personal, intimate, and specific effects of certain pressures than with the pressures themselves.

A piece of music, according to Fugard, becomes obliquely associated with each of his plays as he is writing it. During the period between the first and second productions of *Statements*, he "drove my family mad" listening to the requiems of Mozart and Brahms. Both are celebrations of death, but because of their artistry, "There is also a celebration of a life, a preceder to death. And they also provoked me to thinking of *Statements* as notes rather than the finished thing—simply because I don't think there is as much of a celebration of living there. . . . Any human experience is basically mortal and is doomed. If a man and a woman come together there is the simple fact of human mortality . . . it's already there, it's already spelt out. At a simple level I was trying to show that."[28]

Much of the play was reconceived for the second production, but Fugard's obsession with death persisted: "After all the hymns to Life, now the one to Death. Destruction. Loss. . . . The mystery of Destruction—as great as the mystery of

Creation." On the first day of rehearsal he noted in bold letters: "THE HARD, PURE FACT OF DEATH, THE DIGNITY OF BONES. . . . IT IS. DEATH IS. . . . THE TERRIBLE REALITY CELEBRATED," then added, "A balance between the sacred and profane."[29]

Fugard has called love "one of our useless defenses against Death." (5-7-72) This conjunction of love and death is a common one that goes back in Western literature at least to Tristan and Iseult. "Happy love," writes Denis de Rougemont, "has no history."[30] *Statements* is another chapter in the exploration of unhappy love. The impediments to it, both Philander's marriage and the Immorality Act, make that love all the more passionate. The intrusion of the police marks both the destruction of the Philander-Joubert relationship and its climax. It is the most intense moment they have ever shared and makes them one forever. By suffering the humiliation and degradation of exposure, they become more self-aware than ever before.

Statements is another of Fugard's nighttime journeys. This one ends in nightmare. Again the cast is limited. A second policeman typing the couple's statements was eliminated after the first production. Light is all that is needed to define the library office: A set planned for the London production was gradually stripped away during rehearsal until all that remained were a blanket and a bare floor. Only the policeman wears a costume, though not a uniform; he is a plainclothesman. *Statements* is Fugard's first play to treat middle-class characters only, although there is a great difference between middle-class white and middle-class Coloured. Thus, Joubert and Philander are not outcasts to begin with, like previous Fugard characters, but become so in the eyes of their society through their own actions.

Their relationship had begun simply, innocently—although it took courage for Philander to seek assistance from a white woman in a library he could not legally patronize, and nearly as much courage for Joubert to help him. She has more education and intellectual curiosity than others in the rural village; he too is isolated from his less educated neighbors. Intellectual companionship and stimulation preceded, perhaps even precipitated, the physical attraction between them. Both have also led unfulfilling personal lives: She had long been lonely and admits to having been a virgin prior to knowing him; his marriage is unsatisfactory. In addition to Philander's marriage, Fugard further complicates the affair: Joubert is six years older than Philander; she initiates the sexual relationship; and, the coupling of a white woman and a Coloured man is less expected than that of a white man and Coloured woman.

In a play *ostensibly* concerned with the effects of a heinous law, the audience's sympathy for the lovers might be mitigated by the existence of Philander's wife and child. This complication expands the scope of the play from the effect of a particular law to the nature of passion and loving relationships in general; it also deepens what might otherwise be a simplistic situation—a good man and woman versus an outrageous law. Although the Immorality Act is emphasized in the play's title, Philander's family is a greater impediment than race to his relationship with Joubert. She wants him to "Take me with you. Now," (93) but disconsolately realizes this is impossible not so much because of Philander's race, but because of his family.

The morality of this adulterous relationship puzzled some British reviewers. B.A. Young wrote, "By conventional standards, therefore, their affair is immoral, whatever their color. Inexplicably, this difficulty is left unresolved."[31] *Statements*, however, is concerned with the annihilation of two individuals involved in a loving interpersonal relationship, not simply a cross-racial one. Immorality, whether legal or religious, is not its subject. Because he strives to create "the density and ambiguity of truly dramatic images," (ix) Fugard has a penchant for complications such as Philander's marriage.

One of these "truly dramatic" images revolves around Joubert's appearance. She draws the curtains because she is afraid the neighbors or police will discover her with Philander. By so doing, she also blocks the moonlight and thus avoids fully exposing her body to her lover, which she is afraid to do. Her first speech is delivered "*shyly;*" (81) later "*She moves to him but remains shy and reticent.*" (83) The dramatic ironies of these moments are extraordinary. Joubert is truly modest, even innocent, yet the actress portraying her is performing nude. Joubert does not want Philander to see too clearly the faults of her body, and she objects when his match illuminates the darkness. However, when her arrest is enacted minutes later, the police rush in, expose her with their glaring flashlights, and photographically record her appearance. Later still, she offers a careful description of her body's defects and attributes.

Joubert had initiated the sexual relationship, but throughout the first half of the play she appears quiet, unassuming, uncertain, and weak. Frightened and insecure, she clings to her man. She initially seems much different from Fugard's typically strong women such as Hester and Lena. After du Preez appears, however, Joubert's strength is clear as she undergoes an arduous police examination. She cowers with her lover in the dark, yet forthrightly faces her accusers in the light despite her embarrassment over her body's exposure.

Philander, on the other hand, appears strong at the beginning of the play, later reveals his weakness to Joubert, then grovels abjectly before the police. He is truly obsequious towards them in a way that Styles, for example, never is with Baas Bradley. Philander's affair with a presumably sacrosanct white woman has not filled him with pride. In addition to the feeling of having betrayed his family, he must endure ignominies merely to see Joubert: "Pride doesn't use back doors! . . . Or wait until it's dark. You don't walk the way I do between the location and town with pride." (90)

Statements explores a doomed love affair that might exist anywhere, but in so doing it utilizes South African details that emphasize the chasm between

Joubert and Philander. Joubert knows about the water shortage in the Coloured community: "We're going to have prayers for rain next week." (89) The practical and immediate need of the Coloureds elicits an impractical response from the whites. Joubert's belief in the power of prayer is a typical Fugard juxtaposition of incongruities. It calls to mind Johnnie Smit's claim of "Resurrection" as he sinks into catatonic impotence. In *Statements* there is no question of Joubert's sincerity; she truly believes the prayers will help, and since Philander seems to believe in God, he may believe this as well. Still, applying a supernatural solution to a pressing, utterly basic human problem is deftly ironic. Like Johnnie on his crutches, it might be funny if it were not so pathetic.

As horrible as the water shortage is, Philander sees nothing *especially* unusual about it (given the prevailing way of life). The ordinariness of such conditions in the mind of the insider who lives with them daily makes them even more horrific to the outsider. Du Preez embodies a similarly ironic contrast between what one character considers normal and commonplace, and what other characters and the audience perceive as such. Whether reading a statement or speaking directly to the audience, his language is cool: abstract officialese. It is as unemotional as his demeanor. Snooping outside the library, peering through the window, and exposing the intimacies of other people's lives are all part of a day's work. Du Preez is matter-of-fact about his actions; his behavior is utterly "correct;" he is unaware that his impassivity during the exposure and debasement of others so reveals his own character and the racial consciousness it reflects. His apparent decency intensifies rather than mitigates the nightmare Joubert and Philander experience.

More important than the character of the policeman and the laws and attitudes he represents is Fugard's technical use of him; his arrival completely alters the tone, style, and structure of *Statements*. What had been a fairly conventional psychological play, an apparently realistic love story unfolding straightforwardly in a representational style, suddenly becomes something quite different. Even the language changes; the generally simple and colloquial dialogue of the first half of the play is transmuted into longish speeches of increasing lyricism in the second half. Dialogue is replaced with monologues, which emphasize the increasing separation and isolation of the lovers. The naturalistic explication of their relationship gives way to an abstracted recreation of both their arrest and their reactions to discovery.

Despite the policeman's pivotal part in triggering these shifts, Jonathan Hammond writes, "The role of the policeman stands like an afterthought tacked on the play, never organically involved with the action."[32] Du Preez does stand outside the play like a narrator, but it is clear that Fugard consciously constructed *Statements* in this manner. He uses the policeman as the fulcrum balancing the play's apparently disparate halves.

The introduction of the policeman and the subsequent reactions of Joubert and Philander are not afterthoughts, nor are they of subordinate importance to *Statements*' realistic first half. Rather, the first half is subordinate. The lovers' meandering conversation is really an extended prelude to the twenty crucial seconds when the photographs are taken. Without such an introduction those responses would exist in a void disconnected from the nature of known characters. Whereas the expository introduction of *People* is evident as such, and is the reason the play starts so slowly, in *Statements* it is not until the policeman's entrance that one realizes that much of the dialogue on the library floor is exposition. It seems to *be* the substance of the play as one hears it. *Statements* is simply more skillful in solving this common dramaturgical problem.

Du Preez's entrance is no *coup de théâtre*. Philander's and Joubert's anxieties foreshadow his appearance. Even the title gives away the "fate" of the characters and what might have been a crucial moment of suspense in another play. Additionally, it was originally written for a South African audience, which would immediately recognize the "immorality" of the Joubert-Philander relationship and understand their anxiety. There is less likelihood of mystery-story suspense in Cape Town than in London or New York.

Upon his entrance, du Preez does not direct his attention to Joubert and Philander. Rather, he dictates his statement to the audience. Furthermore, there is no attempt to represent the actual arrest; it is re-created instead. Du Preez merely describes, after the fact, what had happened. Throughout this address he speaks in the past and past perfect tenses.

In between the policeman's statements the audience sees Joubert clinging to a blanket and hears the various statements made by her and Philander. Also evident is the temporal disjunction between their words and actions, and those of the policeman. The statements referred to in the title are those of Philander and Joubert as well as those of du Preez and the prying neighbor. All of these are delivered within a few minutes of stage action, but they have not actually occurred at the same time.

This disjointedness is emphasized by Fugard's effective and self-consciously theatrical use of blazing police flashlights and flashbulbs. Instead of the old directorial solution to a staging or textual problem, "Let's fix it with lights," lights *are* the problem. The flash-sequences are not intended to illustrate what actually happened at the time of the arrest, but to suggest the horror of intrusion that Joubert and Philander subjectively experienced. The play turns surreal as the lights make the nightmare of the lovers palpable; they cannot escape the inquisition that is to follow. The effect of these lights and the camera's "Siss," loud as a gunshot as it advances automatically, are especially startling in the theatre. Coupled with the entrance of the police voyeur, the lights drastically change the mood and initiate the metamorphosis of character about to transpire.

Nudity in the theatre has been used primarily for its shock effect, but in the first half of *Statements* it establishes serenity, beauty, and innocence through

Joubert's shyness. Her frequent complaints about her body underline the fact that this nudity is not an excuse to expose the perfect body beautiful for the titillation of an audience. Rather, it is a means to emphasize the ordinariness of the characters. This changes entirely with the arrival of the police and their probing torches. Frank Marcus has described the shift: "Nudity on the stage can be natural and heartwarming at one moment and turn into obscenity the next. The cruel light of the flashbulbs changed beauty into pornography."[33] (Fugard has called the Immorality Act South Africa's "unique contribution to the world of pornography." [7-23-72]) It is only after the lights shine on Philander that he becomes sexually self-conscious. His attempts to don his trousers become grotesque.

Furthermore, the exact sources of illumination are unclear. The police hide behind their lights and become a disembodied presence, an unseen nemesis. Joubert and Philander are left to direct their confessions to a source of light (and themselves) rather than to other human beings. Philander and Joubert immediately respond to the intrusion of the outsiders by trying to explain their relationship, but their words elicit no reaction. Their affair is doubly inexplicable: As true believers in an abstract and ideal concept of racial purity, the police cannot truly comprehend miscegenation; furthermore, emotional relationships exist outside the pale of rational explanation.

Following Joubert's confession, and her adoption of the question-and-answer technique of a police inquisition as she interrogates herself, Philander also confesses quickly to the shining light. He tries to hide his genitals, but he cannot prevent the emasculation that is to come. In the play's last speech he admits that he has lost a part of himself: "And then I start to give him [God] the other parts. I give him my feet and my legs, I give him my head and body, I give him my arms, until at last there is nothing left, just my hands, and they are empty. But he takes them back too. And then there is only the emptiness left. But he doesn't want that. Because it's me. It's all that is left of me." (108) To some critics, such lyricism has seemed out of place in the mouths of Fugard's earthy characters. However, even though Philander's heightened emotion and diction are more sustained than in any of Fugard's previous works, they are also more clearly appropriate since they are a climax of a sometimes lyrical love affair.

The lame Johnnie Smit on crutches and the childless Boesman suggest two kinds of castration; Philander's is made so palpable it transcends the merely psychological. Like a jackal who chews off his foot to escape a trap, Philander dismembers himself. Fugard calls "every arrest under the Immorality Act a vestigial reenactment of the castration ritual." (7-23-71)

Du Preez is no *deus ex machina* resolving action, but a catalyst precipitating it. The horror of discovery is not simply that of arrest and possible internment, but of exposure and humiliation. Life's most private and intimate moments are not above governmental scrutiny. No legal punishment could be as severe as the suffering and dehumanization Joubert and Philander must endure. Both have been raped.

Loving relationships often end, but seldom so brutally. Joubert and Philander are transformed, metaphorically, into those twitching legs of a frog touched with an electrode that Fugard had noted, or into the snakes chopped into pieces that Joubert mentions: "They were mating at the time. Their . . . pieces kept moving . . . for a long time afterwards." (85) Destruction and an act of beauty—the consummation of human love—are conjoined in a theatrical echo of the Metaphysical Poets' pun on the word "die." Love commingles with death.

Time, its cessation with death, is again one of Fugard's themes, and in this case he reinforces it by manipulating the play's temporal structure. Joubert hints at the inevitability of disintegration through time in her first speech. Stimulated by the last book Joubert had lent him, Philander reflects on the origin of life: "The difference between life and even the most complex of chemical processes . . . [includes] a susceptibility to death. Because life lives, life must die." (82)

Philander's special interest is science, the subject of his correspondence course. He quotes Charles Lyell's *Principles of Geology* and had first come to the library seeking Julian Huxley's *Principles of Evolution*. (The topics are linked: Geology is an evolutionary history of the earth.) This background of science, however basic, opens the play to an outer world of vast and unknown proportions. Philander recounts an emotional experience he had while reading Lyell's phrase "no vestige of a beginning, no prospect of an end": "It was a 'comprehension'— *ja*, of life and time . . . and there in the middle of it . . . at that precise moment . . . in Bontrug, was me. Being me, just being me there in that little room was . . . *(choosing his words carefully)* . . . the most exciting thing that had ever happened to me. I wanted that moment to last forever! It was so intense it almost hurt. I couldn't sit still." (84-85)

In *Statements*, according to John David Raymer, time is seen as something beneficial because with the passage of enough time, all men will be the same color and racial conflict will end: "Errol comes to see himself not as a lonely, isolated, and alienated Coloured man, but as part of an awesome process, as a bright moment unfurled against the immensity of time."[34] Raymer deduces a hopeful and political meaning in Fugard's use of the time-evolution theme, but this is not the only possible interpretation. Raymer's conclusion may eventually prove historically correct, but this does not mean that the consciousness he describes is attained by Philander, or implied by Fugard. Philander sees himself primarily as an individual "being me, just being me." (84) His final speech is not one of group consciousness, triumph, and hope, but of individual guilt and failure. Where his consciousness is broad, it is scientific and cosmic rather than racial.

Statements offers no optimistic epilogue indicating "this too shall pass." Instead of some final victory, it suggests that nature, history, and evolution cannot be affected by individual human action. Morrie and Zach, like Boesman and Lena, are left with each other; Hester, at least, discards some illusions. *Statements* is more pessimistic. Philander and Joubert are utterly alone; according to a stage direction, "*The woman is totally isolated in her last speech, as will also be the case with the man.*" (105) The play is not an essay on heroism and strength under duress, but of the degradation, dehumanization, and ultimate destruction of more or less average individuals.

Despite Fugard's early problems with *Statements*, perhaps because of them, it became his favorite play: "It almost escapes into the area of freedom." After seeing a college production in 1980, he admitted, "it still surprises me that I wrote that play."[35]

Fugard had long perceived himself as a composite director, actor, and writer, but after the American premieres of *Sizwe Bansi* and *The Island* he stated, "The most significant sense I have of myself is as a writer. Circumstances have also made me a director and actor, and I've lived very uneasily for a long time with those three different functions. . . . I've now decided I'm not going to try to be a jack of all trades, but try to be a specialist in one."[36] He claims no longer to be interested in acting, though he appeared in four recent films, including two of his own, took over the part of Steve shortly before the South African opening of *A Lesson from Aloes*, and plans to perform *The Blood Knot* again with Zakes Mokae.

Following the 1971 London premiere of *Boesman and Lena*, through the productions and tours of *Sizwe Bansi* and *The Island*, Fugard had only worked collaboratively in rehearsal rooms rather than privately at his desk. (*Statements* was only a partial exception.) At the end of this period he said: "I think I've exhausted that experience for myself. . . . Working collaboratively requires a very special energy, a very special sobriety, concern, and accuracy in keeping company with your actors and in going through the mine-fields with them. It's to the extent that I don't have that energy, or am no longer capable of that accuracy, that I won't be working so intimately in collaboration any longer."[37]

In addition, it seems clear that the "statement" made by Fugard, Kani, and Ntshona in *Sizwe Bansi* and *The Island* is fundamentally different from those in Fugard's own creations. The narrator of *The Coat* informs the audience, "We want to use the theatre. For what? Here it gets a bit confused again. Some of us say to understand the world we live in but we also boast a few idealists who think that Theatre might have something to do with changing it. These attitudes imply something of a purpose to our work." (8) They do not, however, coincide with Fugard's own purpose; he is no idealist.

Fugard admits that the personal statement he wants to make is not the same as the one he, Kani, and Ntshona had made. This difference is most clearly manifest in the hope of meaningful social and political change with which *The Island* ends. Fugard says, "It's not a difference that has broken us up in any way, because I think I'll be working in some way with John and Winston for the rest of my life, but the energies we use are very different energies."[38] All three plays that comprised the Royal Court's South African Season are concerned with survival and with the dehumanization of man. In the two that are fully collaborative, *Sizwe Bansi* and *The Island*, all the characters maintain their pride, manhood, and sense of self. *Statements* is not so optimistic: Joubert and Philander are broken by external pressures.

Politics and Fugard's Critics

Why do people always expect authors to answer questions? I am an author because I want to ask questions. If I had answers I'd be a politician.
                                                              —Eugene Ionesco

Lewis Nkosi recalls that in the Sophiatown period of 1958-59, "Athol Fugard gave no signs of being directly interested in politics. Indeed, one might say he rather despised politics and politicians. If he did not, he certainly distrusted them. Far more directly, Athol was interested in learning about how we lived and in practicing his art, and the politics of the South African situation touched him on these two levels."[39]

With the exception of *Mille Miglia, Dimetos,* and *The Drummer*—Fugard's only scripts not specifically set in South Africa—all his work has some overt relationship to that society. Fugard's characters are always influenced by the South African environment, but it is not until the collaborative plays that politicized situations, even specific laws, emerge from the background into the foreground. In these plays apartheid moves from the wings to centerstage.

It is no surprise that the South African milieu is part of Fugard's work. No artist can ignore his time and place, and in South Africa this inevitably leads to characters and situations rife with racial and political overtones. Alan Paton writes that, "Race is not a plot, or a structural pattern, or an obsession; it is of the very stuff of our lives, and it is life that is the making of a story." Nadine Gordimer notes similarly that all writing by South Africans is profoundly influenced by the politics of race: "There is no country in the western world where the creative imagination, whatever it seizes upon, finds the focus of even the most private event set in the overall social determination of racial laws."[40]

This preoccupation with race is not a recent development in South African writing. The title character of William Plomer's novel *Turbott Wolfe* (1925) says, "There would be the unavoidable question of color. It is a question to which every man in Africa, black, white, or yellow, must provide his answer." In his

142

autobiography *Down Second Avenue* (1959), Ezekiel Mphahlele writes, "I now realize what a crushing cliché the South African situation can be as literary material."[41] In particular, both interracial friendship and miscegenation have been common literary subjects. Gordimer calls friendship between a young black and a young white, as in Sol Plaatje's *Mhudi* (1930), "the literary wish-fulfillment of what South African society could be, would be, if only the facts of the power struggle conveniently could be ignored." Alan Lennox-Short calls miscegenation "this well-worn South African theme."[42] Throughout his work, Fugard emphasizes the need for love between men; that so universal a theme has such political overtones is a piercing indictment of his homeland.

The mere presence of these themes and relationships throughout Fugard's work does not distinguish him from his contemporaries at home, does not mean that he is a political writer, and does not mean that South Africa is his primary subject. In a letter from the period between *No-Good Friday* and *Nongogo*, Fugard writes, "Playwrights must be left to write about subjects of their choice, and not feel obliged to wave a social banner every time they start writing. . . . I do not deny that a good play can have a strong measure of social comment. What I do object to is making this a yardstick of good theatre . . . and the danger of expecting it every time we go to the theatre."[43]

Asked in 1967 about his sense of political commitment, Fugard admitted it was something he often thought about: "Shouldn't I move closer on the problem, the South African problem, than I have? This is my dilemma. . . . I have very strong feelings about it, but at the same time the moment I start to function as a writer on this level, I think flatly, I think superficially—the magic goes out."[44] This quandary has continued to trouble him. After noting Ernst Fisher's description of the Marxist artist being "commissioned by his society," Fugard once asked himself, "Do I want a commission? Have I got one? Must I function without one? Is my context as artist irremediably bourgeois? How do I align myself with a future, a possibility, in which I believe but of which I have no clear image? A failure of imagination." (2-26-68)

As urgent as concerns with race and repression or biology and sociology may be, they are superceded in importance by the primordial needs of man alone in a world he would like to call his home, aware of his imminent death, searching for meaning, love, and maybe even happiness. Preconceptions of South African society and Fugard's supposed political concerns have prevented many critics from seeing past the specific social context of his plays to the universal quandaries they dramatize.

No artist can turn away from his time, but nor can he totally immerse himself in it. Fugard usually starts by focusing upon his "one little corner of the world,"[45] but he never ends there. The South African society of his plays is as much a metaphor as a particular historical place, however precisely and evocatively it is drawn. The setting is a kind of ready-made objective correlative given form through Fugard's selection of details. His concern is with the plight of all men—one heightened by particular South African pressures, but nevertheless common to men in all societies.

Similarly, his use of race is symbolic of the isolation and alienation of all men. In Fugard's plays race may be a cause of divisiveness, but it is the effect that concerns him. His downtrodden itinerants, outcasts, and paupers are images of the extreme situation that confronts the entire species.

Still, many critics persist in writing about Fugard as if he were a didactic social realist, or the creator of inspirational political history in dialogue form. South African Mervyn Woodrow claims that "Fugard succeeds in spite of himself. . . . I am convinced that Fugard's root motivation is political, that his intention is to create propaganda in favor of the 'victims of a social order.' . . . It is a pity that Fugard, by confining his attention to the lowest social order of mankind and to misfits and derelicts within that order, thereby excluding a large section of mankind, is at the same disadvantage as all other writers of propaganda plays. With the best will in the world many of us simply cannot identify with the majority of his characters."[46]

Literal-minded critics often have difficulty seeing through the exterior of a play to its substance, and are thus unable to fathom a playwright's choice of a particular situation or character. *Waiting for Godot* might be viewed as a story of the disaffection caused by unemployment and *Woyzeck* as a dramatization of a proletariat's predisposition to murder, but such reductive interpretations are obviously ludicrous. Morrie, Hester, Lena, Milly, and Sizwe are more than poor lost souls. Their dispossession is comparable to that of Didi and Gogo, Woyzeck, or Lear on the heath. If Woodrow can identify only with characters like himself, what does he make of Othello or Oedipus? Surely it is no more difficult to empathize with society's outcasts than its warriors and rulers.

Misapprehension of Fugard has not been limited to South Africans, which J.W. Lambert notes, writing from London: "Mr. Fugard's pictures of life in the dustbins of South African society have been widely hailed for the wrong reasons; readers of many reviewers of them might easily suppose that [*Sizwe Bansi, The Island,* and *Statements*] were also mere propaganda exercises." In America, Raymer writes about many aspects of Fugard's work, but he believes that in *Sizwe Bansi,* a "message" play, Fugard's intent "is to educate the world about the South African situation in hopes that support will be given to those who would bring about change there." Raymer ignores that the play was created for South Africa and that Fugard, Kani, and Ntshona were surprised, even bewildered, that it interested people elsewhere. Audiences may infer a message, but it is not necessarily one that Fugard, Kani, and Ntshona intended. Kani says, "It is for the audience to call a play political, not for the artist to intend it so. . . . These plays are called political because they show our lives, not because we are politicians."[47]

Boesman and Lena is also, in Raymer's view, primarily a socio-political work:

"What Fugard says in this South African parable is that although white men would love to get rid of their non-white population, they cannot do so. Nazi methods have failed in the past. The only way living specters like Boesman and Lena will vanish from South Africa is when rights are given to suppressed groups by the Pretoria government."[48]

Raymer praises Fugard as a political writer and Woodrow criticizes him for being one, but Fugard has been especially attacked from the left for the inadequacy of his presumed political statements. He is too political for some critics and not enough so for others. After praising *Boesman and Lena*'s memorable image of the human degradation engendered by a racist regime, Michael Billington adds, "It seems to me not quite enough for the white liberal dramatist to offer his colored contemporaries his pity, his compassion, his despair. What surely is needed in the context of South Africa, is an affirmation of the fact that the country's tragedy is man-made and therefore capable of change: in short, some political gesture."[49]

Blacks have also criticized Fugard's presumed politics. Ezekiel Mphahlele claims that Fugard's politics "stink" because, "not only does a white man speak for the African, but he also simply says that the situation is bad and he does nothing to transcend that." Fugard has never claimed to be speaking "for" anyone other than himself; Mphahlele also seems to object to Fugard even writing "about" blacks. Fugard has a simple response to those who believe his race disqualifies him from writing truthfully about others: "If the nature of human experience changes with a man's skin color, then the racists have been right all along."[50]

Fugard's plays are dominated by the immutable metaphysical dilemma of the individual rather than by the remediable social-historical problems of the collective. He writes in the introduction to *Three Port Elizabeth Plays*, "Today's future barely includes tomorrow." (xxv) It is this absence of hope in Fugard's work, as well as the implicit lack of faith in the efficacy of concerted action, that have especially provoked critics of his presumed political stance. This is largely due to the incompatibility of two world views.

Marxists such as R.K. complain that since no alternative is offered within the situation faced by Sizwe Bansi, the play does not reflect "objective reality." The "reality" of Fugard's plays pleases leftists no more than it does conservatives like Woodrow. After suggesting that Sizwe Bansi is representative of eighteen million blacks, R.K. backtracks and objects to Fugard's emphasis on the individual instead of the collective. Such emphasis is, among other things, a twentieth-century vestige of the continuing vitality of psychologically oriented Romanticism. R.K. would undoubtedly prefer the chorus-as-protagonist of the ancient Greek plays or of plays like Lope de Vega's *The Sheep Well* and Hauptmann's *The Weavers*.

R.K. ascribes Fugard's deficiencies to his presumed existentialism, which R.K. views narrowly: "This philosophy of despair sees the individual as being helplessly cut-off from society, locked in his own private torment, the perpetual victim of hostile forces."[51] Apparently, the racial consciousness that John and Winston exhibit throughout *The Island* is insufficiently collectivist. R.K. rejects Fugard's fatalism, a profound belief in the ineluctability of man's condition, yet he implicitly exhibits faith in another kind of fatalism: the inevitable victory of history, vindication through time.

R.K., and others who condemn Fugard's plays for being individualistic, despairing, uninspiring, anti-revolutionary, and so on, assume both that Fugard *should* write another kind of play and that he *could* do so. They imply that his vision could be easily abandoned, traded in for a credo compatible with their own. Such ideological objections indicate a refusal to accept Fugard's assumptions. The plays are evaluated not on their own terms, but on the basis of the critic's preconceptions of what art should be. In 1974, Fugard stated, "I'd like to believe that a play can be a significant form of action, but I've never been able to convince myself."[52] Two years later he accepted that writing was a form of action, but even so he saw only two categories of action: "1. The one which will produce immediate returns (political pamphlet). 2. The long-term investment (story-telling)." (9-76)

The question of Fugard's presumed political statement has been especially debated since his more forthright use of the South African context in the collaborative works. Still, the "political" label reduces a complex talent to a facile classification and limits the scope of Fugard's achievement. He is keenly aware of "the dangers of the political category, of appearing to have a good liberal conscience in an ugly situation. This cheapest of all the pigeonholes has by and large been mine."

Artists are never the best judges of their own accomplishments, nor of their intentions, but Fugard has repeatedly said, "I am not using the stage as a political platform."[53] He also considers himself naïve politically. Asked about the message of his work, he replies, "I don't have any."

Sartre asserts that, "The 'engaged' writer knows that words are action. He knows that to reveal is to change and that one can reveal only by planning to change. He has given up the impossible dream of giving an impartial picture of Society and the human condition."[54] Fugard's picture is hardly impartial, but it does not encompass the possibility of significant change.

In one of his many inner debates about segregated theatres, Fugard wonders about the old argument that a single audience member might be changed by what he saw: "Art can give meaning, can render meaningful areas of experience, and most certainly also enhances. But, teach? Contradict? State the opposite to what you believe and then lead you to accept it? In other words, can art *change* a man or woman? No." (6-25-63) Because a work of art is influenced by its milieu does not mean it will influence that milieu. Perhaps it should not. Leslie Fiedler writes, "A successful poem is a complete and final act; if it leads outward to other action, it is just so far a failure."[55]

146

asking Q!

Fugard writes, "As always was, is and will ever be—somebody must ask the question that can't be answered." (3-6-73) No political, economic, religious, philosophical, or scientific system can provide a satisfactory answer to Lena's "why?" Social solutions are irrelevant for the simple reason that the problems that concern Fugard are ultimately metaphysical rather than social; attributing a single cause to his characters' disaffection is reductive. If his men and women were removed from their South African context, only details of their plight would have to be altered. Not the essence. Like Ibsen, Fugard is "more of a poet and less of a social philosopher than people generally tend to suppose."[56]

During the London production of *Boesman and Lena* Fugard had noted, "Here in England the critical response too, although very favorable, has been that Fugard is painting a picture. I just haven't had, really, here in England, the depth of response that I encountered in America, where a few critics really did crash through beyond those externals and say, as one critic said, 'This is a love story;' another critic said 'No, this is a metaphor of the condition of man, in a sense'—which was great, really great, important to me."[57]

If apartheid were abolished, the oppressed people of South Africa might be better educated, clothed, fed, and housed; some of their problems would be meliorated. It is doubtful, however, that the profound intellectual and psychological needs that are the ultimate source of man's alienation, the cause of his quotidian struggle, and the subject of Fugard's plays, would be affected.

Having completed a collaborative trilogy, Fugard abandoned the challenges of actors in a rehearsal room for those of a blank sheet of paper. In his next play, *Dimetos*, he would again be misperceived by British reviewers.

He argues that H. F. addresses mainly universal questions

147

VI

Artisan and Artist Alone

One of the novelties I have given to the modern drama consists in converting the intellect into passion.　　　　　—Luigi Pirandello

Shortly before *The Island* was performed in South Africa, Fugard commented, "I've written intuitively about the clock ticking—suddenly it's actually ticking for me in a very personal sense. I feel a sense of panic and I have to be very careful that my writing is not informed by it." By the time *The Island* and *Sizwe Bansi* had opened in England and America, Fugard had decided to stop making plays in a rehearsal room with actors: "I think, finally, those experiences don't give me the opportunity for the very personal statement that I want to make. That whole experience coincided with a period when I thought of myself as being very alive, and I'm not being funny when I say that I'm now becoming conscious of dying, and to the extent that I think I'm dying, I would like to use my words, and my time, and calculate my effect very, very carefully."[1] Returning to blank paper, Fugard worked alone, and in *Dimetos* and *The Guest* he wrote about man alone.

148

Head, Hands, and Heart Divided: *Dimetos*

*The more incommensurable and incomprehensible a poetic creation
may be, the better.* —Johan Wolfgang van Goethe

While Fugard was writing *The Blood Knot* in Port Elizabeth in 1961, Sheila gave him the first volume of Camus's *Notebooks*. He was especially thrilled by one enigmatic paragraph: "Dimetos had a guilty love for his niece, who hanged herself. One day, the little waves carried on to the fine sand of the beach the body of a marvelously beautiful young woman. Seeing her, Dimetos fell on his knees, stricken with love. But he was forced to watch the decay of this magnificent body, and went mad. This was his niece's vengeance, and the symbol of a condition we must try to define."[2] Fugard admits being amazed that these five sentences filled him with such awe: "I was immediately possessed and am still acutely conscious of that moment. It was probably the most purely seminal experience in all my writing. This, literally, was the one little sperm that fertilized the egg, whereas with the other plays it was five sperm crawling into the same egg. My other work has been spawned by people, incidents, or images I knew rather than by something I read."

More than a decade passed before Fugard tried to define Dimetos's condition, but there were no abortive attempts in the meantime. When asked to write a play for the 1975 Edinburgh Festival, he recalls, "I thought about appointments I hadn't kept and what I wanted to do next. I knew I would do something with Dimetos someday. Suddenly, I felt that time had come. I was again feeling limited by both being defined as a political writer and by the ways I had used space, time, and the stage to tell a story. I thought, 'If I'm going to do this, I need to give it a new direction.' " By February 1975 Fugard was immersed in his new play. "It has now become compulsive, any intrusion on my time in the shed is resented and even out of the shed a part of me lives constantly with the images already defined, the challenges to which I have not yet responded." (2-75)

Dimetos opens *in media res* as Dimetos and his orphaned niece Lydia rescue a horse from an abandoned well. Lydia, Dimetos (an accomplished engineer), and Sophia, his housekeeper, had come to the remote province from an unnamed city five years earlier. They are visited by Danilo, who beseeches Dimetos to return to the city to help solve its water shortage. While awaiting his decision, Danilo is drawn close to Lydia. At first she responds to his kiss, then resists as he struggles with her violently. Upon learning that Dimetos had been watching but did nothing to stop Danilo, Lydia hangs herself.

The second act transpires many years later. Dimetos and Sophia have exiled themselves by the sea, where Danilo again finds them. Lydia's death had long been on his conscience until he realized that Dimetos had had a guilty love for

149

her and had conspired to make Danilo his surrogate. As the putrefaction of a decaying sea mammal on the beach becomes unbearable, Dimetos grows mad. Lydia's voice prompts him to tell a story. Narrating the dream of a man who thought he was a horse, Dimetos becomes more and more obsessed with his useless hands and ends the play laughing madly.

Before beginning the play, Fugard knew nothing about the story of Dimetos except Camus's cryptic statement. Moreover, unlike most of Fugard's work, only a few incidents from his own life found their way directly into the play. An abandoned well on his property had been so dangerous that he planned simply to fill it in, but Lisa discovered a family of frogs living at its bottom. She and her father determined to rescue the frogs first, but the collapsing sides of the well prevented them from climbing into it. Instead, they rigged up a device using long ropes and one of Fugard's fishing nets to haul up the frogs one at a time. A year later, a horse fell into a similar well at a neighbor's house, and Fugard watched it being pulled out with ropes and pulleys. Finally, the play is dedicated to Lisa, about whom Fugard quips, "Our relationship isn't incestuous, but . . .".

Both the idea for *Dimetos* and the spirit behind it derive from Camus, who writes that "myths are made for the imagination to breathe life into them."[3] Camus's few words, in turn, breathed life into Fugard's imagination. The narrative of *Dimetos* is archetypal: A man possessing special powers exiles himself and his faithful companion—not to a pastoral retreat but to a desolate primitive province. After committing a grave sin, he moves on to the sea. Turning his back on other men, on civilization itself, he reflects upon the nature of society and, especially, the purpose and meaning of life.

Because myths are usually ambiguous rather than explicit, they compel us, as Garrett Hardin writes, "to get our own thoughts straight as we try to deduce what the maker of a myth *might* have meant." The greater the myth (or the work of art) is, the greater the number of interpretations, often contradictory ones, it elicits. These creations are artistic Rorschach tests in which we find ourselves. In approaching them, the critic should be frank and admit, as Anatole France once advised, "I am going to speak about myself apropos of Shakespeare, apropos of Racine, or of Pascal, or of Goethe."[4]

As myths are simultaneously simple and ambiguous, so the seemingly simple story of *Dimetos* is textured with layers of meaning. The play's complex metaphors are infinitely suggestive, multifarious, and timeless. The characters, including Dimetos himself, are more sketched than sculpted. The writing is more suggestive than assertive, and throughout the play Fugard poses hypotheses instead of concluding proofs.

Dimetos defies immediate comprehension not because it is intentionally obscure, but because it is a profound work of pure, unencumbered imagination without simple analogues in the everyday world. The play's broad canvas and fugal interweaving of related subjects and metaphors make it Fugard's densest and most ambitious work to date. On the face of it at least, *Dimetos* conforms to Coleridge's definition that great works of literature are those that contain the most content in the least space.

Dimetos's profession is the fulcrum of several themes. As an engineer, he creates by manipulating material. As a scientist, he is capable of abstract speculation. When he is employed by a society, he applies his skills for the benefit of a civilization, perhaps to help it progress. Dimetos is armed with knowledge both of the abstract laws of physics and of the practical means to implement them by applying hands to the six basic machines—level, pulley, inclined plane, wedge, screw, and wheel. He says, "There is nothing more beautiful than a man making something and making it well, than a pair of hands urgent and quick with a need and behind those a guiding intelligence. Do you know what bridges that mysterious distance between head and hands, bringing them so close together that they are almost one? Caring. . . . I don't care any more. . . . Usage blunts a tool, but when that happens you sharpen it. It's not as simple as that with," Sophia interrupts, "The heart, Dimetos," but he continues, "Head, hands, and heart." (17*) The play centers on the scope and, especially, the limits of Dimetos's head, hands, and heart. Through these innate basic tools man builds his life, but in Dimetos they no longer work together harmoniously.

Dimetos has a guilty love, but he evinces more passion towards objects than people. No longer concerned with the human applications of the laws and machines of physics, he prizes them abstractly, aesthetically, in and of themselves—form without function. When he explains that the horse at the bottom of the well was trapped because it fell victim to gravity, Lydia says she wants none of his old facts. Dimetos insists, "They are all that really matter. They'll help you understand a lot more than falling horses little one. That law holds the universe together." (7) Dimetos also becomes a helpless victim of a force attracting him: Lydia. The consequences are indeed grave. Lydia wonders why he hides his feelings, but Dimetos claims there isn't much to hide. When Sophia perceives that Danilo has upset him, Dimetos wonders, "Is it that obvious?" (15) He is more concerned with exhibiting an emotion than experiencing one.

Before going down the well, Lydia has to remove her dress in order to move about freely with the horse. Dimetos's attraction to her, however, is prompted by something far more complex than either the sight of her body or the clichéd interpretation of a woman riding a horse. Rather, the horse's trust of Lydia and its cooperation with her echo Dimetos's description of men working in unison. It is this unity of purpose, itself a sexual image, that seems most to have excited Dimetos's imagination. While in the act of resolving the horse's problem, Lydia inadvertently stimulates Dimetos's.

It is typical of Fugard's use of paradox that Dimetos is ruled more by coolness

*All textual quotes from *Dimetos: And Two Early Plays* (Oxford: Oxford University Press, 1977).

than passion, despite his guilty love. *Dimetos* is not a pathological study of incest and passion. Lydia represents a desire in Dimetos for communion. He is guilty of nothing more than voyeurism, but this is especially apposite since the palpable actions of his past have been replaced by the intangible contemplations of his present.

Lydia may comprehend neither the sexual impulse behind Dimetos's voyeurism nor the reasons he has prolonged Danilo's stay. Nevertheless, she kills herself because her uncle has betrayed their relationship by failing, in her eyes, to protect her. Shortly before hanging herself with a rope knotted the way Dimetos had taught her, she conjures up the horse and says, "You didn't know that men make holes in the world. You thought it was safe. So you trusted it." (37) Dimetos made a hole in Lydia's world by betraying her trust.

Dimetos is yet another of Fugard's plays focusing upon a family, although here it is an extended rather than a nuclear one. Sophia's bond to Lydia seems at first maternal. The quiet intimacy of their game of naming ten beautiful things evokes more than the relationship of a nanny to her charge. However, as Lydia's relationship with Dimetos erodes, so does her relationship with Sophia. When they play the naming game a second time, Sophia does so mechanically, and her hands seem different to Lydia.

Sophia's relationship with Dimetos is still more complex. Fugard notes, "Dimetos sees her as sister-in-law, not woman."[5] Although she has spent decades with him, she is unsure of her role and wonders, like so many of Fugard's previous characters, who she is. Yet despite her importance in the play, Sophia's function in much of the first act is rather shadowy. Her insistence upon learning who tore Lydia's dress, and relief upon learning that it was Danilo, suggest that she had suspected Dimetos. However, it is not clear in the first act alone that her counsel to Lydia also applies to her relationship with Dimetos: "To love is a position of weakness, to be loved a position of power." (36) Sophia's second-act admission of complicity in Lydia's death is a surprise to the audience.

As Sophia has been less than forthright with Lydia, so Dimetos lies to Danilo by claiming he is working, inspired by another man's need. In fact, he no longer works, no longer cares about the needs of others, and is no longer inspired; the horse's rescue reminds him of the time he did care and was inspired.

Dimetos's profession is again the key to an important set of interrelated themes: scientific technology, progress, and action. Charles A. Beard calls technology the fundamental basis of modern civilization, and goes on to write, "Of all the ideas pertinent to the concept of progress . . . none is more relevant than technology. . . . The idea of progress is both an interpretation of history and a philosophy of action."[6] Yet, however much technology has raised man's hopes for the solution of his problems, it can never satisfy his deepest desires. Dimetos's scientific knowledge allows him to understand, sometimes to master, parts of the outer universe; it cannot help him fathom or control his inner soul.

Natural mysteries can be explained scientifically, but the mysteries of life cannot. By the time he realizes this, madness has dawned. *Dimetos* explores the impossibility of answering philosophical questions and needs through science.

As with other Fugard characters who enter from the outside, Danilo functions as a catalyst. He forces Dimetos to reflect back upon his past faith in civilization, upon his former concern with its future and the practical needs of other men, and upon the passionate sense of purpose that had once animated his life, in severe contrast to his now blunted sensibility. Since he is a link to the city and civilization, Danilo reminds Dimetos of their nature and precipitates discussions of them and of the idea of progress. Danilo admits his mission is a selfish one and that "Cities have no morality except their own survival," (11) but he still hopes to recruit Dimetos away from rural primitivism back to urban civilization.

The two worlds seem at first entirely different to Danilo, but not to Dimetos—even though he relies totally upon the facts of science while the provincials are ruled by superstition and religion. Danilo considers them primitive and uncultured; Dimetos responds to the primeval nature of their struggle for existence. His obsessions with basic tools and laws of physics correspond to the utterly fundamental difficulties the valley faces.

He even suggests to Danilo that the valley has been refreshing and stimulating, but in so doing Dimetos lies again, if not to Danilo then to himself. He may have sought the good life through Rousseau-like retreat to a primitive world, but he has not found it there. Dimetos does not experience happiness in either civilization or nature.

Recounting his thoughts about the city while viewing it from above, he says, "Was the city finally an organism, something more than just the sum total of all the individual lives it contained . . . or was it still only a machine, a system of forces that could be controlled? . . . I didn't [decide]. Because a third possibility occurred to me. That I was looking at the creation of a modern Daedalus into which Theseus has gone without his ball of twine." (22) Dimetos's uncertainty about the nature of the city and, implicitly, his role in it, had apparently contributed to his decision to leave it. In addition, he seems also to have sought a renewed life of action. He tells Danilo he didn't come to the valley to talk; he had initiated the horse's rescue by admonishing the locals to use their hands rather than their tongues.

However, the valley has resolved neither Dimetos's aimlessness nor his desire to act. Idleness has become a way of life. Lydia says of the rescue, "It was good to have something to do again today." (21) Nevertheless, throughout the first act Dimetos at least appreciates the working hands and purposeful direction of others. By the end of the play virtually all meaning has disappeared. Even his hands, which Sophia has often enjoyed watching, "have come to an end. That's a lament worthy of a poet." (40) The sea, Dimetos's new-found playmate, confirms his now fixed vision of the absurd. Holding up a stone, he says, "This almost perfect shape is without a purpose. Form without function. The sea is a clever but mad craftsman, Sophia. His is the ultimate mockery. You should relax. He ridicules my hands and all they did more than you ever will. A colossal and totally absurd energy. I imagine there is more in one tide pushing up that beach than a man uses in a lifetime. The energy in one wave could build a wall. But what does it do instead? . . . polish stones until they disappear." (40) Shortly before this sea reduces shells to nothingness, Dimetos gathers up the grit to sell to farmers. He is finally working again, as a scavenger.

Dimetos and Danilo are often contrasted, but as the play progresses Danilo increasingly resembles Dimetos. In the years that pass between the two acts, Danilo loses his sense of purpose and his faith in progress, in intelligence, and in the possibility of finding permanent solutions to the crises of the city. His absolute transformation is clear after Dimetos asserts that Danilo once had vision, a rare quality Danilo had previously praised in Dimetos. Danilo replies, "A few old cranks and their young followers still keep that word alive. The rest of us muddle along as best we can. I came across a theory the other day which struck a responsive chord. The City of the Living—our metropolis—has its origins in the City of the Dead—the necropolis. That is how it all started, apparently, with burial grounds . . . a permanent place not for the living, but the dead. Sometimes I think it's on its way back to being that." (43)

As in most of Fugard's previous work, time is again an important theme. Danilo links it to Dimetos's reference to Daedalus when he asserts, "Man is the only animal to be trapped by time. That's the real labyrinth." (23) In addition, time is inextricably linked with concepts of progress, but time also leads inevitably to decay. Loss of faith in progress is tantamount to loss of faith in tomorrow. During Danilo's defense of progress, Lydia is adamant that she wants tomorrow. However, after secrets begin to intrude into her relationships with Sophia and Danilo, she wishes that "tomorrow was yesterday" and wonders why nothing is forever, which prompts Danilo to promise that he will retrieve her lost faith in tomorrow.

His attempt to do so coincides with the summer solstice, "the day the sun stood still." (36) Dimetos counsels Lydia, "When you wake up . . . all that happened will already be yesterday. Time is not always our enemy, Lydia. What shall we do tomorrow? . . . We've so much time left." (36-37) His advice implies that "this too shall pass," but before it does, things may get worse. Lydia hangs herself immediately after this conversation; she puts an end to her time. Instead of diminishing with time, the mammal's putrefaction worsens.

Dimetos is resigned to waiting out "what's left of my time." (38) He says that selling shell-grit is "my last apprenticeship, Danilo. To the sea. My Master's only tool is time." (42) As his madness intensifies he muses, "Time is passing . . . nowhere to nowhere . . . Time is at work." (50) Trying to make a machine for the last time, Dimetos chooses one "that will stop time." (50) Before resigning in defeat, he admits, "Time stinks. Time stinks!" (51) which it does in this play both literally and figuratively.

The final moments of *Dimetos* are the most intricate in the entire play, indeed, in anything Fugard has written. The play's themes are woven throughout every scene, but they meld with dazzling precision in Dimetos's final monologue and create the most powerful stage image in Fugard's entire *oeuvre*. Defeated by his inability to create a machine that will stop time, Dimetos asks what he must do. Lydia's disembodied voice replies, "Find your hands. Look at them. They are useless. The only tool a man can make that will help him hold time, is a story." (51) Early in the play Dimetos had said, "I'm an engineer, Lydia, not a story teller. An artisan, not an artist." (7) Of Lydia's rescue of the horse he had commented, "If I was an artist I'd turn my hand to modelling that." (28) Bereft of the use of his hands, Dimetos becomes not a sculptor but the teller of an archetypal story beginning "once upon a time," pivoting upon "there was," concluding "for ever after." The voice's last advice is "You've made your tool, Dimetos, Now comes the hard part. Use it." (51)

As the artisan becomes an artist, ephemeral words become his palpable tools. Dimetos creates something from nothing, a story of a man who dreamt he was a horse that, in turn, dreamt it had hands. A voice addresses the disembodied hands as *Dimetos* ends, "Close that powerful hand on a thing. Yours. Hold it! . . . Now give it away. Don't be frightened. Only to your other hand. . . . That was a terrible second when they were both empty. One still is. Find something. Quickly! Now comes the hard part . . . so listen carefully. Each must give what it has got to the other, at the same time. You must give and take with the same action. Again . . . and again . . . (*Dimetos's hands juggle. He starts to laugh . . . and laughs and laughs.*) And now, because your gaiety is so great, the last skill of all. Hold them out, and wait . . . ." (52-53)

Empty hands are a central image in many Fugard plays,[7] but none of his characters is as obsessed with hands as Dimetos. He remembers men by their hands rather than their faces or personalities. The hands of a potter and smith are memorable, but those he will longest remember belonged to a juggler who had explained his trade with a paradox: "Learn to give and take with the same action." (25) Dimetos has no patience with beggars, who take but do not give. Empty hands have always angered him since they mean a man has ended up useless, yet this is precisely how Dimetos ends.

The image of hands echoes back through the entire play, and as *Dimetos* ends, the meaning of "ending" also reverberates. Lydia says to Dimetos of the horse in the well, "He has got a story even if you don't care what it is, and you did give it a happy ending." (7) Before hanging herself, she repeats, "For all its holes the world is still worth it—because Dimetos makes happy endings." (37) Dimetos's own story ends closer to Lydia's than the rescued horse's. He is left awaiting infinity with his empty hands, as mad as Lear on the heath. It is a climax without a denouement.

Dimetos's solitude may be compared to Fugard's own desire to work alone following his exhausting collaborative period. Dimetos's inability to work is similar to the blocks many writers sometimes experience. Fugard has never indicated that he considers *Dimetos* to be either directly autobiographical or thematically concerned with the nature of being an artist. Indeed, he claims there are fewer incidents from his personal experiences in it than in any previous work. However, Fugard's musings on the artist's impotence—"Is my context as artist irremediably bourgeois?" (2-26-68) and "I'd like to believe a play can be a significant form of action, but I've never been able to convince myself"[8]—make it inviting to read a personal statement into Dimetos's final failure. Much of the play deals with the effect of his art (science) upon his life as a man. As with all artists, he becomes primarily an observer and interpreter—of himself, other men, and the surrounding world.

There are numerous parallels among it and other plays that focus upon scientist-creators who are also artist figures. Dimetos, Solness, Faust, Prospero, and Prometheus are all rebellious dreamers, intellectual brooders, and creators suffering a conflict between their lives and their art, a conflict they have largely willed themselves. They possess practical scientific skills that allow them to control at least part of nature, if not their inner souls. These skills either have been or might be applied practically for the good of mankind. Far from indicating Fugard's ability consciously to imitate other authors, these similarities point out a continuing fascination with certain ideas throughout the history of Western dramatic writing. Some of man's obsessions are universal and the ways of depicting them archetypal.*

In preparation for the Edinburgh Festival premiere scheduled for August 27, 1975, *Dimetos* was presented at the University of the Witwatersrand and at The Space for a week of "final rehearsals of a play in progress." Although Fugard had vowed not to work in total collaboration with his actors as he had with *The Island* and *Sizwe Bansi*, *Dimetos* evolved, in part, as *Statements* had. "The definition I took into rehearsal was a very primitive one," he says. "Enormous discoveries occurred in that rehearsal room that made their way into the text, especially through working with Yvonne." (Bryceland was cast as Sophia.) During the week at The Space, according to Astbury, "Athol chopped and changed, wrote and rewrote."[9]

B.A. Young wrote of the Edinburgh production at the Church Hill Theatre, "Athol Fugard has freed himself from his obsessive concern for the problems of his own people, and the result is disastrous." Ned Chaillet added, "Thick South

*These literary parallels are discussed more fully in Appendix B.

African accents and the unexpected non-political nature of the play worked together to bring about general disappointment and denouncement." Far from denouncing *Dimetos*, Harold Hobson praised it passionately as "exciting, perfectly directed, and beautiful to look at. . . . It is the best play I have seen in Britain this year. . . . Because of its exceptional technique and texture it demands a readjustment of conventional attitudes to drama. But so, when we first encountered them, did Joyce and Beckett and Pinter and Duras."[10]

Despite generally poor reviews in Edinburgh, Fugard noted, "My faith in the complex of central images [is] totally intact." (9-75) He reworked the play and a second production, again under his own direction, opened the following year with Paul Scofield as Dimetos, Ben Kingsley as Danilo, Celia Quicke as Lydia, and Bryceland again as Sophia. After a short run at the Nottingham Playhouse, this production moved to London's Comedy Theatre where it opened May 16, but closed quietly within four weeks. Again, most of the critics were cool. John Elsom wrote, "This production more so than the version which eventually emerged at Edinburgh, is a failure." Chaillet, however, became more appreciative after seeing *Dimetos* the second time: "In the past year, with the single exception of Edward Bond's *The Fool*, it would be impossible to find a more serious, not to say dour, new play on the English stage, nor a play with more latent power. . . . *Dimetos* will certainly grow in importance, though in its present form it may forever elude an entirely satisfactory production." Astbury's appreciation of *Dimetos* also increased with time: "When I first read the play I did not understand it at all, especially the final image. . . . Those last lines have become the most important lesson I am learning. The definitive production is yet to be done but I think it is his most important play."[11]

The "political" expectations of the British critics to which Chaillet refers were no doubt formed by their prevailing opinions of *Sizwe Bansi*, *The Island*, and *Statements*, which had played London the previous year. Once before such preconceptions of Fugard had influenced a play's reception: *People* had gone unproduced for five years until it, like *Dimetos*, premiered in Scotland. Fugard believes, "The problem I had with *Dimetos* arose out of the expectations created by my other work: It meant *Dimetos* wasn't seen or read for what it is."[12] He adds, "My advice to any young writer would be, 'work under a nom de plume and change it every time you write. Make the critics look at your work without any expectations.' The way to do *Dimetos* in America is to change the name of the author. Say it is by the Hungarian, Lohta Draguf " (Fugard's name spelled backward).

There are basically two ways of perceiving the essence of everything Fugard has written: Either he dramatizes the universal pain of consciousness or he chronicles specific socio-political causes of that pain. The latter view explains parts of much of his work, but the former encompasses the essence of all of it. Like Gide, Fugard might plead with his interpreters, "Please do not understand me too quickly." *Dimetos* has not been understood at all. In writing that Fugard "has utterly departed from his previous subject matter,"[13] A. Christopher Tucker indicates that he misunderstands either Fugard's previous work or *Dimetos*. Its form and means are newer than its subject and ends.

The play's themes place it firmly in the center of Fugard's work. He is again concerned with man's responsibility to man, with love, albeit a "guilty" one, with time, with the plight of modern man and his lonely suffering, and with his inability to comprehend fully his being, his purpose, and the structure of the world. Science, progress, and civilization are new themes for Fugard, but in many ways *Dimetos* is more similar to "The Family" than to either *Sizwe Bansi* or *The Island.*

Dimetos has been criticized because it does not have a specific South African social or political context, but in some ways it is Fugard's broadest social and political play: the society being civilization as a whole, and the political system being that served by the technocratic metropolis. It is also his most scathingly critical play. Dimetos is Fugard's first character to possess sufficient skill and power to benefit others on a large scale; his inability to care about his fellow man invites censure. Most of Fugard's characters elicit respect and sympathy.

Despite the continuity of thematic leitmotifs, *Dimetos* is a stylistic departure. None of Fugard's other plays spans as long a period of time, nor is any other written in so many scenes or such brief ones. Instead of a strong woman at its center, the play revolves around a fragile man. Most significant of all, *Dimetos* is the only Fugard work not concretely grounded in time and place. It only implicitly transpires after the industrial revolution, let alone in the twentieth century.[14] Nor is the geographical setting indicated. The specificity of contemporary Port Elizabeth has been replaced by generalities of an infinite universe. Fugard has frequently praised Beckett, and their themes are often similar, but for the first time he resembles Beckett in another way: *Dimetos* leaps immediately to the macrocosm without the interpositioning of the microcosm.

Many of Fugard's previous plays conform to the neo-Aristotelian unities of time and place, but of all his plays, *Dimetos* most resembles Greek tragedy. He admits, "Greek tragedy, primarily that of Sophocles, has greatly influenced me, following the statement of Camus. The staging recalls Greek settings, and the language of the play often uses poetic images, since the inspiration is not that of a rational idea but one arising from profound human feelings." Fugard made a cursory search through Greek mythology to find the story of Dimetos, but did not discover Camus's apparent source in the Dimoetes of Parthenius.[15]

Like the Greek tragedies, *Dimetos* is remorselessly general, highly literary and seemingly static, and dominated by diction more formal and restrained than that in any of Fugard's other plays. Dimetos's emotional impotence obviously influences the texture of Fugard's dialogue, but the coolness of the language is deceptive. Passion exudes from Fugard between the lines as well as from his characters on the lines themselves.

He admits that the critical response makes *Dimetos* his one failure, but it is not a failure in his mind; he sometimes calls it his favorite play. He is, however, critical of his direction of the play. Following the London premiere, he vowed never to direct again (though he changed his mind after completing his next play). In 1980, he said of *Dimetos*, "I'm living quietly with the sense of having one more appointment with that play as a director. The right moment will come. It will take four actors with very very special qualities to get me back to it." If Fugard does direct the play again, he may need to find clearer dramatic images and action to project its intense intellection.

The text of *Dimetos* is not faultless either. The symbolism of the decaying mammal, suggested by Camus, is rather heavy-handed. However, on the whole, the play is more nebulous than explicit. Sophia is especially murky. She complains that she has little identity and is only an appendage of Dimetos's life, but the same is true of her role in the play. Her grievances often seem arbitrary since Fugard neither prepares a context for them nor makes sufficient dramatic use of them.

The state of mind and perceptions of Dimetos are not always self-evident either, but then they cannot be. The arc he traverses, and with him that of the entire play, is towards an understanding of his head, hands, and heart. Because his incomprehension is the very mainspring of the play, audiences must be enticed by it instead of befuddled—an enormous challenge for any production, since spectators often prefer proofs to hypotheses and reassuring affirmation to disturbing denegation.

Dimetos is ethereal, but its rarefied atmosphere coincides with its themes and the loftiness of its thought. No single interpretation can contain its many layers, yet despite this, perhaps because of this, *Dimetos* insistently imposes itself upon the imagination as indelibly as it did upon Fugard's own.

"Intellectual," "abstract," and "philosophical" are often considered pejoratives when applied to a play, but these are the very qualities that distinguish much of Fugard's work. Animated abstraction is an oxymoron that describes the special vitality of *Dimetos*.

It has been performed in Germany, and a second time in South Africa, but never in the United States. *Dimetos* is the kind of play that will remain an underground classic until a producer unconcerned with commercial success, a director with vision, and a commanding actor collaborate to rescue it from oblivion. Why, the critics will then ask, has this masterpiece been neglected? Following the London opening, Hobson wrote, "That *Waiting for Godot* triumphed over contemporary critical and popular disapproval . . . is a good augury for what will eventually happen to Mr. Fugard's *Dimetos*."[16]

Suffero Ergo Sum: *The Guest*

Hell hath no limits, nor is circumscrib'd
In one self place. But where we are is hell,
And where hell is there must we ever be.   —Christopher Marlowe

For his next project Fugard returned to a concrete setting in time and place, 1926 on a South African farm. As in *Dimetos*, he again focused upon a white middle-class man in self-imposed exile from civilization, but this time his protagonist is a naturalist rather than an engineer, and a practicing writer instead of simply an artist figure. Fugard recalls the genesis of *The Guest: An Episode in the Life of Eugène Marais* as follows: "Ross Devenish asked me in London if I'd ever thought about doing a film on Marais. My own interest in natural history goes right back to my childhood and among the first books on the subject I'd read were Marais's. I'd also known his poetry for a long time. Ross's suggestion was such a valid possibility that the idea quietly grew." Devenish first mentioned the project in the fall of 1973. By the following spring Fugard had begun to outline his new script. He told a reporter he wanted to get away from racial problems to write about other emotions. After Fugard admitted that he had an addictive personality, the newspaper deduced that the new play would be about gambling.[17]

Eugène Marais was born in Pretoria on January 9, 1872. He was educated in English, but after beginning his career as a journalist, he wrote in Dutch and later in Afrikaans, then in transition from a vernacular to a written language. After travelling to London in 1896 to read law, he began his lifelong study of the subconscious mind by learning hypnosis and reading widely in biology and psychology. Following the Boer War, Marais briefly practiced law in Johannesburg, and in 1907 moved to the Waterberg, a remote part of the Transvaal, where he studied the chacma baboon in its natural habitat.

Marais felt little pride in his newspaper articles about his experiences, and long hoped to publish a serious work on the psychology of primates, especially on the subconscious. Addiction to morphine prevented completion of this work, but the unfinished manuscript of *The Soul of the Ape*, long thought lost, was eventually discovered and published in 1969. (This "soul" connotes "mind" in Afrikaans rather than "spirit" as it does in English.) Marais also wrote poems and stories that, although few in number, remain highly regarded. "Winternag," the one Afrikaans poem that most English-speaking South Africans have read, marks him as one of the founders of Afrikaans literature. Fugard notes that perhaps six of his poems "totally define and suddenly express the range, power and intensity of the Afrikaans language."[18]

The episode from Marais's life that Fugard and Devenish eventually selected runs as follows: Under the supervision of his friend, the physician and popular

Afrikaans poet A.G. Visser, Marais retreats to Steenkampskraal, the farm of Oom Doors and Tant Corrie Meyers and their three children, Doorsie, Louis, and Little Corrie. There he hopes gradually to end his addiction. His erratic behavior and schemes to get more drugs have a corrosive effect on the family, but Marais gradually reduces his dependence and returns to his writing, parts of which are quoted throughout the film in voice-overs during dreams and flashbacks. Despite the marked improvement of his health and nearly total withdrawal, he finally secures an extra supply of morphine, returns to his habit, and forces Oom Doors to have Visser remove him from Steenkampskraal.

The Guest is Fugard's second period piece based upon historical characters and events, but he found the facts less troublesome than he had in Mille Miglia: "That little episode at Steenkampskraal was very thinly documented, just a little hearsay evidence about what actually transpired. I had the freedom to fill in the gaps." Only two short chapters of Leon Rousseau's biography of Marais, Die Groot Verlange (The Great Yearning), which Fugard and Devenish read in manuscript form, describe Marais's visit to the farm.[19]

Like much of Fugard's previous work, The Guest focuses intensely upon a character's anguish. Its most powerful language is not Fugard's dialogue, however, but Marais's prose in the voice-overs, and even these words are not as potent as the film's images. Fugard and Devenish had adapted Boesman and Lena for the screen, but it remains a film version of a play; The Guest is thoroughly conceived as a film and could not easily be adapted for the stage. Its haunting images cannot be indicated in a text, even one accompanied by still photographs. Fugard and Devenish thoroughly exploit the potential of their medium by finding an appropriate camera style, framing individual shots with great precision, and creating a visual leitmotif through the use of recurring images of windows and reflections.

The rural setting of Steenkampskraal, coupled with Marais's interest in nature, might have led to travelogue-style emphasis on the beauty of the Highveld. The film does contain shots of the setting sun and expansive farm vistas, but the look of The Guest is as bare and stripped-down as any of Fugard's plays, as stark as life itself at Steenkampskraal. Although shot in color, much of The Guest feels like a black-and-white film.

It opens with the mournful tones of Bach's Cello Suite #1. Doors's hearty welcome to the farm elicits an uncertain stare from the impassive Marais, and in meeting the family he can do no more than extend a listless hand. Both he and Tant Corrie are dressed in black and white, as they will be throughout the film. The room Marais is to share with Louis and Doorsie is also stark; its bare walls have been white-washed rather than painted. The room's narrowness and the low doorway into it make it feel like a prison cell, foreshadowing the claustrophobia Marais will experience.

A close-up of Marais reveals his emaciation. His cheeks are so hollow that the skull beneath seems ready to puncture the skin—a Giacometti image, sculpted not in bronze but in bone. Marais projects unmitigated pain until he prepares an injection, which establishes the pattern for these moments throughout the film: Nervous eagerness to get the drug into his bloodstream is followed by a radiant countenance as his facial muscles relax when the drug takes effect. Each injection is followed by a voice-over in which Marais quotes his writings with cool detachment.

Marais's state of mind is presented both objectively and subjectively, often-times simultaneously. The detached tone and apparent objectivity of the voice-overs contrast with their actual subject, the pain of consciousness. The audience perceives life as he does, and sees him as he cannot.

Camera shots of his bedroom window are sometimes from Marais's point of view, and sometimes he is the object of view. In the first of these he carries a candle and approaches the window in response to Louis's tapping. Instead of seeing Louis, Marais sees his own elfish reflection. It is an image of self-centered isolation. He has elected not to join the family for dinner, and even when attempting to peer outside, sees only himself. Once Marais begins to improve, he is viewed through his bedroom window, which is now open. In the most horrific image of the film, after Marais returns to heavy morphine use, he recites poetry to his reflection in this window. When this cuts to an image of him seen through the window, his face is distorted, as if seen in a funhouse mirror. As Marais himself uses a magnifying glass to study a termitary, the window serves as a kind of microscope slide through which the various transformations of Marais, the specimen, are studied. This use of windows as mirrors may have been suggested by Marais's own verse: "knows't thou now me? Hast in a mirror looked, and knowest thou thee?"

This emphasis on windows leads to one point of confusion in the narrative. In an early dream sequence experienced from Marais's point of view, a baboon appears at a window, presumably that of Marais's bedroom at Steenkampskraal. In a later dream, baboons again appear at this window, and Marais chases them into the night. The window of this dream, which is only slightly smaller than the one on the farm, is actually that of his hut at Waterberg, where he had observed the baboons twenty years previously. Although Marais does look younger and in better health, it is not clear enough that the dream is a flashback to another place. Moreover, because it is insufficiently clear that these scenes transpire in Waterberg, one wonders how the baboons made their way to Steenkampskraal: Perhaps these are only imaginary baboons? The script labels these Waterberg scenes "dreams," attempts to evoke morphine dreams perhaps, but they might also be called flashbacks or self-reflections.

The transition out of this sequence is also muddled. Marais's pursuit of the baboons bleeds into his attempted escape from the farm, although one might think he is still chasing baboons. The direction in the script reads, "*Marais flee-*

ing. For a moment a sense of continuity between this and the preceding dream sequence." (42*) The creation of a parallel between the two scenes is undermined by the fact that during his flight from the farm the veld is burning. The image seems symbolic, as if this too were part of Marais's imagination. In fact, the veld is simply being prepared for the spring rains. Fugard admits that the burning veld image is one of the film's flaws.

Repeated use of windows and reflections to create a dual perspective is one aspect of *The Guest*'s style. Another is the juxtaposition of sharply contrasting points of view. The evening of his first night at Steenkampskraal, Marais brusquely sends Doors from the room. When Doors next visits, however, Marais launches into a sorry story as he tries to wheedle extra pills from him. The innocent credulity of Doors is vividly juxtaposed with the intensity of the con game hatching in Marais's mind. In a later scene, Marais watches Little Corrie swinging in a tree that is viewed against the backdrop of the veld; in the foreground of this frame of human innocence and natural beauty is his emaciated appearance and indifferent stare.

Visual juxtaposition is used two other times when Marais argues with Doors for more drugs. The beginnings of these segments are heard offscreen as the camera fixes upon other family members. There is no escape from their guest. In the most powerful juxtaposition of all, which follows Marais's relapse, Doors's reading of the Bible to his family is drowned out by Marais's incoherent babbling, maniacal laughter, and crazed recitation of verse. Afrikaans piety intermingles with Marais's Afrikaans poetry and Shakespeare. This clash of temperaments, values, and psyches succinctly encapsulates the effect of Marais's visit upon the nexus of this family's relationships.

Another form of juxtapositions is the use of voice-overs, which often suggest the similarities between man and animal. These similarities are also indicated during the dream preceding Marais's attempted escape from the farm: *"The man is rapidly losing his self-assurance and is identifying more and more with the animals. . . . He abandons himself to total animal terror."* (42) This man-as-animal image intensifies during the escape itself. Growing fatigued, Marais scurries ahead on all fours. When he is finally captured, Doorsie hauls him into the house like a dead carcass and locks him in his room. Its windows are then boarded up. Only Tant Corrie seems to remember that Marais is a human being. She orders Doorsie to unlock Marais's door.

This segment marks Marais's nadir, but his condition soon improves to the point that he returns to work. When he had prepared his first injections the melted pills had almost overflowed a teaspoon, but as the number of pills decreases, the spoon seems to grow larger. His recovery is also evident in his ap-

*All quotes from *The Guest: An Episode in the Life of Eugène Marais* (Johannesburg and London: Ad. Donker, 1977).

pearance. In the early scenes Marais's face is bony, but by the time he and Visser examine a baboon cranium, the fleshiness of Marais's face masks his skull as it did not in the first close-up. Unshaven and slovenly in the early scenes, he begins to take better care of himself and dons an immaculate white suit for the visit of his former mistress, Brenda. By then the weather has changed as well, from winter to early spring. The landscape had been bleak when Marais had arrived, and though the prospects for his recovery had then been bleak as well, he now seems to have his life under control.

In contrast to the false gregariousness of his con game with Doors to get more pills, Marais does eventually become more friendly with the family, though Louis always remains suspicious. The shots of Marais by himself that had served to emphasize his isolation become less frequent. Marais's warmth is clearest in his relations with Little Corrie and Doorsie; he becomes their science teacher during walks in what he refers to as his real home, the veld. Little Corrie's wish that it were green prompts Marais's advice, a projection of the way he hopes others will perceive him: "You must learn to see and love it for what it is. Don't ask it to be something else. It's dry, but not dead. There's a lot of life down there." (73)

Despite Marais's moments of intimacy with Little Corrie, Doorsie, and Tant Coorie, none of Fugard's previous intruders into a domestic routine is as disruptive as Marais. The effect of the past upon the present is as evident in *The Guest* as in many of Fugard's previous works, but here the effect is physiological as well as psychological.

While Fugard has often concentrated on a character's journey towards increased consciousness, in *The Guest* he focuses on the anguish of Marais's already-existing consciousness, which has led to his addiction. Such, at least, is Marais's theory about addiction, although it might instead be called his justification for it. Indeed, the thematic core of the play is an examination of the interrelationship between consciousness and suffering: "The pain of the survival struggle has a single focus . . . the consciousness. Both man and the baboon experience consciousness as something based on pain and suffering." (41) Not even sleep provides relief. While dreaming, Marais opens his mouth in a silent scream as loud as that of Mother Courage.

Fugard had long been drawn to the examination of pain. In a letter to Yvonne Bryceland written before *The Guest*, he noted, "Our most important duty is to bear witness to pain."[20] Tsotsi, Hester, and Lena experience their existence through pain, and in all three it is associated with their state of consciousness, which is gradually heightened through the course of each work. *Hello and Goodbye* is informed by the pain suffered by Fugard's father. This pain, though purely physical like the Smit patriarch's, is indistinguishable from Marais's, which is physiological and mental. In *Hello and Goodbye* Fugard had also touched upon the desperate dependence upon pills when Johnnie describes his father's anxiety about having enough medicine.

Suffering is inextricably linked to consciousness, but Fugard never implies that man would be better off without consciousness. Having acquired it, he does not have the choice of returning to a blissful state of ignorance. Marais has lived out the verse from Ecclesiastes that Doorsie quotes: "For in much wisdom is much grief: and he that increaseth knowledge increaseth sorrow." (68) Consciousness, the pain of individual existence, is one of man's primary characteristics. In a section of Marais's *The Soul of the White Ant* not actually quoted in *The Guest* but implied throughout it, he writes, "If pain were to disappear from this earth, life would soon cease. Without pain organic matter cannot exist."[21] Sometimes it cannot exist *with* pain.

On first glance Marais seems to be the antithesis of Dimetos, the one feeling too much, the other too little. Yet there is an inherent paradox in Marais's addiction. Morphine initially displaces the intrinsic feeling of pain with an extrinsically created feeling of euphoria, but this is short-lived: "Continuous use of the drug resembles sluggish mental anaesthesia rather than positive happiness." (25) This anaesthesia is similar to Dimetos's blunted sensibility. In the end, Marais has simply traded the normal pain of consciousness for the more intense, abnormal pain of addiction. By bathing in scalding water he induces one type of pain to block his brain from experiencing another.[22]

Upon his arrival at Steenkampskraal, Marais needs ten pills in both the morning and evening. He gradually reduces this to one pill per day. Even so, he asserts, "It's as much a part of me now as the spelling of my name." (70) As total recovery appears near, Marais loses interest in the apparent goal of his stay at the farm; the morphine is as much a response to his anguish as the cause of it. He argues with Visser that his real ailment is life itself, then quotes an ancient Egyptian papyrus: "Title: Dialogue between the writer and his soul. In it the writer came to the conclusion that the very existence of life was founded on sorrow and pain, and that there was ultimately only one perfect remedy . . . to put an end to one's existence. The Sotho have a nice turn of phrase for that . . . *peli n'daba* . . . 'end of dialogue'. " (71)

Nietzsche writes, "The thought of suicide is a great consolation: by means of it one gets successfully through many a bad night." Camus believed that the fundamental question of philosophy is judging whether life is or is not worth living: "As soon as one does not kill oneself, one must keep silent about life. . . . If you are convinced of your despair, you must either act as if you did hope after all—or kill yourself. Suffering gives no rights."[23]

Suffering gives Marais no rights, but he does not keep silent about his life either. Rather, he projects his suffering into his writing. Instead of silence, he ultimately chooses Camus's other alternative. After Marais departs Steenkampskraal, a text superimposed upon the screen reads, "Ten years later, on the farm 'Pelindaba' in the Pretoria District of the Transvaal, Eugène Marais, suffering acutely again from withdrawal symptoms, shot himself." (79) Even within the time scheme of the film he seems to yearn for self-destruction or, at least, to be incapable of avoiding it. Marais craves immediate gratification, perhaps because he has faith in nothing else. As he says to Doorsie, "My mother died in my arms. Just before the end there was an expression . . . a look in her eyes. I asked her what it was she saw. She said . . . 'Nothing. There is nothing.' " (68)

It took Devenish two-and-a-half years to raise the money for the film, but throughout this period—both while writing *Dimetos* and while reworking it for the second production—Fugard continued working on the script, which was restructured five times. According to Devenish, the funding crisis "was quite beneficial for the film itself, because it gave time for the idea to ferment. If you look at the scripts, the original one was not as good as the final one we used."[24] Principal filming lasted seven weeks and was finished in September 1976. Fugard himself played Marais and considered it "possibly the most demanding and challenging role I have ever attempted." (9-76)

The Guest was aired by the BBC on March 5, 1977, and was awarded two prizes the following month at the Locarno Film Festival: one for Devenish's direction and another for Fugard's performance. Although *The Guest* was ready for distribution that April, including a print dubbed into Afrikaans, it was not generally released until the following September.

The Blood Knot marked Fugard's emergence as a major writer as well as the beginning of a truly significant South African theatre. *The Guest* was a similar milestone for the South African cinema. The reviews boasted, "At Last a South African Masterpiece," "A Giant Leap for South African Films," and "Easily Best S.A. Film Ever Made."[25]

Coleridge claims that "deep thinking is attainable only by a man of deep feeling." Nietzsche adds, "The tragic artist is not a pessimist—it is precisely he who *affirms* all that is questionable and terrible in existence."[26] Both statements apply as much to Fugard as to his protagonist in *The Guest*.

Both Marais's poems and his writings on animals argue that his suffering, even his final fate, was perfectly natural. The nature referred to in the titles of Fugard's next two works is not as harsh and permits survival, at least for a time.

VII

Surviving a Drought

Tales easily understood are not well told.   —Bertolt Brecht

Throughout most of Fugard's career, he has created a daily routine for his writing. While living with his parents in their cramped Bird Street apartment, the routine included a late-night walk down Bird Street and around St. George's Park. In June 1964 he moved to Skoenmakerskop, seven miles down the coast from Port Elizabeth. The cottage was named The Haven and Fugard lauded its "view of the sea and the silence and privacy I've wanted so long. I feel ready for work." (6-64) A few months later he bought the little house, which he had only been renting: "My mom helped us out to organize a little building society bond." Fugard built himself a garden shed "that became my sort of private world." Even after the Fugards moved in 1974 to The Ashram, their seven acres on Sardinia Bay, "the shed" stuck as the family name for the place Fugard writes. "It sounds less pretentious than 'studio,' " he says. The phrase also conjures up a place for arduous labor.

At Skoenmakerskop, a typical day of writing was structured around his daughter: "I'm not the most strong-willed person and Lisa's school-going created a nice discipline. I'd get up, make breakfast, and take her to school, which meant I'd be back home by 8:30. I'd then work straight through the morning until stopping to putter about the garden, plant a tree, care for the animals, and take a nap. I'd write again at night. The morning writing would be very disciplined, but at night I'd just let it rip. I found this routine seriously disrupted when Lisa's schooling came to an end."

Fugard's regimen now includes weekly fishing trips and regular bicycle expeditions of forty to fifty kilometers. The writing day itself is dictated by an old clock, handmade in London by Charles Frodsham: "By noon, I've finished my morning session and Sheila's finished her morning session, and we sit in the shade of one of our trees, drink a little bit of white wine, and watch the birds. That's all the drinking I do until Charles Frodsham says its six o'clock and I can have my one whiskey and a couple of carafes of red wine and supper. When I'm working, I don't smoke a single cigarette. I just stay with my pipes."[1] Wine and whiskey, rather than gambling, had been the manifestations of Fugard's "addictive personality," as he called it before writing The Guest, but since January 1, 1983, he has given up alcohol.

As he begins a new play and must start to write a new character, Fugard says, "I walk around like a cripple. Then the accident happens. It comes at one line which I just know is right out of a character's mouth, and it's like having a tuning fork. It gives me absolute pitch in terms of that character, and whenever I'm in doubt about my character I look at that line again. I get its rhythm, I feel the way it's structured, why it fits his mouth so well. I think the same thing operates for an actor."[2] Sometimes Fugard uses another image to describe his writing—that of taking out his characters and winding them up to see what they will do that day. Early in his career he worked with charts while writing a play: "There would be a column for external events, a column, say, for Boesman and key words in terms of his responses to the external event, and another column for Lena and her response to external events—and her response to Boesman's response. I don't do that kind of charting now at all."

Some of Fugard's projects have germinated for years, but however long this gestation lasts, he says that, "Upon sitting down to put pen to paper I take about a year, sometimes nine months. My formula has always been, 'Once upon a time there was . . .' . " When he first makes a commitment to writing something new, he adds, "I'm seized with a terrible, really frightening impatience to get it down because everything I write and think relates to the play I'm on at the moment. It's got to be seen now, you know, not next year. There might be a different society next year." The collaborative works, of course, evolved differently, and each play has been subject to adjustment in the rehearsal room. Aside from his actors, however, Fugard admits, "I've never listened to anybody's advice. Never. I operate totally out of something inside myself."[3] Sheila does not see the plays until they are in production, and, Fugard says, "the same goes for me with her writing." During production periods, of course, Fugard adheres to a rehearsal rather than a writing schedule.

The writing of *A Lesson from Aloes* took much longer than Fugard's usual nine months to a year. Observations that would become part of the play date back to February 1961, and over the next ten years Fugard made several attempts to write it. After working on it for four weeks in 1966, he noted, "Most worrying of all is a lethargy and prosaicness in my thinking. I am skating on the surface, instead of sounding its depth." (11-66) In 1970 he noted, "as conceived so far, the characters are too 'helplessly innocent,' too passively victimized by the situation I've created." (6-70)

Another attempt miscarried in 1971 and Fugard abandoned the idea, he thought forever. Like most writers he has been blocked from time to time, and in 1977 noted, "These past months I have been trying to live through one of the most intensely experienced crises of my life. If Sheila and Lisa were to read that sentence they would stare at me in amazement, so effective has been the disguise of my inner agony, my death in life. As I write this I still see no light. But maybe tomorrow. . . . Who knows. The 'crisis' is, quite simply, the total extinction of my creativity. Without it I find living a pain I can only describe as intolerable. I have feared for my sanity." (5-77)

Whose Home?: *A Lesson from Aloes*

My country doesn't need me. I need my country.   —Athol Fugard

Five months later, the idea of *Aloes* returned to Fugard yet again. The following March he noted, "I've got an appointment that I really must keep. Something that I've been thinking about for a long time. . . . It's entrenched in the life of South Africa. . . . They'll be able to put me back in the pigeonhole. P. for politics."[4] By July of 1978, fourteen months after his "crisis," he had finished a rough version of the play.

The plot of *Aloes*, which is far more convoluted than any of Fugard's others, runs as follows: Sitting outside their humble Port Elizabeth home in 1963, Afrikaner Piet Bezuidenhout and his English-speaking wife Gladys await a visit from Piet's old friend and political ally, Steven Daniels, and his family. They are Coloured. Gladys wonders why none of the old comrades has visited over the past six months since her return from a place not yet specified. Piet insists the police raids following Steve's arrest and the banning of the congress to which they had both belonged are probably the reason. After recounting the midnight raid by the Security Branch police who had read and removed her diaries, Gladys admits that she fears they will return. She has spent the day trying to hide her current diary. Piet recounts the time he first met Steve, during a bus boycott, then reveals Steve's plan to leave South Africa for England. Piet acknowledges that others seem to suspect that he is the one who informed on Steve.

Act Two opens two hours later. Piet has given up hope that Steve will ever arrive, but at last he does—without his family. The friends swap stories until Steve, responding to Gladys' prompting, asks if Piet were in fact the one who had betrayed him to the police. Instead of denying the accusation, Piet insists he has nothing to say. After having led Steve to believe that Piet really was the informer, Gladys admits that she lied and proclaims that Steve is not the only one who has been victimized. She retires to her bedroom, and Piet explains that following the raid and the loss of her diaries she had become paranoid and was admitted to a clinic. After Steve departs uneasily, Piet comforts Gladys. She reveals that her diary is entirely blank and that she must return to the clinic.

Despite some recurrent elements from past plays and Fugard's reliance again upon only three characters, *Aloes* is much different from his previous plays. There are few of the usual verbal flourishes and, most important of all, the play's scope is narrower and its meaning more obvious than had been his habit.

Gladys's first line, "I'm awake," (3*)[5] reflects her state of mind. She is utterly lucid most of the time despite her emotional illness. Her persistent probing uncovers secrets and lies. She believes the truth is purgative; her credo is "it's better to have these things out in the open." (70) By the end of the evening she admits her own lies and deceptions and elicits those of Piet and Steve.

Piet is more resigned and accepting than Gladys. The truth he seeks is simple and factual. As the play opens he is trying to identify the species of one of the aloes he keeps as a hobby. Names are more than labels for Piet. Knowing the right one makes him feel more at home in the world. Naming is epistemological for Piet, as it had been for Boesman; it is the way he knows and understands.

Fugard considers having a name one of the crucial facts of existence, and he admits, "I've often thought about how unique an identity is."[6] Queeny tries to hide the name that describes her past; Tsotsi recovers his name; Hester is missing the meaning of hers; Robert Zwelinzima gives his up; and Philander sees himself as a man without a name. *Aloes* is, in part, an extended definition of the identity of an aloe and its lesson. The play also questions whether or not the name "informer" should be applied to Piet. Among other things, of course, an informer names names.

In Gladys's mind, Piet's name has a strong, "earthy" sound. Although he lives in the city now, Piet's thoughts frequently return to the farm he was forced to leave because of drought. Nurturing plants is one link to farming, so are the aloes themselves, which survived the drought Piet himself could not. Despite moving to the city, the drought in Piet's personal life had continued until he met Steve. Fugard calls this meeting "the one miracle in Piet's life." It was, says

---

*All quotes are from *A Lesson from Aloes* (New York: Random House, 1981).

Piet, "like rain after a drought." (42) Steve's tie to the sea is as strong as Piet's to the land.

Like his father before him, Steve is forced to leave a home that has shaped his identity. Despite all he has suffered, Steve's bond to South Africa is as visceral as Piet's, a fact which Gladys is slow to comprehend. She assures him that he is fortunate to be leaving, but Steve has doubts. Packing for the trip has prompted him to examine his roots, even to the point of working out his exact relationship to a simple-minded aunt, "my father's brother-in-law's sister-in-law." (63) Steve demands that Piet explain the reasons he, Steve, is emigrating, perhaps because he is not so sure himself. He hides his ambiguous feelings behind his blustering insistence that he has paid his debts in full and owes his country nothing. Piet perceives what his friend may not: "You're arguing with yourself, Steve." (67) Steve hopes Piet really was the informer because it will be "easier going next week . . . if I can throw away our friendship like all that junk on my lounge floor." (73)

Steve's exile is only technically voluntary: He is forced to leave because he cannot earn a living. Idle for four years, his hands have become softer than his wife's. Holding them up he says, "They might as well fall off for all they mean in my life now." (67) Steve's empty hands are not as powerful an image as Dimetos's, but they do represent both his loss of self-sufficiency and one kind of emasculation. The police had taunted him with the more literal kind after he had tried to hide an erection. Their threat of actual castration had been followed by figurative ones, prompting Steve to consider suicide: "They had laughed at my manhood and every reason I had for diving out of that window." (72) Along with the use of his hands, Steve has lost the sense of purpose that had given his life meaning. During internment he had tried to determine, vainly, what he had ever accomplished to make it all worthwhile.

Gladys has no sense of purpose either. At the time she had met Piet, she recalls, "Nothing seemed more without purpose than the Gladys Adams I looked at in the mirror." (23) The first time she and Piet had been together he had quoted Thoreau: "There is a purpose to life, and we will be measured by the extent to which we harness ourselves to it." (22) For a time, Piet had rescued Gladys from an isolated, arid life as numbing as that of Camus's stranger. She had written in her first diary, "My mother died today. I haven't cried yet and I don't think I'm going to." (23)

Steve and Gladys share more than a loss of purpose, although he does not recognize their kinship until she confronts him with her pain: "Politics and black skins don't make the only victims in this country." (74) Gladys's victimization is horribly ironic since she had never been enthusiastic about "The Cause." Nevertheless, she has suffered at least as much as Steve: Her symbolic rape (the seizing and reading of her diaries) is countered by his symbolic castration; electroshock therapy is as horrific as police torture; Steve's imprisonment is mirrored by her hospital confinement; the normal lives of both have been destroyed. Their status at the end of the play is also similar; Fugard notes, "Steve's going to take a physical journey out; Gladys is going to travel into herself."[7]

Piet, on the other hand, has maintained both his faith in Thoreau's words and his sense of purpose. He refuses Steve's toast to "a lost cause." It is Piet's unassailable faith in himself that immunizes him from assault and gives him the strength of character to refuse to respond to Steve's suspicion that he is the informer.

Gladys's reasons for exciting Steve's suspicion may be jealousy of a friendship whose easy intimacy she and Piet have never quite enjoyed, but when she apologizes for wrecking everything, Piet replies, "There was nothing left to wreck." (77) His denial seems paradoxical since he has esteemed the friendship so highly. However, once Steve's mistrust is manifest, it is clear to Piet that more than the foundation of their friendship has been cracked; the mistrust destroys whatever might have been. As Dimetos says, "Desertion does more than just terminate a loyalty, Sophia. It makes a lie of whatever loyalty there had been." (15) Because of this mistrust, because "there was nothing left to wreck," Piet refuses to allay Steve's suspicion.

Piet is the common figure in the play's two relationships, a friendship and a marriage, but Fugard considers Gladys the center of *Aloes*. His initial attempts to write the play failed as long as he perceived Piet at the center: "There were no ambiguities in Piet's experience—however dramatic that had been. . . . Now, if *Aloes* does work, it works because at the center of the play is an experience that is full of dark ambiguities, and that is the experience of Gladys—her whole relationship to South Africa. It is *her* play."[8]

The police raid had been horrible, but, as Fugard says, "All my characters are moving toward self-realization. If there had been no raid, Gladys's sense of self, her recognition of herself, would have been different. Subsequent to it, she achieves self-realization of a much higher order." Her transformation is not entirely bleak: She finally admits precisely what had transpired at the clinic; she stops hiding from Piet the fact that her diary is blank and thereby reveals that words have failed her as they have him; and she will return to the clinic voluntarily. Finally acknowledging her secret temptation to turn her violence against herself, Gladys will at least, like the aloe, continue to live. Her lesson and that of the entire play is survival.

Fugard had been drawn to the subject before. Benson reports that "survival" is his favorite word. Asked to describe the common theme of *Sizwe Bansi*, *The Island*, and *Statements*, he replied, "Survival, a question of surviving a very harsh and very mutilating environment."[9] Never before, however, had he depicted three distinct modes of survival nor brought together in a single play members of three of South Africa's population groups. At a certain level, Piet, Steve, and Gladys are allegorical representatives of all Afrikaners, Coloureds, and English-speakers. Fugard uses double and triple points of view in the many stories the three tell about their pasts. These stories reach the audience through a prism of perspectives, a different one for each character on stage. While all the stories provide narrative information, they never do only this since the intimate revelations sometimes expose the person addressed as much as the person telling the story. In addition, a character's story is sometimes directed to himself (rather than to anyone else on stage) and thereby becomes a form of interior monologue. For example, Piet's story of how he met Steve is surely one Gladys has heard many times before. Realistically, he need not go into such detail to refresh her memory, but Piet is actually talking to himself more than to Gladys, as if to reassure himself that his current drought may also end. (The vividness with which he portrays Steve also heightens the audience's eagerness to meet him.) Similarly, when Gladys tells Steve she has been to England many times, she is not so much lying to him as enacting a wish fulfillment.

Except for Gladys's recounting of the time she had met Piet and her narration of the raid, her stories and Piet's center on moments they did not share—a subtle reflection of both the state of their marriage and the isolation they feel. Piet had been alone in his room after leaving the farm; Gladys had been isolated in the clinic to which she will return; Steve's banning had limited his association with others and his internment had imposed even greater solitude. *Aloes* ends with yet another image of isolation: While Steve trudges back to Gelvandale, Gladys is alone in her bedroom and Piet by himself in his yard. The betrayal of the informer has transformed the public lives of Piet and Steve and infected them and their families with suspicion and fear. Two loving relationships, a friendship and a marriage, have been permanently altered.

After completing a rough draft of *Aloes* in July 1978, Fugard immediately selected Marius Weyers and Shelagh Holliday as Piet and Gladys. Steve proved difficult to cast, but Fugard eventually chose Paul Jacobs. However, shortly before the November 30 opening at Johannesburg's Market Theatre, Fugard stepped into the role himself. (Only a few months earlier he had said, "I think my days of acting are over now. I do not have the discipline to act seriously."[10]) *Aloes* was next performed at Montreal's The Centaur in January 1980 and then in New Haven, Connecticut, opening March 28, 1980 at the Yale Repertory Theatre. (Fugard was then on a semester-long fellowship from the Yale University-Wesleyan University Southern African Research Program.) His Yale production with Harris Yulin, Maria Tucci, and James Earl Jones proved so popular that it moved to New York that spring. The South African production opened in London at the Cottesloe to mixed reviews on July 10, 1980.

Fugard says of *Aloes*, "I draw no comparisons, but I would like to believe

I am keeping company with a certain sort of Chekhovian approach to the theatre." He does not think he has been imitative of Chekhov, "but rather through an inevitable progression on my side, I've had recourse to dialogue in which the most important things being said on stage are not being said with words."[11] The New York Drama Critics Circle named *Aloes* "Best Play" in 1981, but it is significantly weaker than Fugard's other mature work, let alone comparable to Chekhov.

Aloes is the most intricately plotted of Fugard's plays and the only one in which narrative revelations assume great importance. Generally, Fugard poses postulates to be queried rather than questions to be answered factually, but by the end of *Aloes* those questions that are raised are resolved. Furthermore, questions such as what happened to Gladys, whether or not Piet is the informer, and why Steve is leaving, rouse compassion and puzzle-solving curiosity, but they are not as engaging or disturbing as Lena's ontological questions or Dimetos's compulsion to fathom his empty hands. In short, psychological and intellectual ambiguity give way to narrative fact. The reliance of *Aloes* upon unraveling secrets makes it the closest thing to a melodramatic mystery Fugard has ever written. It leaves an impression of cool manipulation by an omniscient author who fetters his characters to a very short leash as he simply re-orders those narrative puzzle pieces he had scrambled at the start.

The lesson of the aloe is equally disappointing. In his previous work Fugard had imbued selected objects with a complex of meanings: Morrie's alarm clock and suit of clothes, Shorty's silkworms, the boxes Hester and Johnnie unpack, Sizwe Bansi's passbook and photograph, Dimetos's ropes and hands. The aloe is more prosaic than any of these; additional resonances do not accrue to it through the course of the play. As a symbol, it is utilitarian—like the plant itself— but it has no beauty. The aloe is too simple a symbol to bear the weight expected of it since it has no meaning outside of its ability to survive a harsh environment. Instead of being evocative, it is demonstrative.

Fugard realizes that in *Aloes*, "One has to look underneath the relative domesticity of the seemingly bland surface, underneath the level of the dialogue to find the event: the action and the movement and the shift of tensions."[12] Indeed, there are some muted moments throughout the play that demonstrate his mature craftsmanship: the revelation of part of Piet's character through his habit of either ignoring difficult questions or trying to change the subject; his wordless yet heartfelt disappointment at the beginning of Act II when it seems that Steve will not arrive—which effectively sets up the infectious comraderie his subsequent appearance instigates; the residual charisma in Steve that convinces an audience he truly had been a political leader; the awkward formality of Gladys's relationship with him as suggested by her persistence in calling him "Steven" until her final goodbye.

However, these are minor accomplishments. The look beneath the domesticity and flat dialogue of *Aloes* is not sufficiently rewarding. The play's pace is glacial until Steve's arrival in Act II. He injects vitality and humor and raises the level of domestic conversation, but the disparate energy levels of the two acts make them appear to belong in different plays. Instead of developing inevitable momentum from the first scene on, *Aloes* stops and starts until the last third of the second act when, at last, sufficient history of the characters has been seeded, and they can battle one another without restraint or self-evident calculation.

While struggling to get the play right in one of its early forms, Fugard noted, "An aggravating factor is the more blatant politics of this idea—and the bellyful of clichés about S.A. that I've got to vomit out of my system before I can start writing meaningfully."[13] However hard he might have tried, these elements were neither evacuated nor made less blatant.

Given apartheid's entrenchment, it seems harsh to call any dramatization of the human toll it exacts clichéd, but the lesson of *Aloes* is not fresh. Instead of offering new perceptions, or casting the old truisms in fresh language or form, Fugard relies upon assertions that are embarrassing not because they are untrue, but because they have become banal. Piet explains his first and most important lesson from Steve: "Bad laws and social injustice are man-made and can be unmade by men. It's as simple as that. We can make this a better world to live in."(35) (None of Fugard's other characters is so optimistic.)

In the first scene Gladys complains that a conversation with Piet has become a catalogue of South African disasters. *Aloes* becomes one too. Fugard had often exploited these disasters previously, but never as both means and end nor in quasi-catalogue form. *Aloes* is a parable delivered as a sermon. Even the mildly fresh statement that whites can suffer as much as blacks and Coloureds smacks of piety. The play's very title betrays its didactic nature.

Fugard reconceived the center of the play, at least for himself, when he decided Gladys's situation was more ambiguous than Piet's, but *Aloes* is unambiguous and Gladys's quandary is more limited and less compelling than that of any of Fugard's other protagonists. Although pathology is not Fugard's primary subject, her plight can be attributed to *it* rather than to conditions suffered by every man. Gladys's innocent victimization makes her pathetic rather than heroic. Morphine addiction is also a pathological condition, but Fugard's use of it in *The Guest* is entirely different. It is a given aspect of Marais rather than a secret climactically revealed. Moreover, the film does not emphasize the addiction itself so much as the consuming pain Marais suffers—a pain that, not coincidentally, is universal whereas Gladys's victimization is narrowly South African.

Six months after the American premiere of *Aloes*, Fugard stated, "I'm tired. I must be ruthless and make no accommodation. I want to cut down to the bare bleached bone without any meat on it." An artist's desire for purity and refinement is problematic only when too much is cut away or too little exists to begin with, when bare becomes barren. The bones of *Aloes* are not nourishing enough.

In a climactic moment Piet says, "I've got nothing to say." (71) In *Aloes*, Fugard has too little to say, and says even that too baldly. Instead of evolving with organic ease, *Aloes* gives the impression of having been forced into being. Given its history of aborted early drafts, this may be the reason it exists at all.

The completion of all of Fugard's work has depended, he says, "on a correspondence, a relevance, between the external specifics of the play—the 'story' as such—and my sense of myself at the time." (xiii) He also notes, "In the plays that come out of my own private relationship with paper, the seminal idea, the seminal image, has always been autobiographical."[14]

This is especially true of *Aloes*. Fugard admits, "A hell of a lot of me is invested in the character of Piet Bezuidenhout. I know that now, after the event. I was never conscious of it while I was writing."[15] Piet is pure Afrikaner; Fugard calls himself a bastardized Afrikaner whose Afrikaner mother was the dominant cultural influence in his life: "My essential response to South Africa at its most meaningful level is that of an Afrikaner." *Aloes* bears the dedication "In celebration of Elizabeth Magdalena Potgeiter," who died in 1980, shortly before the play's American premiere.

After moving from the Bird Street flat to Skoenmakerskop, Fugard wrote Mary Benson on December 12, 1964, "I've never realized fully how much of an Afrikaner I really am, until this moment when I kicked off my shoes and stood barefoot on the earth. I keep looking at my toes to see if roots haven't appeared. All this plus the sea—an even greater passion that the earth." Fugard has never had to endure droughts as severe as Piet's, but at the Ashram he is totally dependent on rainwater.

Fugard recognizes a number of similarities between himself and Piet: "I certainly love my country in the same way he does. I share his sense of commitment, and I share his passion for naming all aspects of that little part of the world. I also like to know the names of the aloes growing on my little bit of land."[16] His notebook descriptions of the coast, of shell-collecting, and of fishing suggest that his link to nature, especially the sea and sun, is umbilical. His awe at the beauty of mating cobras became one of *Statements'* central images, and he is fond of walking local roads with Lisa to remove snakes that seek the warmth of the tarmac, thus preventing them from being crushed by passing cars. As an actor, he handles snakes in both *The Guest* and *Marigolds in August*.

Fugard speaks of his land—not its government, laws, or values, but the physical place itself—as a Muscovite does of Mother Russia. His attachment to South Africa is as visceral as it is passionate. On the first night of his long hitch-hiking trip at age 21, the prospect of leaving home for the first time had filled him with panic and loneliness. Asked in 1963, the year in which *Aloes* is set, if he would leave the country should it turn into a "Second Algeria," Fugard became enormously depressed and wrote in his notebook, "We all live here loving and hating. To leave means that the hating would win—and South Africa needs to be loved now, when it is at its ugliest, more than at any other time. By staying I might be able to do this." (6-9-63) His perseverance was tested four years later when his passport was withdrawn, yet Fugard persistently holds that "the thought of leaving my country permanently was, and remains, intolerable."[17]

Fugard's bond to South Africa is also an artistic one since the creative stimulus of his writing depends on his continued residence there. He says, "My essential identity is that of a writer. Since I can't write outside South Africa that identity always ends up being a little undernourished when I'm away." Emigré writers have been so common over the last century that with only some exaggeration they might be called the norm: from Ibsen, Conrad, James, Pound, Eliot, and Joyce to Beckett and Solzhenitzyn. Fugard's 1959 trip to Europe had been short-lived, but even at home he lives, like Genet, outside the mainstream of his society, a kind of exile in his own land.

Like Piet, Fugard has also been suspected of being an informer—or so the Security Branch police have tried to make him believe. Attempting to put a wedge between him and Kani and Ntshona, the S.B. has related Fugard township stories supposedly told by Kani and Ntshona that cast suspicion on him. Like many South Africans, he has often been in the company of suspected informers. In the early 1960s the Fugards attended a gathering of politically minded friends, among them the real Steve Daniels, who had broken his banning order to attend. After the S.B. arrived and arrested the man, those who remained "knew that one of us was most probably an informer and had tipped off the police before hand. Most people settled on the wrong man."[18] At least one Serpent Players session entirely devoted to discussing informers, "brought Piet very vividly to mind." (6-10-70) At another time Fugard worked with Kani and Ntshona on an improvised piece called The Informer.

Fugard's identification with Piet is not complete. He says, "I wish I were like Piet. He's a good man." Fugard thinks he himself is not. He contends that his best attributes are to be found in his writing.

The similarities between Fugard and Piet are not the only autobiographical aspects of Aloes. During rehearsal for the South African premiere, Fugard explained that he had used his own experience of a Security Branch search rather than the one Piet had actually endured: "Four of them trooped in and went through the house. One of them sat down and was, in fact, the first person to read Sheila's poetry." Like Gladys, Sheila Fugard had also suffered a nervous breakdown. Fugard alluded to it in rehearsal when he explained that he knew from personal experience that Piet would watch Gladys every second, "because if there is anything he can do to prevent it happening a second time, he will do it. . . . Also, it's something he mustn't let her know he's doing. He must keep it very secret because people in Gladys's condition pick it up very quickly and resent it and hate it."[19]

Given the process of refraction through which every writer distills and manipulates personal experience to make it fit his work, Gladys should not be equated with Sheila nor should the Bezuidenhout marriage be equated with that of the Fugards. Fugard cites one of the changes he made in the character of Piet, whose real-life model kept a fish pond with plastic fish, lilies and octopuses. After Fugard asked him, "Why not real ones?," Piet had replied, "I want no more responsibilities for living creatures." "For me as a writer," Fugard explains, "this was a dead end. I had to shift to aloes. Now there's a slender vestige of hope."

A final autobiographical element of *Aloes* is associated with Steve's sense of emasculation, which has a number of antecedents in Fugard's work. Zach says, "Two legs and trousers, I'm a man;" (12) Sizwe adds, "I'm a man. I've got legs;" (35) and Philander experiences figurative castration during which he loses his legs. This leitmotif might be interpreted as a metaphor for the treatment of South Africa's blacks and Coloureds, but standing on his father's crutches, Johnnie Smit is also an image of emasculation—as well as a clue to Fugard's persistent interest in it. In his notebook he writes about his own father, "He started to say something then floundered and drowned in another flood of tears. He eventually got it out. 'Don't let them do anything to my leg. Don't let them take it off.' So that's it. Behind the bland, withdrawn expression, that is the terrror of the midnight hours—that the second leg, his final vestige of independence, of manhood, would go." (5-15-61) Manhood figures again prominently in his next work, *Marigolds in August*, as it had so often in the past.

Aloes is a weak play and an autobiographically oriented one, but no causal relationship necessarily exists between the two. Fugard's next play, *"Master Harold". . . and the boys*, is far better—and far more autobiographical.

August Postures: *Marigolds in August*

Your hands are dirty.
Better dirty than void.   —Bertolt Brecht

For his next project, originally titled *S'kop 5*, Fugard again collaborated with Ross Devenish to film an original screenplay. The script was written with John Kani and Winston Ntshona in mind, but when filming was first scheduled to begin they were not available. In October 1977, the money Devenish had raised fell through, as it did again in 1978, only four days before shooting was to commence. A year later Devenish scraped together the financing for a third try. (With a budget of only $150,000 at his disposal, Devenish refers to the film as "poor cinema," an echo of Grotowski.) This time Kani and Ntshona were able to play the parts intended for them, and Fugard played the other major role as the three acted together for the first time. Rehearsals began in May of 1979 and shooting in June. *Marigolds in August* was completed later that year and was first exhibited in 1980. As with *Aloes*, it won a number of awards but cannot be counted among Fugard's best works.

Marigolds centers on Daan, a black gardener and odd-job man whose territory in the white village of Skoenmakerskop outside Port Elizabeth is invaded by Melton, a black man looking for work. Daan chases him away, but Melton returns the next day. This time Daan pursues him into the bush and forces Melton to accompany him on a visit to Daan's Coloured friend, Paulus, who lives off the land. Paulus mediates between the two by getting Daan to understand Melton's plight, but when Daan offers one of his day jobs, Melton refuses; this does not solve his long-term problem of supporting his family. Instead, he steals food from a shop in the S'kop neighborhood where Daan works.

For *The Guest* Fugard had "wanted very much to make a film that had its roots here, in the country in which it would be made." (8) The same was true for *Marigolds*: "There is a gross neglect of South African material by local moviemakers and imitation of foreign ideas in my country. This is one reason I like working with Ross. He has the courage to put the South African scene across honestly. Who else would put so much effort into making a movie about an ordinary black South African gardener? Ross has a way of getting the South African scene across like few others can."[20]

As in much of his previous work, Fugard knew his setting and characters intimately. He had lived in Skoenmakerskop, Melton had squatted on his land, (2-73) and he had employed the real Daan as a gardener: "He is one of the people I was destined to meet—without him I would not be the same person. To me, he is a great man—he has the stature of a Lear. The film's central theme is to present Daan, the mere laborer, the invisible black man, as the real human being he is—in all his complexity—to explore his situation, questions, conflicts and relations with his fellow men. It asks the question, 'If my life is OK, what do I do about somebody else's life? Where does my responsibility to other people end' "[21]

Fugard had posed this question in a number of plays and twice articulated it in prose. In an introduction to *The Blood Knot* he writes, "If there is a human predicament this is it. There is another existence and it feels, and I feel it feels, yet I am impotent."[22] In his notes on *Orestes* he adds: "the moment of discovery, of finding 'another,' is for me one of the absolutely elemental experiences in life. What after all does Heaven or Hell start and end with except the 'other'?" (4) The compression of the action of *Marigolds* into thirty-six hours and its concentration on only three characters are also reminiscent of Fugard's previous work. This time, as in *Sizwe Bansi*, man can do more than stand by and watch. Daan and Paulus do not physically assist Melton in the burglary, but they do offer their advice.

Marigolds opens with Daan embarking upon the six-mile trek from the Walmer location where he lives to S'kop. He is in his late forties, has a bad cough, and walks with a severe limp. No one offers him a lift, not even when he doffs his cap and smiles expectantly as a car stops to pick up a jogger. After finding a pair of spectacles with thick lenses, Daan shows them to a group of S'kop housemaids. One of them says pointedly, "Go put them back where you found them. Somebody is walking around blind." (21*) Daan's suspicion of Melton and his jealous protectiveness of his own turf make him, of course, blind to Melton's problems. The journey he courses in the film is towards understanding of "the other."

Fugard recalls, "Ross and I had long discussions about whether or not we actually wanted to see the world through those spectacles." They decided against using the optically distorted view of the glasses, but the world seen throughout the film from the perspective of Daan, Melton, and Paulus is distorted anyway, skewed by the sharp contrast between the standard of living of the whites and the harsh existence of Daan, Paulus, and especially Melton.

Instead of spectacles, Fugard and Devenish make effective use of windows, as they had in *The Guest*, and other panes of glass behind which the white world lives. The driver who picks up the jogger is heard, but she remains hermetically sealed within her sedan. Even when the car is viewed through the rear window she is entirely hidden by the headrest. Since Daan's territory is the garden rather than the inner precinct of the madam's house, he must eat his lunch straddling the doorway. When Melton knocks at a door seeking work, a white man appears behind it without ever opening it; his gestures through the window pane indicate that he has no work to offer, but his actual words cannot be heard.

In the next shot, Melton approaches a house in which four women playing cards are seen through a picture window. (Lisa and Sheila Fugard are among them.) Walking towards the window, Melton appears as a reflection in it. He hears the women's sedate music, but they do not respond to his attempt to gain their attention. Their obliviousness to his presence, to his very existence, is the most poignant moment in *Marigolds*; the reflection shot is the most interesting cinematographically.

The separation of black and white worlds is also evident when a white madam pays Daan one rand and a bottle of ship-sherry for his day's labor. Her voice is heard, but standing in her doorway as she reaches toward Daan, only her white hand is seen. Melton's burglary climaxes with the shattering of glass as he sweeps a collection of framed photographs onto the floor. One of these is of a wedding party in formal wear, a reminder of, and contrast to, Melton's own wife.

His odyssey had begun after the burial of one of his children when his wife had challenged him, "Find work, you're a man, why don't you do something." (22) This is one of a dozen references in the play to being a man, which is the

*All quotes from *Marigolds in August* (Johannesburg and Cape Town: Ad. Donker, 1982).

film's major theme, especially as it pertains to Daan's relationship with Melton, but also through the repeated appearance of three Xhosa boys, the abakwetha, who are living in the bush as part of their *rite de passage* to manhood. Daan admires Paulus for a number of reasons, including his fearlessness in handling the poisonous snakes he traps and sells, but when he first mentions him to one of the housemaids he says, "That's a man." (25) With a silly look of fawning admiration he also tells Melton that Paulus is a man and later concurs when Paulus intones, "To be a man! It's a big work, hey Daan." (54) Daan, like Melton, has "gone to the bush" as the abakwetha must; he is already a man as his culture defines it, but he must undergo a second ritualistic passage as he learns first to understand Melton's plight, then to help resolve it. Paulus serves as his mentor.

Whites in the film do not recognize the individuality or humanity of the blacks working for them, do not even comprehend the presence of "the other" or his feelings, but the same is true of Daan's relationship with Melton. Under Paulus's guidance, however, Daan eventually concludes, "Me and you. Ja! There is me, but there is also you." (52) He finally articulates the dilemma, but cannot yet resolve it.

Instead of accepting Daan's offer of a day's work, Melton surrenders his passivity and decides to take matters into his own hands by breaking into the shop. Because his passbook is not in order, Daan knows the burglary will lead to his own arrest when the police begin their questioning. The quarreling that ensues between him and Melton persists until Paulus invites the abakwetha to the fire: "Don't worry. There are no men here. Only whitemen's boys. Come and join us. Real men help each other. Real men don't laugh when somebody else is in trouble." (58)

The rest of the film is denouement: Daan warns Melton about a dog at the shop, and Paulus hands him a rock wrapped in cloth to break the window. Having learned to project himself into the dilemma of another man, Daan then identifies with a cobra and pays Paulus for its freedom as he releases it back into the bush. In contrast, Paulus reveals that he must leave the freedom of the bush because it has been declared a Nature Reserve. Despite the lightness of his complexion, Paulus will not try to pass for white as he once had. Daan realizes that he, Paulus, and Melton are all like marigolds planted in August, at the end of the South African winter when a hostile environment makes survival all but impossible. Following the burglary sequence, Daan shares with Paulus the spectacles he had found, and the two laugh uproariously as a quotation from Swedish poet Tomas Tranströmer is superimposed on the screen: "Two truths draw nearer each other. One comes from inside, one comes from outside, and where they meet we have the chance to see ourselves."

Marigolds received its first major screening in February 1980 at the Berlin Film Festival, but not without incident. The Soviet delegation, apparently unaware of Fugard's opposition to apartheid, protested the presence of a South African film, and Devenish withdrew its national designation. *Marigolds* subsequently won a Silver Bear award as a "stateless" production as well as Russian prizes for Fugard and Devenish. Following the deletion of expletives that the censor demanded, the film was released in South Africa where it won awards for best film, director, editor, and actor (Winston Ntshona as Daan). The London reviews following a July 1980 opening were also generally favorable.

Despite this positive reception, *Marigolds* is weaker than most of Fugard's previous works. He admits, "We found the metaphor and camera style for *The Guest.* I don't think we did for *Marigolds.*" Its shortcomings, however, are not primarily cinematographic. Cross-references exist throughout Fugard's canon, but to anyone familiar with his previous work, *Marigolds* comes across as an encyclopedia of past images, themes, and perceptions that are recycled more out of habit than necessity. The presence of common elements in a number of works is as likely to indicate the consistency of a writer's vision as the bankruptcy of his imagination, but what had been insistently vital and evocative in Fugard's previous work is arbitrary and flat in *Marigolds.* What had been thematic continuity now seems mere repetition.

Some of this can be attributed to the persistence of certain problems in the daily lives of the South African outcasts and underlings Fugard so frequently depicts. Melton has as much trouble finding work as Sizwe had; Boesman and Lena, Steve Daniels's father, and Melton have all been forced from their homes; Daan is likely to be implicated in a burglary just as Boesman, equally innocent, had feared he would be accused of Outa's death; the fact that laughter so threatens one's manhood (whether it be Boesman's, Steve Daniels's, or Melton's), is a telling indictment of a society in which men are frequently treated as boys. Infant mortality had been horrifically evoked in both *Boesman and Lena* and *Aloes;* the film medium gave Fugard an opportunity actually to depict a child's burial. Being a man had been as important to Sizwe Bansi as it is to Daan and Melton, but in the earlier work Fugard had not sounded this note with such clarion insistence or, at least, there were enough overtones in any given scene or speech so that no single assertion seemed baldly tendentious.

Had *Marigolds* been written by Lohta Draguf, to whom Fugard had suggested ascribing *Dimetos,* such comparisons could not be made. Even in isolation, however, *Marigolds* is wanting. In his role as mentor, Paulus must understand much that Daan does not. Nevertheless, he is far too sage and seems to have walked into the film not from the bush but from a Dale Carnegie course. Nor is *Marigolds* distinguished by a light touch. For every moment of subtlety—such as the barely audible tinkling piano scales, presumably from a white child, as Daan and a maid converse—there are two others in which Fugard and Devenish give the audience emotional marching orders—such as when Melton chases a monkey from a trash can so he can scavenge in it for food. The leaden obviousness of such moments undermines their truth.

Marigolds succeeds in creating compassion and pity for the desperate lives of Daan, Paulus, and Melton as well as understanding of the "crime" Melton commits. The external authenticity of the film makes it almost seem to be *cinéma vérité*, but this same quality also has a distancing effect. *Marigolds* simply documents the sociological and psychological reality of three sorry men instead of universalizing that reality. The characters of Fugard's previous work generally face dilemmas of every man, but in *Marigolds* this generalizing principle breaks down. It is a passive portrait that fails either to involve or implicate an audience because it is too much about "them," too little about us.

Marigolds is so direct, simple, and without nuance that it also seems crude. Fugard had hoped to present Daan "in all his complexity," but instead, *Marigolds* is literal and self-explanatory. Many of its failings are similar to those of *Aloes*. Perhaps, therefore, they portend a shift not so much in Fugard's skill as in his intentions. Metaphor, connotation, and heightened language have given way to denotation, explication, and flattened prose. Like *Aloes*, *Marigolds* is so naked it does not bear up to repeated exposures. Even if its naïveté is intentional, the final artifact is jejune.

Fathers and Son
"Master Harold"... *and*
the boys

"Trash is what people is dat puts dirt on de head er dey fren's en makes 'em ashamed.". . .
It was fifteen minutes before I could work myself up to go and humble myself to a nigger; but I done it, and I warn't ever sorry for it afterward, neither. I didn't do him no more mean tricks, and I wouldn't done that one if I'd 'a' knowed it would make him feel that way.   —Mark Twain

Fugard's next play was a five-minute mime commissioned by the Actors Theatre of Louisville for its annual festival of new plays. It was part of *The America Project*, an evening of short plays on America by foreign playwrights. *The Drummer* captures a moment in the life of an urban bum who discovers a pair of drumsticks as he works his way through a pile of rubbish. Surrounded by the noises of the city, he begins to tap the sticks idly on a trashcan lid. As he becomes engrossed in his drumming, he first empties the can, then turns it upside down to make it reverberate even more. Holding his drumsticks at the ready, "He chooses a direction and sets off to take on the city. He has discovered it is full of drums . . . and he has got drumsticks."* Fugard's only other extended use of mime occurs at the beginning and end of *The Island*.

In an introductory note to his three pages of stage directions, Fugard describes the model for *The Drummer*, whom Fugard had seen only once, in Times Square: "He was moving effortlessly through the congested traffic beating out a tattoo with a pair of drumsticks on anything that came to hand. . . . He wasn't beg-

*For the complete text see Appendix A.

184

ging. In fact in his relationship to the world around him the roles of giver and receiver seemed to be just the reverse. He was very joyous . . . defiantly so! . . . and seemed to have a sense of himself as being extravagantly free."

Fugard completed the play in 1979. In his undated cover letter to ElizaBeth King, Louisville's literary manager, he wrote, "Enclosed with this letter is a response to the intimidating invitation from the Actors Theatre which reached me via my good friend and agent, Esther Sherman. If it means nothing to you please do not hesitate to crumple it up and throw it into your wastepaper basket. I will be the first to understand. . . . My mandate to the actor is simple . . . find two drumsticks and with the help of those find first joy, and then courage."

Fugard's uncertainty about the piece, which he considered calling *The Beginning*, proved to be unfounded. *The Drummer* was first performed by Dierk Toporzysek, under the direction of Michael Hankins, on February 27, 1980. In contrast to *Dimetos*, Fugard's only other commission, the reviews were largely enthusiastic. *The Drummer* was generally considered the best playlet in *The America Project*. It is the only one of his plays Fugard has never seen performed.

Asked if the exuberance of *The Drummer* marked a new direction in his writing, Fugard replied, "I think that actually from now on all I'm interested in is what I can celebrate. I've dealt with my pain. I've dealt with the misery of my county as much as I can. Now I'm just going to laugh and laugh and laugh and laugh." His prediction proved to be half right: In his next play, *"Master Harold". . . and the boys*, he continued to probe his own pain, more autobiographically than ever before, but he did so with more humor and laughter than in any previous work.

For fifteen years Fugard's mother had employed a man named Sam Semela at her Jubilee Boarding House and at the St. George's Park Tea Room. Fugard was especially fond of Semela, "But there was an ambivalence in my relationship with him: a love-hate thing. I couldn't come to terms with his difference. And as a little white boy, ten or eleven years old, I had authority over this powerful mature man of about twenty-eight." After a rare quarrel between them, precipitated by something now forgotten, Fugard began bicycling home, burning with resentment: "As I rode up behind him I called his name, he turned in mid-stride to look back and, as I cycled past, I spat in his face. Don't suppose I will ever deal with the shame that overwhelmed me the second after I had done that." (3-61)

Semela was Fugard's only friend from the age of six through secondary school: "It was a very close, shared, celebratory friendship—the man and the boy. Him being the man, incidentally." According to Fugard, Semela "radiated all the qualities a boy could look to and recognize as those of a man. I thought, 'I can model myself on that.' As I started reading, Sam started reading. He and I evolved theories, such as one about the shapes of good heads and bad heads, with such relish and enjoyment—things that a father and son should do."[1] After Fugard had finished reading a book, Semela would take it back to New Brighton to read himself.

Fugard has described the spitting incident in several interviews and had tried unsuccessfully for many years to write a play about Semela and another black waiter who had worked for his mother. *Master Harold* finally began to take shape after Fugard added an adolescent white boy to the scenario. In a letter dated October 8, 1981, a few days after completing "a reasonably substantial second draft," he expressed his satisfaction when, "I wrote the last words, a stage-direction . . . *[The men dance!]* . . . and then predictably a period of self-doubt. That always happens." *Master Harold* is a long one-act, but when Fugard wrote that it was not a "big" play, he did not mean its length: "There are none of the resonances of *Aloes*, for example. In fact I'm tempted to subtitle it: A Personal Memoir. If it succeeds at all I think 'poignant' will be the right adjective. It is also meant to have a lot of gentle humor. I faced the writing of that with considerable trepidation. But bit by bit my touch came back and I now even find myself laughing at my own jokes. I do realize that that could possibly be the onset of senility."[2]

Master Harold is set in 1950 in the St. George's Park Tea Room. As Sam Semela helps Willie Malopo practice his steps for the upcoming ballroom dancing championship, they are joined by Hally, a precocious seventeen-year-old whose mother runs the tea room. He and Sam soon begin a variation on their favorite game—Hally teaching Sam. They also recall their comraderie of the past. Hally turns to an essay he must write, but the banter of Sam and Willie about the dancing championship interrupts his concentration until he realizes the championship itself could be the subject of his essay. Hally's excitement is demolished when he learns in a phone call from his mother that his alcoholic and crippled father has returned home from the hospital. Sam scolds Hally for his unfilial reaction to this news, and Hally responds savagely. He orders Sam to address him as "Master" Harold, then repeats one of his father's racist jokes, and finally spits in Sam's face. Before Hally heads home, Sam's ire subsides and his fatherly concern returns. He and Willie are left alone to dance together.

As might be expected, Fugard's twelfth full-length play shares many traits with his previous work. He again focuses upon an intense relationship and the impediments to it; happy memories quickly give way to the recovery of the past through its vivid re-creation; characters again play with the language they love; games are initiated and roles assumed; important offstage characters precipitate onstage action; hopes and dreams are entertained, then shattered; and a character's consciousness and self-awareness are deeply transformed. Fugard's finest work is extraordinarily simple, but never more so than *Master Harold*, whose central action is nothing more, apparently, than a brief eruption between a man and a boy.

Many writers begin their careers autobiographically and become more "objective" through time. For Fugard, the process has been the reverse. In his Township Trilogy of *No-Good Friday*, *Nongogo*, and *Tsotsi* he presents lives that were sympathetically imagined and authentically reinvented, but that were, of necessity, vicariously observed rather than directly lived. Fugard's own experiences clearly inform *The Blood Knot*, *Hello and Goodbye*, and *Boesman and Lena*, but none appropriates the drama of his own life as unabashedly as *Master Harold*. Like O'Neill before him, he uses his family not merely to lacerate it, but to exorcise his own furies. Even so, the action of *Master Harold* has a more cohesive form and clearer meaning than the actual events of Fugard's life because they have been ordered into a work of art rather than a precise historical recapitulation.

Hally is the audience's conduit into the emotional world of the play. His adolescent rebelliousness as he teeters on the fulcrum between childhood and adulthood is immediately and universally recognizable. However, far from glorifying his younger self, Fugard exposes Hally's condescension, conceit, self-pity, and general oblivion to these personal shortcomings. The intentional insults of the climax are subtly foreshadowed by the racist remarks Hally blithely makes throughout the play. These seem all the worse because they are so unthinking: spontaneous projections of his patronizing sensibility.

Despite his cocky, pseudo-intellectual pretensions, Hally takes genuine pleasure in sharing with Sam what he has just learned—whether it is mathematics, vocabulary words, history, literature, or geography. The exchanges between teacher and pupil early in the play establish their warmth and closeness. When Sam and Hally laugh at a common memory, the laugh becomes an emblem of all they have shared. Apparently, Hally has no friends his own age. Although the servant quarters at the Jubilee had been his home-within-a-home, his family-within-a-family, the Jubilee years "are not remembered as the happiest ones of an unhappy childhood." (24*) Were it not for Sam, Hally might have had no happy memories, but he does have one more special than all the rest—the day Sam gave him a kite.

The story of the kite is reminiscent of the reenacted car ride in *The Blood Knot*: a pivotal scene reaffirming the bond between a pair of characters by reminding them of a shared moment in the past. As a set piece, the kite story is as physically and emotionally palpable, joyous, and evocative as any scene Fugard has written. It is also a great deal more than a set piece. Hally thinks flying the kite must have appeared strange: "Little white boy in short trousers and a black man old enough to be his father flying a kite. It's not every day you see that." (31) This is the only time Hally even obliquely refers to Sam as if he were his

*All quotes are from *Master Harold". . . and the boys*, (New York: Alfred A. Knopf, 1982).

father, but the comparison exists throughout the play and has already been implied within this scene: Hally's initial fear of being mortified should others see him with Sam and the jerry-made kite has precisely the same roots as the embarrassment he has felt when his mother wears an evening gown. Such typically adolescent discomfort pales beside the public humiliation he had experienced while carrying his drunken father down a crowded Main Street. Sam recalls, "That's not the way a boy grows up to be a man! . . . But the one person who should have been teaching you what that means was the cause of your shame. If you really want to know, that's why I made you that kite. I wanted you to look up, be proud of something, of yourself." (58)

The story of the kite also reveals that Hally is a promising raconteur. He himself realizes it would make a nice short story, "The Kite-Flyers," if there were only a twist in the ending. (It turns out there had been a twist, but Sam had hidden it from Hally; Sam had left Hally alone on a bench at the time because it was whites-only.) Hally also thinks the kite incident could be the start of a novel called *Afternoons in Sam's Room* that would include other stories. He may also have a knack for yet another form of writing. After recalling the look and feel of Sam's room, he says, "Right, so much for the stage directions. Now the characters." (27)

Hally savors the taste of words, sometimes pretentiously, but always sincerely. His inventive mind is also evident in his approach to his school assignment. Instead of settling for a pedestrian topic, Hally's imagination, like Fugard's when he was a decade older, seizes the simple life around him and perceives the universal truths embodied by the concrete particulars in the lives of blacks.

As extraordinary as the story of the kite is, *Master Harold* contains another set piece equally vivid. This time it is Sam's turn to tell a story, and he etches a detailed portrait of the 1950 Eastern Province Open Ballroom Dancing Championships. Sam's utopian vision of the dance floor as the embodiment of an ideal life fills the budding writer with admiration; the idyllic dreamworld of a dance floor becomes a metaphor for a world without collisions. Hally subtitles his essay "Ballroom Dancing as a Political Vision."

The banter over the kite had ended when Hally's mother had phoned to say his father *might* come home. The phone rings a second time: His father *will* come home. The intoxicating trance of the imagined ballroom is destroyed by this intrusion of reality. The imagined world that Sam and Hally have created disintegrates. Hally might have predicted as much: "Just when things are going along all right, without fail someone or something will come along and spoil everything. Somebody should write that down as a fundamental law of the Universe. The principle of perpetual disappointment." (35) Even Hally, however, could not forsee the cataclysm about to follow.

The reverie of a world without collisions ends, and Hally tears up the notes for his essay. His father has returned home and so will he, but not as a supportive, rejoicing Neoptolemus. Hally says, "Home-sweet-fucking-home. Jesus, I hate that word." (51) (*Master Harold* is one of Fugard's few scripts not set in the place its characters call home.) Hally's disaffection is more than merely intellectual, and in an emotional outburst he names a new competition to replace that of the ballroom: "the All-Comers-How-To-Make-A-Fuckup-Of-Life Championships." (51) Sam admonishes Hally, "It's your father you're talking about," (52) but Hally responds with his own caution: "Leave me and my father alone." He refuses to heed his own warning.

Hally displaces the shame he feels toward his father and directs it at a safer object, Sam. As Hally's shame turns to rage, he repeatedly tries to bait Sam, but the older man's steadfast refusal to respond only makes the boy angrier. First, Hally insists that Sam remember he is "only" a servant. Then he demands that Sam address him as Willie does, with "Master." Although Sam addresses Hally's mother with an obsequious "Madam," he now vows to Hally, "If you make me say it once, I'll never call you anything else again." (54) Next, Hally repeats his father's joke about a "nigger's arse" not being "fair." Because of all the wordplay previously, there is no doubt that Sam understands the pun.

Finally, in a deft reversal of the expected dynamics of the situation, when Sam lowers his trousers to show just how "fair" his backside is, it is Sam who keeps his dignity and Hally who is made to feel ignominious. When he spits in Sam's face, desperately trying to save face and preserve his pride, Hally demeans only himself. Willie responds with "a long and heartfelt groan," an utterly appropriate response from the one character who lacks the facility with English possessed by the other two.

Sam knows that, "The face you should be spitting in is your father's," (56) and he restrains his instinct to hit Hally who is only, as Willie reminds him, "Little *white* boy. Long trousers now, but he's still little boy." (57) Sam's anger gives way to a sense of defeat and of the failure of the promise he had made to himself after carrying home Hally's drunken father—that Hally should not be ashamed of himself. Now Hally will be doubly ashamed: of his denial of his natural father and his betrayal of his surrogate one. He is ready to slink back home meekly.

Despite his previous vow, Sam addresses the boy informally: "I've got no right to tell you what being a man means if I don't behave like one myself, and I'm not doing so well at that this afternoon. Should we try again, Hally?" (59) Sam has done more than turned the other cheek. His generosity and plain humanity in offering Hally a second chance is an act of hope, not just for this black man and white boy but for all of estranged humanity.

Hally says that he oscillates "between hope and despair for this world," (15) but for the most part he manifests his despair. As the student exchanges roles with his teacher, Sam counsels him, "You don't *have* to sit up there by yourself. You know what that [whites-only] bench means now, and you can leave it any time you choose. All you've got to do is stand up and walk away from it." (59-60) Sam's challenge leaves Hally and the audience some hope, not of the collective consciousness and concerted action suggested by *Sizwe Bansi* and *The Island*, but of the possibilities of the individual human spirit and consciousness. Having instigated a cathartic eruption, it is Hally's choice either to come of age and be initiated as a man, or to remain a boy.

Sam and Hally are not entirely reconciled, but before heading home Hally begins to rise from his absolute nadir. For the audience, the emotional ascent continues as the jukebox, the only visually exciting object in the spartan cafe, comes to life with the Maurice Sigler and Al Hoffman song, "Little Man, You've Had a Busy Day."[3] *Master Harold* opens with Sam and Willie alone on stage, and so it ends as they dance together, a final image of harmony among men. Gliding across the floor, the pair embody Sam's earlier advice: "The secret is to make it look easy. Ballroom must look happy Willie, not like hard work." (5)

The same is true of Fugard's craft in this compact, simple, and powerful drama. Following as it does the severely flawed *Aloes* and *Marigolds*, *Master Harold* is a convincing answer to those who might have predicted the erosion of Fugard's skill and power.

Fugard says of the play, "I was dealing with the last unlaid ghost in my life, who was my father. Our relationship was as complex as Master Harold expresses it in the play. I had a resentment at his infirmity and other weakness but, as Master Harold says, 'I love him so.' " Fugard had tried before to confront the ghost of his father in *Hello and Goodbye*. Unlike Hally, or Fugard himself, Johnnie Smit never emancipates himself, never acheives emotional autonomy, and never finds his own identity. Instead of leaving his own father for university, Fugard says, "I could have been weak enough to decide not to go." Instead of going to railroad school, Johnnie "stopped, thought about his father, and went back. And that's a mistake."[4] Johnnie is chronologically older than Hally, but developmentally younger. In *Marigolds*, too, Fugard explores a variation on the adolescent-adult relationship by juxtaposing Daan's journey of self-discovery with the *rite de passsage* of the abakwetha.

Fugard's father-son relationship—both in life and on stage—begins as that of every manchild, but is further complicated by the presence of two fathers: black and white, strong and weak, warm and distant, adopted and natural. The one's race and the other's infirmity are physical "liabilities" beyond control. The son feels the social prohibition against striking the biological father, even figuratively (especially since he is disabled), yet that same society fosters his trampling of the surrogate father because he is black. Hally's demand to be called "Master" is a proclamation of racial superiority, but it is also a proclamation of emancipation by an adolescent who yearns to become an adult.

In adolescence, a son realizes his full physical power at the very time his father's power begins to wane. Because Hally's father has long been a cripple, this particular pattern does not apply. (He never flew a kite with his son, let alone played ball in the backyard.) However, in most other ways Hally's struggle for maturity is prototypical. The innate power of this archetypal father-son conflict is one reason for *Master Harold*'s impact.

It is not clear in his quote above which "weakness" of his father Fugard considered most disabling. He bequeathed Fugard his love of music and storytelling, but the son also "inherited" alcoholism and, for a time at least, bigotry. Fugard stopped drinking about the time he began writing *Master Harold*. And like many children, he rejected his father's politics—not to retreat as an underground revolutionary, but to step forward as an impassioned opponent of apartheid—and adopted Sam Semela's openness, compassion, and lucidity.

Parts of *Master Harold* were written at Fugard's mountain retreat in New Bethesda, four-and-a-half hours from Port Elizabeth. This little village near Middelburg, where Fugard was born, is located in the mountains behind Graaf Reinet. In 1984 Fugard purchased his burial plot there. While working on *Master Harold* in New Bethesda, he notes, "I suddenly realized that the chair I was sitting on had been in my mother's tearoom on the afternoon I was writing about. That same chair!" It was according to Fugard, "one of the easiest writing experiences I've ever had. The actual time involved was the same as for the others, but the writing did not involve any of the desperations and traumas I've taken for granted to be an inevitable part of the process." He adds, "The experience was a painful one, but the crafting aspect of it was just one of the most serene, effortless exercises I've ever experienced. . . . In the course of writing the four drafts I never tore up a single page."[5]

Fugard describes his process of writing early in his career as "pouring it out and taking on a process of reduction," but with *Master Harold*, "it was not a question of pouring, it was a question of building." As an example, he cites a sentence in the first and second drafts that read, "You should have taken his crutches away from him." In the third draft it became, "You and the nurses should have taken his crutches away from him." In the published script the sentence runs, "Then you and the nurses should have held him down and taken his crutches away from him." Fugard explains, "Now that's a radically different process to what would have happened if I had been dealing with a moment like that during *The Blood Knot*. That would have been a speech a page long. Which I would have then had to try to cut, reduce, edit, shift, and I would not have had enough sense to know how to reduce it to just one sentence. Because it is a complete picture—isn't it? In that one sentence. I now work very sparingly as a writer. Almost too sparingly I think, at times."[6]

After finishing the second draft, Fugard faced the question of where to produce the play, which, as usual, he planned to direct himself. In a letter dated October 8, 1981 he writes, "I am going to break a past pledge and not do it in S.A. first. I won't get the actors I need here and I'm also certain that there are things in the play that will fall foul of the local censors." Fugard probably had in mind both the baring of Sam's bottom and the casting of Hally, who must look young enough to pass as a teenager, yet have the emotional range and technique of a veteran. In addition to these problems, Fugard sought a first production abroad because *Master Harold* is so introspective and personal a play: "I've always had a sense that the plays that lie behind me—*Aloes*, *Boesman*, and the others . . . that S.A. was half owner of the rights. This one belongs to me; this one's mine."[7] Although Peter Hall offered a production at Britain's National Theatre, Fugard turned instead to Lloyd Richards and the Yale Repertory Theatre, which had presented the American premiere of *Aloes*.

When Fugard began working on the script, he assumed he could achieve the same shocking effect without actually including the spitting incident. Not until the third draft did he write, "Hally spits in Sam's face." This moment was also avoided during the first two weeks of rehearsal until Fugard took it on himself and stopped rehearsal: "I just turned quietly on Zakes (Mokae), took his head in my hands in a very loving gesture, and I just spat that face wet. I just spat it wet, and the poison was out . . . because I also went on you see."[8] Fugard himself also demonstrated how Sam should drop his trousers.

Master Harold premiered in New Haven on March 12, 1982 with Mokae, Danny Glover as Willy, and Željko Ivanek as Hally. Jack Kroll wrote, "If there is a more urgent and indispensable playwright in world theatre than South Africa's Athol Fugard, I don't know who it could be." Three months later, after *Master Harold* had opened at the Lyceum Theatre on Broadway, Frank Rich asserted, "There may be two or three living playwrights in the world who can write as well as Athol Fugard, but I'm not sure that any of them has written a recent play that can match *Master Harold*."[9] The play received both the Drama Desk Award and the Outer Critics' Circle Award for Best Play of 1982.

The dramaturgy of *Master Harold* is so deft that it may barely be discerned— proof in itself of its skill—yet Fugard's refined craft is present even in minor moments throughout the play. Consider the textures of this brief exchange:

Hally: It doesn't have to be that way. There is something called progress you know, we don't exactly burn people at the stake anymore.
Sam: Like Joan of Arc.
Hally: Correct. If she was captured today she'd be given a fair trial.
Sam: And then the death sentence.

In only a few lines, Fugard introduces the idea of progress, indicates the extent of Sam's learning, and finishes the beat with a joke on both South African justice and the idea of progress.

Fugard's contrapuntal skill is not limited to his dialogue. The rainy weather outside the cafe suggests the gloominess of Hally's mood, contrasts with the day Sam and Hally shared a kite, and, on a literal and realistic level, explains why no customers visit. Also, while the play focuses on Sam and Hally, Willie remains present even when he has nothing to say. Washing the floor on his hands and knees, his trousers rolled up like a schoolboy's, he is an inescapable reminder of the role blacks are expected to play.

Critics, and Fugard himself upon occasion, have noted the slow beginning of some of his plays. It takes some time for the relationships and issues of *Master Harold* to engage also. In the meantime, however, it is energetically propelled by its humor, much of it "gentle" as Fugard predicted, but a great deal of it broad and hilarious—more so than even Fugard has realized in either his comments or his production. It is unquestionably the funniest play he has written.

When his mother died in 1980, Fugard received a warm letter of condolence from Semela although the two had not seen each other in fifteen years. *Master Harold* bears the dedication "for Sam and H.D.F." Shortly before the scheduled opening of the play in South Africa, Fugard asked John Kani to contact Semela and give him an airline ticket for the Johannesburg premiere. Kani, who was cast as Sam, "arrived at the Semela family residence to find all the furniture piled outside, as it is in the tradition of the Xhosa people when the head of a household dies."[10]

IX

Truths the Hand
Can Touch

Poetry, therefore, is a more philosophical and a higher thing than history: for poetry tends to express the universal, history the particular. —Aristotle

In everything he has written, Athol Fugard's ultimate concern is the universal plight rather than the particular South African one. Man's isolation, his lonely search for warmth, intelligibility, and meaning in an alien world, his avowal of human dignity, affirmation of his identity, and temporary recourse to dreams and illusions before embracing a world bereft of consoling myths—these are themes so fundamental that they cannot be delimited to a single society that will someday crumble from its inherent contradictions.

Fugard's revolt is against the irremediable human plight and not against social conditions created by men and therefore amenable to correction by men. Free as he is as a member of the privileged caste in a racial society, his conception of man is not one of liberty and autonomy. The promise of human potential is overshadowed by the fact of human limitation. Neither individual nor collective action holds promise for altering man or his world; Fugard's ken dismisses absolutely the confident optimism of both social engineers and revolutionary missionaries of either the political or religious variety.

In general, his characters learn not to cure their ailments but to live with them. They do not affirm their plight, but resign themselves to it. Their struggles are not resolved, because solutions to their fundamental quandaries do not exist. Fugard's plays do not build to shattering climaxes followed by reassuring denouements; the high point of a play is likely to be a solitary moment of lucidity and the consciousness that results from a subtle insight. The plays affirm nothing but man himself. Fugard is a secular writer whose characters find meaning and reassurance, if at all, by reaching out to one another.

His men and women are voyeurs of their own lives. Often insecure, they search for their identities by reliving their pasts, but they learn that they cannot escape time, the present, however much they might try to do so through dreams and illusions about the future. Boesman and Lena expressly declare that the "here and now" is all they have, but the same is implicitly true for all of Fugard's characters.

One of his personal observations helps explain the persistence of this emphasis on the here and now: "Christmas morning—Lisa bewildered and confused by her new toys, all of which are a great success, particularly the tricycle. Otherwise, nothing. The celebration of that birth 2,000 years ago is totally without meaning to me, and its 'message' one of those illusions, those 'hopes' that I have no place for in my life. I would have done better to say I have no time for it—because that is the point surely to these hopes: the time they steal from a man's one and only life." (12-25-63) This preoccupation with time's evanesence can also be inferred from Fugard's increasing consciousness of his mortality. South Africa, too, has shaped his obsession with the present: "Like everyone else in this country, black and white, my horizons have shrunk, and will continue to do so. Today's future barely includes tomorrow. At times I see the situation deteriorating still further to the point where even the thought of tomorrow will be a luxury."[1]

Relationships in Fugard's plays are usually interdependent. He ascribes his fascination with two-character plays to the fact that he is "staggered by the mysterious and unresolvable equation of 'self' and 'the other'. "[2] His preference for small-cast plays leads inevitably to an emphasis on his characters' personalities and the intense emotional relationship between siblings, mates, or friends.

Such basic relationships are merely one instance of Fugard's focus upon essentials. Stanley Kauffmann's comment on *Boesman and Lena* can be applied to much of Fugard's writing: "The play's epic quality derives from the wide and simple arch of its compass: shelter, food, fire, children, quarrels, dependence, ego needs, death, endless pilgrimage."[3] Above all else, Fugard is preoccupied with love and death, the one as uncertain as the other is inevitable. These are common themes, but Fugard dramatizes them with such intensity that one is forced to experience them anew. As they are gradually revealed to an audience, his women and men demand attention, sympathy, and, finally, respect.

Influences and Cross-Currents

A writer goes to previous writers not for technique but for spirit. —D.H. Lawrence

T.S. Eliot writes, "We dwell with satisfaction upon the poet's difference from his predecessors, especially his immediate predecessors; we endeavor to find something that can be isolated in order to be enjoyed. Whereas if we approach a poet without this prejudice we shall often find that not only the best, but the most individual parts of his work may be those in which the dead poets, his ancestors, assert their immortality most vigorously. . . . No poet, no artist of any art, has his complete meaning alone."⁴

Eliot's observations should be remembered by theatre critics especially. Great modern playwrights such as Büchner, Ibsen, Strindberg, Pirandello, and Beckett are often revered for their contributions to the "development" of drama, an unfortunate term that implies the theatre has "progressed" as a result of their innovations. This unintentionally suggests that the state of the art has continuously "improved" since the merely nascent works of the Dionysian Festival and that its growth can be plotted as a series of causes and effects. "Development" may also imply that some objective measure of an artist's achievement and contribution actually exists. Such thinking suggests a comparison between artists and athletes: With time and sufficient training some playwright of the future may eventually run the theatrical equivalent of the three-minute mile.

Fugard cannot be considered either a stylistic or thematic innovator. He has acknowledged the influence of O'Neill, Williams, Brecht, Kierkegaard, and Grotowski. He has also expressed his admiration for Dostoevsky, Chekhov, and Tolstoy and modern American poets such as Pound, Lowell, and Stevens. Some of Fugard's links to Büchner have been mentioned in regard to *The Family*, and those to Grotowski in the discussion of the collaborative period.

Even before *Aloes*, when Fugard acknowledged his esteem for Chekhov, numerous similarities between them had been evident. External resemblances include the use of intense family relationships (and deceased parents) in domestic settings. Fugard's women, like Chekhov's (and Shaw's), tend to be stronger than his men. Substantive similarities between the two are more revealing. Despite their use of apparently conventional dramatic structures, plot, in the sense of a series of significant concatenate "actions," is seldom very important except, ironically, in the one play about which Fugard has invoked Chekhov's name. (*The Three Sisters* is a play about what the Prozorovs do not say or do while they do not go to Moscow. Similarly, *The Seagull* is the story of the non-reconciliation of Nina and Konstantin. Chekhov's last play is framed by what does not happen while the cherry orchard is not saved.) As critics have often noted, subtext is triumphant throughout Chekhov's work; Fugard has sometimes achieved similar subtlety and ambiguity. In the works of both, however, meaning is not projected Faulkner and Fugard populate their work with diverse characters, whether the categories are tenant farmer, planter, Indian, and Negro, or black, white, and in single momentous events—the melodramatic endings of Chekhov's early works not withstanding—but in the incidents of daily life, mundane comings and goings. Fugard's and Chekhov's plays present the resounding tinkle of anti-climax, non-action, and non-response.

The triumph of Chekhov's characters is sometimes the simple one of enduring the present. If his plays affirm anything it is the constancy of time—not the advance of progress but the march of time, the process of life, and with it death. In some of Chekhov's plays the present is only affirmed after attempts to escape into the past or future prove futile. The Moscow of *The Three Sisters* represents both past and future. Morrie and Zach's farm, like Moscow, is a dream that cannot be fulfilled.

A final similarity between Chekhov and Fugard is the misapprehension by some critics of their true subjects, especially the overemphasis on the social significance of their work. Chekhov has been called (and not only by Soviet critics) a precursor of the Revolution, a writer who condemned the leisured and indolent rural gentry as he predicted the rise of the peasants and workers. Both Chekhov and Fugard are misunderstood because of a confusion between external details and internal substance, between context and subject.

Both write about *homo sapiens* through close examination of specific individuals firmly rooted in a particular time and place. Chekhov's plays clearly emanate from Czarist Russia, and Fugard's are usually grounded in apartheid South Africa. (It remains to be seen whether each period happens also to be pre-revolutionary.) Both make acute observations about those societies, but this specificity is a means, not an end. The real meaning of their work must be understood by induction, by movement past the specific to the general. Ultimately, Chekhov's estates and Fugard's Port Elizabeth shanties are—like O'Neill's or Hawthorne's New England, Williams's New Orleans, and Faulkner's Mississippi, among scores of examples—imaginative fictional constructs.

Fugard first read Faulkner in his late teens and acknowledges his influence as follows: "There was obviously for me just this one remarkable discovery, at a certain point in my life, of a great writer who had taken the very simple, very specific stories, and had made astonishing literature out of it. And, more than anybody else, Faulkner turned me around in the sense that, where I'd been looking at American plays and European experiments, suddenly he gave me total security to turn around and look at the specific, the humble specifics of an Eastern [Cape] Province world."[5]

The similarities between the American South and South Africa are often exaggerated or over-simplified, but both slavery and apartheid obviously put intense pressure on relations between disparate sections of the population. Both Coloured. Their characters are always in close touch with nature (even in Fugard's

197

urban settings the veld is nearby). Fugard shares with Faulkner a love of the outdoors—and with Chekhov a fondness for planting trees. Their characters are isolated, obsessed with time, and aware that modern society is a wasteland, though Faulkner's men and women tend to see the past as preferable to the present, while Fugard's often look to the future. Each author consciously manipulates time to emphasize that it is as much a subjective experience as an objective measure.

Fugard and Faulkner have similarly mixed feelings about their homes. Faulkner says of the South, "Well, I love it and hate it. Some of the things there I don't like at all, but I was born there, and that's my home, and I will still defend it even if I hate it."[6] It is obvious that Fugard, too, loves his homeland as much as he hates it.

Fugard's Port Elizabeth plays are not a cycle in the way that Faulkner's Yoknapatawpha novels and stories are. Even the interrelationship of *The Family* was an afterthought. However, in both Faulkner and Fugard, their repeated abstractions of the places they were born and lived invites expectations of an exact correspondence between their fictional worlds and the real ones on which they are modelled. Although such expectations are understandable, they are misleading because the correspondences can only be literal, whereas the works themselves are figurative.

Fugard describes himself as a regional writer: "I think there are writers—maybe all writers—who work in the specifics of one time and place. And if they're any good as writers, then finally a few universals will emerge in the course of their writing about the specifics."[7] He believes that starting with a specific is the most effective form of storytelling, but he also admits to being surprised at times that his regional obsessions have had significance for others. This ability to imbue specifically South African characters and situations with universal meaning is one of Fugard's highest achievements, as well as an indication of his mastery of his chosen material. Like Faulkner, Synge, and Lorca, other writers labeled "regional," his intimacy with the sights, sounds, and smells of a particular microcosm assists him in transmuting an isolated moment into a cosmic metaphor.

In addition to Faulkner, Fugard is most indebted to two other Nobel laureates. He says, "Camus belongs to a very special category in terms of influence on me, shared by only one other person. And that's Samuel Beckett. They're both men who've shaped my craft and sharpened my thinking."[8] Both have been invoked frequently in preceding chapters. Their influence does not consist simply of the stimulation one writer provides another, but of the meeting of remarkably similar sensibilities and aesthetics, with those of Camus and Beckett nourishing and reinforcing the perceptions that Fugard instinctively believed to be true. The cross-currents between them and Fugard are too numerous to analyze comprehensively, but several must be noted.

Fugard admits that Camus was a kind of lateral ancestor, *l'homme du midi*, the man of the south: "When I first encountered the articulation of that almost pagan, sensual life lived out in the sun, next to a sea, with warm rocks being, in a sense, the ultimate reality, it struck a resonance in me that persists to this day."[9] The numerous references in Camus's notebooks to the Mediterranean Sea and sun are paralleled by Fugard's descriptions of the physical beauty of his homeland. Both were raised in families with dominant women, both worked as journalists, and both wrote and directed for amateur theatre companies they helped found. Fugard may also have felt an implicit kinship since both were raised in European cultures transplanted to Africa and in societies that maltreated the indigenous people. Wealth might have secured separation from the aborigines, but the modest circumstances of their childhoods assured regular contact.

Far more important than their similar backgrounds is their intellectual compatibility. While reading Camus's notebooks, Fugard wrote in his own, "Camus sounds out and charts the very oceans of experience, feeling, and thought on which I find myself sailing at this moment. His importance to me is monumental. Reading Camus is like finding, for the first time, a man speaking my own language." (8-63) After finishing *The Myth of Sisyphus*, Fugard noted, "Impossible to describe the excitement, the total sympathy that exists for me with Camus's thinking." (12-63)

In that book, Camus writes, "A world that can be explained even with bad reasons is a familiar world. But, on the other hand, in a universe suddenly divested of illusions and lights, man feels an alien, a stranger." Fugard's plays project isolated men and women who toy with hopes and dreams before discarding them as illusory, then embracing lucid consciousness. The parallels to Camus are obvious: For him, hope is a fatal evasion. He focuses upon Sisyphus during his walk back down the hill to retrieve his rock, the time he can reflect on his plight: "If this myth is tragic, that is because its hero is conscious. Where would his torture be, indeed, if at every step the hope of succeeding upheld him?"[10]

After exploring some caves once inhabited by the original inhabitants of the Cape, Fugard became depressed and wrote in his notebook, "I feel those lives must have been unconscious. Revolt (meaning) can only come with consciousness. I am sure I would have felt differently if there had been paintings on the wall—because in that I would have seen consciousness. Without that consciousness even the sunlight and sea become as black as the night that stuffed the inside of the caves. Consciousness—the sun in man's life—our only light. Without consciousness we become victims instead of actors—even if it is still only a question of acting victims. And in this make-believe of our lives the audience is self." (12-25-63) This consciousness and revolt have clear analogues in Camus, who calls consciousness not the sun but the light in man's life.

A final similarity between Fugard and Camus is their shared perception of the role of the artist. Camus writes, "The world I live in is loathsome to me, but I feel one with the men who suffer in it. . . . [One] ambition that ought to belong to all writers: to bear witness and shout aloud, every time it is possible, insofar as our talent allows, for those who are enslaved as we are."[11] Fugard notes similarly, "My life's work is to witness as truthfully as I can, the nameless and destitute of this one little corner of the world."(9-7-68)

Fugard says that he doesn't want to meet any writers he admires, but he and Beckett did meet in a London pub where they discussed cricket and Fugard's pipe—a Kapp and Peterson, the kind Pozzo smokes in *Godot*. Fugard recalls, "He was exactly what I'd expected, an incredibly reserved man with a passionate connection to his work." Beckett's impression of the meeting has gone unrecorded. However, although he usually insists that even his short dramaticules be performed by themselves, Beckett gave the Royal Court permission to produce a double bill of *Not I* and *Statements*, which he had seen and liked in Paris.

Beckett probably holds sway over more serious playwrights than anyone else, perhaps more writers of all kinds. Still, Fugard's relationship to him is a special one even if Beckett's immediate leap to the general and unspecified is the exact opposite of Fugard's reliance upon concrete particulars. After reading *Malone Dies*, Fugard noted, "I wanted to start writing again the moment I put it down. Beckett's greatness doesn't intimidate me. I don't know how it works—but he makes me want to work. Everything of his that I have read has done this—I suppose it's because I really understand, emotionally, and this cannot but give me power and energy and faith." (12-62) It is only a slight simplification to say that Camus was the formative influence on the context of Fugard's work, and Beckett the dominant influence on its style. (This formulation overlooks the compatibility of the world views of Camus and Beckett.)

The similarities between Beckett and Fugard include their use of only a few characters, a spare set if any, and a limited number of properties. Because their plays are intimate, they are best produced in small theatrical spaces. Their characters are often possessed by their pasts and dredge up apparently irrelevant memories of them. Beckett's emphasis upon basic bodily functions can be compared to Fugard's preoccupation with man's fundamental needs. In the works of both, the terms of existence are simply given. Attempts to provide causal explanations are fruitless and irrelevant since the emphasis is often on the fact that existence *is* inexplicable and irremediable. At the end of *The Blood Knot* Morrie says of the game, "It will pass the time," (96) which is precisely the function of the games played by Didi and Gogo, Hamm and Clov. Like the Unnamable, Fugard's characters search for themselves and "go on," neither saved nor damned but left alone to face eternity. Both Fugard and Beckett present an image of man in an extreme situation. Even if Hamm had his pain killer, it would provide no more ultimate comfort than Marais's morphine (or Chekhov's characters' valerian drops). Deirdre Bair considers Beckett's chief preoccupations "the problem of identity, the obsession with words, the nameless teller of tales."[12] She might also have added the dramatization of metaphysical anguish, which, along with the search for both identity and the right word, is prevalent throughout Fugard's work.

The modern dramatic genre of inaction, passivity, and impotence discussed in regard to *Boesman and Lena* did not originate with Beckett, but he is its leading figure. With physical action minimized in such static plays, language is heightened, paradoxically through its spareness. Throughout Fugard's career, like Beckett he has sought greater simplicity and purity.

He also echoes at times Beckett's style of stichomythia, as in *The Blood Knot*:

Zach: Why did you come back?
Morris: I was passing this way.
Zach: Why did you stay?
Morris: We are brothers, remember. (18-19)

Zach: I can never have her.
Morris: Never ever.
Zach: She wouldn't want me anyway.
Morris: It's as simple as that.
Zach: She's too white to want me anyway.
Morris: For better or for worse. (61-62)[13]

Of all contemporary playwrights, Beckett is most clearly a poet in the theatre, as Fugard and others have called him, but despite the wordiness of the early plays, Fugard may also be best remembered for the texture and evocative power of his language. This is true of the notebooks as well as the plays.

Language and Style

Style consists in force of assertion. If you can say a thing with one
stroke unanswerably you have style. —George Bernard Shaw

Critics have often commented on Fugard's language, but there is no consensus on whether or not it is heightened and, if it is, whether or not this is appropriate. John Simon writes, "Fugard manages, furthermore, the difficult feat of finding a language for Lena that is neither flatly naturalistic nor unduly and unconvincingly poeticized. That there are a few lapses is not surprising—what is surprising is that they are so few." Martin Gottfried writes similarly about *Sizwe Bansi*, "Fugard's writing is simply gorgeous, which comes as no surprise considering his past plays. . . . He can have characters say the most heroic and poetic things without ever seeming literary." However, Jean Marguard writes that passages of poetic, if desolate, reverie in *Hello and Goodbye* are "improbable in the mouths of such essentially inarticulate characters."[14] Critical opinion is sharply drawn: Fugard's writing must be either poetic or naturalistically mimetic.

Were Fugard a purely naturalistic writer, Marquard's criticism would be appropriate, since in that case one-to-one correspondence between social status, level of education, and the way characters express themselves might reasonably be expected. However, such demands reveal a basic misunderstanding of Fugard's tactical use of society's outcasts and underlings. Their socio-political stature is an analogue for the alienation of all men, not a causal determinant of their actions or speech. It is as absurd to call Fugard's language inappropriate or "out of character" as it would be to say the same of Büchner, Brecht, or Beckett. An obsession with what is presumed to be a photographic image of reality undermines the credibility of extraordinary language.

In addition to Fugard's language, his specificity and concreteness is the stylistic element that most distinguishes his work. Dryden's comment that when Shakespeare "describes anything, you more than see it, you feel it too," might also be applied to Fugard. Most of the plays had begun with a concrete image—a shantytown perched on a fetid lake that is home to two brothers, a woman with a suitcase, a prisoner's coat, a lonely woman walking on the road, a smiling man with a pipe and cigarette, a police photograph. Moreover, Fugard has always needed to assimilate the specific details of a situation before writing about it. He calls a published extract of *Boesman and Lena*, a first attempt "to define the physical context and elements of a new play. If there have ever been 'universals' in my writing they have had to look after themselves. I concern myself with the 'specifics.' When the fire-blackened paraffin tin, or Boesman's flea-ridden mattress, or the mud between Lena's toes means something to me, things might start to happen. It's been this way with anything I've ever written." With the exception of *Dimetos*, Fugard has always created a palpable context for his plays. He has repeatedly cited a phrase from Camus that has always moved him: "[Camus] talks about the 'truths the hand can touch.' I'm very frightened, very nervous, about a slightly religious element in my nature and so I always hang on to the tangible."[15] This religious element is seldom evident in any of his work after *Tsotsi*, perhaps because he is an "agnoceros," as Lisa once described him. Sheila Fugard is devoted to Zen Buddhism, but Fugard is not—although he does have a mantra that he uses.

Fugard understands the characters and world of his plays as intimately as the drops of pond water he studies for hours with his daughter's microscope. His characters possess such concrete quirks, compulsions, and ways of expressing themselves that they persist in the imagination as tangible entities. Abrahams praises the precision of Johnnie Smit's characterization: "Such details set him palpably before us, and in them if anywhere lies the proof of Fugard's genius for *incarnation*, the essential dramatic power."[16] In addition to being one of Fugard's most pronounced attributes, this ability to create irrepressibly vital characters also helps account for the success actors have had portraying his roles.

Language and Style

Fugard's notebooks are filled with subtle details that locate the conversations and incidents he describes. Such details are not embellishments; rather, they help explain why the thing Fugard saw or heard so interested him. His first entry in his first notebook, which evolved into *The Blood Knot*, indicates his ability to conjure up the essence of a place: "Korsten: The Berry's Corner bus, then up the road past the big motor-assembly and rubber factories. Turn right down a dirt road—badly potholed, full of stones, donkeys wandering loose, Chinese and Indian grocery shops—down this road until you come to the lake. Dumping ground for waste products from the factories. Terrible smell. On the far side, like a scab, Korsten location. A collection of shanties, pondoks, lean-tos. No streets, names, or numbers. A world where anything goes."

The context of each play is clearly suggested, but little more than a bare stage is required. Such simplicity complements the basic themes and questions that are the focus of the work. Stripped of decorative set pieces, each play—and the audience's experience of it—is concentrated on the primal struggle of the characters. The few properties that are needed become extraordinarily important. There are no merely cosmetic accoutrements to distract from Fugard's intimate probing of essential human dilemmas.

Most of Fugard's plays begin with a single character on stage, the absolute minimum to make theatre. Like the Greek tragedians, he usually requires only two or three more. The intense focus that a small cast provides is one of its attractions. Fugard explains, "First of all, I write in the context of the South African theatre, and the more economical my plays are the easier it is for them to get performances. Secondly, my major influence is music; the most important composers to me being those who use one or two instruments; Bach, say, in his unaccompanied violin sonatas or cello suites. And so I think of actors as instruments. I've become an economical writer through circumstances and through personal predeliction. I always strive for very tight plays. The tighter I can write them, the deeper I can get."[17] For similar reasons no play has a subplot.

Fugard claims that he has learned more about writing plays from Bach's unaccompanied violin sonatas and his harpsichord and cello suites than from any writer except Beckett. Fugard has composed virtuoso scores for his actors. The impact of his work is largely due to its concentration on a few characters in a simple setting as they struggle to comprehend the utterly fundamental problems that besiege them.

Critical Reputation

*A critic knows more than the author he criticizes, or just as much,
or at least somewhat less.*   —Henry Cardinal Manning

*When my critical mood is at its height, personal feeling is not the
word: it is passion: the passion for artistic perfection, for the
noblest beauty of sound, sight, and action—that rages in me.* —George Bernard Shaw

As early as 1966, Abrahams wrote that Fugard "stands in virtual isolation as a native master of the medium." A decade later Nadine Gordimer observed that "significant South African drama in English has been created, single-handed, by Athol Fugard." An American reviewer has called him "South Africa's leading playwright—indeed, internationally speaking, its leading artist,"[18] although Paton and Gordimer may be more widely known. Given the stature of South African theatre, such praise is hardly surprising. Fugard is certainly the best-known South African playwright, but he is also the only one widely known outside the country.

Some critics have ventured to evaluate him in a larger context, with Robert Berner going so far as to claim that he "may very well be the most distinguished dramatist writing in English today." This is surely an exaggeration as long as Beckett continues writing, but at least Berner errs on the side away from parochialism. Emphasis on Fugard's nationality has distorted evaluation and limited the appreciation of his work. Martin Gottfried, for one, has recognized this and suggested in 1974 that Fugard's reputation had been slighted because "the American-British theatre environment is so provincial that a playwright from any culturally different country is rarely accepted on equal terms, even when he writes in English. Were Fugard American or English and writing about white people, he would have long since been accepted as the major contemporary playwright he is. Instead, he is just someone you hear from once in a while. It is ridiculous and wrong."[19]

Faulkner concluded his Nobel Prize address in 1950, "The poet's voice need not merely be the record of man, it can be one of the props, the pillars to help him endure and prevail." In his Nobel citation seven years later, Camus was praised as a defender of "those silent men who, throughout the world, endure the life that has been made for them." The Swedish Academy cited Beckett in 1969 for "a body of work that, in new forms of fiction and the theatre, had transmuted the destitution of modern man into his exaltation."[20] Man's destitution and final exaltation are also hallmarks of Fugard. Like his characters, his dramatic achievement will long endure because his language, dramatic images, and characters possess the imaginative complexity to shock an audience, actor, and reader into fresh recognition with each encounter.

In *Tsotsi*, Fugard writes of the cripple Morris Tshabalala, "This man, this half-

man, this unsightly and disfigured remnant of a man Tsotsi recogr
the certainty of his unnumbered years as being the true figuration of life. rκ
was a symbol of this precisely because he was bent, and broken, and so without
meaning that other men had abandoned him. This was the final reality to life.
Everything else was just rouge and lipstick on an ugly face." (77) Yet in so writing,
Fugard celebrates and immortalizes the Morris Tshabalalas of the world. He is
only one of Fugard's images of the entire species. Fugard's dual vision leads him
to depict palpably the horror of the world and at the same time to celebrate
the men and women isolated in it. He compels us to be more than passive voyeurs;
his characters' epiphanies of self-recognition become our own.

Lena muses, "Sometimes loneliness is two . . . you and the other person who
doesn't want to know you're there." (183) Throughout the play she reaches out
to Outa, to Boesman, and through them to the audience. Hell is sometimes other
people, but communicating with them mitigates its isolation. Fugard is fond of
quoting a Pascal *pensée* about a group of men chained together in a cell. Every
day at dawn the man at the end of the chain is executed: "Those left behind
read their fate in the opening and closing of the door. Pascal says 'this is man's
condition.' All right, you've got twenty-four hours before it happens—what can
you do? You can weep, feel sorry for yourself, beat the ground. Or you can put
out your hand and touch the man next to you and say, what is your name? You
have the possibility of defying that condition even though defiance might look
stupid."[21] Fugard's characters, like the condemned men, tap one another on the
shoulder to begin a dialogue. Fugard does the same with audiences around the
world.

Popular literature assumes that questions can be answered, that everything is
clear and definite. It provides answers equally clear and definite, and usually affirmative and reassuring. People, according to Laudisi in Pirandello's *Right You
Are (If You Think You Are)*, "want the truth—a truth that is: Something specific;
something concrete! They don't care what it is. All they want is something
categorical, something that speaks plainly." Lena learns that such a truth "doesn't
explain anything."

Enduring works of literature are more concerned with a search than its conclusion, and may therefore be more disturbing than consoling. Fugard shuns
melodramatic sentimentality and entirely good or bad characters. He also avoids
moral judgments and prefers, instead, those complex human predicaments that
have no simple solutions, indeed no solutions at all. "If the world were clear,"
writes Camus, "art would not exist." Fugard says, "I don't believe there's a simple
trite answer to everything. I think that if I ever did write a play that had simple
answers, but maybe I have, that play wouldn't really qualify in my regard."[22] His
preoccupation with unanswerable questions suggests that the world is
unknowable, but in wrestling with that conclusion through the creation of a

work of art, a kind of clarity emerges, even when the final answer is that there is none.

Great works of art are intensely affecting not because they contain something new, but because they create experience anew, thus confirming what is already known somewhere deep within us. Even those works that reveal the depths of a living hell provide a sense of exhilaration as a result of one's presence in the midst of artistic greatness. In a sense, it is not the heroism of Oedipus, Lear, or Lena that is affecting. The true champions are their authors who have experienced each search and loss more acutely than any audience, more so than even the characters who embody that search and loss, yet have withstood it all. This is a kind of meta-theatre; we are affected by the agent as well as his created object, and glimpse the potential both of a character's human greatness and of a creator's artistic greatness. Order may not exist in the universe, but it does in the work of art.

Fugard's work resounds with philosophical overtones, but his writing is so deeply rooted in the basic human relationships of a particular time and place that there is never the arid abstractness that "philosophical" sometimes implies in a work of art. He makes us feel the sensation of ideas. All great plays are problem plays and plays of ideas. This does not mean that they are didactic, that the playwright has a particular lesson to espouse, but that he recognizes the existence of a question. The best modern playwrights are not programmatic philosophers, but (to borrow Eric Bentley's term) thinkers. Fugard's plays are supreme examples of what can happen when a skilled writer and craftsman is compelled to ask why. In his best writing, the questions are so well put, so basic, alluring, and ultimately unanswerable, that his plays will long remain important works of art, and deeply affecting ones.

APPENDIX A:

The Drummer
by Athol Fugard

Note: I only saw him once, but that was enough. His immediate identity was that of a bum . . . what looked like an old army overcoat with a bit of rope serving as a belt and a head of wild, unwashed and uncombed hair. I remember one seemingly incongruous detail—a length of bright yellow material, tied around his neck, which he wore like a cape.

It was a very busy hour in Times Square, New York, and he was moving effortlessly through the congested traffic beating out a tattoo with a pair of drumsticks on anything that came to hand. In the half hour or so that I followed him he dealt in this fashion with a series of manholes in the street, passing motorcar bonnets, lampposts on the pavement and one mail box. He wasn't begging. In fact in his relationship to the world around him the roles of giver and receiver seemed to be just the reverse. He was very joyous . . . defiantly so! . . . and seemed to have a sense of himself as being extravagantly free.

A pile of rubbish on a pavement, waiting to be cleared away. This consists of an over-filled trash-can and a battered old chair with torn upholstery on which is piled an assortment of cardboard boxes and plastic bags full of discarded junk.

Distant and intermittent city noises. These will increase in volume and frequency as the action demands.

A bum enters. He walks over to the pile of rubbish and starts to work his way through it . . . looking for something useful in terms of that day's survival. He has obviously just woken up and yawns from time to time. After a few seconds he clears the chair, sits down, makes himself comfortable and continues his search.

One of the boxes produces a drumstick. He examines it and then abandons it.

A little later he finds a second drumstick. He examines it. Remembers! He scratches around in the pile of rubbish at his feet and retrieves the first.

Two drumsticks! His find intrigues him.

Another dip into the rubbish but it produces nothing further of interest.

Two drumsticks!

He settles back in his chair and surveys the world.

An ambulance siren approaches and recedes stage right.

He observes indifferently.

A fire engine approaches and recedes stage left.

He observes.

While this is going on he taps idly on the lid of the trash-can with one of the drumsticks.

He becomes aware of this little action.

Two drumsticks and a trash-can!

It takes him a few seconds to realize the potential.

He straightens up in his chair and with a measure of caution, attempts a little tattoo on the lid of the can.

The result is not very impressive.

He makes a second attempt, with the same result.

Problem.

Solution!

He gets up and empties the trash-can of its contents, replaces the lid and makes a third attempt.

The combination of a serious intention and the now-resonant bin produces a decided effect.

He develops it and in so doing starts to enjoy himself.

His excitement gets him onto his feet.

He had one last flash of inspiration.

He removes the lid from the can, up-ends it, and with great bravura drums out a final tattoo . . . virtually an accompaniment to the now very loud and urgent city noises all around him.

Embellishing his appearance with some item from the rubbish . . . a cape? . . . and holding his drumsticks at the ready he chooses a direction and sets off to take on the city.

He has discovered it is full of drums . . . and he has got drumsticks.

The Beginning

APPENDIX B:

Literary Ancestors of *Dimetos*

Dimetos and Ibsen's Solness are both attracted to young women, want to find a new home, and suffer conflicts between personal, familial, and professional responsibilities. Both can be viewed, in part, as autobiographical projections of their authors. Most important of all, both have been practical builders. They evoke the first engineer, Daedalus, although neither Dimetos nor Solness can extricate himself from a predicament of his own making. Solness's fall from his tower suggests his affinity with Icarus, another overreacher bent on elevating himself to a higher plane in order to attract attention. Dimetos seeks anonymity instead.

Both Dimetos and Faust are scientists who are disaffected with their present ways of life. Filled with intellectual curiosity and dissatisfaction with what seems to be the meaning of existence, they strive to discover a vaster significance for life. Both eventually realize the mind's limitations and that no amount of knowledge can provide ultimate answers. Dimetos and Goethe's Faust struggle to resolve the conflict between sensual urges and higher impulses.

Still, the similarities between Faust and Dimetos are far from complete. Instead of tempting Dimetos with access to new worlds, Danilo tries to induce him to return to the old one; his suit is hardly Mephistophelean. Dimetos is acted upon less by outside agents than by inner ones dredged up by his isolated self-reflection. Both Faust and Dimetos are keenly aware of the limitations of what they possess, but this does not create in Dimetos an insatiable desire for new knowledge and skills. Dimetos scoffs at the "vision" Danilo ascribes to him and does not even value what he once possessed. Faust is an ambitious overreacher, but Dimetos has no ambition, no sense of purpose whatsoever. While Goethe's *Faust* mirrors the Age of Reason, *Dimetos* echoes the Age of Unreason. Where Goethe's Faust is benevolent and affirmative, Dimetos is, if not misanthropic and negative, skeptical and uncertain.

Dimetos is closer to Marlowe's Faustus in showing "the tragedy of wasted human material."[1] In his last scene, Marlowe's Faustus also tries to stop time. As the clock strikes behind him, he pleads, "Stand still, you ever-moving spheres of heaven, That time may cease and midnight never come. . . . O *lente, lente, currite noctis equi*," which translates, "O slowly, slowly run, ye horses of night."

Both Prospero and Dimetos have become strangers to the practical affairs of state and live outside the mainstream of society in deliberately unidentified locales that are intimately associated with primitive nature. Prospero has not ex-

209

iled himself, but his negligence of civic duties makes him partially responsible for his banishment. Both he and Dimetos are introspective and often prefer contemplation to action. Both are voyeurs, have loyal servants, and are charged with the care of young women whom both contrive to join with a man. Miranda and Lydia are also assaulted sexually, though neither attack is consummated. Prospero and Dimetos are scientists able to fathom and manipulate secrets of nature, and in both of their plays science is linked with art. In both *The Tempest* and *Dimetos* the audience is constantly reminded of time. Both plays end with monologues and are set against aqueous disasters, a tempest and a drought. Although *The Tempest* is usually thought to end happily, Prospero anticipates giving a third of his thoughts to his grave. Moreover, his strength has grown faint. Dimetos's scientific strength is shown to be faint even before it is "o'erthrown." His suffering is closer to the abstract mental anguish of Ariel than the concrete physical pains of Caliban.

Of all *Dimetos's* dramatic ancestors, the *Prometheus Bound* of Aeschylus is so close that Fugard might have had it in mind, if only subconsciously. In addition to mentioning Theseus and Daedalus, himself a smith, Dimetos refers to another mythological character. After praising the hands of a metalworker, he adds, "The last time I saw him he was at work on a chain—for one of the ships in the harbor—forging each link as if it was the one destined for Prometheus." (24) The reference, of course, is to the opening of *Prometheus Bound* when Hephaestus chains Prometheus to a rock. Hepheastus uses the same language as that for fettering a horse.

Both *Prometheus Bound* and *Dimetos* are given remote settings that seem to be on the very edge of the world. As Io is condemned to wander the earth because of a love, so Dimetos exiles himself from place to place because of his guilty love. Throughout the play he contemplates the uses of hands; Io's suffering will be ended by a touch of Zeus's hand.

The strongest links between the plays are their central characters, both of whom will their fates. Prometheus was the first technologist, "the father of 'progress' before the word was coined." The fire he gave man became the basis for all the applied sciences, "the teacher of each craft to men."[2] Prometheus enlightened man through the gift of intelligence as well as that of fire and instructed mankind in the practical arts, including the use of horses.

Prometheus embodies the wisdom of the juggler. He steals fire but gives it to man; instead of simply contemplating nature's workings, he teaches them to others. He is the man of action rather than words; he effects good instead of merely talking about it. Thus, it is poignantly ironic that this restless doer is bound to a rock, able only to speak. Until unbound, he is as physically powerless as Dimetos is spiritually and emotionally impotent. The one struggles with Zeus on Olympus, the other with demons in his heart.

Prometheus's anguish is the result of helping man; Dimetos's is due, in part,

210

to neglect of his fellow man. Prometheus is the original philanthropist. Instead of denying man, he affirms that man is worth loving and worth saving from the destruction Zeus had planned for him. Dimetos embodies the fact that the opposite of love is not hate but indifference. He doubts where Prometheus hopes.

In addition to their narrative and thematic similarities, each of the plays discussed above (except *Prometheus Bound*) has been interpreted as an autobiographical portrait of its author. Each protagonist confronts his death and muses on himself, his art, and the world with such passion that he appears to have been written from the inside out, thus suggesting the author's total and intimate understanding of his character, perhaps even personal identification with him. In addition, all of these plays are extremely difficult to stage successfully, in part because of their penchant for abstraction and inner action. *The Master Builder* and *Faust* are often considered "closet dramas."

Fugard has never discussed the parallels between these plays and *Dimetos*, but he has acknowledged the direct influence on it of one writer besides Camus. On the dedication page of *Dimetos* he quotes William Blake's poem "With Happiness Stretch'd across the Hills"[3]

> May God us keep
> From Single vision & Newton's sleep!

Fugard has expressed his admiration for many artists, but seldom his love of Blake. Whenever in London, however, he visits the Blake Room of the Tate Gallery. Fugard says, "I think Blake is unquestionably one of the most profound prophets in terms of the spiritual waste of our civilization. He knew where technology was going to take us."

Blake opposed Newton because he believed that Newton's closed scientific system usurped the province of the artistic imagination and vision of reality. Instead of perceiving artistic imagination as a reflection of external nature, Blake believed that external nature was an imitation of the artistic imagination. Newton posed so serious a threat because Blake believed that art was the tree of life, and science the tree of death. Donald Ault writes, "In the fallen world science presents a real threat to Eternity not only because of its capacity to usurp imaginative drives toward organization and image but also because it seems to pose the finite problems through which 'progress' is possible; for Blake such progress is only movement into deeper delusion."[4]

To Blake, the machines of the industrial revolution were comparable to the mechanics of Newton; as science threatened to supplant the imagination, so machines could become the master of man—a fear of Blake's that grew deeper after Watt defined horsepower in 1782. Blake wondered if horses would be deemed more valuable than men.[5] Although Blake's life spanned the industrial revolution, he made his living as a printer, by using his hands.

During rehearsals of *Dimetos* in London, Fugard took Yvonne Bryceland to the Tate Gallery to view Blake's color print *Hecate*: "I wanted to deal with a moment in the play and I said to Y, 'just look at this very carefully. Give yourself ten, fifteen, twenty minutes, as long as you need, then come back and describe it.' What exists in *Dimetos* [49-50], with one or two refinements, is her verbatim recall of that terrible image of somebody at hell's gate."

APPENDIX C:

Production Chronology of Works by Athol Fugard

The following list includes the opening dates of the world and American premieres of each work through 1983.

Plays

Klaas and the Devil
October 3, 1956   Scopus Club, Cape Town

The Cell
May 26, 1957   Labia Theatre, Cape Town

No-Good Friday
August 30, 1958   Bantu Men's Social Centre, Johannesburg

Nongogo
June 8, 1959   Bantu Men's Social Centre, Johannesburg
December 3, 1978   Manhattan Theatre Club, New York

The Blood Knot
September 3, 1961   Dorkay House, Johannesburg
March 2, 1964   Cricket Theatre, New York

Hello and Goodbye
October 26, 1965   Library Theatre, Johannesburg
November 11, 1968   Theatre de Lys (ANTA Matinee Series), New York

The Coat
November 28, 1966   Dunne Hall (Hill Presbyterian Church), Port Elizabeth

People Are Living There
March 13, 1968   Close Theatre, Glasgow
November 18, 1971   The Forum (Lincoln Center), New York

Boesman and Lena
July 10, 1969   Little Theatre, Rhodes University, Grahamstown

June 22, 1970   Circle in the Square, New York

PRODUCTION CHRONOLOGY

Orestes
   March 24, 1971   Castlemarine Auditorium,
                                            Cape Town

Statements after an Arrest under the
Immorality Act
   March 25, 1972   The Space, Cape Town
Revised version:
   January 22, 1974   The Royal Court, London
   February 6, 1978   Manhattan Theatre Club, New York

Sizwe Bansi Is Dead
   October 8, 1972   The Space, Cape Town
   October 11, 1974   Long Wharf Theatre, New Haven

The Island
   June 1973   The Space, Cape Town
   October 27, 1974   Long Wharf Theatre, New Haven

Drivers (Adapted from *Mille Miglia* by David Muir)
   July 1973   The Space, Cape Town

Dimetos
   August 27, 1975   Church Hill Theatre, Edinburgh

A Lesson from Alocs
   November 30, 1978   The Market, Johannesburg
   March 28, 1980   Yale Repertory Theatre, New Haven

The Drummer
   February 27, 1980   Actors Theatre of Louisville

"Master Harold" . . . and the boys
   March 9, 1982   Yale Repertory Theatre, New Haven

Feature Films

Boesman and Lena
   July 1973   Berlin Film Festival (Fringe Festival)
   September 1973   Atlanta Film Festival

The Guest
   March 5, 1977   BBC (under the title *The Guest at*
                                           Steenkampskraal)
   April 3, 1978   Filmex (Los Angeles Film Festival)

Marigolds in August
   February 29, 1980   Berlin Film Festival
   June 20, 1984   Film Forum, New York

Notes

A single note has been assigned to each paragraph in the text, even when more than one source is cited.

Introduction

[1] In Ernest Cole, *House of Bondage* (New York: Random House, 1967), p. 8.
[2] Margaret Bacon, "Writing in a Troubled Land," *Antioch Review*, 25 (1965), pp. 446-47.
[3] Mary Benson, *South Africa: The Struggle for a Birthright* (1963; rev. New York: Minerva Press, 1969), p. 170.
[4] Muriel Horrell, *South Africa: Basic Facts and Figures* (Johannesburg: Institute for Race Relations, 1973), p. 26.
[5] Lewis Nkosi, "The Prisoner," in Ezekiel Mphahlele ed., *African Writing Today* (Middlesex: Penguin, 1967), p. 299.
[6] *Report of the United Nations Commission on the Racial Situation in the Union of South Africa* (New York: United Nations General Assembly, Eighth Session, Supplement No. 16, 1953), p. 93.
[7] See International Defence & Aid Fund, *South African Prisons and the Red Cross Investigation with Prisoners' Testimony* (London: 1967). Political prisoners are classified Group D.

Chapter I

[1] *Three Port Elizabeth Plays* (New York: Viking, 1974) p. 25. These lines have been eliminated from Fugard's cut version of the text.
[2] *Ibid*, p. vii.
[3] From a BBC 2nd House program entitled "The Life and Works of Athol Fugard," first telecast Nov. 20, 1974 (Tristram Powell, Producer).
[4] Craig Raine, "An Interview with Athol Fugard," *Quarto*, No. 9 (Aug. 1980), p. 9.
[5] Mary Benson, "Keeping an Appointment with the Future: The Theatre of Athol Fugard," *Theatre Quarterly*, 7, No. 28 (1977), p. 77.
    Christopher Ford, "Life with a Liberal Conscience," *Guardian*, July 17, 1971, p. 8.
[6] BBC, "Life and Works."
[7] Robert M. Wren, "Profile: Athol Fugard, In Segregated South Africa, A Vision of Shared Hopefulness," *Africa Report*, 15, No. 7 (1970), p. 32.
[8] Benson, "Keeping an Appointment," p. 77.
    Raine, p. 9.
[9] Wren, p. 32.
    "Fugard Avid Reader from Early Age," from the Fugard collection of the National English Literary Museum and Documentation Centre at Rhodes University, Grahamstown, South Africa (hereafter abbreviated NELM).
[10] Glenda (Fugard) Swart, "My Brother Athol," NELM.
[11] Raine, p. 9. Versveld was a charismatic Catholic existentialist who had similar roots

NOTES

to Fugard, according to Dennis Walder in *The Varied Scene: Aspects of Drama Today*, prepared for The Open University, Arts: A Third Year Course, Drama (Walton Hall, Milton Keynes: The Open University Press, 1977), p. 70.

[12] Ford.

Benson, "Keeping an Appointment," p. 77. On April 10, 1981 the University of Natal gave Fugard an honorary Doctorate of Literature. Two years later, Yale University named him a Doctor of Fine Arts.

Pogrund's quotes throughout this chapter are from his "Nights When *Tsotsi* Was Born," *Rand Daily Mail*, Feb. 11, 1980.

[13] Barrie Hough, "Interview with Athol Fugard, Port Elizabeth, Oct. 30, 1977," *Theoria*, No. 55 (Oct. 1980), p. 37.

[14] This letter and the following ones of Oct. 12, 1953, Oct. 28, 1953, Nov. 18, 1953, and Feb. 6, 1954 quoted below are all from NELM.

[15] "Students' 30-Pound World Trip," *Eastern Province Herald*, May 21, 1954.

[16] Fugard long thought his ruse coincided with the Feast of Ramadan, which in 1953 occurred in June. He does not believe too long a period elapsed between his arrival in Port Sudan and the beginning of his sailing career, which can be dated to Oct. 1954. Assuming the banks actually were closed for a Moslem holiday, this was probably for the festival of sacrifices connected with the Great Pilgrimage between the tenth and thirteenth of the Islamic month of Dh-ulhijja, August 22-25 in 1953. The holiday could also have been Muharran, New Year, Sept. 10, 1953.

[17] Wayne Grigsby, "The Cost of Bearing Witness," *Macleans*, Jan. 21, 1980, p. 46.

[18] Colin Smith, "White Man on a Tightrope," *Observer*, Jan. 6, 1974, p. 8.

[19] In the preface to *Three Port Elizabeth Plays*, Fugard says he spent two years as a seaman in the Far East (p. vii). Sometimes he has said he was at sea for eighteen months. (Since he went to sea in Oct. 1953, this would mark the end of his sailing career as some time between April and Oct. 1955.) In fact, Fugard had returned to Port Elizabeth by May 21, 1954 when the *Eastern Province Herald* published an article on his experiences ("Student's 30-Pound World Trip.") Therefore, his entire trip lasted only about one year, with about half of that at sea.

[20] Mel Gussow, "Witness," *The New Yorker*, Dec. 20, 1982, p. 89.

[21] Fugard, "Caught in a Typhoon," NELM.

Fugard, "Turning the Pages of History in Graveyards," *Port Elizabeth Evening Post*, May 28, 1954.

[22] Benson, "Keeping an Appointment," p. 77.

[23] "Three One-Act Plays in Programme," *The Argus* (Cape Town), Oct. 4, 1956.

[24] Naseem Khan, "Athol Fugard," *Ink* (London), July 23-29, 1971, p. 27.

[25] From my correspondence with Grütter, May 22, 1977.

[26] Benson, "Keeping an Appointment," p. 78.

[27] Correspondence with Grütter.

[28] Benson, "Keeping an Appointment," p. 78.

[29] *Ibid.*

[30] The high incidence of exile and suicide among this group is not unusual in South Africa. T.T. Moyana writes that in addition to black and Coloured exiles such as Ezekiel Mphahlele (who has since returned to South Africa), Dennis Brutus, Lewis Nkosi, Mazisi Kunene, Bloke Modisane, Alex La Guma, Peter Abrahams, Alfred Hutchin-

216

son, Arthur Nortje, Todd Matshikiza, and Noni Jabavu "some English and Boer writers too have left, among them well-known names like Roy Campbell, William Plomer, Laurens van her Post, Dan Jacobson, and C.J. Driver. Many writers have committed suicide: including three Afrikaner poets, according to one source, and at least twice as many black writers among them the journalists Can Themba and Nat Nakasa. The leading and prize-winning Afrikaner writer Breytenbach has lived in exile in Paris, because he married a Vietnamese. . . . Every single writer worth the name has had to suffer in some way from the heavy hand of the law, because he is a writer." "Problems of a Creative Writer in South Africa," in *Aspects of South African Literature*, ed. Christopher Heywood (London: Heinemann, and New York: Africana Publishing, 1976), p. 89. In 1975, Breytenbach returned to South Africa in disguise and was given a nine-year prison sentence for being part of a conspiracy to overthrow the government. He was released in 1982. Can Themba did not commit suicide.

[31] Lewis Nkosi, "Athol Fugard: His Work and Us," *South Africa: Information and Analysis,*" No. 63 (May 1968), p. 2. All Nkosi quotes in this section and the next are from this article.

[32] All Mokae quotes throughout this book are from an interview in Los Angeles, Aug. 22, 1980.

[33] From my correspondence with Brulin, July 2, 1980.

[34] Dora Sowden, "African Drama," *Rand Daily Mail*, Sept. 18, 1958, p. 6.

[35] Robert Hodgins, "Interview with Athol Fugard," *Newscheck*, July 21, 1967, p. 25. Hough, p. 39.

[36] Mary Benson, "One Little Corner of the World," *yale/theatre*, 4 (Winter 1973), p. 58. NELM. Fugard did, however, suggest that Alton Kumalo produce them for his Themba Theatre Company. See "Interview with Alton Kumalo," in Stephen Gray (ed.) *Athol Fugard*, Southern Africa Literature Series, No. 1 (Johannesburg: McGraw-Hill, 1982), pp. 119-20.

[37] Bob Leshoai, "Theatre and the Common Man in South Africa," *Transition*, No. 19 (1965), p. 45.

[38] B.S., "Rev. *A Kakamas Greek*," *Algemeen Handels Blad* (Rotterdam), June 2, 1960. "*A Kakamas Greek* Nu in Amsterdam," *Het Parool*, June 2, 1960.

[39] Correspondence with Brulin, July 2, 1980.

[40] D.K. "Rev. *De Honden*," *Elsevier* (Amsterdam), Nov. 19, 1960. Hans Van Straten, "Rassendrama Grijpt Publiek Naar Keel," *Het Vrije Volk* (Rotterdam), Nov. 14, 1960.

[41] "South Africa's Play about Things as They Are," *The Times*, Dec. 11, 1961, p. 5. The uncredited author of this article is Mary Benson.

[42] Fugard, *Three Port Elizabeth Plays*, p. viii.

[43] Fugard, *Notebooks: 1960-1977* (NY: Alfred A. Knopf, 1984), p. viii.

[44] Raine, p. 11.

[45] Stephen Gray, "The Coming into Print of Athol Fugard's *Tsotsi*," *Journal of Commonwealth Literature*, 16 (Aug. 1981), p. 60.

[46] Shark's protection racket is supposed to prevent just such murders. See *No-Good Friday*, p. 138.

[47] David Hogg, "Unpublished Fugard Novel," *Contrast*, 12, No. 1 (1978), p. 76.

Chapter II

[1] Undated, NELM.

[2] Dec. 16, 1960, NELM.

[3] Jonathan Marks, "Interview with Athol Fugard," yale/theatre, 4 (Winter 1973), p. 70.

[4] Fugard, Three Port Elizabeth Plays, p. viii.

[5] Hodgins, p. 29. Fugard's own encounter with moths near a gasoline station (12-60) is repeated by Morrie (p. 63).
Marks, "Interview," p. 69.
Benson, "One Little Corner," p. 58.

[6] Zach wants to drive "to hell and gone," (49) which is precisely the name of the game Tsotsi remembers from his childhood (134).

[7] Fugard's knowledge of insects is also evident in his next play, People Are Living There, in which he uses silkworms as a symbol of metamorphosis.

[8] Raine, p. 10.

[9] Marks, "Interview," p. 66.

[10] Raine, p. 11.

[11] Athol Fugard, The Blood Knot (New York: Samuel French, n.d.), p. 4.

[12] Hodgins, p. 28.

[13] Lewis Nkosi, "Athol Fugard: His Work and Us," South Africa: Information and Analysis, No. 64 (May 1968), pp. 5, 7, 8.

[14] All Simon quotes throughout this book are from an interview in Los Angeles, July 16-17, 1982.

[15] Oliver Walker, "Stark Tragedy of a Coloured Man," Johannesburg Star, Sept. 5, 1961.

[16] G.V.L., " 'Blood Knot' is Superb Theatre," Rand Daily Mail, Nov. 9, 1961, p. 8.
James Ambrose Brown, "Rev. The Blood Knot," Sunday Times (Johannesburg), Nov. 12, 1961.

[17] Nadine Gordimer, "Plays and Piracy: A Discussion," Contrast, 3, No. 4 (1964-65), p. 55.
Khan.

[18] BBC, "Life and Works."

[19] Soon after arriving she says, "Twelve years ago next month. I worked it out in the train. I was twenty-two." (111) She also says, "1937. Six years old." (144) If she were born in 1931, Hester would have been twenty-two in 1953. If that were twelve years prior to her return home, Fugard apparently meant to set the play in 1965 when it was completed and first produced. However, Hester also implies she was away from home for fifteen years (127), and in Johnnie's opening monologue he refers to 1963 as if it were the date of the play's setting. He also says his chance to go to railroad school, in 1958, occurred perhaps ten years previously. (153) Fugard is aware of these discrepancies: "I slipped up on some arithemetic."
    A similar mathematical error exists in Nongogo. Before beginning his door-to-door rounds, Johnny leaves some of the material he has bought with Queeny. He plans to sell the rest at a 50% mark-up. He returns with twelve pounds, the original eight plus four pounds profit. However, he still has some material left over. Either his mark-up is greater, or he returns with less money. Fugard says of such mathematical errors, "I usually slip up and my petticoat shows in things like that."

[20] Hodgins, p. 29.

[21] Some of the ways *Hello and Goodbye* reflects Afrikanerdom are noted by Lionel Abrahams, "Hello and Goodbye," *The Classic*, 2, No. 2 (1966), p. 76, and by John David Raymer, "Eight Recent Plays by South African Dramatist Athol Fugard: His Method, His Development as a Playwright, His South African Context, and the Major Influences upon Him," Diss. Ohio University, 1975, pp. 91-93.

[22] Benson, "Athol Fugard and 'One Little Cortner of the World,' " *yale/theatre*, 4 (Winter 1973), p. 58, and Ronald Hayman, "Janet Suzman: Intelligence and Emotion," *The Times*, Oct. 13, 1973, p. 11.

[23] Abrahams, p. 72.

    Hodgins, p. 24.

[24] "Athol Fugard Writes an Open Letter to Playwrights," *Forward* (Johannesburg), Sept. 1962.

    Anti-Apartheid Movement declaration, London, June 25, 1963. For debate on the boycott see, for example, a series of letters that appeared in *The Times* in 1968, on May 7, 9, 11, 17, and 18.

[25] Fugard, *Three Port Elizabeth Plays*, p. xvii.

[26] *Ibid*, p. xviii.

    BBC, "Life and Works."

[27] Fugard, *Three Port Elizabeth Plays*, p. xix. For some of his thoughts on why his passport was removed, see Donald Prosser, "What's behind the Passport Ban?," *Eastern Province Herald*, June 9, 1970.

    "Athol Fugard and Don Maclennan: A Conversation," *English in Africa*, 9, No. 2 (1982), p. 10.

[28] Dorrian McLaren, "Athol Fugard and His Work," Diss. University of Leeds, 1974, p. 45.

[29] Hodgins, p. 27.

[30] Frank O'Connor, *A Short History of Irish Literature* (New York: G.P. Putnam's Sons, 1967), p. 11.

[31] In the Samuel French edition, the old man's Xhosa is translated; he claims to be looking for relatives. However, in the theatre he is incomprehensible except to some audiences in South Africa. Furthermore, Fugard has admitted that providing a translation for this edition was a mistake. Neither Yvonne Bryceland, who created the role of Lena, nor Ruby Dee, who played her in the American premiere, was given a translation. Had Fugard wanted Lena and the audience to understand Outa's words, he would have made him speak in broken English. According to Fugard, each actor playing Outa should make up his own lines.

[32] Boesman's pleasure in misfortune, including his own, is especially clear in the film version of the play. As a bulldozer demolishes the shantytown at the beginning of the film, Boesman shrieks with laughter. He puts a license plate around his neck, begs a cigarette butt from one of the workmen, and gleefully leaps about the rubble saying, "*Dankie* [thank you] *Baas, dankie Baas.*" Lena is not amused by his behavior, but the workmen are. The use of a bulldozer for a "slum clearance" is reminiscent of the end of *Tsotsi*.

    The film also shows Boesman selling bait, he and Lena trekking to the mudflats, and the mudflats themselves. This especially pleased Fugard: "If there is one thing the film finally does which the play should have done but doesn't do, is just to explain why Boesman ends up on those mudflats. They are like a little oasis of freedom, of serenity, just that one pulsing rhythm of the tides, the river coming up, the river going down—birds, silence. But totally ringed by industrial Port Elizabeth. You have something going round and round like a record turning, with something happening very fast on the periphery and the nearer you get to the center, to that spinning, is a point of total stillness." (McLaren, p. 41). Fugard has also used this record image in his teleplay, *Mille Miglia*, broadcast by the BBC.

The BBC was also interested in filming *Boesman and Lena*, but Fugard elected to work with a South African production team—Ross Devenish as director and Johan Wicht as producer. Fugard expanded the action to cover two days and two nights, but he cut some of his dialogue: "One has been able to stay a lot closer to the bone of the experience and not try to adorn it with clever words and pretty smiles, striking metaphors and things like that." ("Fugard in New Medium," *The Pretoria News*, Jan. 24, 1973, p. 18.) Filming began in Dec. 1972 and continued, mostly at night, for seven weeks. It was shot on an island in the Swartkops River. At the Atlanta Film Festival, it received a silver medal in the foreign picture category and also a gold medal as a special Jury Award.

[33] Khan.

[34] Stanley Kauffmann, *Persons of the Drama* (New York: Harper & Row, 1976), p. 205.

[35] Khan.

[36] A highly effective detail was added to the death scene in the film. After beating Outa, Boesman collapses on top of the corpse. Juxtaposed over this somberness is the gay sound of voices from a motorboat cruising the river.

[37] McLaren, p. 39.

[38] This uncertainty about their marital status is appropriate since many facts about their past are unclear, and when factual "truths" are revealed, they explain nothing.

In an earlier draft, Boesman and Lena are clearly not married. Lena claims that Boesman had said they would be married in church. Boesman replies he must have been drunk that day. (Fugard, "Extract from a Work in Progress: First Sketch for the Opening of Act I," *Teater S.A.*, 1, No. 2 (1968), insert, p. 10.)

Although this extract covers only nine pages, it is worth noting some of the changes Fugard made in the text. The first line of the play remains "Here," but in the earlier version it is a simple statement by Boesman, perhaps an order, rather than a question from Lena. The next line runs, "Is he still there?," apparently in reference to Outa. Fugard's decision to cut any foreshadowing of Outa's appearance and to introduce him only after establishing the relationship between Boesman and Lena is a sound one. In a similar way, mention of "the babies that never lived" was cut from the early pages so that Lena's subsequent description for Outa of the birth carries more weight because it is more of a surprise.

[39] Alain Robbe-Grillet, *For a New Novel: Essays on Fiction*, trans. Richard Howard (New York: Grove Press, 1965), p. 17.

[40] Marks, "Interview," p. 67.

[41] "Action" is a treacherous term in any discussion of drama. Francis Fergusson notes, "The distinction between plot and action is fundamental, but it is very difficult to

make in general terms. . . . Aristotle does not explain [it]." (*The Idea of a Theatre: A Study of Ten Plays, The Art of Drama in Changing Perspective* [New York: Doubleday, 1953], p. 242). By action, Fergusson writes, "I do not mean the events of the story but the focus or aim of psychic life from which the events, in that situation, result." (p. 48) Thus, every play has an action or, in Aristotle's terms, "is an imitation of an action," and strives to achieve unity of action.

My use of the term is more literal and limited. Instead of using it inclusively as something inherent in all drama, I use it exclusively to distinguish *Boesman and Lena* and plays like it from more conventional works. My meaning is similar to that of Racine and Corneille—the result of action: "the overt deeds, chains of events reportable as facts, which action produces." (Fergusson, p. 61). Such results are missing in *Boesman and Lena*.

If, as Fergusson argues, every play has an action that can be expressed by an infinitive, for most plays, the verb is transitive; in *Boesman and Lena* and static plays like it, the verb is intransitive. The action of *Boesman and Lena* is "to search," but Fugard's characters seek without finding, struggle without resolution, and act without effect.

[42] Khan.

[43] Hough, p. 44. Fugard has added, "By the same token, *Statements* could be in Afrikaans and *Aloes* too, at least between Piet and Steve." Similarly, there are moments in *No-Good Friday, Nongogo,* and *Sizwe Bansi* where black characters converse in English when, in realistic terms, Zulu or Xhosa would be more appropriate.

[44] Albert Camus, *The Myth of Sisyphus: And Other Essays,* trans. Justin O'Brien (1952; rpt. New York: Vintage, 1955), p. 5.

[45] John Gassner, *The Theatre in Our Times* (New York: Crown Publishers, 1954), p. 65.

[46] In a short scene added to the film, Boesman's prostration before whites is clearly shown when he sells fishbait.

[47] BBC, "Life and Works."

[48] Friedrich Nietzsche, *The Birth of Tragedy,* trans. Francis Golffing (Garden City: Doubleday & Co., 1956), pp. 51-52.

Ibid., p. 102.

[49] From a private conversation, New Haven, Connecticut, July 1977.

[50] Jean Branford, "Fugard Play Joy Shines Off Misery," *Cape Argus,* July 12, 1969, in Gray (ed.), *Athol Fugard,* p. 80.

[51] Fugard, "Extract from a Work in Progress," pp. 2-3.

[52] BBC, "Life and Works."

Raine, pp. 9, 11.

[53] Quoted in Benson, "Athol Fugard," p. 58 from a letter Fugard had written Benson.

[54] Sigmund Freud, *Civilization and Its Discontents,* trans. Joan Riviere (New York: Doubleday, 1958), p. 17.

[55] Samuel Beckett, *Proust* (1931; rpt. New York: Grove Press, n.d.), p. 59.

[56] Quoted by Richard Gilman in his introduction to Franz Xaver Kroetz's *Farmyard and Other Plays* (New York: Urizen Books, 1976), p. 18.

[57] BBC, "Life and Works."

Chapter III

1 Fugard, "Extract from a Work in Progress," p. 1.
2 Fugard, *Boesman and Lena: And Other Plays* (Oxford: Oxford University Press, 1978), p. xi.
3 Milly's reference to puberty is clearer in an early version of the script: "It happened. The thing boys don't know about that happens to girls. Suddenly it was there. I sat on my bed with my body, being brave—but I didn't know it anymore, if I liked it anymore. I mean me. To be me. It used to be fun, to be small. But suddenly I had to be careful because I was getting big." ("People Are Living There," *Contrast*, 5 (July 1968), p. 45.
4 James Ambrose Brown, "Fugard's Millie Lives Again in Sharp New Focus," *Cape Times*, May 15, 1972, p. 7.
5 Peter Wilhelm, "Athol Fugard at Forty," *To the Point*, June 3, 1972, p. 39.
6 Johnnie in *Hello and Goodbye* also has a scoring system. He tells Hester, "That was a very good description. My journey to P.E. on the S.A.R. I'd give you eight out of ten." (113)
7 "People," *Contrast*, p. 31.
   See Gray, *Athol Fugard*, p. 43.
8 Martin Gottfried, "Rev. *People*," *Women's Wear Daily*, Nov. 21, 1971.
9 "People," *Contrast*, p. 31.
10 Murray Biggs, "Prison and the South African Theatre of Athol Fugard," unpublished paper, p. 10.
11 During a talk at the Yale School of Drama, New Haven, Connecticut, Oct. 10, 1974.
12 Henri Bergson, *Laughter*, trans. by arrangement with the Presses Universitaires de France (1900; rpt. New York: Doubleday, 1956), p. 71.
13 Horace Walpole, *The Letters of Horace Walpole* (Oxford: Clarendon, 1903-05), 9: p. 403.
   J.L. Styan, *The Dark Comedy: The Development of Modern Comic Tragedy* (Cambridge: Cambridge University Press, 1968), p. 47.
14 Fugard may have had in mind these words from Chaplin's *My Autobiography*: "We must laugh in the face of our helplessness against the forces of nature—or go insane." (New York: Pocket Books, 1966), p. 327.
   Camus, *Sisyphus*, p. 90.
15 Undated, but sometime in 1962.
   M.M. Levin, "Reps Disagreed over Athol Fugard Play," undated, NELM.
16 In *Scottish Daily Mail*, quoted in "Fugard Scores Big Success," unnamed South African newspaper, March 15, 1968, NELM.
   Terry Herbst, "Brilliant New Fugard Play Marks a New Era in South African Theatre," *Cape Times*, June 16, 1969, p. 11.
17 Richard Watts, "A Sad Birthday Party," *New York Post*, Nov. 19, 1971.
18 From a letter dated Oct. 20, 1980.
19 Undated, sometime in 1963.
20 The famous monastery at Monte Cassino, founded in the fifth century, was located about eight miles south of Rome. It could have been part of, in Serge's words, "the cradle of ancient civilization." (266) In 1944 it was virtually destroyed by Allied bombs because the Germans had occupied positions near the abbey. The Germans survived; many of the monastery's art treasures did not.

[21] During this research, Fugard obviously read Jenkinson's article "Fright" in Michael Frewin (ed.), *The International Grand Prix Book of Motor Racing* (New York: Doubleday, 1965), p. 197.

[22] NELM, also the source for Midgley's two letters that follow, which are, respectively, undated and July 24, 1968.

[23] Benson, "Athol Fugard," p. 59.

Michael Billington, "Philosophy of Moss," *The Times*, Aug. 6, 1968, p. 9.

[24] Sylvia Clayton, "Mille Miglia Was Brighter Says Moss," *Daily Telegraph*, Aug. 6, 1968.

[25] Athol Fugard, *The Coat* (Cape Town: A.A. Balkema, 1971), pp. 2, 3.

[26] Keith Dewhurst, "rev. *Mille Miglia*," *Guardian*, Aug. 6, 1968, p. 4.

Tom Stoppard, "Fact Fiction and The Big Race," *The Observer Review*, Aug. 11, 1968, p. 20.

[27] Benson, "Keeping an Appointment," from the original transcript, edited out of the published version. The text has since been published in *Modern Stage Directions: A Collection of Short Dramatic Scripts* edited by Stephen Gray and David Schalkwyk (Cape Town: Mashew Miller Longman, 1984).

Chapter IV

[1] "An African Theatre in South Africa," *African Arts*, 3 (Summer 1970), p. 43.
"Theatre," *The Classic*, 1, No. 1 (1963), p. 65.

[2] Letter to Mary Benson, undated, sometime in 1962.
Ibid.

[3] "Theatre," p. 65.

[4] Benson, "Keeping an Appointment," p. 80.

[5] Undated letter to Benson.

In his introduction to *Three Port Elizabeth Plays*, Fugard inaccurately dates the first performance as May 1963. The cast included: Norman Ntshinga, Humphrey Njikelana, Welcome Duru, Mike Ngxocolo, Simon Hanabe, George Mnci, Sylvia Mapela, and Sarah Blauw. Actors involved in subsequent productions included: Gwyn Mjuza, Sipho Mguqulwa, Mable Magada, Fats Bokholane, Lloyd Moikwana, John Kani, Winston Ntshona, George Luse, Mulligan Mbiquaney, Mangaliso Grootbroom, and Nomhle Nkonyemi.

On the program with *The Cure* was *A Place of Safety*, an original play by Peter du Preez, a professor of psychology at Rhodes. Fugard directed the cast drawn from the university and also played a part.

[6] My thanks to Ian Ferguson for this letter.

[7] All quotes from Allister Sparks, "The Eager New Actors," *Rand Daily Mail*, July 24, 1965.

[8] For another account of this episode see Richard Hall, "Brecht Play Starts Africa Race Row," *The Observer*, May 17, 1964.

[9] Athol Fugard, "African Stages," *New York Times*, Sept. 20, 1964, II, p. 3. For another version of the Rhodesian encounter, in which Fugard's threatened deportation is attributed to his keeping company with two black actresses in a bar, see Louis Calta, " 'Blood Knot' Production Pleases Playwright Who Fled Rhodesia: Atholl [sic] Fugard, South African Avoided Being Deported after Racial Incident," *New York Times*, May 27, 1964, p. 44.

[10] Undated, probably Dec. 1964.

[11] Fugard, *Three Port Elizabeth Plays*, pp. xi-xii. For further details of performance conditions in South Africa see Vandenbroucke, "Chiaroscuro: A Portrait of the Theatre in South Africa," *Theatre Quarterly*, 7, No. 28 (1977), pp. 46-54.

[12] Athol Fugard, "South African Playwright Finds Peace on Crete," *Port Elizabeth Evening Post*, Oct. 1, 1966.

[13] Fugard, *Statements: Three Plays* (London and Cape Town: Oxford, 1974), p. viii.

[14] Markland Taylor, "Fugard Waves through Flames," *New Haven Register*, Oct. 13, 1974, p. 1D ff.

[15] Fugard, *Three Port Elizabeth Plays*, p. xi.

Rob Amato and Skhala Xinwa, " 'The Serpent Players': Rev. of Two Productions (1970)," in Gray, *Athol Fugard*, p. 83.

[16] Fugard, *Statements*, p. ix.

[17] Fugard, *Three Port Elizabeth Plays*, p. xi.

Nancy Plaatjies, "A Note on the Serpent Players and Their Performance of 'The Terrorists' or 'The Just' by Albert Camus," *S'ketsh'* (Summer 1972), p. 30.

[18] "The Crisis of African Theatre," *Business South Africa*, 8 (April 1973), p. 33.

[19] Fugard, *Three Port Elizabeth Plays*, p. xii.

BBC, "Life and Works."

[20] *Ibid.*

"Theatre-Go-Round," *S'ketsh'* (Summer 1974-75), pp. 5, 6.

[21] C.S.M., "Good Acting from New Brighton," *Port Elizabeth Evening Post*, Aug. 16, 1963.

[22] Wilhelm, pp. 38, 39.

[23] Jonathan Marks, "A Man Who Commits Provocative Acts of Theatre," *Yale Reports: News from the Yale Repertory Theatre*, 4, No. 4 (1980), p. 3.

[24] Raine, p. 13.

Doris Whitbeck, "He Puts South Africa on Stage," *Hartford-Courant*, March 10, 1982, p. C1-2.

[25] Marks, "Interview," p. 64, 71. For more of Fugard's comments on actors see "Fugard on Acting, Actors on Fugard," *Theatre Quarterly*, 7, No. 28 (1977), pp. 83-87.

[26] A partial list of these includes: Drama Desk Awards to Colleen Dewhurst (1970) for Hester and Ruby Dee (1971) for Lena; the same performance earned Dee a 1971 Obie (Off Broadway); Yvonne Bryceland, the 1971-72 Gallery Club trophy (Johannesburg) for her Lena; Janet Suzman, Best Actress, 1973 *Evening Standard* Award (London) for her Hester; Benji Francis, Best Actor, 1975, Durban Critic Circle for his Morrie; John Kani and Winston Ntshona, 1975 Tony Awards (Broadway) for *Sizwe Bansi Is Dead* and *The Island*; Robert Christian, a 1976 Obie for his Zach; Zakes Mokae, 1982 Tony Award for Sam in *'Master Harold' . . . and the boys*. The old saw that there are no bad actors but only bad parts is patently false, but it is surely true that good parts make good actors look even better.

Critics have frequently praised the acting in Fugard's plays: Stanley Kauffmann called Ruby Dee's Lena "the best performance I have seen in the American theatre since Judith Anderson's Medea", (*Persons of the Drama*, [New York: Harper & Row 1976], p. 207); the *Boesman and Lena* in which Dee appeared was called "the best-acted play in New York" (Clive Barnes, "Rev. *Boesman and Lena*," *New York Times*, June 23, 1970, p. 30); Michael Coveney wrote about *Statements*, "the acting of Miss

Bryceland and Mr. Kingsley is as good and no doubt better than any other in London at the moment" ("Rev. *Statements," Financial Times,* Jan. 30, 1975, p. 3); Irving Wardle wrote of Bryceland's performance in that production, "pain of this intensity is rarely heard on the English stage" ("Rev. *Statements," The Times,* Jan. 23, 1974, p. 13); Robin Malan called the performances of Fugard, Bryceland, Ken Leach, and Gillian Garlick in the original South African production of *People,* "above anything seen on Cape stages not in months but years" ("Rev. *People," Teater S.A.,* 1, No. 4 [1969], p. 15); Robert Cushman wrote of *Sizwe Bansi,* "And truthfully, you have never seen such acting" ("Drama's Invalid," *Observer,* Jan. 13, 1974, p. 24); and Jack Kroll called Kani and Ntshona in *Sizwe Bansi* and *The Island,* "one of the most extraordinary acting companies I've seen" ("The Beloved Country," *Newsweek,* Dec. 2, 1974, p. 98). Kroll wrote that in *People,* Diana Davila "gives one of the most moving performances I have seen in a long time" ("Rev. *People,*" Newsweek, Dec. 6, 1971, p. 121.)

27 Fugard, *Statements,* p. ix.

28 Benson, "Keeping an Appointment," p. 81.

29 Athol Fougard [sic], "The Blood Knot," *Contrast,* 2, No. 1 (1962), p. 29.

30 Marks, "Interview," p. 66.

31 Fugard, *Statements,* p. x. Technically, part of this statement is Fugard quoting himself in slightly modified form from the earlier Marks, "Interview," p. 64.

32 Fugard, *Statements,* p. x.
   Ibid. and Benson, "Keeping an Appointment," p. 81.

33 Marks, "Interview," p. 66.
   Benson, "Keeping an Appointment," p. 81.

34 In conversation, Dublin, Aug. 10, 1976.

35 Terry Herbst, "Theatre Laboratory Takes Its First Faltering Steps," *Cape Times,* March 20, 1971, p. 8.
   Carole Abramovitz, "Fugard's 'Orestes' 'Powerful, Uplifting, Devastating . . .'," *Cape Times,* April 1, 1971, p. 81.

36 Fugard, *Statements,* p. xi.
   Benson, "Keeping an Appointment," p. 81.

37 As Fugard often does, probably because he is writing from memory, he has slightly misquoted the original. Pound calls an image, "that which presents an intellectual and emotional complex in an instant of time." Ezra Pound, "A Few Don'ts by an Imagist," *Poetry,* 35 (1913), p. 203.
   Hugh Kenner, *The Poetry of Ezra Pound* (1951); rpt. Krauss Reprint Co., 1968), p. 39.

Chapter V

1 Brian Astbury, *The Space/Die Ruimte/Indawo* (Cape Town: Fine, 1980), n.p.
   Ibid.

2 BBC, "Life and Works."

3 *Ibid.*

[4] Michael Coveney, "Challenging the Silence: Athol Fugard Talks to Michael Coveney," *Plays and Players*, 21 (Nov. 1973), p. 35.

[5] From an unpublished interview conducted by Gresdna Doty, London, 1981.

[6] Michael Venables, "Exciting New Indigenous Play," *Rand Daily Mail*, Nov. 24, 1972, p. 27.

[7] "Art is Life and Life Is Art: An Interview with John Kani and Winston Ntshona of the Serpent Players from South Africa," UFAHAMU (Journal of the African Activist Association), 6, No. 2, (1976), p. 7.

From Doty's interview.

[8] Quoted in Vladimir Klima's *South African Prose Writing in English* (Prague: The Oriental Institute in the Publishing House of the Czechoslovak Academy of Sciences, 1971), pp. 76-77.

"Panel on South African Theatre: From the Proceedings of the Symposium on Contemporary South African Literature," *Index: A Quarterly Journal of Africanist Opinion*, 6 (Spring 1976), p. 50.

[9] Mary Benson, "Dramatist," *Christian Science Monitor*, April 3, 1974, p. 9.

The preacher says of the dead man, "But in his life, friends, he walked the roads of this land. He helped print those footpaths which lead through the bush and over the veld . . . footpaths which his children are now walking." (28) The lines echo *Boesman and Lena*.

[10] In his book, Astbury writes, "*Sizwe Bansi*—Athol Fugard—Directed by 022/223725 (Athol Fugard) Cast: N.I. 3964702 (John Kani), N.I. 3811863 (Winston Ntshona)." Zwelinzima is given Ntshona's number.

[11] Alan Seymour, "Rev. *Sizwe Bansi*," *Plays and Players*, 21 (Nov. 1973), p. 52.

Irving Wardle, "Drama of Brotherhood," *The Times*, Sept. 21, 1973, p. 17.

[12] Astbury.

[13] Pat Williams, "Athol Fugard," *Ink*, July 24, 1971, p. 10. Fugard has used this pet phrase on numerous occasions.

Mshengu, "South Africa: Where Mvelinqangi Still Limps (The Experimental Theatre of Workshop '71)," *yale/theatre* 8 (Fall 1977), p. 46.

[14] BBC, "Life and Works."

[15] Albert Camus, *The Plague*, trans. Stuart Gilbert (New York: Random House, 1948), p. 278.

[16] Richard Findlater (ed.), *At the Royal Court: 25 Years of the English Stage Company* (Derbyshire: Amber Lane Press, 1981), p. 158.

[17] Peter Rosenwald, "*Separate Fables*," Guardian, Jan. 8, 1974, p. 10.

[18] Ibid. Kani also says that *The Island* started "out of what we call 'bullshit' talk, when we sit around and don't feel like rehearsing . . . and we're playing on a blanket because Winston was wearing navy blue trousers which would pick up the grass, so we spread the blanket on it." "Art Is Life," p. 17.

[19] From Doty's interview.

[20] BBC, "Life and Works."

[21] Camus, *Sisyphus*, p. 90. Harry, the old prisoner who has turned to stone, is also like Sisyphus: "A face that toils so close to stones is already stone itself." (p. 89)

[22] Mel Gussow, "To Fugard, Playwriting Is 'Defiance,' " *New York Times*, Dec. 17, 1974, p. 30.

Raine, p. 13.

[23] *Ibid.*

[24] BBC, "Life and Works."

[25] Astbury.

[26] Owen Williams, "Honesty, Integrity, but Dullness in Play," *Cape Argus*, March 29, 1972, p. 17.

[27] Benson, "Keeping an Appointment," p. 81.

[28] For *Dimetos* the music would be Bach's Toccata and Fugue in D Minor. Fugard says, "Once you get past the fugue into the toccata you can actually see a cathedral being built, you are actually inside the head of an engineer." A Bach cello concerto is used in *The Guest*, the first time since *No-Good Friday* nineteen years previously that Fugard calls for music in a script. For *"Master Harold"* . . . *and the boys*, Fugard found himself incessantly listening to Mozart's Great Mass in C Minor.

Wilhelm, p. 39.

[29] "Rehearsal Log for the London Premiere of *Statements after an Arrest under the Immorality Act*," pp. 1, 2. (NELM)

Ibid., p. 10.

[30] Denis de Rougemont, *Love in the Western World*, trans. Montgomery Belgion (rev. New York: Harper & Row, 1956), p. 52.

[31] B.A. Young, "Rev. *Statements*," *The Financial Times*, Jan. 23, 1974, p. 3. Also see, Harold Hobson, "Rev. *Statements*," *The Sunday Times*, Jan. 27, 1974, p. 29.

[32] Jonathan Hammond, "A South African Season: *Sizwe Bansi, The Island* and *Statements*," *Plays and Players*, 21 (March 1974), 43.

[33] Frank Marcus, "In the Act," *Sunday Telegraph*, Jan. 27, 1974, p. 32.

[34] Raymer, p. 195.

[35] Raine, p. 13.

[36] "At Yale."

[37] *Ibid.*

[38] *Ibid.*

[39] Nkosi, "Athol Fugard: His Work and Us," p. 2.

[40] Alan Paton, *Knocking on the Door: Shorter Writings*, selected and edited by Colin Gardner (Cape Town: David Philip, 1975), p. 140.

Nadine Gordimer, "English-Language Literature and Politics in South Africa," in Heywood (ed.), *Aspects of South African Literature* (London: Heinemann; New York: Africana Publishing, 1976), p. 100.

[41] William Plomer, *Turbott Wolfe* (1925; rpt. London: Hogarth, 1965), p. 68.

Ezekiel Mphahlele, *Down Second Avenue* (1957; rpt. Garden City: Doubleday, 1971), p. 207.

[42] Gordimer, "English-Language Literature," pp. 107-08.

Alan Lennox-Short, *English and South Africa* (Cape Town: Nasou, n.d.), p. 57. South Africa's best-known novelists have written about miscegenation: Paton in *Too Late the Phalarope* (1953) and Gordimer in *Occasion for Loving* (1963). Also on the subject are Millin's *God's Stepchildren* (1924) and *King of the Bastards* (1950), Jacobson's *The Evidence of Love* (1959), and J.C.B. van Niekerk's early Afrikaans play *Van Riet van Rietfontein* (1929).

As early as 1968, four years prior to *Statements*, Fugard had been thinking about a play in which miscegenation would figure prominently: "It's a play that should have been written. Funnily enough I keep thinking of it from time to time. Its title was *Man without Scenery*, which sounds a bit derivative of Sartre. The plot was very simple: an Afrikaner bus conductor [Danie] by chance meets a Coloured man [Steve] who has a slightly retarded daughter [Lena], and the Afrikaner falls in love with the Coloured girl. The three of them live in relative security until a Group Areas decision totally changes the character of the little world in which they are living." (Benson, "Keeping an Appointment, p. 80.) A trace of this plot can be found in *Aloes* in which a former bus driver named Piet, who is Afrikaner, loves not a re-tarded Coloured girl but an emotionally unstable white woman. For Fugard, Piet and Danie "are the same character in a sense. There isn't as direct a connection between the Steve of *Aloes* and Steve in *Man without Scenery*," to which Fugard also refers as "the Fairview play."

[43] Athol Fugard, "Must S.A. Plays 'Protest'?," *Port Elizabeth Evening Post*, undated, NELM.

[44] Hodgins, p. 29.

[45] Benson, "Athol Fugard," p. 55.

[46] Mervyn Woodrow, "A Critical Consideration of English Plays Written in South Africa, with Special Reference to the Emergence of a Dominant Theme," Diss. U. of Pretoria, 1972, pp. 82-83.

[47] J.W. Lambert, "Plays in Performance," *Drama*, No. 112 (Spring 1974), p. 22.
Raymer, p. 153.
Kani and Ntshona spoke at the Yale School of Drama, New Haven, Connecticut, Nov. 8, 1974.

[48] Raymer, p. 135.

[49] Michael Billington, "Rev. *Boesman and Lena*," *Plays and Players*, 18 (Sept. 1971), p. 49. Billington later praised *Sizwe Bansi* as a "profoundly political play." *The Guardian*, Jan. 9, 1974.

[50] "Panel on South African Theatre," p. 54.
Marks, "Man Who Commits," p. 2.

[51] R.K., "Sizwe Bansi Is Alive and Struggling for Freedom," *African Communist*, No. 58 (1974), p. 126.

[52] Taylor, p. 4D.

[53] "Plays Not Anti-South African—Fugard," *East Province Herald* (Port Elizabeth), Feb. 5, 1974, p. 11.

[54] Jean-Paul Sartre, *What Is Literature?*, trans. Bernard Frechtman (New York: The Philosophical Library, 1949), p. 23.

[55] Leslie Fiedler, "Symposium on the State of American Writing," *Partisan Review*, Aug. 1948, p. 886.

[56] Michael Meyer, *Ibsen: A Biography* (Garden City: Doubleday, 1971), p. 774.

[57] Marks, "Interview," p. 68.

Chapter VI

[1] McLaren, p. 4.
"At Yale."

[2] Albert Camus, *Notebooks: 1935-1942*, trans. Philip Thody (New York: Modern Library, 1965), p. 136.

[3] Camus, *Sisyphus*, p. 89.

[4] Garrett Hardin, *Promethean Ethics: Living with Death, Competition, and Triage* (Seattle: University of Washington Press, 1980), p. 5.

Anatole France, *On Life and Letters*, trans. A.W. Evans (New York: John Laney, 1911), I, p. viii.

[5] "Original Notes of *Dimetos*," p. 1 (NELM).

[6] J.B. Bury, *The Idea of Progress: An Inquiry into Its Origin and Growth* (1932; rpt. New York: Dover Books, 1959), pp. xx, xi.

[7] Johnnie Smit refers to "my two helping hands useless and empty." (103) Barend, in *The Occupation*, possesses "*big hands—so empty.*" (260) Philander imagines himself without anything except his hands, which are empty, and they too are surrendered. In a pivotal speech in Fugard's next play, *Aloes*, Steve Daniels says of his hands, "They might as well fall off for all they mean in my life now." (67) The emptiness of Fugard's own hands was especially disturbing when his mother once entered the hospital: "The past twenty-four hours have been sheer hell. Nothing to record but the stupidity of my helplessness. To stand by with empty hands . . .". (12-24-63)

[8] Taylor, p. 4D.

[9] Astbury.

[10] B.A. Young, "Rev. *Dimetos*," *The Financial Times*, Aug. 29, 1975.

Ned Chaillet, "Rev. *Dimetos*," *Plays and Players*, 23 (Aug. 1976), p. 26.

Harold Hobson, "A Play to Remember," *Sunday Times* Sept. 7, 1975, p. 37.

[11] John Elsom, "Atonement," *Listener*, 95 (June 3, 1976), p. 711.

Chaillet, p. 27.

Astbury.

[12] Raine, p. 10.

[13] A. Christopher Tucker, "Athol Fugard," *Transatlantic Review*, No. 53/54 (1976), p. 88.

[14] Hints suggesting the time the play is set are not conclusive. It takes Danilo a day to reach Dimetos in the first act and more than a day in the second, but his mode of travel is unspecified. The city's concrete and stormwater systems are mentioned in the play, but these do not specifically date it either: Concrete ruins of the Roman Empire are still extant and the modern type of structural concrete dates to 1850; drainage systems date back even further. Dimetos's reference to a tap for water in the city probably sets the play within this century.

There is, in fact, a place in Port Elizabeth from which the city can be viewed much as Dimetos does in gazing down from the old fort.

While reworking the play for its second production, Fugard did give it a specific setting in his imagination: Bethesda in the Karoo for Act I and Mossel Bay for Act II. "The play now reads (and could be so staged) as either present or past." (2-76)

[15] Tucker, p. 89.

For a discussion of the parallels among Camus, Fugard, and Parthenius see Richard Whitaker, "Dimoetes to Dimetos: The Evolution of a Myth," *English Studies in Africa*, 24, No. 1, (1981), pp. 45-59.

[16] Harold Hobson, "Tales of Passion and Destruction," *Sunday Times* May 30, 1976, p. 37.

[17] "Fugard Plans New Play—On Gambling," *Cape Times*, Apr. 18, 1974, p. 10.

[18] Ben Shepard, "Marais—A Mind in the Wilderness," *The Listener*, Mar. 10, 1977, p. 299.

[19] Rousseau's book was subsequently translated into English as *The Dark Stream: The Story of Eugène N. Marais*," (Johannesburg: Jonathan Ball, 1982).

[20] Astbury.

[21] Eugène Marais, *The Soul of the White Ant*, trans. Winifred de Kok (New York: Dodd, Mead & Co., 1937), p. 106. Marais's other publications include, among others, *The Soul of the Ape* (New York: Atheneum, 1969); *My Friends the Baboons*, trans. de Kok (1939; rpt. Cape Town and Pretoria: Human and Rousseau, 1971); and "Notes on Some Effects of Extreme Drought in Waterberg," *South African Smithsonian Annual Report*, 1914 (Part 1), pp. 511-22.

[22] This scene follows immediately after his success in getting the remaining pills from Doors, but it is not as clear as it could be that he is taking the bath to counteract the pain of withdrawal.

The help Visser had given Marais and Brenda is also enigmatic. Visser says, "Your doctor doesn't remember a thing, and he hopes for his sake that you will do the same." (59) He is referring to an abortion, but it is impossible to glean this from his elusive words unless one already knows about this incident in Marais's life. The scene with Brenda is the weakest in the film and could easily have been cut.

[23] Friedrich Nietzsche, *Beyond Good and Evil*, trans. Marianne Cowan (Chicago: Henry Regnery, 1955), p. 86.

Camus, *Notebooks: 1935-1942*, pp. 21, 28.

[24] "The Art of the Possible—An Interview with Ross Devenish," *The Blood Horse*, No. 6 (Dec. 1981), p. 73.

[25] These sources are, respectively, Daniel Raeford, *Rand Daily Mail*, Sept. 14, 1977, p. 6; Percy Baneshik, *The Star*, Sept. 15, 1977, p. 11; and Barry Liknaitzky, *Cape Times*, Sept. 16, 1977, p. 8.

[26] Samuel Taylor Coleridge, *Collected Letters*, ed. Earle L. Griggs (Oxford: Oxford University Press, 1956), II, p. 388.

Friedrich Nietzsche, *Twilight of the Idols*, trans. R.J. Hollingdale (Middlesex: Penguin Books, 1968), p. 39.

Chapter VII

[1] Gussow, "Witness," pp. 86-87.

[2] Ross Devenish, *Athol Fugard: A Lesson from Aloes*, BBC-RM Productions, 1979. This is a Devenish film of the rehearsal period leading up to the premiere of *Aloes* at Johannesburg's Market Theatre.

[3] Fugard, *The Coat*, p. 3.

Marks, "Man Who Commits," p. 1.

[4] Gussow, "Fugard Balances,"

[5] The opening image of *Aloes* echoes *Endgame*. Sitting perfectly still in her sunglasses, Gladys resembles Hamm, who is also sedentary and in dark glasses. Her "I'm awake" suggests a readiness to interact with the man taking care of her that can be compared to Hamm's first line, "Me to play."

[6] Wilhelm, p. 38.

[7] Raine, p. 13.

[8] Benson, "Fugard's *A Lesson from Aloes*: An Introduction," *Theater*, 11, No. 2 (Spring 1980), p. 6.

[9] Benson, "Athol Fugard," p. 58.
    BBC Radio, "Kaleidoscope" (Radio 4), Jan. 2, 1974.

[10] "Fugard Writes Again," *Pretoria News*, July 25, 1978, p. 2. Devenish's film of the rehearsal period documents many of the difficulties Jacobs had with the part of Steve.

[11] Marks, "Man Who Commits," p. 3
    Raine, p. 13.

[12] Marks, "Man Who Commits," p. 3.

[13] Benson, "Fugard's *Aloes*," p. 6.

[14] BBC, "Life and Works."

[15] Raine, p. 11.

[16] Patricia Barnes, "Athol Fugard's South African Conscience," *The Times*, June 30, 1980, p. 11.

[17] Fugard, *Three Port Elizabeth Plays*, p. xix.

[18] David Richards, "The Agony and the Irony: Playwright Athol Fugard and the Sorrows of South Africa," *The Washington Post*, Nov. 8, 1971, p. M1.

[19] Devenish.
    Ibid. Fugard's maternal grandmother died at the Fort England Mental Home in Grahamstown.

[20] "RM Productions: *Marigolds in August*," photocopied press hand-out, n.d., n.p.

[21] *Ibid.* Much of the material in this hand-out is found in "To See an Invisible Man," *Rand Daily Mail*, July 26, 1979, p. 11.

[22] Fugard, *The Blood Knot* (Samuel French), p. 4.

Chapter VIII

[1] Raine, p. 11.
    Gussow, "Witness," p. 55.

[2] Letter to Russell Vandenbroucke, October 8, 1981.

[3] As originally scripted, the song was to have been sung by Lena Horne. After Fugard learned that she had never recorded it, as he had presumed, she expressed her willingness to do so—without a fee. However, the Yale Repertory Theatre would not pay the cost of a recording session. A Sarah Vaughan recording was used instead. Fugard had hoped to use Horne's rendition as a form of gratitude both for her voice and for her praise of him when he had received a Best Play award from The New York Drama Critics' Circle for *Aloes*.

[4] William B. Collins, "A Master's Play of Tragic Import Is Brought Here," *The Philadelphia Inquirer*, March 21, 1982, p. 10-M.
    BBC, "Life and Works."

[5] Gussow, "Witness," p. 87.
    Letter to Vandenbroucke.
    "Athol Fugard and Don Maclennan," pp. 3-4.

[6] *Ibid.*, p. 9.

[7] Letter to Vandenbroucke.

"Masterful Fugard: Athol Fugard's *"Master Harold"* . . . *and the boys,"* *Yale Reports*, 6, No. 4 (1982), p. 1.

[8] "Athol Fugard and Don Maclennan," p. 6.

[9] Kroll, "Masters and Servants" (rev. *"Master Harold"*), *Newsweek*, March 29, 1982, p. 52.

Rich, "Rev. *'Master Harold','"* *New York Times*, May 5, 1982.

[10] Joseph Lelyveld, *"Master Harold* Stuns Johannesburg Audience," *New York Times*, March 24, 1983, p. 22.

Chapter IX

[1] Fugard, *Three Port Elizabeth Plays*, p. xxv.

[2] Fugard, *Orestes*, p. 4.

[3] Kauffmann, p. 206.

[4] T.S. Eliot, "Tradition and the Individual Talent," in *Selected Essays: 1917-1932* (New York: Harcourt, Brace, Jovanovich, 1932), pp. 4, 5.

[5] Hough, p. 43. Faulkner had had a similar insight: "I discovered that my own little postage stamp of native soil was worth writing about, so I created a cosmos of my own." (Quoted in the documentary film *William Faulkner: A Life on Paper*, written by A.I. Bezzerides, directed by Robert Squier.)

[6] Michael Millgate, *The Achievement of William Faulkner* (New York: Random House, 1966), p. 278.

[7] Khan.

[8] Raine, p. 10.

[9] *Ibid.*

[10] Camus, *Sisyphus*, p. 5.

Ibid., p. 7.

[11] Camus, *Resistance, Rebellion, and Death*, trans. Justin O'Brien (New York: Modern Library, 1963), p. 62. Camus has expressed the same idea a number of times. See *The Plague*, p. 278, *Notebooks: 1935-1942*, p. 97, and Herbert R. Lottman, *Albert Camus: A Biography* (New York: Doubleday, 1979), p. 61.

[12] Deidre Bair, *Samuel Beckett: A Biography* (New York and London: Harcourt, 1978), p. 521.

[13] Such rhythmic patter is also found in *People*:

Shorty: You said you hate me.

Milly: I exaggerated.

Shorty: So you like me?

Milly: No need to go to the other extreme. Let's just say you're also human and leave it at that. (61)

[14] John Simon, *Uneasy Stages: A Chronicle of the New York Theatre 1963-1973* (New York: Random House, 1976), p. 263.

Martin Gottfried, "Fugard Copes with Africa," *New York Post*, Nov. 14, 1974.

Jean Marquard, "Fugard Revival," *Snarl*, 1 (Aug. 1974), p. 6.

[15] Fugard, "Extract from a Work in Progress," p. 1.

BBC, "Life and Works." The Camus phrase "truths the hand can touch" is from "Summer in Algiers" in *Lyrical and Critical Essays*, ed. Philip Thody, trans. Ellen Conroy Kennedy (New York: Vintage, 1955), p. 90.

[16] Abrahams, p. 74.

[17] Taylor, p. 4D.

[18] Abrahams, p. 72. Hodgins notes, "Athol Fugard is, flatly, the best playwright South Africa has." (p. 24) Lindy Wilson has given him the same title in her review of *Boesman and Lena* in *South African Outlook*, 99 (Aug. 1969), p. 129.

Nadine Gordimer, "English-Language Literature," p. 114.

Clive Barnes, rev. *Statements, New York Post*, Feb. 6, 1978.

[19] Robert L. Berner, "Athol Fugard and the Theatre of Improvisation," *Books Abroad*, 50 (Winter 1976), p. 81.

Martin Gottfried, " 'The Island' Joins 'Sizwe Bansi,' " *New York Post*, Nov. 25, 1974.

[20] Francis Lee Utley, Lynn Z. Bloom, and Arthur F. Kinney (eds.), *Bear, Man, and God: Seven Approaches to William Faulkner's "The Bear"* (New York: Random House, 1964), p. 171.

Camus, *Resistance*, p. v.

Bair, p. 606.

[21] Benson, "Athol Fugard," p. 59. In explaining why he has allowed his play to be produced in segregated theatres, Fugard has also cited this idea of reaching out and speaking to the man next to him.

[22] Camus, *Sisyphus*, p. 73.

BBC, "Life and Works."

Appendix B

[1] J.W. Smeed, *Faust in Literature* (London: Oxford, 1975), p. 16.

[2] Hardin, p. 6.

David Green (trans.), *The Prometheus Bound* (Chicago: U. of Chicago Press, 1956), line 111.

[3] Found within a letter to Thomas Butts. Geoffrey Keynes (ed.), *Complete Writings of William Blake: With All the Variant Readings*, from a letter to Thomas Butts, (London: Nonesuch Press, 1957), pp. 816-19.

[4] Donald Ault, *Visionary Physics: Blake's Response to Newton* (Chicago: U. of Chicago Press, 1974), p. 51.

[5] J.B. Bronowski, *William Blake and the Age of Revolution* (New York: Harper & Row, 1965), p. 95.

Bibliography

By Fugard

Fougard [sic], Athol. "The Blood Knot." *Contrast*, 2, No. 1 (1962), pp. 29-44.

Fugard, Athol. "African Stages." *New York Times*, Sept. 20, 1964, II, p. 3.

The Blood Knot. New York: Samuel French, n.d.

Boesman and Lena: And Other Plays. Oxford, London, and New York: Oxford University Press, 1978.

"Caught in a Typhoon in the Pacific." NELM.*

The Coat. Cape Town: A.A. Balkema, 1971.

"The Coat: An Acting Exercise from Serpent Players of New Brighton." *The Classic 2*, No. 3 (1967), pp. 50-68.

Dimetos: And Two Early Plays. Oxford, London, and Melbourne: Oxford, 1977.

"Drama of P.E.'s Night School for African Adults." *Port Elizabeth Evening Post*, June 18, 1954.

Drivers. Adapt. David Muir from *Mille Miglia*.

The Drummer. (See Appendix A.)

"Extract from *People Are Living There*." *The Classic*, 1, No. 2 (1963), pp. 49-67.

"Extract from a Work in Progress: First Sketch for the Opening of Act I." *Teater S.A.* 1, No. 2 (1968), insert 1-12.

"Fugard on Acting, Actors on Fugard." *Theatre Quarterly*, 7, No. 28 (1977), pp. 83-87.

"Fugard on Fugard." *yale/theatre*, 4 (Winter 1973), pp. 41-54.

"The Gift of Freedom." In Findlater, Richard (ed.), *At the Royal Court: 25 Years of the English Stage Co.* Derbyshire: Amber Lane Press, 1981, pp. 157-60.

The Guest: An Episode in the Life of Eugène Marais. Johannesburg and London: Ad. Donker, 1977.

"Letter from Athol Fugard." *The Classic*, 2, No. 1 (1966), pp. 78-80.

"Letters." NELM.

"Life aboard a Tramp." *Port Elizabeth Evening Post Weekend Magazine*, July 3, 1954.

Marigolds in August. Johannesburg: Ad. Donker, 1982.

"Marigolds in August." RM Productions; photocopied press hand-out, n.d.

"Must S.A. Plays 'Protest'?" *Port Elizabeth Evening Post*, NELM.

"Notebooks." *The Classic*, 3, No. 4 (1971), pp. 66-82.

Notebooks: 1970-1977. New York: Alfred A. Knopf, 1984.

"The Occupation." In Cosmo Pieterse (ed.) *Ten One-Act Plays*. London: Heinemann Educational Books; New York: Humanities Press, 1968, pp. 255-293.

"The Occupation: A Script for the Camera." *Contrast*, 2, No. 4 (1964), pp. 57-93.

"Open Letter to Playwrights." *Forward* (Johannesburg), Sept. 1962.

"*Orestes* Reconstructed: A Letter to an American Friend." *Theatre Quarterly*, 8, No. 32 (1979), pp. 3-6.

*NELM is the abbreviation for the National English Literary Museum and Documentation Centre, Grahamstown.

BIBLIOGRAPHY

"Original Notes of *Dimetos*." NELM.

"People Are Living There." *Contrast*, 5 (July 1968), pp. 31-46.

People Are Living There. New York, Cape Town, and London: Oxford, 1970.

"Rehearsal Log for the London Premiere of *Statements*." NELM.

"Sizwe Bansi Is Dead." In Ronald Harwood. *A Night at the Theatre*. London: Methuen, 1982, pp. 26-32.

"South African Playwright Finds Peace on Crete." *Port Elizabeth Evening Post*, Oct. 1, 1966.

Statements: Three Plays. London and Cape Town: Oxford, 1974.

Three Port Elizabeth Plays. London and Cape Town: Oxford, 1974.

Tsotsi. Johannesburg: Ad. Donker, 1980.

Tsotsi (manuscript). NELM.

"Turning the Pages of History in Graveyards." *Port Elizabeth Evening Post*, May 28, 1954.

"University of Natal 1981 Grahamstown Address and Citation and the Laudation in Presenting Athol Fugard for the Honorary Doctorate." NELM.

"Why Wesker?" NELM.

"Writer's Notebook." *Sunday Tribune* (Durban), Dec. 11, 1966.

"At the Yale School of Drama" (informal talk). Oct. 10, 1974.

Other Sources

Abrahams, Lionel. "Hello and Goodbye." *The Classic*, 2, No. 2 (1966), pp. 72-77.

Abramovitz, Carole. "Fugard's *Orestes* 'Powerful, Uplifting, Devastating . . . ' ." *Cape Times*, April 1, 1971, p. 8.

Aeschylus. Trans. David Green. *The Prometheus Bound*. Chicago: U. of Chicago Press, 1956.

"An African Theatre in South Africa." *African Arts*, 3 (Summe 1970), pp. 42-44.

"Afrikaner Humanist." *Observer*, July 18, 1971, p. 9.

Amato, Rob and Skhala Xinwa. "The Serpent Players: Review of Two Productions (1970)." In Stephen Gray. *Athol Fugard*, pp. 83-85.

"Art Is Life and Life Is Art: An Interview with John Kani and Winston Ntshona of the Serpent Players from South Africa," *UFAHAMU* (Journal of the African Activist Association), 6, No. 2 (1976), pp. 5-26.

"The Art of the Possible: An Interview with Ross Devenish." *The Bloody Horse*, No. 6 (Dec. 1981), pp. 66-76.

Astbury, Brian. *The Space/Die Rumte/Indawo: March 1972-Sept. 1979*. Cape Town: Fine, 1980.

"Athol Fugard and Don Maclennan: A Conversation." *English in Africa*, 9, No. 2 (1982), pp. 1-11.

Ault, Donald D. *Visionary Physics: Blake's Response to Newton*. Chicago and London: U. of Chicago Press, 1974.

Bair, Deirdre. *Samuel Beckett: A Biography*. New York and London: Harcourt Brace Jovanovich, 1978.

Baneshik, Percy. "Rev. *The Guest*." *The Star*, Sept. 15, 1977, p. 11.

Barnes, Clive. "Rev. *Boesman and Lena*." *New York Times*, June 23, 1970, p. 30.

———"Rev. *Statements*." *New York Post*, Feb. 6, 1978.

BIBLIOGRAPHY

Barnes, Patricia. "Athol Fugard's South African Conscience." *The Times*, June 30, 1980, p. 11.

Beckett, Samuel. *Proust*. 1931; rpt. New York: Grove Press, n.d.

Benson, Mary. "Athol Fugard and 'One Little Corner of the World.' " *yale/theatre*, 4 (Winter 1973), pp. 55-62.

———"Dramatist." *Christian Science Monitor*, April 3, 1974, p. 9.

———"Fugard's *A Lesson from Aloes*: An Introduction." *Theater*, 11, No. 2 (Spring 1980), pp. 5-6.

——— " 'A Hunger for Ideas' Moves Them." *New York Times*, Sept. 12, 1965, II, p. 8.

———"The Island Where Men Are [Not] Broken." *The Observer*, April 14, 1974, p. 13.

———"Keeping an Appointment with the Future: The Theatre of Athol Fugard." *Theatre Quarterly*, 7, No. 28 (1977), pp. 77-83.

———"South Africa: The Struggle for a Birthright." 1963; rev. New York: Minerva Press, 1969.

———"South Africa's Play about Things as They Are." *The Times*, Dec. 11, 1961, p. 5.

Bergson, Henri. *Laughter*. Trans. by arrangement with the Presses Universitaires de France. 1900; rpt. New York: Doubleday & Co., 1956.

Berner, Robert L. "Athol Fugard and the Theatre of Improvisation." *Books Abroad*, 50 (Winter 1976), pp. 81-84.

Biggs, Murray. "Prison, and the South African Theatre of Athol Fugard." Photocopy.

———"Time, and the South African Theatre of Athol Fugard." Photocopy.

Billington, Michael. "Rev. *Boesman and Lena*." *Plays and Players*, 18 (Sept. 1971), pp. 48-49.

———"Philosophy of Moss." *The Times*, Aug. 6, 1968, p. 9.

———"Rev. *Sizwe Bansi*." *Guardian*, Jan. 9, 1974.

Black Review. Durban: Black Community Programs, 1972, pp. 201-07; 1973, pp. 104-11; 1974/75, pp. 211-13; 1975/76, pp. 193-95.

Blake, William. *Complete Writings of William Blake: With All the Variant Readings*, ed. Geoffrey Keynes. London: Nonesuch Press, 1950.

"*Blood Knot* Is Superb Theatre." *Rand Daily Mail*, Nov. 9, 1961, p. 8.

Blumenthal, Eileen. "Rev. *Sizwe Bansi* and *The Island*." *Educational Theatre Journal*, 27 (1975), pp. 416-18.

Brand, Adam. "He Plans an African Theatre." *Port Elizabeth Evening Post*, Sept. 30, 1956.

Branford, Jean. "Fugard Play: Joy Shines Off Misery." In Gray, *Athol Fugard*, pp. 80-81.

British Broadcasting Corporation. "Kaleidoscope" [Radio 4], July 19, 1971; Oct. 31, 1973; Jan. 2, 1974.

———"The Life and Works of Athol Fugard." Second House Series, Nov. 30, 1974.

Bronowski, J. *William Blake and the Age of Revolution*. New York: Harper & Row, 1965.

Brown, James Ambrose. "Rev. *Blood Knot*." *Sunday Times* (Johannesburg), Nov. 12, 1961.

———"Fugard's Mille Lives Again in Sharp New Focus." *Cape Times*, May 15, 1972, p. 7.

Brustein, Robert. "Plaudits and Brickbats." *The Observer*, Mar. 25, 1973, p. 35.

———*The Theatre of Revolt: Studies in Modern Drama from Ibsen to Genet*. Boston, Toronto: Little Brown & Co., 1964.

Brutus, Dennis. "Protest against Apartheid." In Cosmo Pieterse and David Munro (eds.), *Protest and Conflict in African Literature*. London: Heinemann, 1969, pp. 93-100.

Bryceland, Yvonne. "I'm Dry—I Think I Need a Rest—Fugard." *Cape Times Weekend Magazine*, Nov. 27, 1965.

BIBLIOGRAPHY

Burns, John F. "Transkei Sets Terms to Free *Sizwe Bansi* Actors." *New York Times*, Oct. 14, 1976, p. 3.

Bury, J.B. *The Idea of Progress: An Inquiry into Its Origin and Growth.* 1932; rpt. New York: Dover Publications, 1959.

Calta, Louis. "*Blood Knot* Production Pleases Playwright Who Fled Rhodesia: Atholl [sic] Fugard, South African, Avoided Being Deported after Racial Incident." *New York Times*, May 27, 1964, p. 44.

Camus, Albert. *Lyrical and Critical Essays.* Ed. Philip Thody. Trans. Ellen Conroy Kennedy. New York: Vintage Books, 1970.

———*The Myth of Sisyphus: And Other Essays.* Trans. Justin O'Brien. 1942; rpt. New York: Vintage, 1955.

———*Notebooks: 1935-1942.* Trans. Philip Thody. New York: Modern Library, 1965.

———*Notebooks: 1942-1951.* Trans. Justin O'Brien. 1965; rpt. New York and London: Harcourt.

———*The Plague.* Trans. Stuart Gilbert. New York: Random House, 1948.

———*Resistance, Rebellion, and Death.* Trans. Justin O'Brien. New York: Modern Library, 1963.

Carroll, Dorothy Connell. "Cultural Boycott—Yes or No?" *Index on Censorship*, 4, No. 1 (1975), pp. 34-43; 4, No. 2 (1975), pp. 5-44; 4, No. 3 (1975), pp. 42-43.

Chaillet, Ned. "One Play Down." *Plays and Players*, 23 (Aug. 1976), pp. 26-27.

Chaplin, Charles. *My Autobiography.* New York: Pocket Books, 1966.

Clayton, Sylvia. " 'Mille Miglia' Was Brighter Says Moss." *Daily Telegraph*, Aug. 6, 1968.

Cole, Ernest. *House of Bondage.* New York: Random House, 1976.

Coleridge, Samuel Taylor. *Collected Letters.* Ed. Earle L. Griggs. Oxford: Oxford, 1956.

Collins, William B. "A Master's Play of Tragic Import Is Brought Here." *The Philadelphia Inquirer*, March 21, 1982, p. 1-M ff.

Coveney, Michael. "Challenging the Silence: Athol Fugard Talks to Michael Coveney." *Plays and Players*, 21 (Nov. 1973), pp. 34-37.

———"Rev. *Statements.*" *The Financial Times*, Jan. 30, 1975, p. 3.

Craig, Randall. "Plays in Performance." *Drama*, No. 111 (Winter 1973), p. 54.

"The Crisis of African Theatre." *Business South Africa*, 8, (April 1973), pp. 32-33.

Cushman, Robert. "Drama's Invalids." *The Observer*, Jan. 13, 1974, p. 24.

Devenish, Ross. *Athol Fugard: A Lesson from Aloes.* BBC-RM Productions, 1979.

Dewhurst, Keith. "Rev. *Mille Miglia.*" *Guardian*, Aug. 6, 1968, p. 4.

E.B. "Fine Story of a Fraternal Bond." *Johannesburg Star*, Nov. 9, 1961.

Eliot, T.S. "Tradition and the Individual Talent." In *Selected Essays: 1917-1932.* New York: Harcourt, 1932, pp. 3-11.

Elsom, John. "Atonement." *Listener*, 95 (June 3, 1976), pp. 711-12.

———"The True and False Pilgrim." *Listener*, 94 (Sept. 4, 1975), pp. 311-12.

Fearn, M. "Modern Drama of Africa: Form and Content, A Study of Four Playwrights." Diss. Northwestern University, 1974, pp. 91-107.

Ferguson, Ian. "Athol Fugard's *Boesman and Lena.*" *Crux*, 4, No. 4 (Nov. 1970), pp. 52-55.

———"Sizwe Bansi Is Dead." *Unisa English Studies*, No. 111, pp. 95-102.

Fergusson, Francis. *The Idea of a Theatre: A Study of the Plays, The Art of Drama in Changing Perspective.* New York: Doubleday, 1953.

Fiddick, Peter. "The Guest at Steenkampskraal." *Guardian Weekly*, 116 (March 20, 1977), p. 21.

ꞁ ıₑᵤₗₑ., Leslie. "Symposium on the State of American Writing." *Partisan Review*, Aug. 1948.

Findlater, Richard (ed). *At the Royal Court. 25 Years of the English Stage Company.* Derbyshire Amber Lane Press, 1981.

Fiskaal, Jan. "Fugard's Play Is Damnably Fascinating." *Cape Times Weekend Magazine*, April 29, 1972, p. 2.

Ford, Christopher. "Life with a Liberal Conscience." *Guardian*, July 17, 1971, p. 8.

France, Anatole. *Of Life and Letters.* Trans. E.W. Evans. vol. 1. New York: John Lane, 1911.

Freud, Sigmund. *Civilization and Its Discontents.* Trans. Joan Riviere. New York: Doubleday, 1958.

"Fugard Avid Reader from Early Age." *Eastern Province Herald*, July 14, 1969.

"Fugard in New Medium." *Pretoria News*, January 24, 1973, p. 18.

"Fugard Plans New Play—On Gambling." *Cape Times*, April 18, 1974, p. 10.

"Fugard Scores Big Success." March 15, 1968, NELM.

"Fugard Writes Again." *Pretoria News*, July 25, 1978, p. 2.

Gala. "Hello or Goodbye, Athol Fugard?" *African Communist*, 57 (1974), 100-05.

Garson, Barbara. "Fugard on the Secret Wisdom of Plants." *In These Times*, May 7-13, 1980, p. 21.

Gassner, John. *The Theater in Our Times.* New York: Crown, 1954.

Gibbs, Garth. "Our Angry Young Man." *Sunday Tribune* (Durban), May 15, 1966.

Gilman, Richard. "Introduction" to Franz Xaver Kroetz, *Farmyard and Other Plays.* New York: Urizen, 1976.

———*The Making of Modern Drama: A Study of Büchner, Ibsen, Strindberg, Chekhov, Pirandello, Brecht, Beckett, Handke.* New York: Farrar, Straus, 1974.

Gold, Ivan. "A Playwright's Novel." *New York Times Book Review*, Feb. 1, 1981, p. 8.

Gomperts, H.A. "Rev. *A Kakamas Greek.*" *Het Parool* (Amsterdam), May 25, 1960.

———"Karaktervol Spel in Stuk oor Apartheid: Premiere bij Puck van Tone Brulins *De Honden.*" *Het Parool*, Nov. 14, 1960.

Gordimer, Nadine. "English-Language Literature and Politics in South Africa." In Christopher Heywood, (ed.). *Aspects of South African Literature.* London: Heinemann; New York: Africana Publishing, 1976, pp. 99-120.

———"Plays and Piracy: A Discussion." *Contrast*, 3, No. 4 (July 1965), pp. 53-55.

———"South Africa: Towards a Desk Drawer Literature." *The Classic*, 2, No. 4 (1968), pp. 64-74.

Gottfried, Martin. "Fugard Copes with Africa." *New York Post*, Nov. 14, 1974.

———"*The Island* Joins *Sizwe Bansi,*" *Women's Wear Daily*, Nov. 21, 1971.

Gray, Stephen (ed.), *Athol Fugard.* Southern Africa Literature Series, No. 1. Johannesburg: McGraw-Hill, 1982.

———"The Coming into Print of Athol Fugard's *Tsotsi.*" *Journal of Commonwealth Literature*, 16 (Aug. 1981), pp. 56-63.

Green, Robert J. "Athol Fugard: Dramatist of Loneliness and Isolation." *Teater S.A.*, 1, No. 2 (1968), pp. 2-4.

———"Athol Fugard's *Hello and Goodbye.*" *Modern Drama*, 13 (1970-71), pp. 139-55.

———"Politics and Literature in Africa: The Drama of Athol Fugard." In Christopher Heywood (ed.). *Aspects of South African Literature.* London: Heinemann; New York: Africana Publishing, 1976, pp. 163-73.

———"South Africa's Plague: One View of *The Blood Knot.*" *Modern Drama*, 12 (1969-70), pp. 331-45.

Grigsby, Wayne. "The Cost of Bearing Witness." *Macleans*, Jan. 21, 1980, pp. 45-46.

Grotowski, Jerzy. *Towards a Poor Theatre*. New York: Simon & Schuster, 1968.

"*The Guest*—A Personal Reminiscence by Director Ross Devenish." *Scenaria* (Supplement), Aug/Sept 1977, pp. 2-3.

Gussow, Mel. "Fugard Balances on Tightrope." *New York Times*, Mar. 18, 1975, p. 15.

———"To Fugard, Playwriting Is 'Defiance'. " *New York Times*, Dec. 17, 1974, p. 30.

———"Witness." *The New Yorker*, Dec. 20, 1982, pp. 47-94.

Hall, Richard. "Brecht Play Starts Africa Race Row." *The Observer*, May 17, 1964.

Hammond, Jonathan. "A South African Season: *Sizwe Bansi, The Island* and *Statements.*" *Plays and Players*, 21 (March 1974), pp. 40-43.

Hardin, Garrett. *Promethean Ethics: Living with Death, Competition, and Triage*. Seattle and Washington: U. of Washington Press, 1980.

"Harsh Comedy on a Lagos Beach." *The Times*, June 29, 1966, p. 7.

Hauptfleisch, Temple, Wilma Viljoen, and Celeste Van Greunen. *Athol Fugard: A Source Guide*. Johannesburg: Ad. Donker, 1982.

Hayman, Ronald. "Janet Suzman: Intelligence and Emotion." *The Times*, Oct. 13, 1973, p. 11.

Herbert, Hugh. "Out of Africa." *Guardian*, Dec. 10, 1979, p. 11.

Herbst, Terry. "Brilliant Fugard Play Marks a New Era in South African Theatre." *Cape Times*, June 16, 1969, p. 11.

———"Theatre Laboratory Takes Its First Faltering Steps." *Cape Times*, March 20, 1971, p. 8.

Heywood, Christopher (ed.). *Aspects of South African Literature*. London: Heinemann; New York: Africana Publishing, 1976.

Hobson, Harold. "Honor Your Partners." *Sunday Times*, July 3, 1966, p. 46.

———"A Play to Remember." *Sunday Times*, Sept. 7, 1975, p. 37.

———"Rev. *Statements.*" *Sunday Times*, Jan. 27, 1974, p. 29.

———"Tales of Passion and Destruction." *Sunday Times*, May 30, 1976, p. 37.

Hodgins, Robert. "Interview with Athol Fugard." *Newscheck*, July 21, 1967, pp. 24-29.

Hogg, David. "Unpublished Fugard Novel." *Contrast*, 12, No. 1 (1978), pp. 60-79.

Horrell, Muriel. *Action, Reaction and Counteraction*. Johannesburg: South Africa Institute of Race Relations, 1971.

———*South Africa: Basic Facts and Figures*. Johannesburg: South Africa Institute of Race Relations, 1973.

Hough, Barrie. "Interview with Athol Fugard: Port Elizabeth, Nov. 30, 1977." *Theoria*, No. 55 (Oct. 1980), pp. 37-48.

Howe, Marvine. "Fugard Opposes Playwrights' Boycott of South Africa." *New York Times*, July 6, 1970, p. 6.

International Defence and Aid Fund. *Black Theatre in South Africa*. Fact Paper on South Africa Series, No. 2, London, 1976.

———*South African Prisons and the Red Cross Investigation with Prisoners' Testimony*. London: Christian Action Publications, 1967.

Jenkinson, Denis. "Fright." In Michael Frewin (ed.). *The International Grand Prix Book of Motor Racing*. New York: Doubleday, 1965, p. 197.

BIBLIOGRAPHY

Jurgens, Heather. "Fugard and Manson." *Teater S.A.*, 1, No. 4 (1969), pp. 6-8.

K., D. "Rev. *De Honden.*" *Elsevier* (Amsterdam), Nov. 19, 1960.

K., R. "Sizwe Bansi Is Alive and Struggling for Freedom." *African Communist*, No. 58 (1974), pp. 122-28.

"A *Kakamas Greek* Nu in Amsterdam." *Het Parool* (Amsterdam), June 2, 1960.

Kani, John and Winston Ntshona. "At the Yale School of Drama" (informal talk). Nov. 8, 1974.

Kauffmann, Stanley. *Persons of the Drama.* New York: Harper & Row, 1976, pp. 208-11.

Kenner, Hugh. *The Poetry of Ezra Pound.* 1951; rpt. Krauss Reprint, 1968.

Khan, Naseem. "Athol Fugard." *Ink* (London), July 23-29, 1971, p. 27.

Klima, Vladimir. *South African Prose Writing in English.* Prague: The Oriental Institute in the Publishing House of the Czechoslovak Academy of Sciences, 1971.

Kroll, Jack. "The Beloved Country." *Newsweek*, Dec. 2, 1974, p. 98.

———"Kentucky Home-Fried." *Newsweek*, March 31, 1980, pp. 70-71.

———"Masters and Servants." *Newsweek*, March 29, 1982, p. 52.

———"Rev. *People.*" *Newsweek*, Dec. 6, 1971, p. 121.

L., D.d. "Rev. *De Horden.*" *Volkskrant*, Nov. 14, 1960.

L., G.V. "*Blood Knot* Is Superb Theatre." *Rand Daily Mail*, Nov. 9, 1961, p. 8.

Lambert, J.W. Plays in Performance." *Drama*, No. 112 (Spring 1974), pp. 22-23.

Lelyveld, Joseph. "*Master Harold* Stuns Johannesburg Audience." *New York Times*, March 24, 1983, p. 22.

Lennox-Short, Alan (ed.). *English and South Africa.* Cape Town: Nasou, n.d.

Leshoai, Bob. "Theatre and the Common Man in Africa." *Transition*, No. 19 (1965), pp. 44-47.

Lester, Elenore. "I Am in Despair about South Africa." *New York Times*, Dec. 1, 1974, II, p. 5.

Levin, M.M. "Reps Disagreed over Athol Fugard Play." NELM.

Liknaitzky, Barry. "Rev. *The Guest.*" *Cape Times*, Sept. 16, 1977, p. 8.

Loder, Robert. "Enriching Theatre in English." *The New African*, 5 (June 1966), pp. 110-11.

Lottman, Herbert R. *Albert Camus: A Biography.* New York: Doubleday, 1979.

M., C.S. "Good Acting from New Brighton." *Port Elizabeth Evening Post*, Aug. 16, 1963.

McLaren, Dorrian. "Athol Fugard and His Work." Diss. University of Leeds, 1974.

Maclennan, Don. "The Palimpsest: Some Observations on Fugard's Plays." In Stephen Gray (ed.). *Athol Fugard. Southern Africa Literature Series*, No. 1.

Malan, Robin. "Rev. *People.*" *Teater S.A.*, 1, No. 4 (1969), p. 15.

Marais, Eugène. *My Friends the Baboons.* Trans. Winifred de Kok, 1939; rpt. Cape Town and Pretoria: Human & Rousseau, 1971.

———"Notes on Some Effects of Extreme Drought in Waterberg, South Africa." *Smithsonian Institution Annual Report* 1914 (Part 1), pp. 511-22.

———*The Soul of the Ape.* New York: Atheneum Publishers, 1969.

———*The Soul of the White Ant.* Trans. Winifred de Kok. New York: Dodd, Mead & Co., 1937.

Marcus, Frank. "In the Act." *Sunday Telegraph* (London), Jan. 27, 1974, p. 32.

Marks, Jonathan. "Interview with Athol Fugard." *yale/theatre*, 4 (Winter 1973), pp. 64-72.

———"A Man Who Commits Provocative Acts of Theatre." *Yale Reports: News from the Yale Repertory Theatre*, 4, No. 4 (1980), pp. 1-3.

BIBLIOGRAPHY

Marquard, Jean. "Fugard Revival." *Snarl* (Johannesburg), 1, No. 1 (Aug. 1974), p. 6.

"Masterful Fugard: Athol Fugard's *'Master Harold'* . . . *and the boys.*" *Yale Reports*, 6, No. 4 (1982), pp. 1-2.

Meyer, Michael. *Ibsen: A Biography.* Garden City: Doubleday, 1971.

"Mille Miglia Method: Moss's Enterprise Rewarded." *The Times*, May 4, 1955, p. 5.

"The Mille Miglia Won by Moss." *The Times*, May 2, 1955.

Millgate, Michael. *The Achievement of William Faulkner.* New York: Random House, 1966.

Mootz, William. "Foreign Playwrights Take Jabs at America, but It's All in Fun." *Louisville Courier-Journal*, Feb. 28, 1980.

Moyana, T.T. "Problems of a Creative Writer in South Africa." In Christopher Heywood (ed.). *Aspects of South African Literature.* London: Heinemann; New York: Africana Publishing, 1976, pp. 85-98.

Mphahlele, Ezekiel. *African Writing Today.* Middlesex: Penguin, 1967.

———*Down Second Avenue.* 1967; Rpt. Garden City: Doubleday & Co., 1971.

Mshengu. "South Africa: Where Mvelinqangi Still Limps (The Experimental Theatre of Workshop '71)." *yale/theatre*, 8 (Fall 1976), pp. 38-48.

"De Negerhut van Oom Tone." *Haagse Post*, Nov. 19, 1960.

Nietzsche, Friedrich. *Beyond Good and Evil.* Trans. Marianne Cowan. Chicago: Henry Regnery, 1955.

———*The Birth of Tragedy.* Trans. Francis Golffing. Garden City: Doubleday, 1956.

———*Twilight of the Idols.* Trans. R.J. Hollingdale. Middlesex: Penguin, 1968.

Nkosi, Lewis. "Athol Fugard: His Work and Us." *South Africa: Information and Analysis*, No. 63 (May 1968), pp. 1-8.

———"The Playwright's War against South Africa." *South Africa: Information and Analysis*, No. 64 (June 1968), pp. 1-8.

Noganta, Mtunzi. "Serpent Players: *The Just.*" *S'ketsh'*, Summer 1972, p. 29.

"*Nongogo*: A Simple Young Man and the Bad Girl." *Drum*, No. 101 (July 1959 [E. Africa, Aug. 1959]), pp. 32-33.

Oakes, Philip. "The Liberty Man." *Sunday Times*, April 7, 1974, p. 38.

O'Connor, Frank. *A Short History of Irish Literature.* New York: G.P. Putnam's Sons, 1967.

"Panel on South African Theatre: From the Proceedings of the Symposium on Contemporary South African Literature." *Index: A Quarterly Journal of Africanist Opinion*, 6 (Spring 1976), pp. 47-57.

Paton, Alan. *Knocking on the Door: Shorter Writings.* Cape Town: David Philip, 1975.

Plaatjies, Nancy. "A Note on the Serpent Players and Their Performance of *The Terrorists* or *The Just* by Albert Camus." *S'ketsh'*, Summer 1972, p. 30.

"Plays Not Anti-South African, Fugard." *Eastern Province Herald*, Feb. 5, 1974, p. 11.

Plomer, William. *Turbott Wolfe.* 1925; rpt. London: Hogarth, 1965.

Pogrund, Benjamin. "Nights When *Tsotsi* Was Born." *Rand Daily Mail*, Feb. 11, 1980.

Poll, K.L. "Uitstekende Voorstelling van A *Kakamas Greek.*" *Et Vaderland* (The Hague), June 4, 1960.

Pound, Ezra. "A Few Dont's by an Imagist." *Poetry*, 35 (1913), pp. 200-06.

Powell, Dilys. "Rage for Freedom." *Sunday Times*, Jan. 17, 1974, p. 37.

Progress through Separate Development. New York: Information Service of South Africa, 1973.

Prosser, Donald. "What's behind the Passport Ban? Dilemma of Outspoken Playwright." *Eastern Province Herald*, June 9, 1970.

Raeford, Daniel. "Rev. *The Guest.*" *Rand Daily Mail*, Sept. 14, 1977, p. 6.

Raine, Craig. "An Interview with Athol Fugard." *Quarto*, No. 9 (Aug. 1980), pp. 9-13.

Raymer, John David. "Eight Recent Plays by South African Dramatist Athol Fugard: His Method, His Development as a Playwright, His South African Context and the Major Influences upon Him" Diss. Ohio University, 1975.

Report of the United Nations Commission on the Racial Situation in the Union of South Africa. New York: United Nations General Assembly, Eighth Session, Supplement No. 16, 1953.

Rich, Frank. "Rev. *Master'Harold.*" *New York Times*, May 5, 1982.

Richards, David. "The Agony and the Irony: Playwright Athol Fugard and the Sorrows of South Africa." *Washington Post*, Nov. 8, 1981, p. M1.

Robbe-Grillet, Alain. *For a New Novel.* Trans. Richard Howard. New York: Grove, 1965.

Rolo, Charles J. "Rev. *Cry, the Beloved Country.*" *The Atlantic Monthly*, 181 (April 1948), p. 112.

Rosenwald, Peter. "Separate Fables." *Guardian*, Jan. 8, 1974, p. 10.

Ross, Laura. "A Question of Certainties." *American Theatre* 1, No. 5 (Sept. 1984), pp. 4-9.

Roter, Danielle. "Athol Fugard: Condemning Apartheid." *Los Angeles Herald Examiner*, Sept. 4, 1981, p. D30.

Rougement, Denis de. *Love in the Western World.* Trans. Montgomery Belgion. New York: Harper & Row, 1974.

Rousseau, Leon. *The Dark Stream: The Story of Eugène Marais.* Johannesburg: Jonathan Ball, 1982.

S., B. "Apartheid: Premiere van de Toneelgroep Puck." *Algemeen Handels Blad* (Rotterdam), Nov. 14, 1960.

————"Rev. *A Kakamas Greek.*" *Algemeen Handels Blad*, June 2, 1960.

S.W., J.v. "Rev. *De Honden.*" *De Groene*, Nov. 19, 1960.

Sartre, Jean-Paul. *What Is Literature?* Trans. Bernard Frechtman. New York: Philosophical Library, 1949.

"To See an Invisible Man." *Rand Daily Mail*, July 26, 1979, p. 11.

Seymour, Alan. "Rev. *Sizwe Bansi.*" *Plays and Players*, 21 (Nov. 1973), pp. 51-52.

Shephard, Ben. "Marais—A Mind in the Wilderness." *The Listener*, March 10, 1977, pp. 298-99.

Simon, John. *Uneasy Stages: A Chronicle of the New York Theatre 1963-73.* New York: Random House, 1976, pp. 263-64.

Smeed, J.W. *Faust in Literature.* London: Oxford, 1975.

Smith, Colin. "White Man on a Tightrope." *Observer*, Jan. 6, 1974, p. 8.

Sowden, Dora. "African Drama." *Rand Daily Mail*, Sept. 18, 1958, p. 6.

Sparks, Allister. "The Eager New Actors." *Rand Daily Mail*, July 24, 1965, p. 8.

Spierdijk, Jan. "Rassenvraagstuk in Driftig Spel van Belg Tone Brulin." *Telegraaf*, Nov. 14, 1960.

Stoppard, Tom. "Fact, Fiction and the Big Race." *The Observer Review*, Aug. 11, 1968, p. 20.

"Student's 30-Pound World Trip." *Eastern Province Herald*, May 21, 1954.

Styan, J.L. *The Dark Comedy: The Development of Modern Comic Tragedy.* Cambridge: Cambridge U. Press, 1968.

Swart, Glenda (Fugard). "My Brother Athol." NELM.

BIBLIOGRAPHY

Tanner, Bill. "Launching the Space." *To the Point*, April 8, 1972, pp. 53-54.

Taylor, Markland. "Fugard Waves through Flames." *New Haven Register*, Oct. 13, 1974, p. 1D.

"Theatre." *The Classic*, 1, No. 1 (1963), pp. 64-66.

"Theatre-Go-Round." *S'ketsh'*, Summer 1974-1975, pp. 4-6.

Thompson, Leonard and Monica Wilson (eds.). *The Oxford History of South Africa*. 2 vols. London: Oxford, 1971.

————Politics in the Republic of South Africa. *Boston and Toronto*: Little Brown, 1966.

"Three One-Act Plays in Programme." *The Argus*, October 4, 1956.

Tucker, Christopher A. "Athol Fugard." *Transatlantic Review*, No. 53/54, pp. 87-90.

Tynan, Kenneth. "Under the Influence." *The Observer Weekend Review*, Feb. 24, 1963, p. 26.

Utley, Francis Lee, Lynn Bloom, and Arthur F. Kinney (eds.). *Bear, Man, and God: Seven Approaches to William Faulkner's "The Bear."* New York: Random House, 1964.

Van den Berghe, Pierre. *South Africa: A Study in Conflict*. Los Angeles: University of California, 1967.

Vandenbroucke, Russell. *Athol Fugard: Bibliography, Biography, Playography*. Theatre Checklist No. 15. London: Theatre Quarterly Publications, 1977.

————"Athol Fugard: The Director Collaborates with His Actors," *Theater*, 14, No. 1 (Winter 1982), pp. 32-40.

————"Athol Fugard's Immense Microcosm," *Los Angeles Times*, Calendar, Aug. 23, 1981, p. 41.

————"A Brief Chronology of the Theatre in South Africa." *Theatre Quarterly*, 7, No. 28 (1977), pp. 44-46.

————"Chiaroscuro: A Portrait of the Theatre in South Africa." *Theatre Quarterly*, 7, No. 28 (1977), pp. 46-54.

————"Fugard and South Africa," *The Guthrie*, May 1983, pp. 18-19.

————"In Dialogue with Himself: Athol Fugard's *Notebooks*," *Theater*, 16, No. 1 (Fall/Winter, 1984), pp. 43-48.

————"Robert Zwelinzima Is Alive," *yale/theatre*, 7, No. 2 (Winter 1975), pp. 116-23.

————"A Selected Bibliography of the South African Theatre." *Theatre Quarterly*, 7, No. 28 (1977), pp. 94-95.

Van Heyningen, Christina and C.O. Gardner. *W.H.D. Manson*. New York: Twayne, 1972, p. 5, 28.

Van Straten, Hans. "Rassendrama Grijpt Publiek Naar Keel." *Het Vrye Volk* (Rotterdam), Nov. 14, 1960.

Van Zyl, J.A. "*Boesman and Lena*." *New Nation*, March 1974, p. 13.

Venables, Michael. "Exciting New Indigenous Play." *Rand Daily Mail*, Nov. 24, 1972, p. 27.

Von Staden, Heinrich. "An Interview with Athol Fugard." *Theater*, 14, No. 1 (1982), pp. 41-46.

Walder, Dennis. "*Sizwe Bansi*." In *The Varied Scene: Aspects of Drama Today*. Walton Hall, Milton Keynes: The Open University Press, 1977, pp. 67-79.

Walker, Oliver. "Stark Tragedy of a Coloured Man." *Johannesburg Star*, Sept. 5, 1961.

Walpole, Horace. *The Letters of Horace Walpole*. Oxford: Clarendon, 1903-1905, vol. 9.

Wardle, Irving. "Drama of Brotherhood." *The Times*, Sept. 21, 1973.

————"Louisville's Standing against the Ugly American Myth." *The Times*, March 21, 1980.

————"Rev. *Statements*." *The Times*. Jan. 23, 1974, p. 13.

BIBLIOGRAPHY

Watts, Richard. "A Sad Birthday Party." *New York Post*, Nov. 19, 1971.

Weales, Gerald. "The Embodied Images of Athol Fugard." *The Hollins Critic*, 15, No. 1 (Feb. 1978), pp. 1-12.

Whitaker, Richard. "Dimoetes to Dimetos: The Evolution of a Myth." *English Studies in Africa*, 24, No. 1 (1981), pp. 45-59.

Whitbeck, Doris. "He Puts South Africa on Stage." *Hartford-Courant*, March 10, 1982, p. C1-2.

Wilhelm, Peter. "Athol Fugard at Forty." *To the Point*, June 3, 1972, pp. 37-40.

Williams, Owen. "Honesty, Integrity, but Dullness in Play." *Cape Argus*, March 29, 1972, p. 17.

Williams, Pat. "Athol Fugard." *Ink*, July 24, 1971, p. 10.

Wilson, Lindy. "Athol Fugard." *South African Outlook*, 99 (Aug. 1969), pp. 129 ff.

Woodley, Ray. "Did *Tsotsi* Shape Fugard's Later Works?" *Sunday Express*, Jan. 13, 1980.

Woodrow, Mervyn Wilbur. "A Critical Consideration of English Plays Written in South Africa, with Special Reference to the Emergence of a Dominant Theme." Diss. University of Pretoria, 1972, pp. 82-102.

————"South African Drama in English." *English Studies in Africa*, 13, No. 2 (Sept. 1970), pp. 391-410.

Woodward, A.G. "South African Writing: A New Play." *Contrast*, 2, No. 1 (1962), pp. 45-50.

Wren, Robert M. "Profile: Athol Fugard, in Segregated South Africa, a Vision of Shared Hopelessness. " *Africa Report*, 15, No. 7 (1970), pp. 32-33.

Xinwa, Skhala. "Serpent Players: Sell-Out." *S'ketsh'*, Summer 1972, p. 28.

Young, B.A. "Rev. *Dimetos*." *The Financial Times*, May 29, 1976.

————"Rev. *Statements*." *The Financial Times*, Jan. 23, 1974, p. 3.

Zwelonke, D.M. *Robben Island*. London: Heinemann, 1973.

Index

Index

Index